G000141417

EVERYBO
DIFFERE

Contents

List of Figures

List of Tables

Preface

Body dissatisfaction in young males and females has increased dramatically in the last few decades. There is an increased prevalence of dieting, disordered eating, smoking and drug taking for weight control, eating disorders, obsessive exercise, excessive weight-lifting and steroid abuse. Children and adolescents have become more susceptible to overweight and obesity over the past three decades, and healthy ways of preventing the interrelated issues of weight problems and body image concerns are now required in order to promote the healthy development of young people.

Self-esteem development is known to be protective for the mental health of young people and a positive sense of self-worth, self-respect and tolerance for differences among others also promotes aspects of social, cultural, spiritual and environmental health.

Positive self-esteem can act as a protective, health promoting factor for children and adolescents as it contributes to positive social behaviours. It acts as a buffer against the impact of negative influences and promotes physical activity. Poor self-esteem can play a critical role in the development of depression, anorexia nervosa, bulimia nervosa, other eating disorders, anxiety, violence, smoking, drug and alcohol abuse, high-risk behaviours, social isolation and suicide.

Conversely, positive self-esteem is protective against these problems and contributes to their prevention, as well as the promotion of positive outcomes such as academic achievement, competence in several different arenas, self-satisfaction, life satisfaction, effective communication and relationships, resilience and coping ability.

My recent research study among 470 adolescents found that the successful implementation of a self-esteem program alone can ward off the development of body image concerns and eating problems in young people, as well as provide a general protective mental health effect.

The body image improvement program was titled 'Everybody's Different' and it forms the basis for this book, which contains the self-esteem theory, research findings and program activities from the original research intervention.

This book sets out in detail how to apply the self-esteem approach in schools, community settings and clinical situations to:

- improve body image
- prevent eating problems and childhood obesity
- foster health, nutrition and physical activity in children and adolescents.

There is information, research outcomes and classroom activities and work sheets about self-esteem development, media literacy for body image improvement, positive ways to teach about health, growth, puberty, food and nutrition, and how to implement school-based obesity prevention programs that are certain to benefit children and 'Do no harm' to otherwise weight-sensitive young people. The program is suitable for use in primary schools, secondary schools and university courses, especially in teacher training and health education.

There is a chapter about childhood overweight and obesity and how they are defined using the body mass index. Limitations in the measurement and definitions of childhood overweight and obesity are explained, common pitfalls experienced by schools are illustrated, and positive ways of motivating healthy eating and physical activity are presented in several case studies from schools.

The important topic of how to combine body image improvement programs and obesity prevention initiatives in school curriculum, school policies and activities, community links and teacher training is also covered in order to give a whole-school approach to promoting overall health among students.

I wrote this book as a summary of my 25 years experience as a nutritionist, health educator, researcher and lecturer in teacher education at the University of Sydney. The contents of this book are all based on sound research evidence and life experiences of teachers, students, parents and health professionals who care for the health and wellbeing of our young people. This book is dedicated to those who give their time and their lives in the service of teaching and those who work for the healthy development of youth.

Dr Jenny O'Dea

Associate Professor in Health Education and Nutrition Education
Faculty of Education and Social Work
University of Sydney

1 Body image and health in children and adolescents

Introduction

This book details body image issues and the ways in which teachers can promote self-esteem, self-acceptance and acceptance of others to improve general health and body image among children, adolescents and tertiary students. The book focuses on self-esteem development and media literacy to promote a positive body image and prevent eating disorders and obesity in young people.

The self-esteem approach of this book helps teachers challenge the current Western belief system that we are valued for our appearance in Western society. How we look and how slim (females) or muscular (males) we are correlates with how successful we are considered to be. This is a very narrow ideal for men and women to achieve and the failure to achieve these extreme body ideals results in a sense of failure, shame, guilt, hopelessness, dissatisfaction and worthlessness—all of which constitute low self-esteem. Low self-esteem predicts eating disorders, depression, anxiety, drug and alcohol abuse, risky behaviours, teen pregnancy and suicide.

This chapter describes body image trends and outlines the many factors that are related to body image in children and adolescents including historical influences, social developments, health implications and the relationship of body image to self-concept and self-esteem.

The meaning of 'child health'

In our role as teachers and health educators, we must remember that child health is a broad concept that encompasses many different aspects of overall health and wellbeing. Child health is so much more than physical health and physical fitness, and is certainly more than just body weight. While these are important, other dimensions also factor when developing a framework to encourage and support the health of children and adolescents. The World Health Organization (1948) defines health as 'a state of complete physical, mental and social wellbeing and not merely the absence of disease or infirmity'.

Physical health often dominates our perceptions of overall health. The idea that health means 'not being sick' is a common viewpoint, but one that is very limited. Physical health encompasses immunity, physical growth, maintenance, recovery from injury, overall function of the senses, susceptibility to disease and disorders, body functioning, stress management and recuperative ability. It also means having a healthy body weight and maintaining normal growth in childhood and adolescence.

Mental or psychological health includes a person's mental status and their mental functioning. Again, the dimensions of mental health encompass not just being mentally ill, but also a sense of psychological wellbeing. Children and adolescents have sound mental health when they feel loved, respected, safe, secure, and have a responsible adult taking care of them. Psychosocial health in children and adolescents is also characterised by a sense of self-worth, self-esteem, self-satisfaction and optimism about their place in the world and their future. Mental health also refers to a sense of resilience where children can develop the ability to learn from their mistakes and failures and are able to grow from experience. Decision making is a vital component of mental health.

Social health is very important for children and adolescents as they need to have interactions and relationships with others in order to lead satisfying lives and buffer the effects of stress and anxiety. Being able to talk to someone about various issues and problems is essential for child health. A strong and stable social network structure promotes overall health in children and adolescents. Feeling accepted and actively involved in cultural activities is an important aspect of health for many young people from various ethnic and cultural backgrounds.

Emotional health refers to a child's ability to identify and express their emotions and to have their emotional needs met. Many children grow up in a home or school environment where the four basic emotions—happiness, sadness, fear and anger—are denied, neglected, ignored, exaggerated or have become dysfunctional. In order for a child to be emotionally healthy, they need to be able to identify and express emotions when appropriate. This means the control of expressing emotions either when it is inappropriate to do so or if it is in an inappropriate manner. Feelings of self-esteem, self-confidence, self-efficacy, trust, love and many other emotional reactions and responses are all part of a child's emotional health.

Spiritual health refers to a child's sense of belonging to the world. A child who is spiritually healthy feels that they have a place in the world, that life is important and valuable with meaning and purpose, and that their destiny will also be meaningful and fruitful.

Body image and health

Health has many different aspects and it includes body image. This section discusses the definition and meanings of body image and how this is reported by Australian children, adolescents and young adults. The importance of developing a healthy body image is presented.

Body image is the mental picture we have of our bodies and how we feel about our bodies. Body image is a concept or scheme that includes feelings and perceptions such as: awareness of the body, body boundaries, attention to parts of the body as well as the whole, size of parts and the whole, position in space and gender-related perceptions.

Body image includes an individual's perception and judgement of the size, shape, weight and any other aspect of the body that relates to body appearance.

Historical influences on body image in Western society

The preference for a slim female ideal has been a relatively recent trend in Western society. The 'beautiful female ideal' from past generations has been consistently plump.

The art world holds testament to the portraits of beauty from past generations. The models of Rubens, Rembrandt, Gaugin and Matisse were all rounded, plump women. Some art critics believe that the supreme of female beauties from the Renaissance, Leonardo da Vinci's *Mona Lisa*, may have been pregnant at the time, suggesting that female roundness and heaviness were considered most beautiful. The fifteenth century women in Europe strived for a pregnant-like body shape because of the social importance of fertility following the plague that depopulated Europe. The famous painting by Jan van Eyck (1434) titled the *Arnolfini Wedding Portrait* shows the exemplification of the fertile look. The bride in the painting is not pregnant, but she strives for a rounded stomach and body shape that fits the physical ideal for women of the times. This fashion look was achieved by wearing a gathered gown worn with stuffing (a pillow) underneath.

Art and fashion from the eighteenth and nineteenth centuries also flattered the round shapes and curves of the fuller, shapely female figure. The bustles, crinoline skirts, upraised breasts; plump arms and necks of the late eighteenth century show a definite preference for fleshy women. Even though tradition in numerous Western cultures led women to portion greater food servings to men and boys at the expense of nourishing the females within the family, a plump and healthy woman was admired as it reflected wealth and success. The fertile female body ideal that persisted throughout the nineteenth century was perceived by historians as an instrument of production. This trend began to change with the fashions of the 1920s that encouraged women to adopt a more boyish, youthful, streamlined and sleek physique, achieved by use of undergarments and dieting.

The late twentieth century has seen a consistent change in the perception of female body beauty. Images of women have become slimmer since the 1950s. Women who Western society have traditionally classified as ideal beauties—fashion models, dancers, artistic models, pornographic queens—have all become significantly thinner. An analysis of the downward trend in weight among *Playboy* magazine models and Miss America contestants during the 20-year period spanning 1959 to 1978 is one example of this (Garner et al., 1980). Women in both groups increased in height and decreased in weight and the authors estimated that the ideal women portrayed during that time were significantly lighter than recommended standard weights. American society was portraying an underweight female ideal and the rest of the world began to follow suit. This study also found that during the same period women's magazines were publishing numerous articles about diet for weight loss. A follow-up to this research spanning 1979 to 1988 found a continuation of the same trend (Wiseman et al., 1992). According to these authors, the ideal American woman had become so thin that she was now approximately 20 per cent below her expected weight and yet magazines were increasingly writing about weight loss diets and weight controlling exercise methods.

More recently, Voracek and Fisher (2002) found an increase in this trend when they analysed the body measurements of the *Playboy* centrefold models in 577 consecutive monthly issues, from the magazine's inception in December 1953 to December 2001. They extracted the centrefolds' anthropometric data: height, weight, and measurements for bust, waist, and hip.

All measures except weight, showed significant changes. Whereas the increase in height merely reflects the well-known secular acceleration trend and an increase in the age of models, all other changes call for attention. Over time, bust size and hip size decreased, while waist size increased. Composite measures of body shape captured the same trends: body mass index and bust to hip ratio decreased, while waist to hip ratio, waist to bust ratio, and androgyny index increased. That is, the shape of the models became less curvaceous and more 'stick' like.

The authors comment that it is of concern that the typical body mass index of *Playboy* centrefolds has further descended below corresponding population levels because it may represent an underweight ideal. They summarise this by saying that the centrefold models' shapely body characteristics have given way to more androgynous ones. These temporal trends are at odds with claims that centrefolds' body shapes are still more 'hourglass' than 'stick insect' and that the maximally sexually attractive female waist to hip ratio is stable.

The changing shape of female fashion models was investigated by Morris et al. (1989). They analysed the height and body measurements of top London models from 1967 to 1987 and found that the ideal had become taller and less curvaceous. Bust and hip size decreased in relation to waist, producing a more tubular and androgynous shape. Over the same period the body shape of female ballet dancers has become significantly thinner and lighter than previous generations of dancers.

An analysis of the weights and apparent percentage body fat of store window display models in fashion shops showed that display figures have become thinner with time and their proportions differ considerably from those of normal weight young women (Rintala & Mustajoki, 1992). This study analysed display mannequins from the 1920s to the 1990s and found that they represented a normal range of body fat before the 1950s but had been considerably less fat since then. The authors suggest that post 1950s mannequins represent an ideal female weight and shape that is much slimmer than the average young woman and that a woman with the shape of a modern mannequin would probably not have enough body fat to maintain a normal menstrual cycle. Art and fashion continue to affect women's body image right up until today. Body image changes with the whims of fashion.

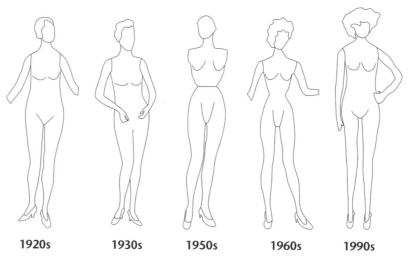

| 1920s | 1930s | 1950s | 1960s | 1990s |

FIGURE 1.1 Pictures of the changing shape of female fashion mannequins

From an early age, children learn that Western culture judges attractiveness and social acceptability using body shape and size as important criteria. The ideals of slimness for males and females and the undesirability of fatness are learned from early childhood.

The results of a 10-year longitudinal study (Gortmaker et al., 1993) suggest that overweight has a negative impact on the lives of young American adults because of resulting adverse economic consequences. They showed that overweight had deleterious effects upon participants' self-esteem and physical health and that overweight participants had a reduced ability to complete formal education, get married or be economically well off. They suggest that discrimination against overweight people in the USA may result in social and economic problems.

Despite research that shows men's ideal of the most attractive female figure is much larger than the ideal held by women, our society still promotes the idea that thin women are more desirable. The classic study of Fallon and Rozin (1985) showed that men have the mistaken belief that women prefer a heavier male stature when in fact females report they like lighter and smaller male standards. Similarly, women incorrectly believe that men prefer thin women. The shape of the male ideal portrayed in the media has become more and more muscular, so much so that the popular press describes the trend towards the mesomorphic look as 'a requirement' for males. Current top male fashion models are clearly mesomorphic and athletic. The ideal man, like the ideal woman, has become slimmer and more muscular. Very similar male and female body size ideals were also found in a study of 1000 Australian university students with the ideal woman being clearly underweight (O'Dea, 1998; 1999). These are illustrated in Figure 1.2. In a separate study of underweight female university students, the women perceived their current body size to be bigger than their ideal body and bigger than the ideal female body. A total of 42 per cent wanted to be slimmer, despite their underweight status.

Only 15 per cent of these underweight women indicated that they wanted to be bigger. Of concern was the finding that half of the women wanted to lose more weight, including those women who were classified as very underweight. There were no cultural differences in these body ideals with women from northern European, southern European and Asian backgrounds having a similar desire for the underweight ideal.

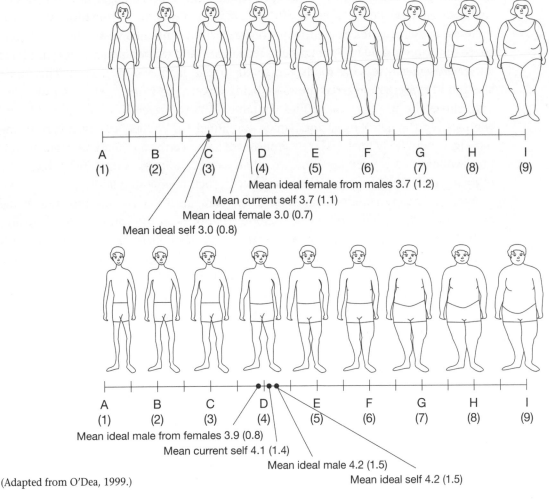

(Adapted from O'Dea, 1999.)

FIGURE 1.2 Body shape preferences used in research studies of young men and women

Social influences on body image in Western society

There is no doubt that ideal images of women in Western society have become much slimmer than those of earlier decades and those of men have become much more muscular. Numerous writers have asked why our society has become obsessed with the thin ideal. One suggestion is the influence of advertising and marketing on the content of magazines and advertising in the print and electronic media. The successful marketing of, for example, diet products, weight loss pharmaceuticals, diet books, gymnasiums and diet magazines requires a constant supply of people who are willing to buy. Magazines rely on advertising revenue for economic survival, so it is no coincidence that the content and images of magazines support the purchase of products that are advertised within. Women's magazines, for example, advertise diet foods and diet products and promote the sale of these products by publishing supporting articles about dieting with images of slim women. The overall impact of this combination is to encourage consumers to purchase products that will help them achieve the slim ideal.

Studies of nutrition-related issues in the Australian media have demonstrated that articles about weight reduction are popular and often contain nutrition misinformation.

In a study of media imagery Silverstein et al. (1986) analysed the body image of males and females appearing on US television. The majority of women characters were thin compared to male characters (69 per cent compared to 17.5 per cent). Overweight women characters were scarce compared to larger men (5 per cent compared to 25.5 per cent) giving viewers the message that it is not acceptable for women to be large or overweight. Analysis of the content of women's and men's magazines also showed that women were being supplied with a constant source of information about the preferred body image for women. Women's magazines contained 96 articles about body shape or size compared to eight in men's magazines, and women's magazines contained 63 advertisements for diet foods compared to one in men's magazines. This study also found evidence of mixed messages being targeted to women who read women's magazines. The women's magazines contained 228 messages about eating and food compared to the men's magazines which contained 10. Women are given very strong messages about body image, as well as messages about eating and food preparation. It is little wonder that women are confused about eating and possess distorted perceptions of themselves, when they receive messages with such double standards.

Western society certainly has created the thin ideal via art, fashion, the media and the advertising industry but this alone has not been the cause of the obsession with slimness. Several researchers have warned that improperly targeted public health initiatives for the reduction of obesity have served inadvertently to promote the belief that most people would improve their health if they lost weight.

Abraham and Mira warned as early as 1988 that health educators and health professionals should weigh up carefully the benefits of weight loss, against the risks of inducing psychological disturbances such as eating disorders and adverse physiological side effects such as dieting, smoking for weight control and severe weight loss. Similarly, Worsley and Crawford (1985) reported that both slim and overweight women had heeded the advice of health authorities regarding exercise, but that the majority were using it as a form of weight control.

Parents and children also have received the wrong message about weight control diets. Lifshitz and Moses, in 1989, described eight children presenting with growth failure after the over-zealous application of a self-administered low-fat, low cholesterol diet. Davis et al. (1978) previously had described 36 cases of retarded growth among British children after long-term weight-reducing diets. Clearly, some of our deliberate and well-meaning public health nutrition messages about weight control and dieting have not been targeted properly in the past and people have acted upon the wrong message about body weight and health. Revision of dietary guidelines for Australians would help clarify some of the information and dispel any misperceptions currently held by Australians about healthy body weight and appropriate weight control practices.

Body image among adolescents

Research into body image among adolescents has shown a continual progression towards a more distorted and negative perception of the body, despite most adolescents being of a normal body weight. Early studies from the USA documented a high frequency of middle to late adolescents who were dissatisfied with their bodies and who perceived themselves as overweight despite the majority being of normal weight. That dissatisfaction with weight and shape is more prevalent among girls was demonstrated in a study from Berkeley, California (Huenemann et al., 1966) in which 43 to 56 per cent of early adolescent girls perceived themselves as fat and 63 to 70 per cent wanted to lose weight, despite only 25 per cent being classified as overweight. A later study found 60 per cent of 17-year-old girls already had dieted and that most had commenced dieting at an average age of 14.5 years. Both these studies from the 1960s demonstrated that girls were actively dieting to lose weight, despite the majority having normal body weights. Since that time there have been numerous studies in several different countries replicating the findings that adolescents, particularly girls, incorrectly perceive themselves to be overweight and that this trend has increased among adolescents since the 1960s. A study of nearly 500 Australian adolescents found a high degree of body dissatisfaction and body image concerns among girls and boys (O'Dea et al., 1996).

Gender differences in body satisfaction and body perception

Several Australian studies have shown that adolescents have a poor body image and that the body image of girls is more inaccurate and negative than that of boys. Biddulph et al. (1984) surveyed 277 girls aged 15 to 16 years and found that 63 per cent were dissatisfied with their body weight and wanted to lose weight despite only 15 per cent being overweight. The study showed that a significant proportion (37 per cent) of girls whose weight fell below the normal reference level wanted to lose weight, that the majority of adolescent girls perceived themselves to be overweight and were actively attempting to lose weight, and that normal weight girls desired ideal weights well below recommended references.

In a sample of Brisbane adolescents in 1985 only 14 per cent of girls aged 11 to 19 years were actually overweight or obese; however, 36 per cent of normal weight girls perceived themselves to be overweight. Dissatisfaction with and misperception of weight increased with age. This inaccurate body perception is a feature of adolescent girls to a greater extent than boys. Of the adolescent boys in the Brisbane study, 22 per cent were overweight or obese, and 17 per cent of normal weight boys perceived themselves to be overweight. Of concern was the finding in this study that 1 per cent of underweight girls perceived themselves as overweight. None of the underweight boys, perceived themselves as overweight. The body image of adolescents, particularly girls, leads them to attempt weight loss, often by dangerous and ineffective means.

Henderson et al. (1981) reported that in the late 1970s, 27 per cent of the teenaged girls in a Tasmanian high school sample were dieting to lose weight compared at the time of interview, to less than 10 per cent of males. Research conducted in Melbourne high schools has found that 57 per cent and 18 per cent of girls and boys respectively had dieted to lose weight and, despite this study failing to measure actual heights and weights of participants, it is probable, based on similar research from the same time, that fewer than 25 per cent would have been classified as overweight or obese.

Similar patterns of body image and dieting among Australian and New Zealand adolescents have been found among 13-year-old girls, 15-year-old adolescents and 12- to 17-year-old adolescents. In their study of 15 year olds, Worsley et al. (1990) reported that 68 per cent of normal weight girls and 19 per cent of normal weight boys held misperceptions about being overweight. Forty-five per cent of girls and 9.5 per cent of boys were currently trying to lose weight—an almost identical proportion to that of O'Dea's sample of younger 13-year-old girls.

Both Worsley et al. (1990) and Wertheim et al. (1992) detected dangerous methods of weight control such as regular use of slimming tablets (3 per cent of girls in the Worsley sample, 2 per cent of girls in the Wertheim sample) and vomiting (5 per cent of girls in the Worsley sample, 3 per cent of girls and 1 per cent of boys in the Wertheim sample). The latter study detected 2 per cent of girls and 2 per cent of boys using laxatives and 1 per cent of girls and 2 per cent of boys using diuretics.

The difference in body image between males and females has become clearer over the past two decades. Earlier studies showed that girls had a poorer body image than boys and were more dissatisfied with their weight than were boys. Adolescent boys perceive themselves as too thin and generally want to be bigger and more muscular, although boys' perceptions have not been as distorted as those of adolescent girls. More recent data from Australian school children illustrate the gender differences showing that of girls and boys respectively, 22 per cent and 31 per cent want to have the same body size, 71 per cent and 34 per cent would have liked to be smaller and 7 per cent and 35 per cent want to be larger (O'Dea et al., 1996; O'Dea & Caputi, 2001).

Age and pubertal differences in body image

The desire to become slimmer and the presence of weight-losing behaviours have been observed in preadolescent children as young as seven years. The majority of studies have shown that body image and eating disturbances among girls increase with age and in particular there is dissatisfaction with upper thighs, buttocks and stomach measurements. Boys generally want to be bigger and taller and are more likely to exercise for weight control than to use other dangerous methods. Among a large sample of 36 320 adolescents in the USA (Croll et al., 2002) the percentage of subjects reporting dieting and disordered eating was significantly less in Grades 7 and 8 than in Grades 9 and 10. Similar results have been found in other studies of adolescents, this trend being particularly marked among females (O'Dea & Abraham, 1999b).

The relationships between stage of pubertal development and body image, body satisfaction and disordered eating have been examined in several studies. The majority of studies report that post-menarcheal girls have poorer body image and higher levels of dieting and eating disturbances related to weight control than pre-menarcheal girls and that this relationship is independent of age. A large study by Killen et al. (1992) of 971 Californian girls found pubertal development (as measured by self-reported Tanner stage) to be associated with eating disorder symptoms. Girls who were more advanced developmentally were more likely to manifest eating disorder symptoms than their less developed counterparts and this relationship was independent of age. The normal pubertal changes that occur among girls in this age group, such as increased body weight and percentage of body fat, may account for the higher rates of body dissatisfaction observed in pubertal girls.

Studies of Australian adolescents (O'Dea & Abraham, 1999a; 1999b) and pubertal girls (Abraham & O'Dea, 2001) repeatedly show an increase in body image concerns and body dissatisfaction around puberty. This is particularly pronounced among girls who become naturally rounder and 'fatter' after their first menstrual period.

Hence, the effective teaching of pubertal growth and development and the normal developments experienced by girls and boys during the adolescent growth spurt is a very important role for teachers. Students need to learn that what is happening to their bodies is normal and expected.

Ethnic differences in body image among adolescents

Adolescents from different ethnic backgrounds in Western societies hold fairly stereotypical perceptions and attitudes towards body satisfaction and body weight with the slim female ideal and the muscular male ideal dominating the body image of most young people. Eating disorders are found among all ethnic groups of adolescents and these disorders know no cultural or ethnic boundaries. Ethnic influences on self-perception and body image have not been investigated thoroughly among Australian adolescents, but it does seem that the slim ideal for young females and the larger ideal for males exist throughout cultural and ethnic groups (O'Dea, 1998). Neumark-Sztainer and her colleagues in the USA (2002) found that African American girls were less likely to desire the slim ideal and reported fewer weight concerns than Caucasian girls or girls from Asian, Hispanic or Native American backgrounds. Several researchers have found a larger, rounder ideal body among young women from Maori or Pacific Islander backgrounds (Becker, 1995).

Social class influences on body weight and body image

Body weight and the prevalence of overweight and obesity are related to socioeconomic factors, although the prevalence of overweight and body image concerns occurs among children and adolescents from all social groups. Studies from the USA show that those of lower socioeconomic status (SES) have a higher prevalence of overweight and obesity and this trend has been found in studies of Australian children and adolescents (O'Dea & Caputi, 2001; O'Dea, 2003). Few studies have properly examined the relationship between SES and body image. The literature presents conflicting results on this issue. The majority of studies have found that socioeconomic status is not related to eating disorders, low body satisfaction, poor body image, dieting to lose weight or disordered eating among females. Story et al. (1991) obtained body image information from adolescents and found no difference in any measure between urban, suburban or rural youth. Other studies indicated that females of higher SES were more likely to display dieting behaviours and the desire to lose weight. A study of Australian teenaged girls revealed no difference between girls from upper or lower socioeconomic groups for measures of body image or eating behaviours (O'Dea, 1994). An average of 37 per cent of girls from both groups perceived themselves as 'too fat' and 42 per cent of girls from both groups reported currently to be dieting to lose weight. A more recent study suggests less weight concern among low income boys and girls (O'Dea & Caputi, 2001). Practitioners working with patients with eating disorders believe that the prevalence of distorted body image and of eating disorders is similar in all social classes.

Self-concept, perceived body weight and body image

Research linking physical attractiveness reported by others, perceived physical attractiveness, body weight and height to self-concept indicates that adolescent self-concept is strongly influenced by body weight and perceived body weight.

Lerner et al. (1991) have shown that 12 year olds with positive body image and high physical attractiveness scores, as rated by others and self-perceived, also had better scores on peer and parent relationships, classroom behaviour and self-concept. Similar results were found by Kenealy et al. (1991) who studied 1018 adolescents. Their respondents with poor body image and low self-attractiveness scores also had low self-esteem. Thornton and Ryckman (1991) have examined the relationship between physical attractiveness, physical effectiveness and self-esteem, and shown that adolescents with higher self-attractiveness and self-effectiveness scores had higher self-esteem. A positive self-image, encompassing a positive body image, appears to be beneficial in helping children and adolescents to achieve an overall positive self-image and self-competence.

Conversely, weight concerns and poor body image may reflect poorly on the overall self-image of girls in particular. In a recent study of early adolescent girls (O'Dea, 2006) who were followed for three years, the heaviest girls had poorer self-concept on all measures including academic, athletic, popularity, romantic, social and behavioural self-concept measures. This trend was stable over the three-year study period. The heaviest 20 per cent were far more likely to have dangerously low self-esteem (a strong predictor of eating disorders, depression, drug taking and teen pregnancy) and they also reported that they thought they were less intelligent, popular, socially acceptable, physically attractive, competent at jobs, athletically competent and romantically attractive than their lower-weight classmates.

The Physical Appearance and Close Friendship scores of heavy girls decreased compared to slimmer girls. This pattern was similar for all other self-concept domains and it shows that several aspects of early adolescent girls' self-image may be adversely influenced by a heavy weight status, even though the majority of girls were heavy compared to their peers, but not necessarily overweight.

The most potent influence on self-concept is body weight (O'Dea & Abraham, 1999a), and this has a particularly negative influence on the self-concepts of females with the greater the perception of overweight, the lower the body satisfaction and self-esteem among adolescents (O'Dea, 2006). Overweight adolescents or those who perceive themselves as such have lower body satisfaction and self-esteem than normal weight or overweight adolescents or those that perceive themselves as such.

Relationship of self-concept to dietary restraint and eating disturbances

Low self-esteem and poor body image are associated with dieting behaviour and eating disturbances and some authors suggest that poor self-concept and body concept scores may be predisposing factors for the development of eating disorders.

It has been suggested also that the transition from high school to college is a vulnerable time for young people, particularly for women, and that it is this change in self-concept that predisposes adolescent girls and young women to eating disorders. A British study (Davies & Furnham, 1986) found that girls whose eating was highly restrained were found to have low body esteem and high dissatisfaction with their bodies; they perceived themselves to be more overweight than less restrained eaters. This pattern was the same for girls aged between nine and 14 years. A finding of concern was that half of each age group was average or below average weight index for age.

Health implications of restrained eating

Dietary restraint during childhood and adolescence can have devastating effects on growth and development. Total nutrient needs are greater during adolescence than at any other time of life, except for pregnancy and lactation. The adolescent growth spurt begins at approximately 11.5 years of age in girls and 13.5 years in boys. During this growth spurt adolescents require large amounts of energy from food to provide for rapid growth of bone, muscle and fat. The quality of the adolescent diet also must improve from the child diet to provide the extra iron required for growth and menstruation and the extra calcium for bone growth to assure peak bone density.

Surveys of Australian adolescents and adolescents in the USA have indicated that intakes of these nutrients are low and may account for the high prevalence of iron deficiency anaemia observed among older girls.

Self-imposed restrictive diets have been shown to result in growth failure in children and adolescents. These include strict vegetarian diets, unsupervised lipid lowering diets and calorie restricted diets. Pugliese et al. (1983) described a group of adolescents with growth failure which resulted from self-imposed restriction of caloric intake arising from a fear of becoming obese. The adolescents had height and weight deficits and delayed puberty but no signs of anorexia nervosa or psychiatric disease. The study showed that caloric restraint in growing children can have severe side effects and that the underlying problem is poor body image and fear of obesity.

Results from a study of adolescent female gymnasts aged 12 years show that caloric inadequacy and excessive exercise caused delayed menarche, short stature and delayed bone age; mean leg length was particularly affected (Theintz et al., 1993). The authors suggest that growth failure was due to inadequate and inappropriate nutrition, defective production of growth hormone, low sex steroid concentrations, and, possibly, damage to the growth plates on the bones caused by overuse and leading to premature fusion of epiphyses. They cite energy deficiency as the underlying cause of hormonal imbalance. The girls in this study passed through the skeletal phase of the adolescent growth spurt with almost no acceleration in growth, thus irretrievably compromising their final adult height. Delayed menarche or amenorrhea (when the menstrual cycle and menstrual periods stop) often are the first signs of energy deficiency and growth failure in adolescent girls.

Several practitioners have reported serious cases of amenorrhea among girls and women who undertake weight loss diets. Studies of athletes and ballet dancers show that loss of body fat and weight and excessive physical activity can result in amenorrhea. Preadolescent girls need to achieve a minimum level of body fat required for the onset and maintenance of a regular ovulatory menstrual cycle. Women should have at least 17 per cent of their body weight as fat in order to reach menarche and 22 per cent in order to have regular menstrual cycles. The hormonal changes associated with weight loss and amenorrhea can lead to loss of bone density in adolescent girls and irretrievable growth failure. Bone mineral density may resume if training decreases and normal menstrual function resumes, but peak bone density will not be achieved if diet and weight are compromised during the time of peak bone density development, which some researchers define as being as early as 15 years.

In addition to growth failure, dieting during the adolescent years may carry health risks or impose potentially dangerous methods of weight control such as starvation, self-induced vomiting, using laxative agents, taking diuretic and slimming tablets and cigarette smoking. As well as these psychological risks, some of the behaviours associated with dieting may be associated with the development of eating disorders such as anorexia nervosa or bulimia nervosa. The poor body image of adolescent boys may lead them to injury caused by weightlifting and the use of anabolic steroids in order to build up their muscle mass. A nationwide study of adolescent males from the USA (Buckley et al., 1988) found the prevalence of anabolic steroid use among 17 year olds to be 6.6 per cent in a sample of 3403. More recently, a study of 1492 adolescents in the USA found prevalences of 7.6 per cent among males and 1.5 per cent among females (Komoroski & Rickert, 1992). One boy from a sample of 400 Australian males aged 14 to 17 years admitted using steroids while another eight said they took 'pills' (O'Dea & Rawstorne, 2001). The use of anabolic steroids can have serious consequences for adolescents, particularly in relation to bone growth, production of sperm, high blood pressure, aggression and risk of physical injury.

Theoretical frameworks that address body image

Discussions of eating disorders and body image disturbances rarely touch upon the broader social context in which these disorders develop. Several feminist authors have attempted to develop theoretical frameworks to explain why body image disturbances have become so prevalent in Western society.

Patriarchy and capitalism

Feminist writers explain body image concerns and eating disorders as a result of our patriarchal social and economic structure. Germaine Greer (1971) suggests that normal pubertal development and sexual liberation are denied to females in our society because our male-dominated society thrives on the powerlessness and passivity of women. This imposed denial of an adolescent girl's sexual power results in her inability to accept her changing female body. Greer believes that this inability to reconcile normal physical and sexual development with social conditioning results in antisocial and self-destructive behaviour.

Other feminist writers such as Naomi Wolf (1991) take this argument one step further by suggesting that thin women have a reduced libido and that this serves to make them less threatening to men and less powerful in our society. The fear of adulthood, intimacy and sexuality is described as a possible explanation in some cases of eating disorders, similar to the theory that obesity protects women from sexual advances.

The perpetuation of the slim ideal for women as a result of male domination is a view held by several authors in that large female bodies are seen as a threat to our traditionally male-dominated culture and the use of small, thin, childlike female models is less threatening to men. Wolf describes dieting as 'the most potent political sedative in women's history'. Susan Faludi (1992) describes the tyranny of slimness as part of the overall 'backlash' upon women in Western society after the economic and political gains seen during the 1960s to 1990s. She believes that the portrayal of the ideal woman in our society as thin, weak, childlike and passive via the use of prepubescent models is an attempt to shift power from women back to men and return to the patriarchal, male-dominated society of earlier decades. Likewise, the body building trend among men can be explained as a male attempt to regain physical, political and economic strength and power by a male population which has been losing it steadily for the past 40 years. Several feminist authors believe that the historical patterns of women's liberation and political gains in the 1920s (the vote), 1940s (participation in the war effort) and 1980s (equal opportunity laws) were all followed by trends towards female thinness as a means to divert feminism, and focus women's attention away from upsetting the status quo.

The role of capitalism in the development of an unrealistic body image, distorted eating and eating disorders is commented upon by numerous authors. Susie Orbach, in *Fat is a Feminist Issue*, describes disordered eating as a result of women using food to repress their needs, reward themselves or obtain control within an economic and social system that devalues women and women's work. Food is used to express feelings that our capitalist society traditionally opposes. Likewise, Ramona Koval (1986) states that women use food as the only way to express control and power from within their otherwise powerless lives.

Our capitalist society has been blamed for the creation and marketing of the slim body ideal and the current mesomorphic ideal for young men. According to Germaine Greer the stereotypical woman has been created so that various industries (fashion, diet products, women's magazines) can rely upon an expanding market, and both men and women have been conditioned to desire these gender stereotypes, thus expanding the market even more. Because the ideal cannot be achieved by the majority of women or men and because it is constantly changed, the continuity of the market is ensured. Marilyn French (1992) describes women's magazines as 'cash cows' that create the ideals sold to women. Similar trends are now observed among magazines aimed at men such as *Men's Health*. Kaz Cooke (1994) says in her expose of the beauty industry, 'not much money can be made by telling women there isn't anything wrong with them and they don't need to buy anything to fix it'.

The examination of social and economic structures such as patriarchy and capitalism as possible causes of body image disorders in our society may explain why girls and women are particularly susceptible, why boys and men are starting to develop eating disorders and body image concerns at an increasing rate and why the trend towards body building has emerged within the last 10 years. The latter is addressed by feminists such as Wolf and Faludi who allude to the idea that body mass equates with strength and power and that the body building men are pursuing a resurgence of the physical, economic and political power they have lost over the past four decades. Camille Paglia (1993) explains the resurgence of body building among men as having numerous roots. First, she describes body builders as seeking the 'Apollonian ideal' and the quest for 'knighthood' as a means of dealing with their embattled masculinity. Men use steroids as a type of 'Faustian bargain' for success, because our society rewards men for being big, strong and dominant and because body building is a type of deviance, rebellion and alienation from establishment values. She believes that body builders undergo a type of 'male bonding' because their actions are confirmed by other men. She also sees body building as a quest for a return to a society that celebrates masculinity as a kind of high art.

Cultural perspectives

The prevalence of body image disturbances in both male and female adolescents has been addressed recently by several authors who explain health-damaging adolescent behaviour in terms of cultural factors. A large study of 36 000 adolescents in the USA (Resnick et al., 1993) focused on protective factors against the quietly disturbed and acting-out behaviours, which represent the major social morbidities of adolescence. Results of multivariate analysis among boys and girls repeatedly demonstrated the protective function of caring and connectedness in the lives of adolescents, particularly a sense of belonging and connectedness to family and school. In addition to these two major factors, the study identified a sense of spirituality and low family poverty, low unemployment, low substance abuse and low domestic violence as factors that protect adolescents against high-risk behaviours and health-damaging behaviours. Socioeconomic status did not differentiate participants as low or high risk after the preceding variables were taken into account. The authors discuss the importance of parenting skills and connectedness to the school environment as essential components of health promotion among adolescents. They point to the effects of capitalism in the USA over the past 20 years as reducing the ability of families to thrive. Economic deprivation was cited as one of the major causes of family stress, even though socioeconomic status did not enter into the multivariate assessments of protective factors against health-compromising behaviours. The authors argue that this sense of belonging is difficult to foster in Western society which is based on materialism and individualism.

Likewise, the impact of culture on the health and wellbeing of youth has been discussed as an important factor in the development of problems among youth such as suicide, mental illness, drug abuse, anti-social behaviour and eating disorders. Eckersley (1993) explains this worsening predicament in terms of cultural inadequacy—that modern Western culture fails to meet the most fundamental requirements of any culture. He argues that our Western culture has increasingly focused upon the trappings of capitalism and the domination of our way of life by science to such an extent that it now fails to provide a sense of belonging and purpose, a sense of meaning, self-worth and a moral framework to guide our conduct. The result is a lack of identity that leads to disillusion, disaffection and discontent, some of which is projected onto the body image. All of these theorists identify broad social contexts as being at the root cause of body image disturbances in Western society. Changing the system appears to be vital to changing the prevalence of eating disorders. This includes allowing women more control over their lives and their bodies, reducing the impact of marketing, providing social support networks for young people and reducing the alienation which appears to be a result of capitalism. Changing the system is almost impossible, but educating people to survive within these social and economic contexts is more realistic. Providing people with skills and coping mechanisms to deal with the body image pressures our society imposes may be the answer to alleviating body image problems in future.

In order to promote a healthy body image and a healthy lifestyle among our students, we as teachers and health educators need to help young people to broaden their self-concept to more than appearance. We need to help our students understand that there is much more to life than the way we look. We can help students broaden their self-image to include relationships, intelligence, personality, hobbies, sports interests, spirituality and cultural pride. Many things make us who we are, not just how we look.

Summary

Health and wellbeing among children and adolescents encompass many dimensions including physical, cultural, psychological, emotional, spiritual and social aspects. Overall health can be achieved by balancing all of these facets of child and adolescent development. Teachers and university lecturers can approach the topic of health and wellbeing using this broad definition in order to provide a framework in which to explore and include all of these important messages.

Body image is an important aspect of health for children and adolescents. Children, adolescents and young adults who experience body dissatisfaction and poor body image are likely to pursue the perfect body ideal by unhealthy means such as fad diets, excessive exercise, cigarette smoking (or refusal to quit smoking) and other more dangerous methods of weight control such as vomiting, starvation, and diuretic and laxative abuse. Some individuals, particularly males, may resort to excessive weight lifting, risky drug taking behaviour or using anabolic steroids to increase strength and muscle mass. Attempted weight loss among children, adolescents and adults has been well documented in the medical literature, with numerous cases of growth failure, nutritional deficiencies, delayed puberty and menarche, and amenorrhoea. Dieting is known to precede eating disorders such as anorexia nervosa and bulimia nervosa.

Body dissatisfaction among both young males and females has increased dramatically since the 1960s, along with an increased prevalence of disordered eating, dietary restraint and other weight-losing behaviours. The irreconcilable conflicts between normal growth, natural body structure and composition and the body ideals of society account for many body image problems. While there is no doubt that obesity accounts for some ill health in Australia, the health and nutrition risks associated with the increasing prevalence of poor body image and the quest for the 'perfect' body must not be ignored and can easily be addressed in schools, universities and communities.

References

Abraham S & Mira M (1988), 'Hazards of attempted weight loss', *Medical Journal of Australia, 148*, 324–5.

Abraham S & O'Dea J (2001), 'Body mass index, menarche and perceptions of dieting among peri-pubertal adolescent females', *International Journal of Eating Disorders, 29*(1), 23–8.

Becker AE (1995), *Body, Self and Society: The view from Fiji*, University of Pennsylvania Press, PA.

Biddulph J, Elliott KV, Faldt JE, Fowler P & Dugdale AE (1984), 'The body image and health-related behaviour of teenage girls', *Journal of Food and Nutrition, 41*, 33–6.

Buckley W, Yesalis G, Friedl K, Anderson W, Streit A & Wright J (1988), 'Estimated prevalence of anabolic steroid use among male high school seniors', *Journal of the American Medical Association, 260*, 3441–5.

Cooke K (1994), *Real Gorgeous: The truth about body and beauty*, Allen & Unwin, St Leonards.

Croll J, Neumark-Sztainer D, Story M & Ireland M (2002), 'Prevalence and risk and protective factors related to disordered eating behaviors among adolescents: Relationship to gender and ethnicity', *Journal of Adolescent Health, 31*(2), 166–75.

Davies E & Furnham A (1986), 'Body satisfaction in adolescent girls', *British Journal of Medical Psychology, 59*(3), 279–87.

Davis D, Apley G, Fill G & Grimaldi C (1978), 'Diet and retarded growth—medical cases of 36 British children', *British Medical Journal, 1*, 539–42.

Eckersley R (1993), 'Failing a generation: The impact of culture on the health and well being of youth', *Journal of Pediatrics and Child Health, 29* (Suppl 1), 16–19.

Fallon AE & Rozin P (1985), 'Sex differences in perceptions of desirable body shape', *Journal of Abnormal Psychology, 94*, 102–5.

Faludi S (1992), *Backlash: The undeclared war against women*, Chatto & Windus, London.

French M (1992), *The War Against Women*, Hamish Hamilton, London.

Garner DM, Garfinkel PE, Schwartz D & Thompson M (1980), 'Cultural expectations of thinness in women', *Psychological Reports*, *47*, 483–91.

Gortmaker SL, Must A, Perrin JM, Sobol AM & Dietz WH (1993), 'Social and economic consequences of overweight in adolescence and young adulthood', *New England Journal of Medicine*, *329*(14), 1008–12.

Greer G (1971), *The Female Eunuch*, Granada, London.

Henderson S, Lewis IC, Howell RH & Rayner KJ (1981), 'Mental health and the use of alcohol, tobacco, analgesics and vitamins in a secondary school population', *Acta Sociomedica Scandinavica*, *63*, 186–9.

Huenemann R, Shapiro LR, Hampton MC & Mitchell BW (1966), 'A longitudinal study of gross body composition and body conformation and their association with food and activity in a teenage population', *American Journal of Clinical Nutrition*, *18*, 325–38.

Kenealy P, Gleeson K, Frude N & Shaw W (1991), 'The importance of the individual in the "causal" relationship between attractiveness and self-esteem', *Journal of Community and Applied Social Psychology*, *11*(1), 45–56.

Killen JD, Hayward C, Litt I, Hammer L, Wilson DM, Miner B & Taylor CB (1992), 'Is puberty a risk factor for eating disorders?', *American Journal of Diseases in Children*, *146*, 323–5.

Komoroski EM & Rickert VL (1992), 'Adolescent body image and attitudes to anabolic steroid use', *American Journal of Diseases in Children*, *146*, 823–8.

Koval R (1986), *Eating Your Heart Out*, Penguin Books, Ringwood.

Lerner R, Lerner J, Hess L & Schwab J (1991), 'Physical attractiveness and psychosocial functioning among early adolescents', *Journal of Early Adolescence*, *11*(3), 300–20.

Lifshitz F & Moses N (1989), 'A complication of dietary treatment of hypercholesterolemia', *American Journal of Diseases in Children*, *143*, 537–42.

Morris A, Cooper T & Cooper PJ (1989), 'The changing shape of female fashion models', *International Journal of Eating Disorders*, *8*(5), 593–6.

Neumark-Sztainer D, Croll J, Story M, Hannan PJ, French SA & Perry C (2002), 'Ethnic/racial differences in weight-related concerns and behaviors among adolescent girls and boys: Findings from Project EAT', *Journal of Psychosomatic Research*, *53*(5), 963–74.

O'Dea J (1994), 'Food habits, body image and self-esteem of adolescent girls from disadvantaged and non-disadvantaged backgrounds', *Australian Journal of Nutrition and Dietetics*, *51*, 74–8.

O'Dea J (1998), 'The body size preferences of underweight young women from different cultural backgrounds', *Australian Journal of Nutrition and Dietetics*, *55*, 75–80.

O'Dea J (1999), 'Cross-cultural, body weight and gender differences in the body size perceptions and body ideals of university students', *Australian Journal of Nutrition and Dietetics*, *56*(3), 144–50.

O'Dea JA (2003), 'Differences in overweight and obesity among 4441 Australian schoolchildren of low and middle/high socioeconomic status', *The Medical Journal of Australia*, *179*, 63.

O'Dea JA (2006), 'Self-concept, self-esteem and body weight in adolescent females: A three-year longitudinal study', *Health Psychology*, *11*(4), 599–611.

O'Dea JA & Abraham S (1999a), 'Onset of disordered eating attitudes and behaviors in early adolescence: Interplay of pubertal status, gender, weight, and age', *Adolescence*, *34*(136), 671–79.

O'Dea JA & Abraham S (1999b), 'Association between self-concept and body weight, gender, and pubertal development among male and female adolescents', *Adolescence*, *34*(133), 69–79.

O'Dea J, Abraham S & Heard R (1996), 'Food habits, body image and weight control practices of young male and female adolescents', *Australian Journal of Nutrition and Dietetics*, *53*, 32–8.

O'Dea J & Caputi P (2001), 'Socioeconomic, weight, age and gender interactions in the body image and weight control practices of 6–19 year old children and adolescents', *Health Education Research*, *16*(5), 521–32.

O'Dea J & Rawstorne P (2001), 'Male adolescents identify their weight gain practices, reasons for desired weight gain, and sources of weight gain information', *Journal of the American Dietetic Association*, *101*(1), 105–7.

Orbach S (1979), *Fat is a Feminist Issue*, Berkley Books, New York.

Paglia C (1993), *Sex, Art and American Culture*, Viking, London.

Pugliese M, Lifshitz F, Grad G, Fort P & Marks-Katz M (1983), 'Fear of obesity: A cause of short stature and delayed puberty', *New England Journal of Medicine*, *309*, 513–18.

Resnick M, Harris L & Blum R (1993), 'The impact of caring and connectedness on adolescent health and well-being', *Journal of Pediatrics and Child Health*, *29*(1), 3–9.

Rintala M & Mustajoki P (1992), 'Could mannequins menstruate?', *British Medical Journal*, *305*, 1575–76.

Silverstein B, Perdue L, Peterson B & Kelly E (1986), 'The role of the mass media in promoting a thin standard of bodily attractiveness for women', *Sex Roles*, *14*, 519–32.

Story M, Rosenwinkel K, Himes JH, Resnick M, Harris LJ & Blum RW (1991), 'Demographic and risk factors associated with chronic dieting in adolescents', *American Journal of Disease in Children*, *145*, 994–8.

Theintz GE, Howald H, Weiss U & Sizonenko C (1993), 'Evidence for a reduction of growth potential in adolescent female gymnasts', *Journal of Pediatrics*, *122*, 306–13.

Thornton B & Ryckman R (1991), 'Relationship between physical attractiveness, physical effectiveness and self-esteem: A cross sectional analysis among adolescents', *Journal of Adolescence, 14*(1), 85–98.

Voracek M & Fisher ML (2002), 'Shapely centrefolds? Temporal change in body measures: Trend analysis', *British Medical Journal*, 325, 1447–8.

Wertheim EH, Paxton SJ, Maude D, Szmukler GI, Gibbons K & Hiller L (1992), 'Psychosocial predictors of weight loss behaviors and binge eating in adolescent girls and boys', *International Journal of Eating Disorders, 12*(2), 151–60.

Wiseman C, Gray J, Mosimann J & Ahrens AH (1992), 'Cultural expectations of thinness in women: An update', *International Journal of Eating Disorders, 11*(1), 85–9.

Wolf N (1991), *The Beauty Myth*, Vintage, London.

World Health Organization (1948), Preamble to the Constitution of the World Health Organization, as adopted by the International Health Conference, New York, 19–22 June 1946, and entered into force on 7 April 1948.

Worsley A & Crawford D (1985), 'Who's dieting? The prevalence of dieting in an Australian population', *Journal of Food and Nutrition, 42*(1), 31–2.

Worsley A, Worsley AJ, McConnon S & Silva P (1990), 'The weight control practices of 15-year-old New Zealanders', *Paediatrics and Child Health, 26*, 41–5.

2 Body image and eating problems among boys and girls

Introduction

Body image problems present as body dissatisfaction including the desire to be slimmer among boys and girls and the desire for greater muscularity among boys and young men. Body dissatisfaction may lead to physically damaging behaviours such as dieting, disordered eating, excessive weight lifting, obsessive exercise and steroid abuse and may also lead to more pronounced and life-threatening eating disorders such as anorexia nervosa and bulimia nervosa. Each condition is characterised by low self-esteem, and hence the focus of this book is the prevention of such problems using a self-esteem enhancing approach.

This chapter provides an overview of the whole spectrum of body image issues among adolescents and young adults. Research findings from studies of body image among young people are presented, with a focus on recent Australian data. Case studies of young people with body image concerns and eating problems are presented to illustrate the many individual, family, social, cultural and biological factors associated with the development of these problems.

Description of body image issues and eating problems

Body image issues and disordered eating exist as a spectrum of disorders. The range of issues spreads from body image concerns, body dissatisfaction and dieting to disordered eating and the psychiatric eating disorders anorexia nervosa and bulimia nervosa. In addition, problems may present with excessive exercise and/or an obsessive drive for muscularity, especially among boys and young men. An outline of the spectrum of body image issues is given below.

Body image concerns

Body image concerns encompass height, weight, shape and body composition. Among girls, body image concerns largely concentrate on dissatisfaction with weight and the desire to be a little or a lot lighter and dissatisfaction with the amount of fat on the abdomen, thighs and hips. Among boys, body image concerns focus on the desire for slimness as well as muscularity. Boys also desire a general increase in height and weight, and this is difficult to achieve physiologically because muscularity and height are largely genetically determined. The issue of desired weight gain and muscularity among boys will be discussed in greater detail later in this chapter. Boys desire a general increase in height and body mass, which is almost always associated with an increased desire for strength and masculinity. Body image concerns may lead to dangerous dieting behaviours, weight-lifting injuries and steroid abuse.

Dieting

Dieting includes various strategies for weight loss (predominantly among girls, but also among boys) and weight gain, predominantly among boys. These dietary methods for weight loss and weight gain may be relatively harmless, such as choosing healthy foods, eating low fat foods and eating more fruits and vegetables, but some dietary methods for weight loss may progress to become harmful. Dieting that incorporates starvation, fasting, exclusion of whole food groups and other extreme fads are likely to be physiologically harmful to the growing child or adolescent.

Disordered eating

This facet of body image concern and eating problems incorporates body dissatisfaction, extreme dietary methods for weight loss or weight gain, including fasting, vomiting, laxative abuse, slimming pills and smoking for appetite suppression and weight control. Patterns of eating may oscillate between 'dieting' and starvation to binge eating. These behaviours are present among males and females.

Eating disorders

Eating disorders such as anorexia nervosa, bulimia nervosa, and Eating Disorder Not Otherwise Specified (EDNOS) are psychiatric disorders which include extreme emotions, attitudes, and behaviours surrounding weight and food issues. Eating disorders are serious emotional, psychological and physical problems that can have life-threatening consequences for girls and boys.

Anorexia nervosa is characterised by self-starvation, fear of eating and fear of fat, and excessive deliberate weight loss. The word anorexia is a medical term, which means 'loss of appetite', but anorexia nervosa refers to 'a loss of appetite that is of nervous origin'. The terminology is a little misleading, as sufferers of anorexia nervosa stop eating and lose enormous amounts of weight, but they do not lose their appetite. Symptoms include a sudden or sustained loss of weight, low body weight and/or refusal to maintain a normal weight for height, body type, age and activity level. Sufferers usually lose more than 15 per cent of their body weight and they refuse to eat and gain weight to maintain a body weight of at least 85 per cent of normal. Despite the weight loss, this condition is accompanied by an intense fear of weight gain or being 'fat' even though he/she may be underweight. The young person may repeatedly report feeling 'fat' or overweight despite dramatic weight loss and this is accompanied with a loss of menstrual periods for at least three consecutive months among girls and young women. Sufferers of anorexia nervosa display an extreme concern with body weight and shape. Some people with anorexia nervosa may experience a disturbance in the way they experience their body weight or shape, they may deny having a low body weight problem and they may have an excessive perception of how important their body weight and shape is to their overall self-evaluation. In other words, they place a huge amount of importance on their shape and weight.

Anorexia nervosa is estimated to affect about 1 per cent of teenaged girls with boys and young men certainly experiencing anorexia nervosa, but at substantially lower rates than teenage girls. It is estimated that one tenth of all anorexia nervosa cases are found in males (Hoek & van Hoeken, 2003). Eating disorders have been medically diagnosed in children as young as eight years of age (Ricciardelli & McCabe, 2001; Robinson et al., 2001), but the vast majority occur in post-pubertal teenage girls.

Bulimia nervosa is characterised by recurrent episodes of binge eating which may present as a cycle of binge eating that is followed by purging. Bulimia is characterised by eating that is out of control and involves eating very large amounts of food at a time. The amount of food is huge relative to normal intakes and constitutes much more than most people would eat in one meal. The eating and drinking binge usually takes place in short periods of time usually within a two-hour period. The binge eating in this disorder occurs at least twice a week for three months and people suffering from bulimia nervosa may try to get rid of food and calories through vomiting, laxative abuse, diuretics (fluid pills) or over-exercising. Symptoms of bulimia nervosa include regular episodes of extreme binge eating which may be followed by purging with laxatives or vomiting. Sufferers of bulimia nervosa report feeling 'out of control' during a binge and they usually eat beyond the point of comfortable fullness. Sufferers may resort to purging after a binge (typically by self-induced vomiting, abuse of laxatives, enemas, diet pills and/or diuretics, excessive exercise or fasting), and then a cycle of frequent dieting, guilt, shame and continued extreme concern with body weight and shape results. Sufferers of bulimia nervosa may be normal weight but are often overweight due to the excessive food intake during food binges. Bulimia nervosa is estimated to affect 2–5 per cent of the young female population (Hoek & van Hoeken, 2003).

An Eating Disorder Not Otherwise Specified (EDNOS)

EDNOS is a term used when the sufferer has signs of disordered eating, yet does not meet all of the diagnostic criteria for anorexia nervosa or bulimia nervosa. This is also sometimes known as a 'subclinical' or an 'atypical' eating disorder. For example, a person could show some of the psychological signs of anorexia nervosa and be losing weight, but still be menstruating and not yet underweight for their height. Similarly, the person's actual behaviours may be very similar to those of someone with anorexia nervosa, but they may not have lost weight and may remain at a normal or overweight level. In this case, the EDNOS is diagnosed on the person's perceptions and behaviours rather than their excessive weight loss or loss of menstruation. When a person is suffering from EDNOS, they may have any combination of dieting behaviours, a negative body image, fear of fatness despite significant weight loss, binge eating (compulsive overeating), purging or over-exercising. The person with EDNOS has an eating disorder that does not quite meet the full diagnostic criteria for anorexia nervosa or bulimia nervosa, but he or she is, unfortunately, well on the way to developing a more serious and life-threatening eating disorder. It is estimated that anywhere between 10–20 per cent of young women may have a sub-clinical eating disorder or an eating disorder otherwise unspecified (Hoek & van Hoeken, 2003), although the extremely secretive nature of these disorders suggests that many women and men suffer these disorders in silence and hence, the prevalence statistics may not reflect actual population rates.

To summarise, the prevalence of anorexia nervosa has been estimated to exist among 1 per cent of young women and is most common among teenage girls (Hoek & van Hoeken, 2003; Patton et al., 1990; Robins et al., 1984). Full syndrome bulimia nervosa has been estimated to range from 2–5 per cent of young women (Ben-Tovim et al., 1989; Fairburn & Beglin, 1990; Hoek & van Hoeken, 2003; Kendler et al., 1991) and is most prevalent among young women aged 18 to their early twenties. Both anorexia nervosa and bulimia nervosa occur in boys and young men and it is a myth that these disorders are only found in females. The lack of data on the partial syndrome eating disorders makes the estimation of their prevalence difficult. Previous studies estimate the prevalence of EDNOS to be around 10–20 per cent of young women and girls (Clinton & Glant, 1992; Hall & Hay, 1991; Hoek & van Hoeken, 2003).

Exercise disorders

Many boys and young men engage in exercise that may become excessive or obsessive (Bamber et al., 2003; O'Dea & Abraham, 2002). Exercise dependence is more prevalent among males (Garman et al., 2004) but females are known to be more likely to exercise for aesthetic (as opposed to health related) reasons.

At present there are no specific diagnostic criteria for exercise disorders. Criteria have been proposed but have yet to be accepted by the American Psychiatric Association.

Some researchers have defined dependent exercisers as engaging in more than six hours of exercise per week (Garman et al., 2004), others use the duration of each session, with 'greater than two hours per day not related to professional career or training' used to indicate an exercise disorder (Abraham & Lovell, 1999). Other authors argue that it is the psychological commitment, and withdrawal symptoms experienced that indicate obsessive exercise behaviours (Pasman & Thompson, 1988).

In our study of young university males, 22 per cent met the behavioural criteria for excessive exercise and another 8 per cent were able to be diagnosed with a clinical eating disorder (O'Dea & Abraham, 2002).

Boys and young men are known to see physical activity as a masculine and effective method of weight loss (Drummond, 2002) and it appears to be the primary method of weight loss and weight control in males (Drenowski & Yee, 1987). This complicates the diagnosis of eating and exercise disorders in males, as they are likely to gain muscle (and therefore weight) and so, are unlikely to attract attention to their behaviour. A dedication to exercise has also become socially acceptable and highly admired, as well as being equated with health and fitness (Phillips & Drummond, 2001).

Body dysmorphic disorder

In some cases, an extreme dedication toward weight gain, in particular muscularity, may lead to the development of muscle dysmorphia. This is a form of body dysmorphic disorder involving a pathological fear of being too small, and a persistent desire for, and engagement in activity to achieve a more muscular body. The type of obsessive behaviour becomes so extreme that it interferes with an individual's social and occupational functioning due to the long periods of time spent thinking about, planning and actually exercising (Pope et al., 1997). Men with muscle dysmorphia differ from other men who train with weights in that they aspire to unrealistic levels of muscularity and body size, have increased rates of body dissatisfaction, may abuse anabolic steroids, consume excessive amounts of protein and creatine supplements, engage in dieting and disordered eating practices and have increased levels of anxiety and mood disorders.

The female athlete triad

This condition is a combination of problems that most often occurs in adolescent or young women athletes (Lerand & Williams, 2006). The three major features of the female athlete triad include dieting and disordered eating, menstrual irregularities or loss of menstrual periods and osteoporosis as a result of low body fat leading to low oestrogen which causes the loss of calcium from bones.

The lack of nutrition and body fat resulting from disordered eating can cause a low level of oestrogen and the loss of several or more consecutive menstrual periods. This low body fat and low oestrogen level in turn leads to calcium and bone loss, putting the athlete at greatly increased risk for stress fractures of the bones. Each of these conditions is a medical concern. Together they create serious health risks that may be life threatening. While any female athlete can develop the triad, adolescent girls are most at risk because of the active biological changes and growth spurts, peer and social pressures, and rapidly changing life circumstances that go along with the teenage years. Males may develop similar syndromes.

Health consequences of eating disorders

Eating disorders are serious, potentially life-threatening conditions that affect a person's emotional and physical health. Eating disorders are not just a 'fad' or a 'phase'. People do not just 'catch' an eating disorder for a period of time. They are real, complex and devastating conditions that can have serious consequences for health, productivity and relationships. People struggling with an eating disorder need to seek professional help. The earlier a person with an eating disorder seeks treatment, the greater the likelihood of physical and emotional recovery. If you think that one of your students has an eating disorder, refer them to the school counsellor or a doctor as soon as possible. The following provides an outline of the many physiological consequences of the eating disorders.

Health consequences of anorexia nervosa

Anorexia nervosa is a cycle of self-starvation where the body is denied the essential nutrients it needs to function normally. Thus, the body is forced to slow down all of its processes to conserve energy, resulting in serious medical consequences. Sufferers of anorexia nervosa have an abnormally slow heart rate and low blood pressure. Because the heart is a large and extremely important muscle, its weakness and loss of mass becomes life threatening because the body cannot effectively pump blood to all parts of the body that require oxygen and nutrients. The heart muscle also requires a good supply of oxygen and nutrients itself. In anorexia nervosa, the risk for heart failure rises as the heart rate and blood pressure levels sink lower and lower. Heart failure is a major cause of death in anorexia nervosa. In addition to the day-to-day self-imposed 'starvation' of nutrients and oxygen to the heart and the rest of the body, the starvation of anorexia nervosa results in a significant loss of brain matter, slowed brain function and reduced bone density, which results in thin, brittle bones and osteoporosis. Long-term sufferers of anorexia nervosa have very low bone density and a high risk for fractures as well as growth stunting, because nutrients are not supplied to growing bones during their period of greatest growth and development. The lack of nutrition and kilojoules in anorexia nervosa result in severe muscle loss and weakness, and severe dehydration, which can result in kidney failure, fainting, fatigue and overall weakness. One feature of anorexia nervosa which often helps the young sufferer finally recognise that they may have some sort of eating problem is the loss of hair. The condition causes dry hair and skin and hair loss is common. Sufferers may pull out handfuls of hair at a time and the quality of their hair and skin becomes dull and lifeless. Sufferers can also be identified by the unusual growth of a downy layer of hair called lanugo all over the body, including the face, which probably grows in an effort to keep the body warm. Some recent reports suggest that long-term sufferers of anorexia nervosa have a shrinkage of the brain matter, which may or may not resume after feeding and weight maintenance. In general the signs and symptoms of anorexia nervosa are the same as severe malnutrition and starvation and the tragic final result may end in heart failure and death.

Health consequences of bulimia nervosa

Bulimia nervosa is a very serious condition as the recurrent binge-and-purge cycles of bulimia can affect the entire digestive system and can lead to very serious electrolyte and chemical imbalances in the body that affect the heart and other major organ functions. Probably the most serious consequence of bulimia nervosa is the electrolyte imbalances that can lead to irregular heartbeats and possibly heart failure and death. Electrolyte imbalance is caused by dehydration and loss of potassium, sodium and chloride from the body as a result of purging behaviours. The imbalance in electrolytes is likely to result in sudden and unexpected heart attack. The abuse of the gastrointestinal tract by repeated vomiting, laxative abuse and consumption of huge amounts of food at one time results in the potential for oesophageal and gastric rupture during periods of bingeing. In addition, sufferers often have damage to the mouth, teeth and throat caused by stomach acid which results in inflammation from frequent vomiting. The young person with bulimia nervosa may have a hoarse, husky voice and sore throat from acid damage to the throat. This is often a clear sign that something is wrong which is noticed by parents, teachers, doctors and dentists. Sufferers frequently end up with tooth decay and tooth staining from stomach acids released during frequent vomiting. Often, the dentist is the first person to detect bulimia in a young patient. Chronic irregular bowel movements and constipation may develop as a result of laxative abuse. In severe cases, peptic ulcers and pancreatitis develop as a result of inflammation and possible infection.

In addition to the severe and life threatening physiological consequences of eating disorders are the social and psychological implications of these incredibly damaging conditions. Young sufferers experience much misery and trauma as a result of an eating disorder. Parents, teachers, siblings and friends also suffer the indescribable misery of watching the young person become consumed and destroyed by the eating disorder. The psychological effects can be severe with depression and suicide possible outcomes of a long-term illness. The young sufferer is more often than not very socially isolated, missing a lot of school and missing out on a large portion of what should be a carefree childhood and adolescence. Some students with eating disorders change school frequently in order to cover up the fact that they have a problem. Many sufferers who are hospitalised spend months away from their normal peer group and in the company of other young sufferers. Some therapists believe this is unhealthy as the young person forms part of his/her identity around the fact that they are a member of an eating disorder peer group. Clearly, the enormous amount of human suffering associated with eating disorders justifies the effort to prevent them arising in the first place. Early detection and treatment is also of great value in helping to stop these insidious diseases running their full course.

Causes of eating disorders

There is no clear cause for eating disorders. Recent research points towards a combination of both 'nature and nurture' in the development of body image concerns and eating problems.

The risk of body image problems and eating disorders among young people is increased under certain individual, cultural and biological conditions and these will now be outlined. It is important to note that every child is different and every case of eating disorders has different origins.

For an excellent detailed literature review of eating disorders and the many factors associated with them, see Wilhelm and Clarke (1998), the National Eating Disorders Association website or Levine and Smolak (2006).

Individual factors

Low self-esteem has been shown to be associated with poor body image and eating disorders, and longitudinal research studies show that poor self-esteem actually predicts whether or not a young person will develop an eating disorder.

Poor self-esteem is known to be an important predictor of body image concerns, dieting, disordered eating and eating disorders (Button, 1990; Button et al., 1996; 1997; McVey et al., 2002; Shisslak et al., 1988; Stice, 2002). In a large, longitudinal study of 594 schoolgirls, Button and colleagues (1996) found that girls with low self-esteem at age 11–12 years were at a significantly greater risk of developing severe eating problems by 15–16 years of age.

In a study of Canadian schoolgirls, McVey and her colleagues (2002) found specific aspects of self-esteem to be strongly associated with disordered eating, namely, low competence ratings for physical activity and high importance ratings for social acceptance by peers. One of the conclusions by the authors of this study was to implement self-esteem strategies among adolescent females in order to lower the importance they place on physical appearance in order to prevent disordered eating. Hence the prevention of body image concerns and eating disorders presented in this book largely focuses on the enhancement and protection of self-esteem.

Other factors associated with the development of body image concerns and eating disorders in young people include depression, trauma, difficulty expressing their own needs and feelings (particularly negative feelings), high or unrealistic personal expectations and perfectionism, unrealistic goals that the person believes will bring love and respect from family and friends and an exaggerated need to gain control over one's life. Many researchers believe that the eating disorders anorexia nervosa and bulimia nervosa have their origins in the structure and function of the brain. There may be a certain area of the brain that is 'damaged' or somehow susceptible to the onset of eating disorders. There may also be a strong genetic component that makes young people susceptible to anorexia nervosa just as genetic predisposition can also carry a susceptibility to other related psychiatric disorders and symptoms such as obsessive compulsive disorder and perfectionism. Clinical practitioners report that taking a family history of a young person with anorexia nervosa can often reveal a strong family pattern of eating disorders, perfectionism and obsessive behaviours (personal communication, Dr Julie O'Toole, 2006). In this way, the biological susceptibility to eating disorders that is related somehow to brain function and structure and genetics is then worsened or 'triggered' by environmental factors such as media advertising of the slim ideal or some sort of trauma or life stress. This area of eating disorders research is continuing and building, but not yet conclusive.

Family factors

There are no typical family patterns, but family discord, family enmeshment, problems with relationships, communication and conflict can make the young person feel unvalued and alone and therefore more susceptible to psychological problems. Some sufferers of eating disorders report a perceived family emphasis on being worthwhile only when they are very good at study or sport, or very well behaved, thin and attractive. This sort of unrealistic expectation from parents and teachers can have a severe impact on some young people who feel worthless if they do not match up to the family or school expectations. Family history of eating disorders is not well researched, but is believed to be common and, in combination with the susceptibility of the brain and genetic predisposition, these 'family' factors can make individuals highly susceptible to eating disorders.

Cultural factors

Eating disorders such as anorexia nervosa have been reported throughout history and are reported in many different countries and cultures all over the world. Factors primarily present in Westernised cultures may promote the unrealistic expectations that lead to or 'trigger' the onset of body image concerns and eating disorders. Media messages that equate thinness with beauty, desirability and success have resulted in a culture which almost exclusively portrays happiness, success and femininity with thinness. There is similar media portrayal of height and muscularity among boys and young men equating to happiness, success and masculinity.

Career demands for a 'perfect' body image may also increase the risk of body image disturbances and eating problems, especially among career paths for models, dancers, actresses, celebrities, sports people, personal trainers, fitness instructors and athletes—both males and females. Research shows that these young people are more frequently affected by eating disorders than those who do not experience work-related weight and body image pressures. Similarly, people with a predisposition towards perfectionism and body image concerns may be attracted to weight-related careers such as dancing or athletics. It is probably no coincidence that the sort of extremely competitive and almost obsessive attitudes and behaviours that promote sporting success also promote body image concerns and disordered eating.

Research suggests more men are suffering from eating disorders because the muscular and lean image of men (Olivardia et al., 2004; Pope et al., 1997). The media is having an effect on men's body image and health in the same way it does on women's. More men, however, are over-exercising in the attempt to develop the ideal body shape. This can cause health problems too as obsessive exercise can lead to injuries, exercising when ill, tired or injured, drug use and social disruption.

In a study of young male university students (O'Dea & Abraham, 2002), we found that 3 per cent of the young men had bulimia nervosa; another 3 per cent were using vomiting to try to control their weight and a concerning 8 per cent had an exercise disorder which caused them to exercise daily for more than two hours for weight control and shape concerns (not related to their sport or job) and kept them away from relationships and social activities. This sort of obsessive behaviour is as equally damaging to the overall health of young people as the more well-known eating disorders such as anorexia nervosa and bulimia nervosa.

Many other factors can trigger an eating disorder if someone is already vulnerable. These include a life crisis or the death of a loved person, family changes, moving home or school, a change of job, beginning university, school problems or a personal failure or perceived failure (Wilhelm & Clarke, 1998).

An eating disorder may also develop when there is a gradual build-up of problems which on their own seem small. The person may interpret each small problem or failure as 'evidence' that they are not worthy and the resulting low self-esteem results in behaviours associated with the eating disorders.

Biological factors

Some researchers suggest that eating disorders may be genetically determined. Substantial effort has been put into the exploration of the biological background of eating disorders, through family, twin and molecular genetic studies. According to a recent review, family studies have shown that anorexia nervosa and bulimia nervosa are strongly familial, and that familial factors appear to be shared by both disorders (Slof-Op't Landt et al., 2005). In their review, twin studies consistently yielded moderate to substantial heritabilities, suggesting that there is a strong genetic link to eating disorders. In addition, there have been gene studies that focused on eating disorders with seven gene linkage regions being identified in genome-wide screens. These results suggest a gene link but while many genetic association studies have been performed, no consistent association between a candidate gene for anorexia nervosa or bulimia nervosa has yet been reported.

Body image concerns and eating disorders in athletes

Several studies suggest that body image concerns and eating disorders are more frequent among athletes and competitive sports people (Beals & Manore, 1994; Sundgot-Borgen, 1993; Wilmore, 1991).

Involvement in organised sports can offer many benefits, such as physical fitness, social interaction, improved self-esteem and body image and encouragement for individuals to remain active throughout their lives. A recent study found that students involved in sports have better food habits and more nutritious diets than those who are not involved in sports or athletics (Croll et al., 2006).

Competitive athletic competition, however, may also cause psychological and physical stress in some vulnerable young people. Likewise, perfectionist, competitive and obsessive young people may do very well at sports. When the pressures of athletic competition are added to an existing cultural emphasis on thinness, the risks increase for athletes to develop disordered eating. Among elite athletes, up to one-third of females report attitudes and symptoms placing them at risk for anorexia nervosa. Though most athletes with eating disorders are female, male athletes are also at risk—especially those competing in sports that tend to place an emphasis on the athlete's diet, appearance, size and weight requirements, such as wrestling, body building, rowing, dance, diving, running and gymnastics (National Eating Disorders Association, 2005).

Factors associated with body image concerns and eating disorders in athletes and sports people

Sports that emphasise appearance or weight requirements are associated with body image concerns and eating disorders—gymnastics, diving, rowing, dance, body building or wrestling, for example, wrestlers trying to 'make weight.' Sports that focus on the performance of the individual rather than the entire team are also likely to contain more than the average number of participants with eating problems. For example, gymnastics, running, endurance sports, figure skating, dance or diving, versus team sports like basketball or soccer (Johnson et al., 1999).

Involvement in weight-related careers, such as fitness trainers, is known to be associated with increased body image concerns and disordered eating in young college males (Phillips & Drummond, 2001). In addition to the pursuit of the slim or muscular ideal required for a certain type of sport, some participants may also have an inaccurate belief that lower body weight will improve performance. This belief is usually inaccurate because severe weight loss and starvation may hinder physical fitness and result in lethargy. Involvement or training for a sport since childhood or being an elite athlete is associated with eating problems, as these patterns appear to become entrenched over time and with age. Low self-esteem, family dysfunction, families with a history of eating disorders, chronic dieting, a history of physical or sexual abuse, peer, family and cultural pressures to be thin, and any other traumatic life experiences may predispose a person to an eating disorder.

Weight loss issues for girls and boys

Weight gain in pubertal girls and boys is a natural consequence of growth. Research studies have found that for every centimetre increase in height, a child or adolescent can expect to have an approximate correlating 0.5 to 1 kilogram increase in body weight. The composition of this weight increase includes fluid (water, blood, spinal fluid), muscle mass, bone and fat. Considering that most growing teenagers will grow 6–8 centimetres per year with a corresponding 3–5 kilogram weight increase, this message is a very important one for students to understand. Unfortunately, many adolescents, particularly girls, do not understand the link between height increase and weight increase and they mistakenly believe that any weight gain must be fat.

In both girls and boys, body composition becomes relatively 'fatter' after the adolescent height spurt when they 'fill out' and lay down muscle and fat. This 'rounding' is perfectly natural especially for females as they attain the adult female shape. The consequence of this rapid adolescent weight gain is often body dissatisfaction and dieting in girls and boys.

It is interesting to note that some male adolescents may begin their growth spurt late in adolescence, with some not experiencing their height spurt until age 16 or 17. Therefore, young men will continue to grow into their early twenties and hence, we often see young college and university males whose height and weight are still increasing. The issue of normal growth in adolescence is dealt with in more detail in Chapter 6.

The role of teachers and lecturers in allaying students' body image concerns and fears is of paramount importance, as this is a crucial stage when dieting and disordered eating may be averted.

The following table lists the weight loss behaviour of 470 young Australian adolescents aged 11–14 years (O'Dea et al., 1996).

TABLE 2.1 Methods of weight loss used by young adolescents

Methods of weight loss used by young adolescents	Males %	Females %
Exercise	58.8	72.9
Not eating between meals	24.3	44.3
Keeping busy	13.3	37.3
Own diet	15.6	35.3
Selecting low joule foods	15.0	32.5
Drinking water before meals	11.0	28.4
Skipping meals	12.7	19.5
Excessive exercise	12.7	19.5
Becoming vegetarian	4.0	16.4
Avoiding situations where there will be food	5.2	14.7
Diet from magazine	2.9	16.1
Taking advantage of illness to avoid eating	3.5	13.7
Natural laxatives, e.g. bran	5.2	11.3
Fasting, starvation	3.5	9.9
Other method	2.9	6.2
Laxatives	3.5	3.8
Trying to vomit	2.3	3.4
Vomiting	1.7	3.8
Smoking	2.3	2.4
Slimming pills	0	2.4
Not swallowing food	0.6	2.1

While the majority of weight control methods were relatively harmless (exercise, not eating between meals, keeping busy to avoid eating because of boredom), it should be noted that this age group of adolescents is pubertal and both males and females at this age would be expected to be growing and developing quite rapidly and weight loss from dieting behaviour may interfere with normal growth and development in these young adolescents.

One of the findings of most concern in this early study was the number of young girls who were engaged in dangerous and harmful weight loss behaviours including fasting (9.9 per cent), laxatives (3.8 per cent), vomiting or trying to vomit (7.2 per cent), slimming pills (2.4 per cent) and smoking cigarettes for appetite suppression and weight control (2.4 per cent). Boys were not exempt from these extreme weight loss methods with around 2.3 per cent of boys engaging in these behaviours.

It was also interesting to note that 16.4 per cent of the girls reported becoming vegetarian in order to lose weight and this is a well-known excuse used by young people with an eating disorder.

In a large study of 1131 children and adolescents aged 6–19 years (O'Dea & Caputi, 2001), we found high rates of weight loss behaviours in primary school children (53 per cent of 6–12-year-old girls and 27 per cent of boys) and in high school children (27 per cent of 12–19-year-old girls and 33 per cent of boys). While the majority of weight loss behaviours were found among heavier children and those who probably would be considered overweight on clinical examination, a consistent proportion of weight loss behaviours were found among normal weight primary school children (28 per cent normal weight girls, 16 per cent normal weight boys) and high school children (45 per cent normal weight girls, 10 per cent normal weight boys).

The results of this large Australian study confirmed earlier reports from my own studies and those of other researchers that primary and secondary school children act upon their largely unrealistic weight concerns and fear of normal pubertal weight gain by attempting to lose weight. The high level of weight loss attempts found among both genders in this study (58 per cent girls, 30 per cent boys) and the use of dangerous weight control methods such as starvation, vomiting, laxative abuse, diet pills and cigarette smoking, confirm the need for primary and secondary school teachers to implement body image improvement and eating disorder prevention programs among children and adolescents.

Weight gain methods in boys

Body image concerns and eating problems have most commonly focused on the weight loss behaviours of girls and the risk of them developing eating disorders. Recent research has focused on the body image concerns of young males and the dangers of some common weight gain methods.

A large study of 397 male adolescents aged 13–18 years was undertaken to investigate the weight gain practices, beliefs and attitudes of male adolescents, their reasons for wanting to gain weight, their sources of weight gain information and any differences between age groups of boys (O'Dea & Rawstorne, 2001). The boys were randomly selected from three government high schools and two Catholic boys schools in NSW.

The inaccuracy of the boys' nutrition knowledge and the inappropriateness of their dietary behaviours is evidenced by the variety of results. Of the 103 boys who had deliberately tried to gain weight in the past 12 months,

0.7%	Lost 2 kilograms
42.8%	Reported no weight gain
31.0%	Reported weight gain of 1–5 kilograms
22.0%	Reported weight gain of 6–10 kilograms
3.5%	Reported weight gain of 11–30 kilograms

A finding of concern in this study was that many of the dietary weight gain methods that had been used by the boys in the past 12 months were unhealthy ways of supporting dietary methods and included, in descending order:

- eating more food and exercising less
- eating more fatty, fried and 'junk' foods
- eating more food in general
- eating more and playing sports or lifting weights
- eating healthy food and exercising more

- consuming protein milk formulas
- consuming more meat, chicken, eggs, plus lifting weights
- fad dietary methods—eating butter, eating more meat, drinking beer, eating chocolate, eating five or more meals per day, eating at night, drinking 'power drinks' eating raw eggs and egg whites
- taking creatine monohydrate, vitamins, minerals, zinc.

The boys' weight gain practices, body image, beliefs and weight-related advice they received from others are listed in Table 2.2.

TABLE 2.2 The weight gain practices, body image, beliefs and weight-related advice received from others among male adolescents aged 13–18 years

Weight gain practices	%
Currently trying to gain weight	27.7
Currently trying to build up my body	59.4
Tried to gain weight in past 12 months	25.9
Beliefs about body	
I feel I should develop my muscles	75.3
I need to build up my body	60.7
Advice from others	
People tell me to gain weight	23.2
People tell me to build up my body	34.3
People tell me to do more exercise	31.2
People tell me I don't eat enough	14.4
Body image	
Too thin	15.4
About right	66.5
Too fat	17.5
Desired weight	
A lot heavier	3.8
A little heavier	34.3
Present weight	31.7
A little lighter	25.9
A lot lighter	3.8

Taking 'drugs' was reported by 20 students and they were identified as 'pills', steroids, fluid pills and insulin. One boy reported taking steroids and one other reported injecting insulin. The boys reported that they were using drugs obtained from gymnasiums but none of the boys were aware that they were at high risk for taking unidentified substances that are peddled by drug dealers, and adverse effects from taking known or unknown substances and infections caused by needle sharing.

The use of steroids is known to cause high blood pressure, high blood cholesterol, acne, gynecomastia (male breasts), aggression ('roid rage'), testicular shrinkage and liver damage.

The reasons for desired weight gain given by boys are listed below in descending order.

- Increased physical strength   67%
- Greater fitness   51%
- Better body image   51%
- Improved sports performance   51%
- Better self-protection   51%
- Improved attractiveness   35%
- Better appearance in front of others   35%
- Increased 'toughness'   35%
- Enhanced self-esteem   35%
- As a hobby   35%
- To fit in with others in peer group   18%

The specific sports related to the boys' desired weight gain were football, soccer, rugby, basketball, hockey and boxing.

The boys received weight gain information and advice from:

- parents   26%
- friends   24%
- gym instructors, sports coaches, swim coaches, YMCA   25%
- teachers   18%
- health professionals   15%
- magazines   14%
- television   13%
- products from gymnasiums   11%
- products from health food stores   10%
- advertisements   10%
- food labels   7%
- books   6%

Interestingly, there were no age differences in any of the weight gain variables studied, suggesting that these behaviour patterns are well-entrenched among teenage boys by early adolescence.

One-third of the boys in the study were actively trying to gain weight using both sensible methods and inappropriate methods such as eating more fatty, fried and 'junk' food, eating more food while exercising less and eating butter. Some weight gain methods were based on nutrition misinformation and could be health damaging (e.g. raw eggs, creatine).

The use of dietary supplements such as creatine monohydrate has not been thoroughly investigated among adolescents. Some studies of creatine usage have warned of possible associated health risks in humans such as kidney dysfunction, stomach upsets, asthmatic symptoms and excessive secretion of insulin in rats. Clearly, the use of potentially dangerous methods of weight gain warrant further investigation.

The results of this study describe in detail the deliberate weight gain practices of young males and their reasons for desired weight gain. This provides valuable information for those working with young people, including parents, teachers, health professionals and sports coaches who require sound nutrition information and education about appropriate growth and weight gain for adolescents.

Teachers, university lecturers and sports coaches may apply these findings to better understand the motives and aspirations of young males; in teacher training, to better educate those who work with adolescent males including parents, teachers, sports coaches and gym instructors; and in health education, to provide information that is age-appropriate, scientifically-based and is of maximum relevance and interest to young people.

Case studies of students with eating disorders

The following real-life case studies illustrate the typical individual, cultural, biological and family factors involved in the development of eating disorders among three young people. These true case studies are presented to help understand how an eating disorder can develop from body image concerns to disordered eating and then to a life-threatening situation that requires urgent medical treatment and attention. All of the young people in these case studies were fortunate enough to have the assistance of parents, teachers, doctors or other adults who were able to help them get the treatment they required to recover from their illnesses. All names, places and personal details in the following case studies have been changed to protect the privacy of the young people involved—adapted with permission from Wilhelm and Clarke, 1998.

Lara

Lara, a 16-year-old girl was taken to her general practitioner by her mother, who was concerned that, after becoming vegetarian the previous year, the girl was now eating all of her meals in her bedroom. Her teacher had also expressed concern that Lara's grades had dropped and she no longer participated in PE classes or sport. Lara had previously considered herself overweight despite her BMI of 22 being quite normal. Her father, brother and several friends had made comments about this. She had taken to wearing loose, heavy clothing in the middle of summer. She was more weepy and irritable. She was now 4 kg underweight (BMI of 17) and her periods had stopped six months previously. A restrictive eating pattern was revealed. Routine blood studies gave normal results.

Lara reported her parents as 'intrusive', and ate in her room because meal times had become 'war zones'. She was having less to do with her friends, some of whom now had boyfriends.

Lara was referred to a local dietitian, who commenced a food diary and sensible eating program and instituted weekly follow-ups. The general practitioner saw the rest of the family for education and reassurance, including recommendations for reading material. The mother said that she herself had experienced short periods of restricted eating (when stressed and during times of change) starting as a teenager. She then expressed grief for an older daughter who had died in a car accident three years previously. Later, her husband aired his feelings about his loss, stating that he had not felt able to grieve openly for fear of distressing his wife. Discussion with the parents also focused on relieving the anxiety around meal time and leaving the responsibility for eating with the daughter.

Lara also benefited from 12 sessions of therapy with a psychologist, aimed at changing her dysfunctional ideas about food, eating and body shape. These positive attitudes to sensible eating were reinforced during school health education classes. During school PE, Lara's teachers praised her participation and helped the whole class to have fun in a non-competitive environment. After two months the dietitian was satisfied with the change in types and quantity of food consumed. Lara was eating with her family, her teachers reported that she was concentrating better and seemed happier. Monthly reviews with the general practitioner and dietitian were organised for the next year.

Dimitri

Dimitri, a 15-year-old boy of Greek origin presented to his local doctor after his teacher had expressed concern to his mother and father. Dimitri's teacher was worried about his dramatic weight loss over the past six months. The teacher was concerned about his dramatic weight loss but also his lack of social interaction, as he was an unusually isolated and quiet boy who spent his lunch hours at school in the library and most of his weekend at home playing computer games. He was overweight prior to the sudden weight loss but a medical examination revealed that he was otherwise well. The parents spoke little English and their son functioned as their interpreter for all business and health transactions. The boy spent at least a day per week out of school taking his parents to various medical or legal appointments. He related as a serious 'pseudo-mature' young man but was not clinically depressed. Examination revealed that he had become 20 per cent underweight, with delayed puberty. He was concerned about his personal fitness and stated that he was secretly engaging in strenuous exercise for about three hours per day in his bedroom.

He was referred to a dietitian, whom he saw regularly. Interpreters were provided for the parents, allowing the boy to resume full-time schooling. On a subsequent visit to the general practitioner, the young man confided his concern about his parents and his relief that they were no longer his sole responsibility. His teachers reported that he became more engaged in school and extracurricular activities and, slowly, Dimitri gained weight and resumed normal growth and pubertal development. Dimitri's PE teacher encouraged and supervised his sensible participation in soccer and weight lifting and this reduced his need for the secret bedroom exercise program.

Emma

Emma is a 19-year-old girl who had recently started university and left home to live in shared accommodation. She presented to her lecturer's office with tiredness, weepiness, erratic sleeping and reported that she was unable to complete an assignment on time. After discussing her lack of sleep, Emma grudgingly admitted to late night food binges and self-induced vomiting, which had been occasional in the past but much more regular since leaving home. She stated that she could no longer control her vomiting and had started taking up to one packet of laxatives per day. Emma was reassured by her lecturer and referred straightaway to the campus doctor and counsellor. She had no physical or biochemical abnormalities.

Emma agreed to take some medication for depression, which led to rapid improvement in mood and gradual improvement in sleep pattern. The counsellor provided an outlet for Emma to express her emotions, fears and to discuss her family issues. The campus doctor showed her a book outlining a self-help program for binge eating that she was prepared to follow under the doctor's supervision. She understood that the dietitian referral was an option, but preferred to 'give it a go' by herself first. She also undertook to stop taking laxatives. She was encouraged to use a problem-solving approach to her current difficulties, as outlined in the self-help book.

After several sessions of counselling, Emma decided to break up a current relationship with a man because 'it isn't going anywhere' and talked to her other lecturers about study-related difficulties. Subsequently, she felt supported by her lecturers and much happier about her ability to cope. She was seen weekly by her campus doctor and counsellor for the first month and then fortnightly for three months. Emma now understands that her eating disorder is triggered by stress and depression and she realises that she needs to take care of herself in order to stay psychologically and physically healthy.

Summary

Body image concerns, eating disorders and obsessive exercise are relatively common among adolescent girls and boys and young adults. The stereotypical slim female ideal and the mesomorphic muscular male ideal are well-entrenched in the hearts and minds of young people who seek the success, admiration, social approval and attractiveness that attaining these ideals offers. Unfortunately, pursuing these body image ideals can be very unhealthy for young people who may damage their physical, psychological and social health in the futile pursuit of bodily perfection. The case studies in this chapter illustrate the physical harm and immense unhappiness that eating disorders can wreak upon young people and their families. The role of teachers and university lecturers in the early detection and referral of the susceptible students in their care is very important as early treatment can help students overcome these extremely dangerous and pernicious conditions. In addition, the prevention of body image concerns and eating disorders among school students and university students is highly desirable and successful preventive efforts will be described in the next chapter.

Recommended websites

http://www.NationalEatingDisorders.org

This website is produced by the National Eating Disorders Association which is the largest not-for-profit organisation in the USA working to prevent eating disorders and provide treatment referrals to those suffering from anorexia, bulimia and binge eating disorder and those concerned with body image and weight issues. This website provides information about programs, products and services of superior quality that support the elimination of eating disorders.

The website also contains information about prevention programs for a wide range of audiences, educational materials and a toll-free eating disorders information and referral helpline.

http://www.thebutterflyfoundation.org.au/content/view/full/54

This website provides information about The Butterfly Foundation, which is a community-based charitable organisation that supports eating disorder sufferers and their carers through direct financial relief, advocacy and lobbying, awareness campaigns, health promotion and early intervention work and professional training in primary and secondary schools. The website also provides information about the BodyThink program for schools which promotes a healthy body image in school students.

http://www.depressionet.com.au

This website provides a comprehensive resource of information; help to access health-care professionals, treatments and tools throughout Australia; and 24-hour peer support via email, messageboards and chat rooms.

http://www.eatingdisorders.org.au/

This website is produced by the Eating Disorders Foundation of Victoria, a non-profit incorporated association founded in the mid 1980s to support those whose lives are affected by eating disorders, and to better inform the community about these disorders. The website provides information, knowledge, support and resources in order to encourage resilience and recovery and lessen the impact of the eating disorder on the quality of life of individuals and families.

http://www.betterhealth.vic.gov.au

This website is operated by the Better Health Channel, which was established in 1999 by the Victorian Government. The information on the site aims to help improve the health and wellbeing of the Victorian community. The website provides very high quality online health and medical information on various health topics.

http://www.daa.asn.au/

This is the website for the Dietitians Association of Australia. The website contains information about food, nutrition and health and it is an excellent resource for students and teachers.

References

Abraham S & Lovell NH (1999), *Eating and exercise examination—Computerized*, Ashwood Medical, Melbourne.

Bamber DJ, Cockerill IM, Rodgers S & Carroll D (2003), 'Diagnostic criteria for exercise dependence in women', *British Journal of Sports Medicine, 37*(5), 393–400.

Beals KA & Manore MM (1994), 'The prevalence and consequences of subclinical eating disorders in female athletes', *International Journal of Sports Nutrition, 4*(2), 175–95.

Ben-Tovim D, Subbiah N, Scheutz B & Morton J (1989), 'Bulimia: Symptoms and syndromes in an urban population', *Australia and New Zealand Journal of Psychiatry, 23*, 73–80.

Button E (1990), 'Self-esteem in girls aged 11–12: Baseline findings from a planned prospective study of vulnerability to eating disorders', *Journal of Adolescence, 13*, 407–13.

Button EJ, Loan P, Davies J & Sonuga-Barke EJS (1997), 'Self-esteem, eating problems and psychological well-being in a cohort of schoolgirls aged 15–16: A questionnaire and interview study', *International Journal of Eating Disorders, 21*, 39–47.

Button EJ, Sonuga-Barke EJ, Davies J & Thompson M (1996), 'A prospective study of self-esteem in the prediction of eating problems in adolescent schoolgirls' questionnaire findings', *British Journal of Clinical Psychology, 35*, 193–203.

Clinton DN & Glant R (1992), 'The eating disorders spectrum of DSM-III-R: Clinical features and psycho-social concomitants of 86 consecutive cases from a Swedish urban catchment area', *Journal of Nervous and Mental Disease, 180*, 244–50.

Croll JK, Neumark-Sztainer D, Story M, Wall M, Perry C & Harnack L (2006), 'Adolescents involved in weight-related and power team sports have better eating patterns and nutrient intakes than non-sport-involved adolescents', *Journal of the American Dietetic Association, 106*(5), 709–17.

Drenowski A & Yee DK (1987), 'Men and body image: Are males satisfied with their body weight?', *Psychosomatic Medicine, 49*, 626–34.

Drummond M (2002), 'Men, body image and eating disorders', *International Journal of Men's Health, 1*, 79–93.

Fairburn CG & Beglin SJ (1990), 'Studies of the epidemiology of bulimia nervosa', *American Journal of Psychiatry, 147*, 401–8.

Garman JF, Hayduk DM, Crider DA & Hodel MM (2004), 'Occurrence of exercise dependence in a college-aged population', *Journal of American College Health, 52*(5), 221–8.

Hall A & Hay P (1991), 'Eating disorder patient referrals from a population region 1977–1986', *Psychological Medicine, 21*, 699–701.

Hoek H & van Hoeken D (2003), 'Review of the prevalence and incidence of eating disorders', *International Journal of Eating Disorders, 34*, 383–96.

Johnson C, Powers PS & Dick R (1999), 'Athletes and eating disorders: The National Collegiate Athletic Association Study', *International Journal of Eating Disorders, 26*, 179–88.

Kendler KS, MacLean C, Neale M, Kessler R, Heath A & Eaves L (1991), 'The genetic epidemiology of bulimia nervosa', *American Journal of Psychiatry, 148*, 1627–37.

Lerand SJ & Williams JF (2006), 'The female athlete triad', *Pediatrics in Review, 27*(1), e12–13.

Levine MP & Smolak L (2006), *The Prevention of Eating Disorders: Theory, research and practice*, Lawrence Erlbaum, Mahwah, NJ.

McVey GL, Pepler D, Davis R, Flett GL & Abdolell M (2002), 'Risk and protective factors associated with disordered eating during early adolescence', *Journal of Early Adolescence, 22*(1), 75–95.

National Eating Disorders Association (2005), 'Eating disorder information index', viewed at: http://www.edap.org/p.asp?WebPage_ID=294

O'Dea J & Abraham SF (2002), 'Eating and exercise disorders in young college men', *Journal of American College Health, 50*, 273–8.

O'Dea J & Caputi P (2001), 'Socioeconomic, weight, age and gender interactions in the body image and weight control practices of 6–19 year old children and adolescents', *Health Education Research, 16*(5), 521–32.

O'Dea J & Rawstorne P (2001), 'Male adolescents identify their weight gain practices, reasons for desired weight gain, and sources of weight gain information', *Journal of the American Dietetic Association, 101*(1), 105–7.

O'Dea J, Abraham S & Heard R (1996), 'Food habits, body image and weight control practices of young male and female adolescents', *Australian Journal of Nutrition and Dietetics, 53*, 32–8.

Olivardia R, Pope HG Jr, Borowiecki JJ & Cohane G (2004), 'Biceps and body image: The relationship between muscularity and self-esteem, depression, and eating disorder symptoms', *Psychology of Men & Masculinity, 5*(2), 112–20.

Pasman L & Thompson KJ (1988), 'Body image and eating disturbance in obligatory runners, obligatory weightlifters, and sedentary individuals', *International Journal of Eating Disorders, 7*, 759–69.

Patton GC, Johnson-Sabine E, Woods K, Mann AH & Wakeling A (1990), 'Abnormal eating attitudes in London schoolgirls: Outcome at twelve month follow-up', *Psychological Medicine, 20*, 383–94.

Phillips J & Drummond M (2001), 'An investigation into the body image perception, body satisfaction and exercise expectations of male fitness leaders: Implications for professional practice', *Leisure Studies, 20*, 95–105.

Pope HG, Gruber AJ, Choi P, Olivardia R & Phillips K (1997), 'Muscle Dysmorphia: An underrecognized form of body dysmorphic disorder', *Psychosomatics, 38*, 548–57.

Ricciardelli LA & McCabe MP (2001), 'Children's body image concerns and eating disturbance—A review of the literature', *Clinical Psychology Review, 21*(3), 325–45.

Robins LN, Helzer JE, Weissman M, Orvaschel H, Gruenberg EM, Burke JD & Regier D (1984), 'Lifetime prevalence of specific psychiatric disorders in three sites', *Archives of General Psychiatry, 41*, 949–58.

Robinson TN, Chang JY, Haydel KF & Killen JD (2001), 'Overweight concerns and body dissatisfaction among third grade children: The impacts of ethnicity and socioeconomic status', *Journal of Pediatrics, 138*(2), 181–7.

Shisslak CM, Crago M, Renger R & Clark-Wagner A (1988), 'Self-esteem and the prevention of eating disorders', *Eating Disorders, 6*, 105–17.

Slof-Op't Landt MCT, van Furth EF, Meulenbelt I, Slagboom P, Meike B, Dorret I & Bulik CM (2005), 'Eating disorders: From twin studies to candidate genes and beyond', *Twin Research & Human Genetics, the Official Journal of the International Society for Twin Studies, 8*(5) 467–82.

Stice E (2002), 'Risk and maintenance factors for eating pathology: A meta-analytic review', *Psychological Bulletin, 128*(5), 825–48.

Sundgot-Borgen J (1993), 'Prevalence of eating disorders in elite female athletes', *International Journal of Sport Nutrition, 3*, 29–40.

Wilhelm KA & Clarke SD (1998), 'Eating disorders from a primary care perpective', *Medical Journal of Australia, 168*(9), 458–63.

Wilmore JH (1991), 'Eating and weight disorders in the female athlete', *International Journal of Sports Nutrition, 1*, 104–17.

Positive body image programs in schools

Introduction

Body image concerns and eating problems among children and adolescents are becoming increasingly targeted for preventive health education and health promotion programs in schools and universities. The current co-occurrence of increasing body image concerns and disordered eating with increasing rates of childhood obesity makes the role of teachers and health educators complicated because of concerns that we must 'Do no harm' in our efforts to ameliorate both issues in schools and universities. Teachers and health educators need to be careful to ensure that the implementation of programs for the prevention of childhood obesity does not inadvertently create food concerns, body image issues, weight stigma, prejudice or eating disorders. Similarly, eating disorder prevention programs must take care not to condone poor food choices, lack of physical activity or obesity, or to glamorise or normalise dieting or disordered eating. This chapter summarises activities from body image programs and eating disorder prevention programs in schools and outlines self-esteem and media literacy approaches that have produced positive results in some large, randomised and controlled interventions. Several suggestions for safe and successful school-based activities and strategies are outlined and discussed.

The need for positive body image programs

Body image problems may be observed among children, adolescents and young people as eating disorders, body dissatisfaction, health damaging weight control practices such as vomiting, fasting, laxative and steroid use and excessive exercise. Anorexia nervosa has been found to affect 0.5–1 per cent of adolescent girls and bulimia nervosa affects 2–5 per cent of girls and young women (Fisher et al., 1995) with sub-clinical partial-syndrome eating disorders being much higher. These sub-clinical partial syndrome eating disorders affect 10–20 per cent of girls and women (Killen et al., 1986). These findings may be inaccurate because of the very secretive nature of these disorders and because young people with eating disorders tend to not participate in research studies about eating disorders (Beglin & Fairburn, 1992).

Disordered eating behaviours, including at least one of the following: fasting, skipping meals to lose weight, diet pills, vomiting, laxatives, smoking cigarettes and binge eating, were recently reported by a staggering 56 per cent of 9th grade females and 28 per cent of 9th grade males (Croll et al., 2002). Reports of dieting, fear of fatness, body image concerns and weight loss attempts, as well as cases of more serious eating disorders have been documented in children as young as seven years old (Ricciardelli & McCabe, 2001).

Body image and eating problems have been consistently more common among girls and young women. More recently, reports show that boys and young men are increasingly reporting these problems (McCreary & Sasse, 2000; O'Dea & Rawstorne, 2001). Young male adolescents are known to be concerned with their body size and shape. These males were found to undertake weight control and weight gain behaviours (for example, fad weight gain diets, inappropriate weight lifting and steroid abuse), which are likely to be hazardous to their health.

In addition to the psychological and physiological consequences of body dissatisfaction and eating disorders, and the obvious economic and social costs of treating such problems, recent studies also show that body dissatisfaction among young people is associated with low self-esteem and depression (Stice et al., 2000). In a large four-year longitudinal study of adolescent females, Stice et al. (1999) observed that elevated body dissatisfaction, dietary restraint and symptoms of bulimia on study entry predicted onset of depression in initially non-depressed girls.

Body image concerns, weight loss behaviours and eating problems pose a serious and increasing threat to the short- and long-term physical, psychological and social health of children and adolescents.

Childhood overweight, body image and eating disturbances

Further to the increase in body image and eating problems among children and adolescents is the concurrent increase in child overweight in many countries worldwide over the past 30 years (Troiano & Flegal, 1995). As overweight, perceived overweight and weight concerns are known to precede dieting, hazardous weight loss behaviour and eating disturbances, the current trend towards the co-occurrence of increasing eating disorders and increasing child overweight is of concern.

It is probable that the increasing rates of child overweight may be one of the factors that have resulted in more dieting and weight loss attempts among young people. Hence, these trends could be expected to continue in tandem.

Further, it appears that children and adolescents who use these extreme weight loss attempts only serve to perpetuate the futile cycle of dieting, purging, binge eating and further weight gain. Among American high school girls of various weights, Stice et al. (1999) found that those who tried extreme methods to lose weight were the most likely to gain weight over time and were therefore at greater risk for obesity. Girls who used more extreme weight loss methods such as laxatives, appetite suppressants, vomiting and fasting gained more weight than those who were not involved in extreme weight loss attempts. Among girls who dieted, the risk of obesity onset was greater than for non-dieters, irrespective of their actual weight at the beginning of the study. Neumark-Sztainer and her colleagues (2006) found similar results in a five-year longitudinal study of adolescents with dieting and disordered eating predicting obesity and eating disorders five years later.

A major aim of programs to improve body image, eating problems and child obesity is to encourage healthy eating and physical activity among children and adolescents without promoting fad diets, weight loss attempts and the diet-binge cycle.

First, do no harm

A key underlying principle facing those involved in the planning of educational programs to promote sensible eating and prevent body image and eating problems is safety. Teachers, health educators, dietitians, school administrators, nurses, researchers and policy makers, as well as those responsible for food product development, marketing and advertising, need to pay heed to this most basic principle of modern medicine—'First, do no harm'. The literature presents many warnings about the potential to do more harm than good when attempting to prevent eating disorders and child overweight (Garner, 1988; O'Dea, 2000).

We must remember to be very careful not to create adverse, negative effects among children who participate in various 'child obesity prevention' efforts. In particular, obesity prevention programs may inadvertently serve to heighten awareness of body weight, and increase weight concerns and weight loss attempts among children and adolescents. A detailed outline of the potentially harmful, unforeseen outcomes of obesity prevention activities is given in Chapter 8.

Risks associated with eating disorder prevention

Similar to the inadvertent risks associated with child obesity prevention are the risks of eating disorder prevention. The following is a list of potentially dangerous and unintended outcomes from eating disorder prevention programs and body image improvement programs.

Introduction to weight concerns

Students may be introduced to weight concerns, body image issues and fear of fat when these issues did not previously cause them any concern. Teachers may 'create' body image concerns by directly introducing the concept to students.

Suggestion of harmful weight loss techniques

Eating disorder prevention programs, especially those that directly refer to case studies of eating disorder behaviour such as vomiting, starvation, laxative abuse, diet pills and cigarette smoking for weight control, are likely to introduce these issues to children and adolescents in a suggestive manner.

Normalisation of dieting

Students may get the wrong message that dieting and disordered eating are common, 'normal' and socially acceptable. The idea that 'everybody is doing it' makes dieting seem like a normal thing to do.

Smoking

Several research reports confirm that teenaged girls and young women have adopted smoking after receiving messages about its potentially slimming effects (Tomeo et al., 1999) and quitting smoking becomes unattractive because of the fear of weight gain.

Glamorisation of eating disorders

No matter how well meaning prevention programs are, they may inadvertently glamorise and normalise dieting, disordered eating and the slim ideal by using case studies of sufferers who are celebrities (Garner, 1988). The late Princess Diana was probably the most glamorised bulimia sufferer to date.

Creation of fear of fat and fear of food

Parents, teachers, food advertisers and marketers may unwittingly transfer anti-fat messages, weight prejudice, body image stereotypes and fear of food by perpetuating the 'good foods, bad foods' myth and creating negative, frightening messages about food and weight. The use of negative language can contribute to the underlying fear of food, dietary fat and weight gain which precede body image concerns and eating problems. Negative language use can occur when problem-based messages such as 'sugar and fat are bad' and use of the term 'junk' food. Children and adolescents need to know that they can enjoy a variety of different foods in a balanced diet and they need to be enabled to do so in a positive, motivating atmosphere. Negative messages or those that produce guilt, shame or fear of food are likely to do more harm than good (O'Dea, 2000).

Interventions to prevent eating disorders and improve body image

Following is a summary of the major research interventions that have addressed body image improvement and prevention of eating problems among children and adolescents.

The current summary identifies 25 large, controlled, school-based interventions from the USA, Canada, England, Australia, Israel, Switzerland, Sweden and Italy that have attempted to prevent eating disturbances and promote a healthy body image among school-aged children (Table 3.1). Slightly more than half the studies (16 of 25), reported findings about girls only with nine of 25 studies including both genders. The vast majority of interventions (21 of 25), resulted in at least one form of significant improvement and these are marked with an asterisk in Table 3.1. The studies of Killen et al. (1993), Dalle Grave et al. (2001) and Kater et al. (2002) reported no statistically significant results in regard to behaviour change but significant improvements in knowledge were achieved in these studies. The studies of Paxton (1993), McVey and Davis (2002), McVey et al. (2003b) and Ghaderi et al. (2005) reported no statistically significant intervention effects. No studies reported adverse effects.

Early studies, before 1995, focused on using an information-giving approach by providing female students with knowledge about eating disorders, facts about the dangers of dieting, nutrition information, analysis of the social construction of body ideals and cultural stereotypes of the perfect body (Killen et al., 1993; Moreno & Thelan, 1993; Paxton, 1993). These early studies reported increased knowledge of eating disorders and weight control issues but did not report body image improvement or reduction in eating disorder behaviour. Nevertheless, these early studies paved the way for later researchers to design more successful interventions. The study of Neumark-Sztainer et al. (1995) introduced strategies of behaviour modification for weight control and development of skills in media analysis and assertiveness. This study reported a decrease in bulimic tendencies and improvement in eating patterns among Israeli schoolgirls.

More recent interventions have produced moderate improvements in beliefs, attitudes and behaviours such as body image, body dissatisfaction, self-image and dieting as well as increased knowledge (Table 3.1). Some of these successful approaches and programs are outlined below.

Media literacy interventions

Media literacy programs focus on educating young people about the media's artificial creation of the 'perfect' body by the perpetuation of 'perfect' images of women and men who are almost always stereotypically slim and muscular. This type of strategy aims to increase students' awareness about body stereotypes in the media and suggest ways of combating media messages and trends such as suggesting advocacy roles. A media literacy program conducted among Girl Scouts (Neumark-Sztainer et al., 2000) resulted in a decrease in the internalisation of the ideal body. The same study also found improved self-efficacy related to being able to impact weight-related social norms.

An earlier program that had included media literacy conducted with girls nine to 10 years of age (Smolak et al., 1998) found improved knowledge of nutrition, effects of dieting and causes of body fat. However, it did little to change the students' eating, exercise or weight control behaviours. Interestingly and very importantly, this study did show an improvement in the students' attitudes and beliefs about fat people and two years later, several of these effects were still present (Smolak & Levine, 2001).

TABLE 3.1 A summary of large, controlled, school-based intervention studies of eating disorders prevention and/or body image improvement programs among children and adolescents

Study/description	Results	Conclusions and implications for school-based applications
Moreno & Thelan, 1993* Female students aged 13–14 years in junior high home economics classes in USA. 30 interventions and 74 controls in Study 1 and 50 interventions and 65 controls in Study 2. Videotape of 6½ minutes depicting a conversation between two sisters about bulimia nervosa and harmful effects of bingeing and purging and suggestions for sensible weight management and resisting peer pressure to diet. Video presented by clinical psychology student in Study 1 and home economics teacher in Study 2.	Improved knowledge of bulimia and disordered eating behaviours. Reduced intentions to diet.	Program was successful in changing knowledge of bingeing, purging, dieting and other disordered eating behaviours. Effectiveness of home economics teacher versus psychologist was equivalent. Video was well received by students and teachers. Suggestion that 'short' programs need to be continued with 'booster' sessions. Suggestion of using peer-led sessions.
Paxton, 1993 Year 9 female students aged 14 years in Australia. 107 interventions and 29 controls. Program of five classes addressing media images of women, determinants of body size, healthy and unhealthy weight control and emotional eating. Conducted by two psychologists.	No significant effect on dietary restraint, eating and weight control behaviours, bulimia, drive for thinness, body dissatisfaction, body image or self-esteem.	Author concludes program to be ineffective among Year 9 girls due to their body image already being entrenched. Media impact on girls needs to be tackled. Short-term school programs need to be supplemented through other educational methods or anti-dieting media campaigns. Suggestions that peer leaders may be beneficial in program presentation. Suggestion that programs should target younger students.
Killen et al., 1993* 6th and 7th grade female students aged 11–13 years in USA. 438 interventions and 400 controls. Program to instruct about harmful effects of unhealthful weight regulation; promotion of healthful weight regulation through sound nutrition and physical activity; and develop coping skills to resist media body image messages. 18 lessons of slide shows depicting case studies of seven girls illustrating normal pubertal development, ineffectiveness and dangers of dieting, skill development to counteract cultural pressures promoting dieting and thin body ideal, promotion of healthy eating and physical activity.	Knowledge of weight regulation principles, growth and development cultural influences and dangerous weight loss methods increased in intervention group. No effect on dietary restraint, bulimia, weight concerns, body mass index or eating behaviours.	Authors conclude that program failed to reduce unhealthful weight regulation and promote healthy behaviours. Suggestion that screening and then targeting high-risk girls may be most beneficial.
Neumark-Sztainer et al., 1995* 269 Israeli girls aged 15–16 years in 10th grade. 126 interventions and 143 controls. Ten-week program among boys and girls, but only data from girls analysed. Topics included adolescent development, healthy eating, physical activity, behaviour modification for weight loss, advertising, body image and the media, eating disorders, assertiveness.	Increased knowledge of nutrition and more regular meal patterns. No effect on body satisfaction, weight loss methods or food preferences. Reduced onset of unhealthy dieting and bingeing among girls who had not tried this before.	High student and staff satisfaction with program. Students prefer interactive activities. Authors conclude that program helped to prevent onset of some unhealthy behaviours but no effect on reducing existing unhealthy behaviours. Therefore, suggestion for early prevention in younger girls. Suggestion for greater focus on changing self-perceptions, self-esteem.

* Studies with at least one significant change.

TABLE 3.1 (Continued) A summary of large, controlled, school-based intervention studies of eating disorders prevention and/or body image improvement programs among children and adolescents

Study/description	Results	Conclusions and implications for school-based applications
Buddeberg-Fisher et al., 1998* 314 Swiss students, 14–19 years who had scored relatively high on risk of disturbed eating. Ten classes received three health promotion lessons, 10 classes were controls. Lessons included beauty ideals, pubertal development, healthy eating, nutrition, eating disorders and their treatment. 90-minute lesson each month for three months. Delivered by adolescent psychiatry staff.	No intervention effect for overall group of male and female students for eating attitudes, physical distress or psychological impairment. Girls with highest eating disorders scores improved on physical impairment symptoms.	Recommendation that prevention programs address students' cognition, emotions and behaviour. Important to capture the interest of male and female students as well as those who do not have any symptoms of eating disorders. Lack of 'blinding' may have biased the results. Future studies should focus on students' self-perceptions, identity and relationships.
Smolak et al., 1998* 222 male and female 5th grade students aged 9–10 years in USA. Ten classroom lessons on knowledge of nutrition, body fat and dieting, attitudes about fat people and body esteem and behaviours such as healthy eating and exercise.	Knowledge of nutrition, effects of dieting and causes of body fat improved. Attitudes towards fat people improved.	Authors conclude that behaviour change such as eating and exercise patterns, weight reduction attempts and teasing fat children was not changed by the program.
Santonastaso et al., 1999* 254 Italian schoolgirls aged 16 years. 154 interventions, 154 controls. Four, 2-hour sessions each week for one month. Conducted by psychiatrist and psychologist. Lessons on pubertal weight changes, importance of physical appearance and body image, relationships, information about eating disorders and dieting, and attitudes towards food and dieting.	At 12 months after the intervention, low-risk girls' body dissatisfaction decreased, but high-risk girls did not. No effect on BMI or other aspects of eating disorders.	Authors conclude that a program including information about eating disorders does not encourage unhealthy eating attitudes or behaviours. Schools should implement coping skills to help students deal with media and social pressure to diet and be slim. High-risk girls may need more help.
O'Dea & Abraham, 2000* 470 male and female students in Australia aged 11–14 years. Interactive self-esteem program including stress management, building positive sense of self, analysis and rejection of cultural and media gender stereotypes (student led) and building self-esteem. No mention of eating, food or disorders. Blinding of students and teachers.	Improved body satisfaction and decreased importance of social acceptance, physical appearance and athletic ability. Improved physical self-esteem in females. Less weight loss and dieting in intervention girls. In high-risk students, improved body image, drive for thinness and physical self-esteem.	Positive student and teacher evaluation. Self-esteem development can improve body image in male and female adolescents. Important to include males. Involving parents, especially fathers, seems to help female students. Focusing on positive approach rather than a negative, problem-based approach appears to be beneficial among young adolescents.
Neumark-Sztainer et al., 2000* 226 girls in USA aged 9–11 years attending Girl Scouts. Six sessions dealing with pubertal development, positive self-assessment, self-esteem, media awareness of body image ideals, media literacy and advocacy.	Program increased knowledge related to their body weight and reduced desire for the thin ideal. Self-efficacy to impact weight-related social norms increased. No effect on dieting or other behaviours.	Authors reported high program satisfaction. Longer follow-up suggested. Girl Scout groups appear to be a suitable place for such programs.

* Studies with at least one significant change.

TABLE 3.1 (Continued) A summary of large, controlled, school-based intervention studies of eating disorders prevention and/or body image improvement programs among children and adolescents

Study/description	Results	Conclusions and implications for school-based applications
Phelps et al., 2000* 532 Grade 6–8 students aged 11–15 years and 312 9–11th grade females aged 13–16 in the USA. A six-session program was incorporated in the Home and Careers curriculum and delivered by regular classroom teachers. Control group participated in regular music classes. Lessons included historical and cultural influences on body image; increased physical self-esteem; increased personal competence; discussion of pubertal developments; exploration of appropriate weight control and a case study of a woman who had recovered from an eating disorder.	Trend towards reduced disordered eating, body dissatisfaction and drive for thinness, but not statistically significant. Trend towards increased self-esteem and personal competence but not statistically significant. Older girls improved on attitudes and beliefs about sociocultural mores, dysfunctional eating behaviours and future intentions regarding weight control.	Interactive program with older girls was more successful and well received by teachers and girls. Authors conclude that younger children were not able to benefit from self-evaluation type discussion. Small groups (e.g. 6–8) work the best. Teachers need training in active listening, non-judgemental feedback, providing information without 'lecturing' and the ability to allow students to discover their own thoughts and feelings.
Stewart et al., 2001* 752 schoolgirls in Year 9 (13–14 year olds) in the UK. Interactive six-week program of lessons including cultural influences on body image, weight regulation, information about eating disorders, self-esteem, managing stress, healthy eating, non-dieting.	Knowledge of eating disorders increased in both intervention and control girls. Dietary restraint decreased in intervention girls. No intervention effect on weight concern but shape concern and eating concerns decreased in intervention girls.	Authors conclude that intervention produced short-term improvement in dieting and body concerns especially among high-risk girls. Suggestion to continue such programs each year and start with younger children. Suggestion to focus on families and teachers and include boys.
Varnardo-Sullivan et al., 2001* 157 females and 130 males, 6th and 7th grade private school students aged 12–13 years in USA. Body Logic Program I involved school students in interactive sessions about body image, social and media influences, self-esteem, impact of puberty on body image and nutrition. Body Logic II involved parents and high-risk children.	Female participants improved on fear of fatness and avoidance of forbidden foods. High-risk girls also improved. Males improved on fear of fatness. Efforts to attract parents and high-risk students failed.	Recommendation that the program was partially effective but did not attract high-risk students or parents. Suggestion that poor body image and disordered eating may now be considered 'normal' and acceptable in some high-risk students and their parents.
Dalle Grave et al., 2001* 106 Italian students aged 11–12 years. Six 2-hour sessions plus two 2-hour booster sessions presented by psychologists. Program included socio-cultural slim ideal, dieting and its effects, eating disorders and risk factors for eating disorders, self-acceptance.	Increased knowledge of eating disorders. No intervention effect for eating behaviours, dietary restraint, weight or shape concerns or self-esteem.	Authors conclude that program improved knowledge and had no adverse effects. Important to include males. Important to further study with larger numbers.
Smolak & Levine, 2001* Long-term effect of initial Smolak et al., 1998 program investigated using the original 9–11-year-old boys and girls in USA who participated two years earlier compared to an additional group of new controls.	Participants had greater knowledge, used fewer weight control techniques and had higher body esteem. Original controls had scores 'in between' suggesting a 'spill over' effect among original controls.	Girls benefited more than boys. Demonstrates long-term impact. Spillover effect among controls suggests that children discussed what was learned in the program, demonstrating interest and relevance of program.

* Studies with at least one significant change.

TABLE 3.1 (Continued) A summary of large, controlled, school-based intervention studies of eating disorders prevention and/or body image improvement programs among children and adolescents

Study/description	Results	Conclusions and implications for school-based applications
Withers et al., 2002* 218 Australian private school girls in Year 7 aged 12–13 years. Intervention group received a 22-minute video including information about female development, sociocultural and media influences on body image, the harmful effects of dieting and eating disorders, healthy eating and self-image enhancement.	Girls who watched the video made positive changes to drive for thinness and intention to diet and improved knowledge.	Authors conclude that positive changes occurred but one month later only the knowledge changes were maintained. Long-term and booster programs recommended. Other powerful influences such as the media need to be addressed.
Kater et al., 2002* 415 boys and girls aged 9–13 years in USA received an 11–week program. Topics included pubertal changes, genetic diversity, hazards of dieting, nutrition, coping skills, media analysis.	Intervention students improved on most scales but not in comparison to controls. Modest improvement in knowledge and effect of the media.	Authors conclude that knowledge can be improved but not body image suggesting that young students should be included in future programs. Suggestion that adults and school administrators become involved.
Steiner-Adair et al., 2002* 500 girls in 7th grade aged 12–14 years in USA. Eight weekly lessons delivered by teachers, nurses and guidance counsellors. Topics included pubertal changes, weightism, positive self-assessment, self-esteem, media literacy, fad diets and nutrition and coping skills.	Knowledge of issues discussed in the program improved. Body esteem improved. Eating behaviours did not change.	Authors conclude that the study produced some improvement that lasted six months. Program was not harmful. Leaders of programs need to be monitored and trained. Also include school administrators, teachers and parents to support program.
McVey & Davis, 2002 263 girls in Grade 6 aged 10–11 years in Canada. Six-session program on media literacy about dangers of thin ideal and promotion of self-esteem, stress management and peer relation skills. Lessons facilitated by a psychologist (McVey).	No effect on body image satisfaction or eating problems. Both the intervention and control group girls improved on both measures suggesting that the routine school health education curriculum had helped the control girls.	Involvement of parents might be helpful in prevention of disordered eating. Have the teachers deliver the program.
McVey et al., 2004* 258 girls aged 11–12 years in Canada. Replication of McVey and Davis (2002) (listed above).	Program improved body image satisfaction, self-esteem and reduced dieting. Body image satisfaction was not maintained at follow-up.	Authors conclude that their original study was replicated, and especially effective in preventing dieting. Self-esteem enhancement is beneficial for other issues such as smoking and early sexual involvement. Long-term programs and follow-up required.
McVey et al., 2003(a)* 214 girls in Grades 7 and 8 aged 12–13 years in Canada. Ten-session peer support group designed to improve body esteem and global self-esteem and reduce negative eating attitudes and behaviours. Program same as above with addition of a small support and discussion group held at lunch time. Groups led by public health nurses.	Program successful at improving body esteem and weight esteem and reduced dieting. Girls reported many benefits of participation.	Authors conclude that life skills presented in peer support groups were successful at improving body esteem and self-esteem and reducing dieting. Success based on improving resiliency and self-esteem in a peer support setting. Authors suggest programs should also address the school climate by involving teachers, parents and school staff.

* Studies with at least one significant change.

TABLE 3.1 (Continued) A summary of large, controlled, school-based intervention studies of eating disorders prevention and/or body image improvement programs among children and adolescents

Study/description	Results	Conclusions and implications for school-based applications
McVey et al., 2003(b) 282 girls in Grades 7 and 8 aged 12–13 years in Canada. Attempt to replicate previous peer support study (listed above).	Contrary to previous findings, this study did not replicate the previous results. Both intervention and control girls' scores improved for all measures, including body esteem, self-esteem and dieting.	Authors suggest that inability to replicate the previous study results may be due to more girls initially dieting in this group. The program themes and content may have also 'spilled over' to the control group of girls at different schools. Suggestion to include younger children before dieting and disordered eating becomes entrenched. Suggest 'whole' school change.
Wiseman et al., 2004* Females aged 15–16 years in USA (n = 50) and Italy (n = 138). Half received lessons by a psychologist or psychiatrist about healthy living, nutrition, lifestyles of models and celebrities, self-image dieting myths, eating disorders, healthy lifestyle.	Drive for thinness was reduced in the Italian girls. No intervention effect in the US girls.	Follow-up is underway. The body image of 15–16-year-old girls is likely to be well-entrenched. US girls were ¼ African American and known to have low drive for thinness.
Weiss & Wertheim, 2005* Grade 9 girls in Melbourne, Australia. 114 in intervention group and 59 controls. Four 100-minute sessions about body image concerns, eating problems, self-esteem, body esteem, how to counter negative sociocultural influences, dangers of dieting and eating disorders, healthy eating. Sessions conducted by a psychologist, nurse or psychology student.	High risk girls improved on body dissatisfaction, drive for thinness and interoceptive awareness. Trends similar but not significant at three-month follow-up.	No harmful outcomes. High risk may benefit most. Booster sessions required.
Ghaderi et al., 2005 5th grade boys and girls in Sweden. 95 interventions and 58 controls. Students given 'Everybody's Different' program from O'Dea and Abraham study (2000).	Favourable direction of effects was observed but statistical significance not achieved. No follow-up was conducted.	Young children do not particularly benefit from this body image program, but this may be because they are mostly still prepubertal and have not yet developed any body image concerns. Authors suggest that a spillover effect may have caused the improvement observed in the control group.
Wade et al., 2003* 86 boys and girls aged 13–14 years in Adelaide, Australia received lessons on either self-esteem, media literacy or control. Three-month follow-up was conducted.	Media literacy group had lower weight concerns but self-esteem group did not. Results did not hold at three-month follow-up.	Small numbers may have limited the study. Role of teacher style is important.

* Studies with at least one significant change.

Media literacy programs are likely to bring about improvement in students' body image and risk of eating problems by having students understand that media images are unrealistic and often manipulated to create perfection. Students may then reject the media images as largely artificially created and unacceptable.

Another explanation for the moderate improvement in body image shown to result from media analysis is that they help young people to reject media stereotypes of perfection by promoting self-acceptance (O'Dea & Abraham, 2000). Studies that have included media analysis, media literacy and examination of media gender stereotypes have resulted in various improvements in body image. (See Table 3.1, for example, McVey et al., 2003a; 2003b; 2004; Neumark-Sztainer et al., 2000; O'Dea & Abraham, 2000; Steiner-Adair et al., 2002; Varnardo-Sullivan et al., 2001; Wade et al., 2003; Withers et al., 2002). At this stage it is unclear whether media analysis skills help to improve body image in a cognitive manner (for example, by rejecting social norms for the thin ideal) or as a function of improving self-acceptance and self-esteem (for example by encouraging students to accept themselves and reject cultural stereotypes). Further studies should investigate this important area.

Self-esteem development to improve body image

Building child self-esteem is a logical approach to the prevention of body image and eating problems. Self-esteem refers to the child's judgement about his or her overall worth. Children and adolescents with high self-esteem are fundamentally satisfied with themselves as persons, while still able to identify weaker characteristics that may require work to improve. High self-esteem envelops a realistic self-appraisal of the child's characteristics and competencies coupled with an attitude of self-acceptance, self-respect and self-worth.

In addition, studies show that overweight children and adolescents or those who perceive themselves to be overweight, have poorer overall self-esteem and body esteem than their lower weight peers (Cattarin & Thomson, 1994; Patton et al., 1990). Self-esteem protection and enhancement is therefore appropriate and desirable for all children and adolescents but it is particularly relevant in the treatment and prevention of body image problems and eating disturbances, because low self-esteem is considered to be a potent risk factor for these problems (Button et al., 1997; Patton et al., 1999; Shisslak & Crago, 2001).

Self-esteem development and enhancement is also believed to improve the other factors known to contribute to body image and eating problems. For example, development of a positive self-image and a strong sense of self-worth are likely to help children and adolescents became more satisfied with their body shape and size and more resilient and resistant to the unrealistic body image ideals portrayed in the media (O'Dea & Abraham, 2000; Shisslak & Crago, 2001). Children with high self-esteem are better able to cope with teasing, criticism, stress and anxiety, which are all associated with eating problems.

Further, the development of a positive self-image, which includes a broad array of aspects of the self other than physical appearance, is likely to help children value their many different characteristics and those of others. This type of self-image development is likely to reduce children's obsession with perfectionism and the belief that one must be perfect, or strive to be perfect, in order to be valued, accepted and loved. As perfectionism is strongly associated with body image problems and eating disorders (Stice, 2002), it is believed that modifying this risk factor by developing self-esteem may help young people to be more self-accepting and less involved in the futile quest for perfection. A discussion of body image improvement and eating disorder prevention programs that have included a strong self-esteem component is presented in Table 3.1 (McVey & Davis, 2002; McVey et al., 2003a; 2003b; 2004; Neumark-Sztainer et al., 2000; O'Dea & Abraham, 2000; Phelps et al., 2000; Steiner-Adair et al., 2002; Stewart et al., 2001; Varnardo-Sullivan et al., 2001). An example of a school-based self-esteem program, Everybody's Different, follows.

A school-based self-esteem program—'Everybody's Different'

The aim of the Everybody's Different program (O'Dea & Abraham, 2000) is to improve the body image, eating disorder attitudes and behaviours of young male and female adolescents by focusing on developing their self-esteem. The program focuses on expanding Grade 7 and 8 students' self-identity and sense of self-worth by encompassing many aspects of the self and thereby decreasing the emphasis and importance of physical appearance. In addition, the program activities promote themes of self-acceptance, respect, tolerance and reduced self-expectations of perfection. The major program theme is that an individual's uniqueness is to be expected, valued and accepted. A strong message of the program is that everybody is different and nobody is perfect. The secondary school teachers who delivered the program were trained to build self-esteem by adopting a student-centred, cooperative and interactive teaching style, which is known to promote student self-esteem. The educational approach featured the use of student discussion, group work, team work, games, play, drama and a content-free, self-esteem building curriculum in which both the teaching style and the content of educational activities foster a positive sense of self, student involvement, self-efficacy, vicarious learning, exchange of feedback and opinion in a safe, respectful and positive classroom environment in which the students feel that they cannot 'fail'.

The Everybody's Different program consisted of nine weekly lessons. The major content is outlined in Table 3.2.

A study found the Everybody's Different program significantly improved the body image of students who received this program compared to those who did not receive the program. Female students and those at high risk for eating problems particularly benefited from the program, showing improvements in body satisfaction, drive for thinness, physical appearance ratings, reduced dieting and less unhealthy weight loss after the intervention. Social acceptance (peer pressure, popularity), physical appearance and athletic competence were shown to be less important to both male and female students after the intervention, with close friendships becoming more important. Many of the improvements were still present and significant at the 12-month follow-up.

A unique and interesting finding of this new self-esteem program was the improvement in body image among both boys and girls, as well as those who were overweight or at high risk of developing body image or eating problems. This is evidenced by the fact that the improvement in the body satisfaction of high-risk male and female students was still statistically significant 12 months after the self-esteem program.

As body consciousness is often cited as a barrier to physical activity in both boys and girls (O'Dea, 2003), improvements in body image may prove to be beneficial in helping students to be less body conscious and therefore more likely to become physically and socially active. Overcoming this barrier would be hugely beneficial for all children, but particularly helpful in the treatment and prevention of child overweight.

Since the initial findings from this Everybody's Different self-esteem intervention trial, McVey and her colleagues have achieved similar outcomes with 11–12-year-old Canadian girls in the classroom (McVey et al., 2004) and in smaller peer support groups (McVey et al., 2003a), using a self-esteem, self-acceptance, media literacy, life skills approach. These two separate studies implemented the 'Every BODY Is A Somebody' program which includes self-esteem enhancement and self-acceptance strategies, stress management techniques, peer relations skills and media literacy lessons and found improved body satisfaction, global self-esteem and attitudes towards dieting.

TABLE 3.2 An outline of the objectives, methods and approaches in the Everybody's Different program

Major objective	Methods, approaches and activities	Description of how lessons achieve specific objectives
Identify ways of dealing with stress	Group discussions. Students report how they deal with stress. Activities are student-led, not teacher-imposed.	Encourage students to develop healthy ways of coping with stress such as peer, teacher, family and parental support; identification and expression of anger and other emotions; communicating with others in order to solve problems. Enhances peer communication and peer support.
	Relaxation/visualisation exercises and take home tape recordings.	Relaxation promotes positive body awareness, stress control and enhances positive physical sensation.
	Benefits of stress control—student-led discussion and reporting.	Homework activities encourage adoption of positive stress control behaviours and involves positive peer, parental and family support.
Develop skills for building a positive sense of self	Expanding self-image to include a wide array of physical and personal attributes—student-led.	Broadens self-image to include many different aspects of the self. Diminishes importance of physical appearance. Promotes diversity, tolerance, acceptance, respect and develops awareness about the undesirability of prejudice and teasing. Encourages positive self-talk and reduces obsessive, 'all-or-nothing' rigid thinking.
	Awareness and acceptance that everybody is different and nobody is perfect.	Reduces the unrealistic and futile pursuit of perfection.
	Identifying positive self-attributes.	Models peer support.
	Learning to give and receive positive feedback.	Positively involves significant others.
	Positive self-evaluation, identifying and valuing uniqueness in self and others.	Reduces impact of criticism from others by receiving positive support from varied sources.
Explore individuality of self and peers (self-advertisements)	Exploration, discussion, identification and rejection of stereotypes in our society. (Student-led discovery of media images of stereotypes—not teacher imposed. Art activities.)	Examination, discussion and rejection of cultural stereotypes of males and females.
		Rejection of slim/muscular ideals.
		Reinforcement that individuality and diversity are normal and acceptable. Reinforces and models self-acceptance.
Develop acceptance of self and others	Reinforcement that diversity, uniqueness and differences between people are to be expected valued and accepted. (Student presentation of artwork and presentation of main messages/discovery from this activity.)	Media literacy and awareness skills.
		Development of reinforcement of self-acceptance and acceptance of others.
		Reduced importance of physical appearance and enhanced importance of many varied attributes.
Discover, practise and develop communication skills	Peer support (drama activities, role plays, discussion).	Improved identification and expression of emotions.
		Improved peer and parental communication and relationships.
		Expansion of self-expression skills.

The findings of O'Dea and Abraham (2000) have been confirmed by a recent self-esteem intervention with Grade 7 and 8 students in Canada. Findings included body satisfaction improvements in male and female students and improved physical appearance ratings of overweight females (Tsimicalis, 2002). Other studies among adolescent girls that have utilised a predominantly self-esteem building and self-acceptance approach have also been successful in improving the pursuit of the thin ideal (Neumark-Sztainer et al., 2000), reducing dietary restraint, shape concerns and eating concerns (Stewart et al., 2001), reducing dysfunctional eating behaviours (Phelps et al., 2000) and increasing body weight satisfaction (Steiner-Adair et al., 2002). The collective positive results of these studies lends support to the self-esteem approach for the improvement of body image and prevention of eating disturbances in children and adolescents.

Conclusions from programs to date

While there are no firm conclusions about the most efficacious way to prevent eating disorders, body image problems or child obesity, the observation of program outcomes to date provides some firm trends in approaches to prevention.

- **Do no harm**. First, it is clear that iatrogenesis (the tendency to inadvertently harm participants or create unintentional adverse effects) is something that health educators and others involved in preventive activities must take very seriously.
- **Interactive approaches**. The evaluation of the 23 programs in this broad summary of preventive activities to date suggests that interactive, student-centred learning activities are well received by students and produce positive results.
- **Inclusion of boys**. The inclusion of boys in the programs was reported as being important by several authors (see Table 3.1) and positive results were achieved among male participants in the studies of Smolak et al. (1998), O'Dea and Abraham (2000), Varnardo-Sullivan et al. (2001), and Smolak and Levine (2001).
- **Delivery by teachers, not outside experts**. Several programs reported the value of having programs delivered in the regular school environment by a teacher who had some skills in facilitating small group discussion and interactive activities (McVey & Davis, 2002; Moreno & Thelan, 1993; O'Dea & Abraham, 2000; Phelps et al., 2000; Steiner-Adair et al., 2002; Stewart et al., 2001). Peer-led sessions were suggested as potentially useful by Moreno and Thelan (1993), Paxton (1993) and McVey et al. (2003a).
- **Including parents**. The inclusion of parents in a positive way was suggested by O'Dea and Abraham (2000), Stewart et al. (2001), Varnardo-Sullivan et al. (2001), Kater et al. (2002), Steiner-Adair et al. (2002) and McVey et al. (2002; 2003a; 2003b; 2004).
- **Changing the school environment**. Addressing issues of changes to the larger school environment as part of a systems approach to prevention was suggested by Paxton (1993), O'Dea and Abraham (2000), Withers et al. (2002), Kater et al. (2002) and McVey et al. (2003b). This topic is addressed in detail in Chapter 10.

School policy, curriculum and environmental considerations

Development of student self-esteem and media literacy skills in the prevention of body image and eating problems would be very naïve if confined to the individual or to the school classroom.

A child's body image, self-esteem and sense of self-worth, while certainly affected by school curricula and teaching style (for example, authoritarian teaching versus student centred, interactive, inclusive teaching), is also impacted by peers (for example, teasing), attitudes of family, teachers and coaches, school environment, community factors (for example, the media, advertising, sports involvement) and culture (for example, feminist issues, cultural stereotypes, social norms and stigma about weight and shape). An extensive outline of these risk and protective factors for body image and eating disturbances is provided by Shisslak and Crago (2001) in a review of the many factors that affect body image and eating disorders.

School policy changes such as anti-teasing policies are very powerful ways of changing the whole school environment to promote a greater diversity in body shapes and a greater tolerance of individual differences (Levine & Smolak, 2002).

A holistic environmental approach to the prevention of body image and eating problems as well as prevention of child overweight, such as the Health Promoting Schools Framework (O'Dea & Maloney, 2000), theorises that whole communities need to be involved in fostering overall health within school and community environments. A well-known Canadian researcher, Niva Piran has employed a whole-school approach to prevention in her work in ballet schools (1995; 1999; 2001). Several facets of a whole-school approach to prevention need attention, including school curricula, school ethos, school policies and school community involvement. The whole-school approach is outlined in detail in Chapter 10.

Summary

Prevention of body image concerns, eating problems and obesity among children and adolescents via programs in schools and universities is an appropriate health education goal.

Teachers and health educators, no matter how well meaning, must be careful to 'Do no harm' in efforts to ameliorate both issues in schools and universities. This chapter provides an evidence-based approach for prevention from a detailed summary of body image programs and eating disorder prevention programs in schools, and outlines self-esteem and media literacy approaches that have produced positive results in some large, randomised and controlled interventions worldwide.

School staff can also address broader and more ecologically based approaches by focusing on the whole-school environment and the Health Promoting Schools Approach. This particular approach is detailed in Chapter 10.

References

Beglin SJ & Fairburn CG (1992), 'Women who choose not to participate in surveys on eating disorders', *International Journal of Eating Disorders*, *12*(1), 113–16.

Buddeberg-Fischer B, Klaghofer R, Gnam G & Buddeberg C (1998), 'Prevention of disturbed eating behaviour: A prospective intervention study in 14- to 19-year-old Swiss students', *Acta Psychiatrica Scandinavica*, *98*, 146–55.

Button EJ, Loan P, Davies J & Sonuga-Barke EJ (1997), 'Self-esteem, eating problems and psychological wellbeing in a cohort of schoolgirls aged 15-16: A questionnaire and interview study', *International Journal of Eating Disorders*, *21*(1), 39–47.

Cattarin JA & Thomson JK (1994), 'A 3-year longitudinal study of body image, eating disturbance, and general psychological functioning in adolescent females', *Eating Disorders*, *2*, 114–25.

Croll J, Neumark-Sztainer D, Story M & Ireland M (2002), 'Prevalence and risk and protective factors related to disordered eating behaviours among adolescents: Relationship to gender and ethnicity', *Journal of Adolescent Health*, *31*, 166–75.

Dalle Grave RD, De Luca L & Campello G (2001), 'Middle school primary prevention program for eating disorders: A controlled study with a twelve-month follow-up', *Eating Disorders: The Journal of Treatment and Prevention*, *9*, 327–37.

Fisher M, Golden NH & Katzman DK (1995), 'Eating disorders in adolescents: A background paper', *Journal of Adolescent Health*, *16*, 420–37.

Garner DM (1988), 'Iatrogenesis in anorexia nervosa and bulimia nervosa', *International Journal of Eating Disorders*, *4*, 701–26.

Ghaderi A, Martensson M & Schwan H (2005), '"Everybody's Different": A primary prevention program among fifth grade children', *Eating Disorders*, *13*, 245–61.

Kater KJ, Rohwer J & Londre K (2002), 'Evaluation of an upper elementary school program to prevent body image, eating, and weight concerns', *Journal of School Health*, *72*, 199–204.

Killen JD, Taylor CB, Telch MJ, Saylor KE, Maron DJ & Robinson TN (1986), 'Self induced vomiting and laxative and diuretic use among teenagers: Precursors of the binge-purge syndrome', *Journal of the American Medical Association, 255*, 1447–9.

Killen JD, Taylor CB, Hammer L, Litt I, Wilson DM, Rich T, Hayward C, Simmonds B, Kraemer H & Varady A (1993), 'Results of an attempt to modify unhealthful eating attitudes and weight regulation practices of young adolescent girls', *International Journal of Eating Disorders, 13*(4), 369–84.

Levine MP & Smolak L (2002), 'Ecological and activism approaches to the prevention of body image problems', in Cash TF & Pruzinsky T, (eds), *Body Images: A handbook of theory, research, and clinical practice*, Guilford Press, New York, 497–505.

McCreary DR & Sasse DK (2000), 'An exploration of the drive for muscularity in adolescent boys and girls', *Journal of American College Health, 48*, 297–304.

McVey GL & Davis R (2002), 'A program to promote positive body image: A 1-year follow-up evaluation', *Journal of Early Adolescence, 22*(1), 96–108.

McVey GL, Pepler D, Davis R, Flett GL & Abdolell M (2002), 'Risk and protective factors associated with disordered eating during early adolescence', *Journal of Early Adolescence, 22*, 75–95.

McVey GL, Lieberman M, Voorberg N, Wardrope D & Blackmore E (2003a), 'School-based peer support groups: A new approach to the prevention of disordered eating', *Eating Disorders, 11*, 169–85.

McVey GL, Lieberman M, Voorberg N, Wardrope D, Blackmore E & Tweed S (2003b), 'Replication of a peer support program. Designed to prevent disordered eating: Is a life skills approach sufficient for all middle school students?', *Eating Disorders, 11*, 187–95.

McVey GL, Davis R, Tweed S & Shaw BF (2004), 'Evaluation of a school-based program designed to improve body image satisfaction, global self-esteem, and eating attitudes and behaviors: A replication study', *International Journal of Eating Disorders, 36*(1), 1–11.

Moreno AB & Thelan MH (1993), 'A preliminary prevention program for eating disorders in a junior high school population', *Journal of Youth & Adolescence, 22*(2), 109–24.

Neumark-Sztainer D, Butler R & Palti H (1995), 'Eating disturbances among adolescent girls: Evaluation of a school-based primary prevention program', *Journal of Nutrition Education, 27*, 24–31.

Neumark-Sztainer D, Sherwood N, Coller T & Hannon P (2000), 'Primary prevention of disordered eating among preadolescent girls: Feasibility and short term effect of a community based intervention', *Journal of the American Dietetic Association, 100*(12), 1466–73.

Neumark-Sztainer D, Wall M, Guo J, Story M, Haines J & Eisenberg M (2006), 'Obesity, disordered eating, and eating disorders in a longitudinal study of adolescents: How do dieters fare 5 years later?', *Journal of the American Dietetic Association, 106*(4), 559–68.

O'Dea J (2000), 'School-based interventions to prevent eating problems—first do no harm', *Eating Disorders, 8*, 123–30.

O'Dea J (2003), 'Why do kids eat healthy food? Perceived benefits of and barriers to healthful eating and physical activity among children and adolescents', *Journal of the American Dietetic Association, 103*(4), 497–501.

O'Dea J & Abraham S (2000), 'Improving the body image, eating attitudes and behaviours of young male and female adolescents: A new educational approach that focuses on self-esteem', *International Journal of Eating Disorders, 28*, 43–57.

O'Dea J & Maloney D (2000), 'Preventing eating and body image problems in children and adolescents using the Health Promoting Schools Framework', *Journal of School Health, 70*(1), 18–21.

O'Dea J & Rawstorne P (2001), 'Male adolescents identify their weight gain practices, reasons for desired weight gain and sources of weight gain information', *Journal of the American Dietetic Association, 11*, 105–7.

Patton GC, Johnson-Sabine E, Woods K, Mann AH & Wakeling A (1990), 'Abnormal eating attitudes in London schoolgirls: Outcome at twelve month follow-up', *Psychological Medicine, 20*, 383–94.

Patton GC, Selzer R, Coffey C, Carlin JB & Wolfe R (1999), 'Onset of adolescent eating disorders: Population based cohort study over 3 years', *British Medical Journal, 318*, 765–8.

Paxton SJ (1993), 'A prevention program for disturbed eating and body dissatisfaction in adolescent girls: A one year follow-up', *Health Education Research, 8*(1), 43–51.

Phelps L, Sapia J, Nathanson D & Nelson L (2000), 'An empirically supported eating disorder prevention program', *Psychology in Schools, 37*(5), 443–52.

Piran N (1995), 'Prevention: Can early lessons lead to a delineation of an alternative model? A critical look at prevention with schoolchildren', *Eating Disorders, 3*(1), 28–36.

Piran N (1999), 'Prevention in a high-risk environment: An intervention in a ballet school' in Piran N, Levine ML & Steiner-Adair C (eds), *Preventing Eating Disorders: A handbook of interventions and special challenges*, Brunner/Mazel, New York, 148–59.

Piran N (2001), 'Re-inhabiting the body from the inside out: Girls transform their school environment', in Tolman D & Brydon-Miller M (eds), *From Subject to Subjectivities*, New York Press, New York, 219–38.

Ricciardelli LA & McCabe MP (2001), 'Children's body image concerns and eating disturbance—A review of the literature', *Clinical Psychology Review, 21*(3), 325–45.

Santonastaso P, Zanetti T, Ferrara S, Olivotto MC, Magnavita N & Savaro A (1999), 'A preventive intervention program in adolescent schoolgirls: A longitudinal study', *Psychotherapy and Psychosomatics*, *68*, 46–50.

Shisslak CM & Crago M (2001), 'Risk and protective factors in the development of eating disorders' in Thompson JK & Smolak L (eds), *Body Image, Eating Disorders and Obesity in Youth*, American Psychological Association, Washington, 103–25.

Smolak L & Levine MP (2001), 'A two-year followup of a primary prevention program for negative body image and unhealthy weight reduction', *Eating Disorders*, *9*, 313–25.

Smolak L, Levine MP & Schermer F (1998), 'A controlled evaluation of an elementary school primary prevention program for eating problems', *Journal of Psychosomatic Research*, *44*(3–4), 339–53.

Steiner-Adair C, Sjostrom L, Franko D, Pai S, Tucker R, Becker A & Herzog D (2002), 'Primary prevention of risk factors for eating disorders in adolescent girls: Learning from practice', *International Journal of Eating Disorders*, *32*, 401–11.

Stewart A, Carter J, Drinkwater J, Hainsworth J & Fairburn C (2001), 'Modification of eating attitudes and behaviour in adolescent girls: A controlled study', *International Journal of Eating Disorders*, *29*, 107–18.

Stice E (2002), 'Risk and maintenance factors for eating pathology: A meta-analytic review', *Psychological Bulletin*, *128*, 825–48.

Stice E, Cameron RP, Hayward C, Taylor CB & Killen JD (1999), 'Naturalistic weight reduction efforts prospectively predict growth in relative weight and onset of obesity among female adolescents', *Journal of Consulting and Clinical Psychology*, *67*, 967–74.

Stice E, Cameron R, Hayward C, Taylor CB & Killen J (2000), 'Body-image and eating disturbances predict onset of depression among female adolescents: A longitudinal study', *Journal of Abnormal Psychology*, *109*(3), 438–44

Tomeo CA, Field AE, Berkey CS, Colditz GA & Frazier AL (1999), 'Weight concerns, weight control behaviours and smoking initiation', *Pediatrics*, *104*(4 Pt 1), 918–24.

Troiano R & Flegal KM (1995), 'Overweight prevalence and trends for children and adolescents: The National Health and Nutrition Examination surveys, 1963 to 1991', *Archives of Paediatric & Adolescent Medicine*, *149*(10), 1085–91.

Tsimicalis A (2002), 'Evaluation of a Health Promotion Program design to enhance body image and self-esteem in children in grades seven and eight', Queen's University, Unpublished Masters Thesis.

Varnado-Sullivan PJ, Zucker N, Williamson DA, Reas D, Thaw J & Netemeyer SB (2001), 'Development and implementation of the Body Logic Program for adolescents: A two-stage prevention program for eating disorders', *Cognitive and Behavioural Practice*, *8*, 248–59.

Wade TD, Davidson S & O'Dea J (2003), 'A controlled evaluation of a school-based media literacy program and self-esteem program for reducing eating disorder risk factors: A preliminary investigation', *International Journal of Eating Disorders*, *33*, 371–83.

Weiss K & Wertheim EH (2005), 'An evaluation of a prevention program for disordered eating in adolescent girls: Examining responses of high and low risk girls', *Eating Disorders*, *13*, 143–56.

Wiseman CV, Sunday SR, Bortolli F & Halmi KA (2004), 'Primary prevention of eating disorders through attitute change: A two country comparison', *Eating Disorders*, *12*, 24–50.

Withers GF, Twigg K, Wertheim EH & Paxton SJ (2002), 'A controlled evaluation of an eating disorders primary prevention videotape using the elaboration likelihood model of persuasion', *Journal of Psychosomatic Research*, *53*, 1021–7.

4 Developing self-esteem

Introduction

A child's self-concept is constructed from very early in childhood and continues to develop throughout childhood and adolescence from several different domains. Self-concept theorists have identified the multi-dimensional nature of self-concept in children and adolescents including different individual domains such as academic self-concept, athletic competence, social acceptance, job competence and romantic appeal. Promoting a positive sense of self in many different domains is the key to producing overall self-esteem and lowering the importance of physical appearance among children and adolescents. Developing a broad positive sense of self also promotes a positive body image which in turn reduces the risk of eating problems and this is the focus of this chapter.

Recent research about the link between low self-esteem and eating disorders reinforces the early suggestions from the 1980s for a self-esteem approach in the prevention of eating problems. Research interventions testing predominantly self-esteem approaches for the improvement of body image and the prevention of eating problems have produced support for the efficacy, safety and suitability of a self-esteem and self-acceptance approach.

Several recent studies utilising strong self-esteem components as part of their controlled prevention interventions have produced improvements in body image, dieting, internalisation of the thin ideal and attitudes associated with the eating disorders.

This chapter discusses self-esteem as one of the important risk and protective factors in the development of body image concerns and eating disorders, and describes the subsequent use of the Everybody's Different self-esteem program for improvement of body image and prevention of eating disorders. Interventions containing strong self-esteem components from around the world are discussed in relation to their impact on the body image and eating behaviours of adolescents. Applications of the self-esteem approach for the prevention of child obesity are also discussed. Program activities and work sheets for use in the school or university classroom are given.

Self-concept and self-esteem among children and adolescents

Children work to construct their self-concept and their sense of self-worth or self-esteem from the pre-school period through adolescence. Constructing the self-concept is like piecing together a 'personal theory' of what the self is like as an experiencing and functioning individual. The self-concept is subject to continual change as it is exposed to new information and experiences and as the child learns more about himself or herself and the surrounding world. An additional component of self-concept is self-esteem which refers to the judgement we make about the worth of ourselves (Coopersmith, 1967; Harter, 1983; 1988; Rosenberg, 1979). Children and adolescents with high self-esteem are fundamentally satisfied with themselves as a person, while still able to identify weaker characteristics that may require work to overcome. High self-esteem envelops a realistic appraisal of the self's characteristics and competencies coupled with an attitude of self-acceptance, self-respect and self-worth.

The self-concept of adolescents is influenced by several variables. The adolescent self-concept decreases slightly on entry into secondary school and then gradually increases with age (Wylie, 1979), and becomes increasingly differentiated into separate categories related to roles with age (Harter & Monsour, 1992; Marsh et al., 1984; 1989; 1990). Theorists categorise the adolescent self-concept as encompassing several different domains such as academic and scholastic competence, physical and athletic competence, physical appearance, close friendship, romantic appeal, perception of personal behaviour and global self-worth (Harter, 1982; Shavelson et al., 1976). Shavelson classifies academic self-concept further by having separate categories for mathematics, English, science and history (Shavelson et al., 1976). Reviews of the adolescent self-concept suggest that self-concept is multidimensional and measurement must address the many separate dimensions of the total self-concept (Harter & Monsour, 1992; Marsh, 1990; Marsh et al., 2004; 2006) rather than try to allocate one self-esteem score.

Harter's Perceived Competence Scale for Children (Harter, 1982) includes a scale for measurement of importance ratings. This instrument assumes that the importance a child gives to certain areas of self-concept determines the overall effect upon their self-concept. For example, a child may score low on the physical ability/athletic competence subscale of the Harter Perceived Competence Scale, but may also assign a low level of importance to that area of self-concept. The discrepancy between perception and importance of the various dimensions of self-concept in comparison to the actual score affects the overall self-concept. Measurement of the importance assigned to each dimension of self-concept is therefore essential in order to assess general self-concept.

The self-concept of adolescents is also influenced by gender. A study of 14–16-year-old adolescents showed that girls scored lower on the Rosenberg Self-esteem Scale than boys (Harper & Marshall, 1991). The authors suggest that the lower level of self-esteem among girls was the cause of their higher level of reported problems. Studies have reported that differences in specific components of self-concept may exist, and that these effects may be lost when forming a total score (Wylie, 1979). Marsh (1990) presented a review of self-concept research and theory, and states that global measures of self-concept tend to favour boys. This suggestion is supported by the literature. Girls tend to score higher on self-concept measures of reading and general schoolwork, but score lower on physical ability, maths and physical appearance. Physical appearance self-concept (physical self-esteem) scores decline significantly after preadolescence. Girls also score higher than boys for self-concept related to verbal competence, honesty and trustworthiness, and same sex relationships. Boys score higher than girls on perceived emotional stability scales and perceived problem solving ability. Marsh states that these trends are consistent with traditional gender stereotypes.

Self-concept studies of Australian adolescents (O'Dea & Abraham, 1999a; 1999b) produced similar findings to the studies of Marsh. The self-concept scales ranked as most important by male and female students were in order, Close Friendship, Scholastic Competence and Job Competence. Females rated their ability to form close friendships significantly higher and of greater importance than did males. Males had a more positive self-concept related to physical appearance, scholastic competence and athletic competence than did females, although both boys and girls rated athletic competence as the least important of all the aspects of self-concept. Boys also scored higher than females for the discrepancy between self-concept and importance, showing that the boys felt more capable of achieving in the areas of self-concept that were important to them.

A number of studies have identified factors associated with low self-concept in adolescents. Renouf and Harter (1990) and Harter et al. (1992) measured self-concept, depression and social support among 346 young adolescents. Findings showed that depressed adolescents and those who had expressed suicidal thoughts had low self-concept scores and, in particular, low scores for physical appearance, peer likeability, athletic competence, scholastic competence and behavioural conduct. Other researchers have identified the negative impact that depression, anxiety and mood have upon the adolescent self-concept (Taylor & Cooper, 1992; Teri, 1982). A study of Australian teenaged girls showed no differences in global self-esteem scores between girls from middle and lower socioeconomic backgrounds (O'Dea, 1994).

Links between self-concept, age and gender

Self-concept and self-esteem has been studied extensively among adolescents. A large study of 12 266 Australian adolescents (Marsh, 1989) found gender and age differences in self-concept. Marsh found that the self-concept scores of preadolescents were lower than those of children who had entered adolescence and that there was a significant decrease in self-concept scores in pre- and very early adolescence. He suggested that some time in early to middle adolescence, the self-concept begins to rise and this continues during late adolescence and early adulthood. This trend has been confirmed by other authors (O'Malley & Bachman, 1983; Savin-Williams & Demo, 1984; Wallace et al., 1984) and this decline of self-concept in preadolescence is partly attributed to the transition from primary school to high school (Marsh, 1989; Rosenberg, 1979). Changing to a new school environment and adjusting to new expectations from teachers and peers may cause adolescents to question their ability to cope with their behaviour and performance and this may affect their self-concept. It has been suggested that younger children and preadolescent children have an unrealistically high self-concept which becomes more realistic with age and that this 'reality testing' may also account for the decline in self-concept at entry into adolescence (Marsh et al., 1984). Self-concept and self-esteem tend to rise after early adolescence, contradicting the long-held belief that adolescence is a time of serious emotional trauma and turmoil.

Gender differences are apparent between the self-concepts of male and female adolescents. Males tend to score higher on most self-concept categories and on measures of general self-esteem than females. The large Marsh study (1989) found boys score higher on physical ability, physical appearance, mathematics, emotional stability, problem solving and general self-esteem. Girls scored higher on verbal and reading competency, school related self-concept, honesty/trustworthiness and religious/spiritual values. Marsh commented that these gender differences were consistent with traditional sex stereotypes. Scores of male and female adolescents on the Harter Self Perception Profile for Adolescents (Harter, 1988) confirm Marsh's findings. Males in Harter's study scored higher than females on all categories of self-concept except for behavioural conduct. The physical appearance scores of male and female adolescents in the Australian study was the only category of self-concept on which gender differences varied substantially with age (Marsh, 1989; Marsh et al., 2006). The younger females in Marsh's study had greater physical appearance scores than older females. These studies suggest that adolescents' self-concept is already affected by cultural sex stereotypes in preadolescence and that the effects are relatively stable throughout the adolescent years.

The studies of Marsh (1989), Harter (1988), Kimm et al. (1991), O'Dea and Abraham (1999a) and O'Dea (2006) highlight the importance of measuring different aspects of the adolescent self-concept rather than using one overall measure of general self-esteem. Using a multidimensional instrument enables examination of gender, pubertal and body weight interactions with different categories of self-concept. A one-dimensional instrument would not be able to detect such variations. Measuring change in the self-concept must therefore take into account the fact that separate dimensions must be measured and that the overall self-concept is expected to improve from early to late adolescence.

Self-concept and puberty

Several studies have shown that pubertal development affects physical self-concept, with early developing females having a less positive physical self-concept than their 'on time' or late-maturing peers (Abraham & O'Dea, 2001; Alsaker, 1992; Folk et al., 1993; O'Dea & Abraham 1999a). In studies of young adolescents aged 11–14 years old, we consistently found post-menarcheal females to have poorer self-esteem than their pre-menarcheal counterparts (Abraham & O'Dea, 2001; O'Dea & Abraham, 1995; 1999b). The female adolescents who were post-menarcheal had poorer general self-esteem as well as poorer self-esteem related to athletic competence, physical appearance and behavioural conduct. The opposite trend for self-esteem was observed among the young males in the studies with post-pubertal males having the greatest global self-esteem of all adolescents in the studies and post-pubertal females having the poorest. Similar effects of pubertal development upon self-concept have been aspects of the adolescent reported in other studies (Alsaker, 1992; Blyth et al., 1981; Brooks-Gunn, 1984; Folk et al., 1993) and support the suggestion that stage of pubertal development may be more influential than age in influencing the self-concept of adolescents, particularly females.

Self-concept and body weight

Body weight and in particular overweight has been consistently found to be a potent predictor of lower self-esteem in both female and male children and adolescents. Studies of the relationship between self-esteem and body weight in young preadolescent children aged below 12 years have generally found an inverse relationship between self-esteem and measures of body weight, body mass index, overweight or obesity (Coopersmith, 1967; Felker, 1968; Felker & Kay, 1971; Strauss, 2000).

Similar results have been found in studies of adolescents with general self-esteem being lower in overweight or obese adolescents (French et al., 1995; 1996; Kimm et al., 1997; O'Dea, 2006; O'Dea & Abraham, 1999a; Strauss, 2000).

Studies that have failed to find a relationship between self-esteem and body weight may have been limited by the use of a one-dimensional instrument for measuring self-esteem rather than using a multi-dimensional instrument. For example, studies of weight and self-concept among adolescents using single dimensional tools such as the Rosenberg self-esteem scale (Rosenberg, 1965) have not been able to detect any impact of weight upon self-esteem (Gortmaker et al., 1993; Mendelson & White, 1985) and this may simply be due to the insensitivity of the instrument being used. Studies that have included a sub-scale measure of general self-esteem such as body esteem or physical self-esteem have reported strong inverse relationships between actual body weight and these sub-scale measures of physical self-esteem, showing that children and adolescents of greater body weight have poorer body esteem (Hill et al., 1992; Mendelson & White, 1982; 1985), poorer body image (Gardner et al., 1999; O'Dea, 2006) and poorer physical self-esteem (French et al., 1995; O'Dea, 2006; O'Dea & Abraham, 1999a)

Impact of sport and exercise on self-concept

Participation by children and adolescents in physical activity and exercise has been found to be associated with greater self-esteem and physical self-esteem in several studies and in both sexes (Salokun, 1994; Sherrill et al., 1989). Various types of sports and physical activity have been shown to be related to higher global self-esteem and greater physical self-esteem in children and adolescents including participation in swimming (Frankl, 1996; Miller, 1989), creative dance (Radell et al., 1993), baseball (Hawkins & Gruber, 1982), karate and martial arts (Richman & Rehberg, 1986) and yoga (Schime et al., 2006).

Interventions to improve self-esteem have successfully employed children and adolescents aged 9–16 years old in physical activities (Boyd & Hrycaiko, 1997; Goni & Zulaika, 2000; Parishplass & Lufi, 1997). The successful intervention study of Goni & Zulaika (2000) differed from the usual physical education classes in that they focused on identifying individual goals, promoted participative and non-competitive games and praised students at every chance possible during the classes. This type of non-competitive, cooperative approach to physical activity and sport has been previously found to improve self-concept in high school girls (Marsh & Peart, 1988) and young children (Emmanouel et al., 1992).

Self-esteem as a protective factor

Positive self-esteem can act as a protective, health promoting factor for children and adolescents as it contributes to positive social behaviours and it acts as a buffer against the impact of negative influences (Mann et al., 2004). Poor self-esteem can play a critical role in the development of depression, anorexia nervosa, bulimia nervosa, other eating disorders, anxiety, violence, substance abuse, high risk behaviours and suicide. (For an excellent review of self-esteem and mental health promotion, see Mann et al., 2004.)

Conversely, positive self-esteem is protective against these problems and contributes to their prevention as well as the promotion of positive outcomes such as academic achievement, competence in several different arenas, self-satisfaction, life satisfaction, resilience and coping ability.

Self-esteem for the prevention of body image and eating problems

Early writings about the prevention of eating disorders identified self-esteem development as a primary target in the prevention of anorexia nervosa, bulimia nervosa and other associated eating problems. As early as 1984, Bayer suggested the following advice for parents, educators and health professionals involved in the protection of children and adolescents from eating disorders.

> Help young people feel good about themselves and accept themselves ... avoid driving adolescents to excel beyond their capabilities in academic or other endeavours ... provide adolescents with an appropriate but not unlimited degree of autonomy, choice, responsibility, and self-accountability for their actions ...
> (Bayer, 1984).

Similarly, early seminal prevention work by Catherine Shisslak and her colleagues (1987; 1990; 1998) cited low self-esteem as one of the most important factors to target in the prevention of eating disorders. The authors state in their classic paper titled 'Prevention of eating disorders among adolescents' (1990) that

> ... given that poor self-esteem is highly correlated with chaotic eating patterns, teaching alternative methods to enhance self-efficacy may decrease the likelihood of developing high risk eating behaviours (p. 104).

Other theorists and researchers followed the early arguments and suggestions of Shisslak et al. (1987; 1990; 1998) by suggesting the development of self-esteem and self-acceptance in the prevention of eating disorders among children and adolescents (Collins, 1991; Mellin, 1988). Clearly, the development of self-esteem as a protective factor against body dissatisfaction, disordered eating and eating disorders was strongly identified and argued in the late 1980s and early 1990s.

Low self-esteem as a risk factor for body image concerns and eating disorders

Building child self-esteem is a logical approach to the prevention of body image and eating problems. Self-esteem refers to the judgement we make about our overall worth. Children and adolescents with high self-esteem are fundamentally satisfied with themselves as a person, while still able to identify weaker characteristics that may require work to improve. High self-esteem envelops a realistic self-appraisal of the child's characteristics and competencies coupled with an attitude of self-acceptance, self-respect and self-worth. Poor self-esteem is known to be an important predictor of body image concerns, dieting, disordered eating and eating disorders (Button, 1990; Button et al., 1996; 1997; McVey et al., 2002; Shisslak et al., 1998; Stice, 2002). In a large, longitudinal study of 594 schoolgirls, Button and colleagues (1996) found that girls with low self-esteem at age 11–12 years were at a significantly greater risk of developing severe eating problems by 15–16 years of age.

In a study of Canadian schoolgirls, McVey and her colleagues (2002) found specific aspects of self-esteem to be strongly associated with disordered eating, namely, low competence ratings for physical activity and high importance ratings for social acceptance by peers. One of the conclusions by the authors of this study was to implement self-esteem strategies among adolescent females in order to lower the importance they place on physical appearance in order to prevent disordered eating.

In addition to the research literature linking the role of low self-esteem in the prediction of eating disturbances, there are many studies that show that overweight children and adolescents or those who perceive themselves to be overweight have poorer overall self-esteem and body esteem than their lower weight peers (Mendelson et al., 1995; O'Dea & Abraham, 1999a; Strauss, 2000).

Self-esteem protection and enhancement is therefore appropriate and desirable for all children and adolescents but it is particularly relevant in the treatment and prevention of body image problems and eating disturbances, because low self-esteem is considered to be a potent risk factor for these problems. Similarly, self-esteem development is critical in the prevention and treatment of childhood obesity because these children may suffer low self-esteem as a consequence of their weight problem and the stigma associated with weight may result in further self-consciousness and social isolation.

Self-esteem development and enhancement is also believed to improve the other factors known to contribute to body image and eating problems. For example, development of a positive self-image and a strong sense of self-worth are likely to help children and adolescents became more satisfied with their body shape and size and more resilient and resistant to the unrealistic body image ideals portrayed in the media. Children with high self-esteem are better able to cope with the teasing, criticism, stress and anxiety, which are all associated with eating problems (Paxton, 2002).

Further, the development of a positive self-image, which includes a broad array of aspects of the self other than physical appearance, is likely to help children value their many different characteristics and those of others. This type of self-image development is likely to reduce children's obsession with perfectionism and the belief that one must be perfect, or strive to be perfect, in order to be valued, accepted and loved. As perfectionism is strongly associated with body image problems and eating disorders

(McVey et al., 2002; Shisslak & Crago, 2001; Stice, 2002) it is believed that modifying this risk factor by developing self-esteem may help young people to be more self-accepting and less involved in the futile quest for perfection.

Relevance of the self-esteem approach in the prevention of child obesity

The prevention of eating disturbances and body image concerns is vital today, as is the concurrent prevention of child obesity which has more than doubled in the USA over the past 30 years (Troiano & Flegal, 1995). Because overweight, perceived overweight and weight concerns are known to precede dieting, hazardous weight loss behaviours and eating disturbances the current trend towards the co-occurrence of increasing eating disorders and increasing child overweight is of concern. It is probable that the increasing rates of child overweight may be one of the factors that have resulted in more dieting and weight loss attempts among young people. Hence, the two trends could be expected to continue in tandem and prevention of both is required.

Further to the intricate relationship between disordered eating and child obesity is the relationship between weight control behaviours and further weight gain. Recent research supports the thesis that children and adolescents who use extreme weight loss attempts only serve to perpetuate the futile cycle of dieting, purging, binge eating and further weight gain. The phenomena of weight rebound following dietary restriction have been observed in a study of adolescent girls. In their recent large, well-designed, longitudinal study spanning four years, Stice and his colleagues (1999) found that among high school girls of various weights, those who tried extreme methods to lose weight were the most likely to gain weight over time and were therefore at greater risk for obesity. Girls who used more extreme weight loss methods such as laxatives, appetite suppressants, vomiting and fasting gained more weight than those who were not involved in extreme weight loss attempts. Among girls who dieted, the risk of obesity onset was greater than for non-dieters, irrespective of their actual weight at the beginning of the study. This finding has since been replicated in a six-year study of girls in the USA (Neumark-Sztainer et al., 2006).

Clearly, one of the major aims of prevention programs to improve body image, eating problems and child obesity is to encourage healthy eating and physical activity among children and adolescents without promoting weight loss attempts and the diet-binge cycle. For this reason, the self-esteem approach is a relevant and appropriate approach to take in both the prevention of body image and eating problems and the prevention of child obesity, because the two issues are inextricably entwined.

A self-esteem program—'Everybody's Different'

The aim of the Everybody's Different program is to improve the body image, eating attitudes and behaviours of children, adolescents and tertiary students by focusing on developing their self-esteem. The program focuses on expanding students' self-identity and sense of self-worth by encompassing many aspects of the self and thereby decreasing the emphasis and importance of physical appearance. In addition, the program activities promote themes of self-acceptance, respect for self and others, tolerance, diversity, rejection of cultural stereotypes and reduced self-expectations of perfection. The major program theme is that an individual's uniqueness is to be expected, valued and accepted. A strong message of the program is that everybody is different and nobody is perfect.

The five teachers who delivered the program in the original research study (O'Dea & Abraham, 2000) were trained to build self-esteem by adopting a student-centred, cooperative and interactive teaching style, which is known to promote student self-esteem. The educational approach featured the use of student discussion, group work, team work, games, play, drama and a content-free, self-esteem building curriculum in which both the teaching style and the content of educational activities foster a positive sense of self, student involvement, self-efficacy, vicarious learning, exchange of feedback and opinion and a safe, respectful and positive classroom environment in which the students feel that they cannot 'fail'.

The Everybody's Different program consisted of nine weekly lessons. The major week-by-week content of the program is outlined in Chapter 3. The results of research studies utilising the self-esteem approach are outlined below.

Major research study results from Everybody's Different

The original research study to test the efficacy, suitability and safety of the program was conducted among 470 male and female adolescents aged 11–14 years and was published in the *International Journal of Eating Disorders* (O'Dea & Abraham, 2000). A particular focus of the study was to investigate the impact of an eating disorder prevention and body image promotion program among adolescent boys. The program was conducted over nine consecutive weeks, with one to two lessons per week spanning 1–2 hours per week with additional homework activities. Students completed questionnaires before and after the program and then again at 12-month follow up. The follow-up test was designed to evaluate any long-term and enduring effects of the program.

The Everybody's Different program significantly improved the body image of program students compared to controls. Female students and those at high risk for eating problems particularly benefited from the program, showing improvements in Body Dissatisfaction, Drive for Thinness, physical appearance ratings, reduced dieting and less unhealthy weight loss after the intervention. Social acceptance (peer pressure, popularity), physical appearance and athletic competence were less important to both male and female students after the intervention, and close friendships became more important. Many of the improvements were still significant at the 12-month follow up (Drive for Thinness, Physical Appearance Rating, Importance of Physical Appearance, Athletic Competence and Close Friendships to self-concept, deliberate weight loss in control girls versus no deliberate weight loss in intervention girls), although some of the statistically significant effects (Body Dissatisfaction, Currently Dieting to Lose Weight) had worn off after the self-esteem program, the trends remained in the same direction. The long-term results suggest that the initial impact was significant and the long-term impact remained for several variables, but that some effects had worn off after the program was discontinued, supporting the need for continued programs or booster sessions.

A unique and interesting finding of this new self-esteem approach was the improvement in body image among both boys and girls as well as those who were overweight or at high risk of developing body image or eating problems. This is evidenced by the fact that the improvement in the body satisfaction of high-risk male and female students was still statistically significant 12 months after the self-esteem program.

Improvements in body image may prove to be beneficial in helping students to be less body conscious and therefore more likely to become physically and socially active, as body consciousness is often cited as a barrier to physical activity in both boys and girls (Heath et al., 1994; O'Dea, 2003; Piran, 2001). Overcoming this barrier would be hugely beneficial for all children, but particularly helpful in the treatment and prevention of child overweight.

Other research studies that utilise a self-esteem approach

Since the initial findings from the Everybody's Different intervention trial, the impact of an eating disorder prevention program that contains a strong self-esteem/self-acceptance approach in the improvement of body image and eating behaviours has been successfully implemented twice in Canada among Grade 6–8 girls in the classroom (McVey et al., 2004) and in smaller peer support groups, by McVey and her colleagues (2003a). The two separate studies implemented self-esteem enhancement and self-acceptance strategies, stress management techniques, peer relations skills and media literacy lessons and found improved body satisfaction, global self-esteem and attitudes towards dieting.

Other attempts were reported as unsuccessful by McVey et al. (2002; 2003b) with the authors reporting improvement in both control and intervention girls, suggesting either a spillover type contamination of the control group by influences from the school intervention program or the favourable impact of their regular health education classes.

Another recent self-esteem intervention among Grade 7 and 8 students in Canada (Tsimicalis, 2002) aimed to replicate the self-esteem trial of O'Dea and Abraham (2000) and succeeded by producing body satisfaction improvements in male and female students and improved the physical appearance ratings of overweight females.

Eating disorder prevention programs that incorporate strong self-esteem components have also produced some significant improvements in the body image and eating behaviours of adolescent females. The study of Stewart et al. (2001) from England, incorporated self-esteem development and self-acceptance in classroom sessions with topics such as developing a positive body image, building self-esteem and managing stress. While their program was not a purely self-esteem approach, the inclusion of a strong focus on self-esteem development is likely to have helped to produce positive results in dietary restraint reduction and improvement in attitudes to weight and shape.

In a preventive intervention among groups of American Girl Scouts, Neumark-Sztainer et al. (2000) implemented a program with strong self-esteem and self-acceptance themes such as activities to help girls 'positively influence their social environment and empower them to feel better about themselves' and 'improving body acceptance' (p. 1467). Some of the activities in the 'Free to be me' program were similar in content to the self-esteem development program of O'Dea and Abraham (2000), including the positive involvement of parents in activities such as in the 'Feelin' Good' interviews with family members and friends about perceived positive traits and collage pictures that promote positive traits versus those that promote negative traits (p. 1468). The overall approach—which provided psycho-educational material on normal physical development, exercises intended to promote self-esteem and an interactive approach that focused on helping adolescents accept themselves and reject the thin ideal—produced increases in knowledge and decreases in thin-ideal internalisation. This intervention is another example of intervention programs that demonstrate that a strong self-esteem and self-acceptance component is an important and influential feature of eating disorder prevention interventions.

Similarly, the program of Phelps et al. (2000) in the USA included high school based lessons that 'utilised active individual participation and collaborative learning' and 'highlighted strengthening specific personal attributes' (p. 445). Phelps and her colleagues reported a trend towards reduced disordered eating, Body Dissatisfaction and Drive for Thinness and improved self-esteem, but the results did not reach statistical significance.

The study of Steiner-Adair et al. (2002), on the east coast of the USA, included strong components of assertiveness, self-acceptance development and self-esteem. Self-esteem related activities in this intervention included lessons titled 'claiming our strengths; identify admirable women; positive self-assessment; body appreciation; affirmations; 10 things I find beautiful; defining personal values; the power of positive action; coping skills; and how to help a friend' (Steiner Adair et al., 2002, p. 404). The results of this study found that the program resulted in knowledge and weight-related body esteem. Importantly, as in the high-risk group of O'Dea and Abraham (2000), these results were maintained at six-month follow up suggesting a strong and lasting intervention effect following a strongly self-esteem based intervention.

Researchers in Sweden (Ghaderi et al., 2005) also implemented the Everybody's Different self-esteem approach in an eating disorders prevention program with Grade 5 boys and girls. The authors reported that the vast majority of children (90–95 per cent) enjoyed the activities, but the research findings did not show any significant changes that were due to the self-esteem intervention. Instead, the authors reported significant improvements among both the control and intervention groups, suggesting a spillover effect among children outside of class. The inability to produce study effects among this young age group may be due to the low level of body image concerns in this age group of 10–11-year-old children who may not really benefit from the self-esteem development until later in their adolescence when their bodies are changing and their body image concerns are increasing with puberty.

Other recent programs to prevent eating problems and improve body image have reported some positive results. Weiss and Wertheim (2005) presented four 100-minute small group sessions with Year 9 girls in Melbourne, Australia, with a strong emphasis on self-esteem development, body esteem and healthy self-perceptions. This predominantly self-esteem approach resulted in significant improvements in the girls' body image.

Schime and her colleagues (2006) from New York State in the USA, incorporated relaxation, yoga, guided imagery, self-esteem, media and the thin ideal, coping and self-competence into 10 weeks of after school 'Girls' Groups' with 5th grade girls. Despite the absence of a control group, the authors reported important and significant improvements in body image and a reduced drive for thinness among the girls after the intervention.

The self-esteem approach to the prevention of body image concerns, disturbed eating and eating disorders has proven to be a very promising approach in several interventions from around the world involving young male and female adolescents.

Everybody's Different program activities

The following table outlines the Everybody's Different program and activities which are suitable for all age groups of students, ranging from Years 5 and 6 in primary school to Years 7–11 in high school and undergraduate students in the college or university setting.

I have used all of these lessons with various age groups of students, remembering that the way each lesson is delivered is completely up to the judgement of the teacher. Delivery should incorporate student-centred, interactive approaches with a lot of student discussion, working in pairs or threes, or small groups and finishing up with presentation and discussion as a whole group. In the original intervention study, the educational approach featured the use of student discussion, group work, team work, games, play, drama and a content-free, self-esteem building curriculum in which both the teaching style and the content of educational activities foster a positive sense of self, student involvement, self-efficacy, vicarious learning, exchange of feedback and opinion and a safe, respectful and positive classroom environment in which the students feel that they cannot 'fail'.

TABLE 4.1 An outline of the content in the Everybody's Different program

Major objective	Content/Activities	Aim of lessons and activities
Ways of dealing with stress	Group discussions. Students report how they deal with stress. Activities are student-led, not teacher-imposed.	Activities encourage students to develop healthy ways of coping with stress such as relaxation, peer, teacher, family and parental support; identification and expression of anger and other emotions; communicating with others in order to solve problems. Enhances peer communication and peer support.
	Relaxation/visualisation exercises.	Relaxation promotes positive body awareness, stress control and enhances positive physical sensation.
	Benefits of stress control. Student-led discussion and reporting.	Homework activities encourage adoption of positive stress control behaviours and involves positive peer, parental and family support.
Building a positive sense of self	Expanding self-image to include a wide array of physical and personal attributes—student-led.	Broadens self-image to include many different aspects of the self. Diminishes importance of physical appearance. Promotes diversity, tolerance, self-acceptance and acceptance of others, promotes respect and develops awareness about the undesirability of prejudice and teasing. Encourages positive self-talk and reduces obsessive, 'all-or-nothing' rigid thinking.
	Awareness and acceptance that everybody is different and nobody is perfect.	Reduces the unrealistic and futile pursuit of perfection.
	Identifying positive self-attributes.	Models peer support.
	Learning to give and receive positive feedback.	Positively involves significant others.
	Positive self-evaluation, identifying and valuing uniqueness in self and others.	Reduces impact of criticism from others by receiving positive support from varied sources.
Exploring individuality of self and peers (self-advertisements)	Identifying positive features in self and others with a focus on non-physical traits.	Reinforcement that individuality and diversity are normal and acceptable.
Acceptance of self and others	Reinforcement that diversity, uniqueness and differences between people are to be expected valued and accepted.	Development of reinforcement of self-acceptance and acceptance of others.
		Reduced importance of physical appearance and enhanced importance of many varied attributes.

Everybody's Different self-esteem activities

Part 1 Ways of dealing with stress (1–2 lessons)

Activity 1   What is stress?

Activity 2   Relaxation activities (1 lesson to introduce the activity, then regular use during class and at home)

Part 2 Building a positive sense of self, exploring individuality of self and peers

Acceptance of self and others

Activity 1   Ways of developing a positive classroom environment

Activity 2   What makes up a person?

Ways to raise self-esteem among children and adolescents

- Call your students by name. Do not refer to students as 'sweetie', 'love', 'mate' or other titles. The student's name helps them to understand that they are unique individuals.
- Smile and let your students know that you enjoy their company.
- Treat your students with respect—especially when they are disrespectful to you or others. Many children only have the opportunity to learn respect at school.
- Help students identify their unique characteristics.
- Notice your students when they do something **right** rather than only noticing when they do something **wrong**.
- Praise and congratulate their positive behaviours.
- Openly reward the child's positive attitudes, for example, 'I noticed how hard you tried on that task. Well done.'
- Congratulate your students for modest achievements.
- Shake your student's hand, look them in the eye, smile and say 'Congratulations'.
- Do not give up on your most 'difficult' students—they are the ones who need your support and reassurance the most.
- Have firm, but reasonable expectations of children and adolescents.
- Build the child's self-efficacy or sense of mastery by setting them up to succeed rather than fail. Always set some tasks that the whole class can succeed at.
- Expect your students to succeed—never allow your children to think that you don't believe in them or that you don't expect them to behave, try or do their best.
- Recognise, reward and outwardly praise children and adolescents when they behave, attempt tasks and do their best.
- Praise children in front of other significant adults such as parents, relatives or teachers.
- **Never** criticise children in front of others.
- Give children your **whole attention**—do not multi-task all of the time when the child is trying to tell you something.
- Create sensible limitations and reasonable rules.
- Stick by your rules consistently and make it clear that in your classroom (or your home) this is the way we behave.
- Try to give each child some individual, face-to-face attention.
- If children or teens rebuke your rules with comments like 'Mrs Jones doesn't make us do that!' or 'Dad lets us eat what we like when we are at his place', gently reply by saying that it is your job as a teacher (or parent) to do what is best for your students (or children) and that you want them to do what is best for them—because you care!
- Allow children and adolescents to help you in the classroom or at home.
- Give students some meaningful and helpful chores to do and thank them for their assistance.

- Do not compare students with each other, as everybody is different. It is best to reinforce our individual features and unique characteristics.
- Compliment your students or your child for their positive features—'you look very nice today', 'your new haircut looks great', 'your laugh is so infectious', 'your compassion is greatly appreciated', etc.
- Encourage student participation in different activities.
- Praise students for their involvement.
- Explain that paying attention or watching other students perform tasks (vicarious learning) is also a valuable contribution.
- Reinforce that students can learn and be involved simply by watching and paying attention.
- Allow students to state their opinions. If you ask for an opinion, allow students time to come up with an answer. A good way to examine beliefs, attitudes and opinions in class is to give **everyone** a piece of paper on which to write their opinion anonymously.
- Encourage, listen to and respect children's opinions in class and at home.
- If you are watching a television program or video together with your class or your children make an opportunity to discuss it together and listen to their point of view.
- Make a special point of noticing the quiet, reclusive students—often it is only the 'squeaky wheel' who gets our attention in class.
- Celebrate milestones in class when students make achievements or when the whole class makes an achievement.
- Acknowledge student successes inside and outside of the classroom.
- Have an end of term celebration.
- Acknowledge and recognise transitions in your students' lives.
- Bring impressive role models from your community into the classroom.
- Introduce your students to members of the community who can act as sources of information, advice or support.
- Enjoy the company of your students. Allow yourself to enjoy being surrounded by the many and varied personalities in your class!
- Relax and allow your students to see you enjoying your role as teacher.

Summary

Strong self-esteem is a very protective factor among children, adolescents and young adults. Young people with a positive sense of self-worth are likely to do well at school and in social settings. Many positive outcomes are associated with self-esteem and these include positive academic outcomes, mental wellbeing, adjustment, happiness, success, life satisfaction, as well as overall 'health' including mental, physical, social and spiritual dimensions of health.

Self-esteem protects against depression, eating disorders, suicide, drug and alcohol use, risk behaviours and teenage pregnancy.

Conversely poor self-esteem predicts eating disorders and body image concerns. Research interventions testing predominantly self-esteem approaches for the improvement of body image and the prevention of eating problems have produced support for the efficacy, safety and suitability of a self-esteem and self-acceptance approach.

Several recent studies utilising strong self-esteem components as part of their controlled prevention interventions have produced improvements in body image, dieting, internalisation of the thin ideal and attitudes associated with the eating disorders.

This chapter has presented the theory, research and practical aspects of implementing the 'Everybody's Different' self-esteem program for improvement of body image and prevention of eating disorders. Classroom activities for use in schools, universities or community settings aim to help students explore and develop their own self-image and develop a positive sense of self-worth. Each of the activities presented focuses on delivery of lessons in a cooperative classroom with all students participating in some way and all students having a 'voice'. Each of the activities presented in this chapter has been pre-tested in the classroom with primary, secondary and tertiary students.

Part 1 Ways of dealing with stress

Activity 1 What is stress?

- Teacher asks the class to define 'stress'.
- Stress is a demand or pressure placed on people that can make us feel tense, unhappy or uncomfortable.
- When we are stressed, our bodies change to adjust to the situation.
- This is called the 'stress response' and it is a survival instinct in all animals.
- This is also called the 'fight or flight' response.
- Teacher hands out page 66 or puts it up on overhead.
- Discussion of physical effects of stress.

Coping with stress

- In pairs or small groups, students use copies of the work sheet on page 67 to brainstorm healthy ways of dealing with stress.
- Some methods are helpful, e.g. going for a walk or a swim, yoga, taking a shower or a bath, talking to family or friends.
- Some common methods for stress are damaging, e.g. eating, drinking, drinking alcohol, drugs, shopping sprees, etc.
- Examine the pros and cons of healthy versus unhealthy methods of stress control.

Is all stress bad for you?

- No, not all stress is bad.
- The fight or flight response is a helpful survival tool.
- It helps us deal with difficult situations.
- A little stress or anticipation can be helpful, e.g. excitement before a life event such as a holiday, birthday, a family celebration or a performance such as a school concert or play.
- This excitement 'revs us up' and helps us get the job done.
- However, too much stress all the time can become a problem.
- Too much stress can cause:
  - Physical effects, e.g. nervousness, headaches, unable to sleep
  - A feeling that your energy is drained
  - Lowering of resistance to infection, e.g. lots of colds
  - A feeling that you can't handle the situation.

Activity 1 What is stress?

- Stress is a *demand* or *pressure* placed on people that can make them feel tense, unhappy or uncomfortable.

- When you are stressed the body changes to adjust to the situation. This is called the *stress response*.

- This is also called the *fight or flight response*.

What is going on in our bodies when we prepare for fight or flight?

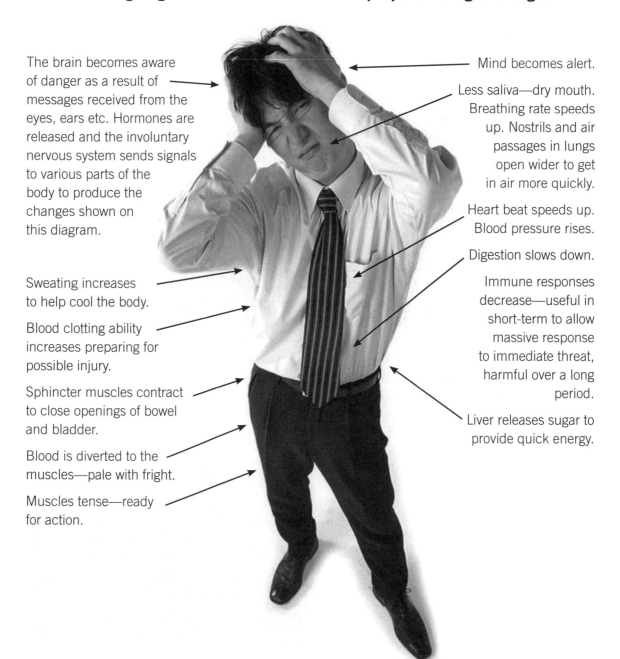

The brain becomes aware of danger as a result of messages received from the eyes, ears etc. Hormones are released and the involuntary nervous system sends signals to various parts of the body to produce the changes shown on this diagram.

Sweating increases to help cool the body.

Blood clotting ability increases preparing for possible injury.

Sphincter muscles contract to close openings of bowel and bladder.

Blood is diverted to the muscles—pale with fright.

Muscles tense—ready for action.

Mind becomes alert.

Less saliva—dry mouth. Breathing rate speeds up. Nostrils and air passages in lungs open wider to get in air more quickly.

Heart beat speeds up. Blood pressure rises.

Digestion slows down.

Immune responses decrease—useful in short-term to allow massive response to immediate threat, harmful over a long period.

Liver releases sugar to provide quick energy.

Activity 1 How can I deal with stress?

What are some of the things that make you feel 'stressed'?

_____

_____

_____

_____

_____

How do you feel when you are 'stressed'?

_____

_____

_____

_____

_____

Can you suggest some healthy ways that help you to relax or feel better?

_____

_____

_____

_____

_____

Activity 1 How can I deal with stress?

Teacher's answers

What are some of the things that make you feel 'stressed'?

- School pressures
- Parents' expectations
- Homework
- Tests and exams
- Keeping up with brothers and sisters
- Brothers and sisters who can be mean

- Some teachers are mean
- Other kids can be cruel
- Trying to adjust to new school
- Coping with puberty
- Physical changes, e.g. menstruation
- Keeping up and fitting in with peers

How do you feel when you are 'stressed'?

- Frustrated
- Helpless
- Worried
- Frightened
- Incompetent
- Unhappy
- Overloaded
- Nervous

- Angry
- Confused
- Physically sick
- Alone
- Inadequate
- Uncomfortable
- Overwhelmed
- Lost

- Hurt
- Pressured
- Hopeless
- Left out
- Unimportant
- Tense
- Burdened
- Headaches

Can anyone suggest methods to relax or feel better?

- Taking a bath (e.g. bubble bath with candles)
- Physical exertion (e.g. riding bike, dancing, jogging)
- Watching TV
- Playing video games or computer games
- Punching a pillow
- Praying or meditating
- Reading
- Taking a shower
- Going for a swim
- Being alone
- 'Escaping' somehow (e.g. go to room)
- Talking to someone (e.g. friends)
- Improving attitude (e.g. looking on the positive side)
- Bashing mattress with cricket bat
- Making a phone call to friends
- Listening to music
- Going for a walk
- Thinking of something nice, remembering nice things
- Looking forward to nice times

Activity 2 Relaxation activities

- Teacher introduces the relaxation activity as a healthy method of reducing stress and a way of helping students feel better physically and mentally.
- Students can sit in their chairs with their eyes closed.
- They can take their shoes off, lie down or sit next to the wall. Some students choose to put their heads down on the desk.

Relaxation guide

- Teacher reads one of the relaxation scripts with relaxation music playing quietly in the background.
- Read the script slowly and quietly when all students are settled.
- It is ideal to have a tape recording of these scripts for students to use in the school library, in the classroom with headphones or to take home to use when they are having difficulty sleeping, when they are worried about exams or for general stress relief and relaxation.
- You can record your own copy of the relaxation tape by reading the script with quiet music playing in the background.
- The relaxation tape can be given to students as a reward or as a way of improving behaviour.

Script 1 Stretching, breathing and relaxation

This is an activity that can help you learn to relax your body and mind by tensing and releasing muscles.

If you ever feel tense while asking a question in class, taking a test or at any other time, you can use this feeling of relaxation to feel better.

Let's begin with you lying on your back on the floor or on your bed.

Wiggle around a little until you find a way of lying down that is completely comfortable.

Now, close your eyes and think of your hands.

Feel the bones inside them.

Feel the muscles that move the bones.

Feel the weight of them on the floor.

Now breathe in, make a fist with your hands and clench tightly and count to five … one … two … three … four … five.

Now breathe out and relax …

Feel the soothing, tingling feeling of relaxation come into your hands.

Breathe deeply.

Release all your tension through your hands …

Now draw up your arms and tighten your biceps as tight as you can.

Breathe in, hold them tightly, one … two … three … four … five …

Now breathe out and relax …

Feel the tension drain out of your arms.

Relax both your arms and feel the tension melting out of them.

Breathe in … breathe out … breathe in and shrug your shoulders now, pushing them as if to push them up through your ears. Hold them tightly one … two … three … four … five—breathe out and relax …

(Pause) Breathe in … and breathe out …

Again, breathe in, shrug your shoulders, now breathe out and let them go and feel all the tension drain out of your body ...

Enjoy how relaxed your body feels ...

(Pause) Breathe in ... and breathe out ...

Continuing to keep your eyes closed, open your mouth as far as it will go, stretching the muscles at the corners of your mouth.

Hold it tightly ... relax.

Enjoy the tingling feeling as the tension dissolves in your mouth.

Now breathe in, tighten the muscles in your chest, stomach and abdomen.

Draw all of the muscles in tightly and hold them tense.

Now let them go ... feel the soothing feeling of relaxation pour in.

(Pause) Breathe in ... and breathe out ...

Now tense the muscles of your legs by straightening your legs and curling your toes. Hold them tightly. Breathe in and breathe out ...

Now relax your legs. Let all of the tension drain out of them.

Enjoy how your body feels, relaxed and without any tension.

(Pause) Breathe in ... and breathe out ...

Your whole body is feeling loose and relaxed now ...

Feel yourself completely supported by the floor and breathe deeply ...

As you breathe in, let each breath fill your body with deeper and deeper feelings of relaxation.

See if there are any places of tension left in your body.

If you feel tense in some area take a deep breath and send the breath to that place ...

Fill that tense area with breath and let the feeling of tension leave your body.

You'll be coming out of relaxation in a moment, and you'll feel rested and alert.

You'll feel happy to be in your body.

I'll count backward from ten to one and, as I do, feel your body becoming alert at your own rate. Enjoy feeling contented in your body.

Ten ... nine ... eight—feel the alertness returning to your body—seven ... six ... five—feel your toes and fingers begin to move—four ... three ... two ... one—now breathe in, stretch your whole body, breath out and relax.

Script 2 Relaxation and escaping

Now we're going on an adventure which will help you clear some of the feelings that make you feel bad, irritated or stressed.

Keep your eyes closed and relax your whole body.

Take a breath and as you breathe out let go of any tension in your body.

Again, breathe in and as you breathe out let all your tensions melt away.

Relax every part of your body.

Imagine you're on a beautiful beach.

The sun is shining gently and it's nice and warm. It feels good on your skin.

A few seagulls are floating on the breeze in the sky.

The water's lapping quietly on the shore of a crystal clear bay.

Down at the water's edge there's a little rowing boat and it's painted your favourite colour.

You slowly walk over to the boat and push it into the water and climb in.

You drift gently out into the bay.

At the bottom of the boat you see a small metal box wrapped in chains.

Inside the box are the things that make you feel stressed, angry, sad or annoyed.

Now you row out to reach very deep water.

You place the oars in the boat, pick up the metal box and hold it over the side of the boat.

Let it drop. It makes a small splash.

Now watch as all your stressed feelings sink out of sight, down, down into the blue depths.

You can feel a sense of relief as your stresses drift away.

You take some time to enjoy the gentle rocking of the boat. Now you take the oars and row back to shore knowing that all your stress is gone, lying on the sea bed.

Very soon you're back on the warm sandy beach feeling very happy with yourself, very contented and very relaxed.

Script 3 Imagery

Close your eyes and relax all of your muscles.

Breathe in deeply and slowly relax with every breath out.

Let your arms and hands go with each breath out.

Now your legs, your chest, let go of any tension, your stomach, your face.

Now take a deep breath and as you breathe out let your whole body relax.

As you enjoy the calm feeling of resting, imagine a closed seed or flower bud deep in your mind.

The flower can be whatever you want it to be. It can be a flower or a tree.

As you imagine this bud, see it slowly beginning to open, the petals or leaves beginning to spread out and separate.

Now let it open fully and completely.

As your mind becomes filled with the image of the tree or flower, you can imagine the rest of its body growing and expanding. Imagine the colours.

Imagine the leaves and branches being your arms.

Imagine the roots reaching down through your body, centring you into the ground.

You feel very healthy and strong.

Remember how good you felt as the flower was opening, how solid and safe you feel connected with the ground.

Whenever you want to feel good you can remember yourself as this beautiful, strong, solid flower or tree.

Now continue to breathe slowly and deeply and relax.

Part 2 Building a positive sense of self, exploring individuality of self and peers

Acceptance of self and others

The aim of these activities is for students to explore and reinforce their individuality. During these lessons students will:

- Expand their self-image by identifying the many different factors which make people different and unique
- Develop respect and tolerance for others by learning to appreciate diversity in others
- Develop a positive sense of self by practising being positive about themselves and others, and giving and receiving positive feedback.

Activity 1 Ways of developing a positive classroom environment

- Remember that the atmosphere and environment in your classroom is largely created by you
- Your students will respond to how you make the classroom feel
- To build self-esteem, your students must feel safe, secure and feel that they have a purpose and sense of belonging
- Students must feel a sense of identity, personal competence and ability
- The topics and activities in this book and especially in this chapter require a respectful, caring and sensitive classroom
- Always let your students know your rules for a respectful and safe classroom
- Remind students that these rules apply inside and outside the classroom and on playing fields
- Try involving students in the development of classroom rules
- Divide students into small groups and have them brainstorm their ideas for classroom rules
- Write all of the suggested rules on the board, have the class prioritise them and agree on a set of class rules
- Use the following to summarise your respectful classroom
  - **R**espect yourself and others
  - **E**quipment is treated with care and replaced after use
  - **S**peak in turn
  - **P**eople are safe in our classroom
  - **E**veryone has a right to be heard
  - **C**lean up after yourself
  - **T**alking things out is important
- Practise being respectful yourself! Practise giving your students a 'voice'
- Listen to and reinforce your students' positive behaviours and their comments, ideas and suggestions. Allow them to participate in their own learning
- Ensure equity by making sure no one dominates discussion or question time
- Encourage openness by ensuring trust and respect
- Developing trust takes time. Keep activities low risk at first

Remember, some students will learn by watching and listening to others.

Activity 2 What makes up a person?

- Brainstorm activity on the board.
- Teacher or lecturer asks if a student can draw 'A Person'. The drawing is done in the middle of the board and the teacher asks the class to describe all of the things that make up a person.
- Student scribes write all of the answers from the class on the board as the teacher keeps asking students for more answers.
- What makes up a person? What makes a human being?
- What are the features that make everybody different? What makes us all unique?
- In general, the complete summary contains:
  - Physical features
  - Personality traits
  - Individual abilities and competencies, skills, hobbies and interests
  - Cultural family background
  - Individual beliefs and attitudes
  - Values
  - Past experiences
  - Character traits such as honesty, trustworthiness etc.
- Teacher or lecturer summarises that humans are complex, diverse and unique and that 'everybody is different'.

What makes up a person?

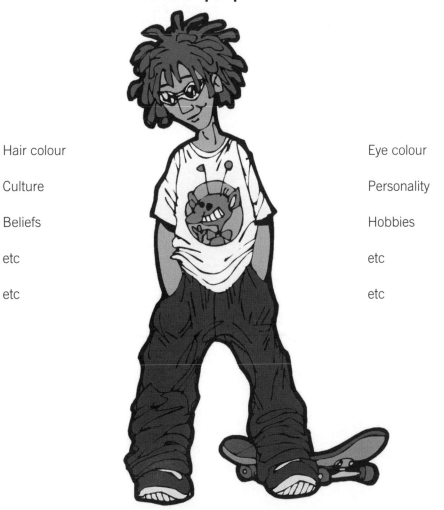

Hair colour	Eye colour
Culture	Personality
Beliefs	Hobbies
etc	etc
etc	etc

Activity 3 Classroom bingo

- Recap 'What makes up a person?' lesson by using the 'Classrooom bingo' work sheet to identify individual traits among classmates.
- Teacher or lecturer asks each student to take a handout of 'Classroom bingo'.
- Students work individually or in pairs. They have to circulate around the room asking fellow students if they fit the criteria in each bingo box. When they find a person with the correct characteristics, they write that person's name in the box and move onto the next box.
- The winner of 'Classroom bingo' is the student or pair of students who can tick off all of the boxes first.
- The lesson summarises and reinforces the message that 'everybody's different', that uniqueness and diversity are normal and acceptable and that we all have many different features including:
  - Physical features
  - Personality traits
  - Individual abilities and competencies, skills, hobbies and interests
  - Cultural family background
  - Individual beliefs and attitudes
  - Values
  - Past experiences
  - Character traits such as honesty, trustworthiness etc.
- Teacher or lecturer summarises that humans are complex, diverse and unique and that 'everybody is different'.

Activity 3 Classroom bingo

Star sign is Virgo	Likes strawberry milk	Can whistle	Has a great sense of humour	Is trustworthy	Loves swimming	Likes rap music	Is taller than you
Has black hair	First name starts with 'R'	Is wearing blue socks	Has brown eyes	Has freckles	Birthday is in July	Has blonde hair	Excellent at spelling
Has a pet that is NOT a cat or a dog	Dislikes swimming	Has a brother	Has a pet mouse	Has brown skin	Plays chess	Plays cricket	Born in Australia
Loves watching the Simpsons	Has white skin	Walked to school today	Star sign is Capricorn	Dislikes strawberry milk	Plays piano	Has red hair	Likes chilli and spicy foods
Green eyes	Has speckles in their eyes	Can't sit still in class	Born overseas	Is very patient	Plays netball or basketball	Has curly hair	Dislikes the Simpsons
Has a dog	Has a younger sister	Wears pyjamas to bed	Has relatives in another country	Has a pet fish	Has an earring	Reads the newspaper	Send his/ her friends emails
Loves broccoli	Dislikes tomatoes	Has completely straight hair	Is shorter than you	Had cereal for breakfast today	Is wearing a watch	Is the same height as you	Star sign is Leo
Plays soccer	Goes to church, synagogue, mosque or temple	Has a pen pal	Is left handed	Has a very calm personality	Speaks a language other than English	Is right handed	Has recently had a haircut

Activity 4 Hand outline activity

- Review 'What makes up a person?' activity with the class and reinforce the messages that everybody is different, unique and that this is normal and expected. Remind students of the broad array of features in humans.
- Life would be pretty boring if we were all the same.
- This lesson we are going to explore the many different features that make us all different.
- You will have the opportunity to observe the positive points in yourself and others. Teacher chooses whether to do this activity in pairs, small groups or as a large group.
- This activity requires a lot of trust and respect within the class, so make certain that students do not write anything negative. Explain that we all have negative features that we would all like to improve upon, but that today we are *only* focusing on *positive* features.
- Teacher demonstrates by tracing their own hand outline on a piece of coloured cardboard.
- The teacher then writes his or her name on the piece of cardboard and writes three positive features of themselves inside the hand outline. Positive features and observations can be physical, for example, brown curly hair, blue eyes, earring in left ear, tall, etc. but should also include some more diverse features such as 'good sense of humour, honest, piano player, easy going' in order to show students how to complete the task.
- In pairs, students do the same, making sure to think broadly about what makes up a person and focusing only on positive observations. Students can help each other in pairs.
- Then students swap hand outlines and write three or more positive observations about their partner in their partner's hand outline.
- Students can then circulate around the class giving and receiving positive comments on their hand outline and doing the same for others.
- It is very important to explain to students that this is an exercise in observing and identifying other people's positive features and it is not necessarily a session of giving compliments to each other.
- Continue this activity, making sure that you as the teacher also make some positive observations about each of your students.
- Returning to the larger group, students discuss whether or not they would agree with what was written about them? Were they surprised? Why or why not?
- Teacher asks students to read some of the comments they received.
- Summarise by stating that we all have positive points about us and that people like us just the way we are. Relax and be yourself!
- Students take their hand outline home for parents, relatives, neighbours and friends to add comments. Hand outlines can also be laminated as many students will keep these for life!

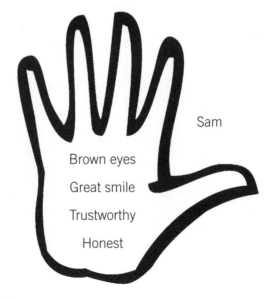

Sam

Brown eyes

Great smile

Trustworthy

Honest

Activity 5 'Introducing the one ... the only ...'

- Students work in pairs to complete the handout 'Introducing the one ... the only ...'
- It is preferable to have students work with others whom they do not necessarily know very well in order to have students get to know each other and learn something about each other. Conversely, this activity also works very well in pairs of students who know each other well. The teacher will have to decide on the best way to deliver this particular activity.
- Students discuss each other's features and they decide what makes the other person interesting and different (e.g. they have a birth mark; they have a certain hobby; they have had various life experiences etc.) and what makes them amazing (e.g. they are talented at certain things; they made certain achievements; they can do quirky things —touch their nose with their tongue) and why they make a great friend (e.g. they are kind, gentle, honest, trustworthy, fun, interesting, brave, helpful, reliable etc.).
- Each student introduces the other to the whole class, beginning with the words 'Ladies and gentlemen, girls and boys, please allow me to introduce, the one, the only ...'
- This activity can be fun, exaggerated and is often hilarious, but the work sheets should also be kept under the watchful eye of the teacher or lecturer before the students read them out to the whole class.
- Summary focuses on the fact that 'everybody's different' and we all have something different, unique and valuable to offer.

Activity 5 'Introducing the one ... the only ...'

Ladies and gentlemen, girls and boys, please allow me to introduce, the one, the only

_____

(name) is

_____

(gender, age, eye colour, hair colour, other descriptive features)

_____

He/she is interesting and different because

_____

He/she is amazing because

_____

And he/she is a great friend because

_____

Ladies and gentlemen, girls and boys, let's have a big round of applause for

_____

Activity 6 Self-advertisements

- Using these aspects of yourself, write an 'advertisement' 'selling' yourself on the Tele-classified advertisement provided.
- If you need help ask a friend or the person sitting next to you.
- The activity this week is to write an advertisement 'selling' ourselves. Teacher does himself/herself as an example. This can be fun and exaggerated, but should also provide some genuine self-disclosure.
- Students take 5–10 minutes filling out an advertisement for themselves. Each is folded the same and placed in the middle of the group circle in a large box.
- Students get a chance to select one each—if they select their own, they have to put it back.
- Students take turns reading out the information and guess who wrote it (this requires a lot of trust and respect; avoid this part of the activity, unless you know your class is ready for this).
- Discuss the concept that we can all make positive comments about ourselves. It is important to focus on our strong points and accept our weaker points.

Homework

Practise observing your own unique positive points and those of the people around you.

Activity 6 Tele-classified advertisement

Are you looking for a friend?

Well I might be just the person you are looking for!

Description:

_____

_____

My strong points:

_____

_____

Particularly talented at:

_____

_____

I am unique because:

_____

_____

I am a good choice of friend because:

_____

_____

Activity 7 What do I admire in others?

- This set of activities involves the exploration of admirable qualities in others.
- First, students are asked to work as a whole group or in pairs or threes to answer the question 'What do I admire in others?' using the work sheet of the same title.
- The teacher does not prompt the students at this stage of the activity as students need to think about these issues themselves.
- The teacher then asks students to present their answers to the class as part of an informal group presentation.
- The teacher then expands on the admirable qualities in others using the handout Teacher's notes—descriptors for 'What I admire or observe about others'. A copy of this handout can be given to students in order to assist them in the completion of the next activity 'Who do you admire?'

Who do you admire?

- Students singularly or in small groups complete the handout 'Who do you admire?'
- This activity works very well as homework, as an assignment or as a group research project.
- Students are encouraged to first think about someone whom they admire and then articulate the admirable features of that particular person. Presentations can be oral, written or as a large poster.
- When deciding who to choose, students should be directed towards people from history, from their local community, from their cultural background or someone who stands out as a truly admirable person.
- Useful websites listing many famous Australians include http://www.abc.net.au/btn/ and http://www.teachers.ash.org.au/jmresources/achievers/australian.html
- Students are discouraged from choosing celebrities unless they can confidently describe something truly admirable about that particular person. For example, they may choose a well-known actress, sports star or performer and then go on to describe their talents, their admirable qualities, their achievements, charity work or the social causes that they support.
- Group projects can focus on people like the early explorers, early scientists, inventors, artists, poets, writers, people who have worked for human rights. Examples of suitable research project subjects would be Mahatma Gandhi, Nelson Mandela, Eleanor Roosevelt, Caroline Chisholm, Mother Teresa, Harriet Tubman, Helen Keller, Martin Luther King.
- Students often write about the admirable qualities of their grandparents and other family members but this activity needs teacher supervision so that students focus properly on admirable qualities of those being studied.
- This activity lends it itself well to student presentations and displays of student work.

Activity 7 What do I admire in others?

Activity 7 What I admire or observe about others

Teacher's notes—descriptors

Uniqueness		
Special talents	Intellect	Personality
Athletic ability	Attitudes/beliefs	Morals/values
Physical appearance	Sense of humour	Hobbies
Aspects of personality		
Skilful	Hardworking	Imaginative
Determined	Practical	Sensible
Reliable	Trustworthy	Honest
Persistent	Artistic	Sociable/fun
Helpful	Sincere	Tolerant
Modest	Happy	Warm
Good natured	Gentle	Smart
Understanding	Kind	Funny
Positive features		
Adaptable	Adventurous	Assertive
Capable	Caring	Cautious
Cheerful	Close	Colourful
Competent	Cooperative	Courageous
Courteous	Creative	Democratic
Efficient	Energetic	Enthusiastic
Forgiving	Friendly	Humorous
Independent	Loving	Open
Organised	Patient	Positive
Powerful	Protective	Relaxed
Resilient	Resourceful	Responsible
Sensitive	Sporting	Supportive
Talented	Thoughtful	Thrifty
Strength	Fun	Active
Helpful	Devoted	Interesting
Flexible	Careful	Trustworthy
Neat and tidy	Good manners	Happy
Brave	Good friend	Collaborative
Self-sufficient	Compassionate	Gracious
Clever	Fair	Hardworking
Lively	Perserving	Sensible
Considerate	Honest	Conscientious
Easy going	Calm	Free thinking

Activity 7 Who do you admire?

- Write down an example of a person whom you admire.
- It may be someone from history, from your school, community or family, someone famous, someone from your past or someone with whom you currently have contact.

Who I Admire

_____

_____

_____

_____

_____

_____

_____

What is it about that person that you admire?

_____

_____

_____

_____

_____

_____

_____

_____

_____

_____

Activity 8 Positive perspectives cards

- As an extension of 'What do I admire in others?' activities, students use 'Positive perspectives cards' to identify positive features of themselves and others. The teacher can use ready made 'strength cards' which are produced by St Luke's Anglicare Innovative Resources (http://www.stlukes.org.au) or students can brainstorm positive features on the board and then make their own cards representing those features on pieces of cardboard. Cards should be laminated for future in-class use.

- Use the list of descriptors for 'What I admire or observe about others' to make the 'Positive perspectives cards' that begin with 'I am ...'. Students can design, colour or illustrate the cards any way they like or they can cut out pictures of animals or other images to illustrate their cards.

- Have students use a thesaurus to come up with new words to create new cards.

- Examples for cards would be,
  'I am strong', 'I am neat and tidy', 'I will try new things', 'I am good fun', 'I am good at sport', 'I help others', 'I am loving', 'I am good at certain things', 'I stick at what I need to', 'I am interesting', 'I am very determined', 'I am brave', 'I am good at making things', 'I look after others', 'I can change', 'I am careful', 'I can be trusted', 'I have good manners', 'I am a good friend', 'I take care of others', 'I stick up for myself', 'I stick up for others', 'I can wait', 'I am a calm person', 'I have a lot of energy', 'I am fair', 'I work hard', 'I look after things well', 'I am honest', 'I think a lot', 'I am sensible', 'I don't waste anything', 'I am easy to get along with', 'I can find ways to do things', 'I tell people what I think', 'I am a good listener', 'I am compassionate', 'I do not judge others', 'I accept others as different to me', 'I have different friends', 'I have lots of different interests', 'I can get along with anybody'.

- Students can choose these cards for themselves, for others and the teacher can choose the card for students.

- Discussion focuses on why students chose the cards for themselves and others.

Activity 9 My social support network

Instructions

- Inside the centre circle write your name.
- In the next circle write down first names of people you have the strongest and closest bonds with:
  - People who have given you strong support throughout your life
  - Those you have warm and close feelings for
  - People you can to talk to
  - People you feel comfortable getting a hug from.
- Inside the next circle write the names of people you like and feel friendly with. This list might include friends, distant relatives, those you haven't seen in a long time or those you would like to get to know better. This list might also include people who you don't see very often, but who you know care about you.
- Inside the next circle write the names of people that you know but are not particularly close to. You might want to see them more frequently and spend more time with them. You would like them to be friends, rather than acquaintances.
- When you have finished, you can quietly observe the people you have in your life who care for you; who are friends with you; and on whom you can rely.
- Remember, you are lucky to have people who care about you and you can always get to know new people, make new friends and get in touch with people who you don't see very often.

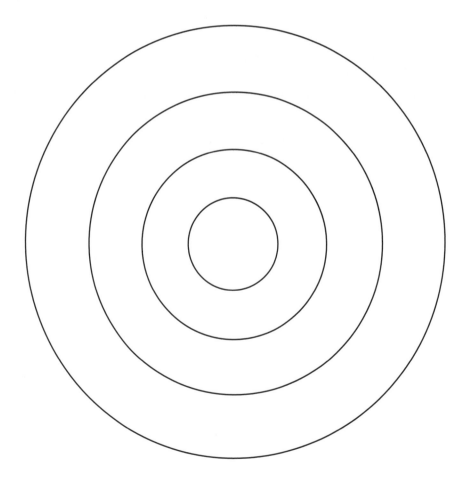

Activity 10 Communication, listening and conflict resolution

- Teacher asks 'What is communication?' and all student answers are brainstormed on the board.
- Communication is the giving and receiving of messages.
- Communication can be verbal or non verbal.
- Teacher asks some volunteer students to give examples of non verbal communication including eye contact, facial expressions, hand gestures, posture.
- Poor communication scenarios—copy, cut out and give these scenarios to your students to perform
    - You are reading a book or doing something else when someone is trying to tell you something—not making eye contact
    - You are talking over the top of a person when they are trying to tell you something—not listening
    - You are yawning or looking bored and uninterested when someone is trying to tell you something—uninterested facial expressions
    - You are slumping over on your desk or lying around looking very relaxed and uninterested when someone is trying to tell you something—poor body language
    - You are looking aggressive and just about to get in a fight when someone is trying to tell you something—aggressive body language

Listening game—Have your class sit in a semi circle or a circle. Give one student a message by whispering it in their ear. Ask the next student in the circle to repeat the message by whispering it to the next person. When the message has been communicated around the room, ask the final student to tell the class the message. Ask the students which message they actually received and try to pinpoint where your message got confused! This is a fun activity that demonstrates that communication is about giving and receiving messages.

- Listening quiz. How well do you listen? Use the quiz to allow students to explore their listening ability
- Fact Files. Use the fact files to give students an opportunity to learn about communication styles—assertive, aggressive and passive
- Use the following case study of Caroline with students working in pairs or threes to discuss how Caroline could communicate aggressively, passively and then assertively.

Caroline goes to Mt Welleton High School and is in Year 8. She shares a bedroom with her younger sister Kate and she is constantly annoyed by Kate borrowing things and not returning them, making a mess in the bedroom and flirting with Caroline's boyfriend. How might Caroline communicate with Kate aggressively? Passively? Assertively?

Activity 10 The listening game

- Copy and cut out the following discussion questions and make them into a class set of cards. You may need to enlarge the photocopy.
- Have students pair up with someone that they hardly ever talk to.
- Tell students that they will be practising their listening skills.
- Allow each pair to select one card and then they each take it in turns to ask each other the question.
- Ask each student to tell what they heard and then ask the other student if they had given an accurate account of what they had actually said.
- Each student is asked to rate the other out of 40 for their listening ability.
- Compare the score out of 40 that they give themselves on the listening quiz with the score out of 40 they got from the student they were supposed to be listening to!

What did you do last school holidays? What was the best thing?	What would you really like to have in your life at the moment?	What do you want to have in your life when you grow up?	Have you ever been bullied? Do you know of somebody who has been bullied?	List all of the things you would like to do to change the world.
What was something really funny that happened to you?	What was the best thing that ever happened to you?	Tell me about your family?	Tell me about your pets. What pets would you most like to have?	Can you remember any of your birthdays? Which one was the best?
What was the best time you ever had?	What is your favourite hobby?	What hobby would you like to do?	Who is someone that you really admire? What do you admire about them?	What is your favourite TV show or movie?

Activity 10 Quick quiz: How well do you listen?

Rate yourself on the following questions by placing a cross in the correct box:

Listening skill	Never (1)	Sometimes (2)	Often (3)	Always (4)
I try to give every person I speak to equal time to talk				
I enjoy hearing what other people have to say				
I wait until someone has finished talking so that I can then have my say				
I listen when I do not particularly like the person talking				
I listen when I do not agree with what the person who is talking has to say				
I put away what I am doing while someone is talking				
I look directly at the person who is talking and give them my full attention				
I encourage other people to talk by my non-verbal messages				
I ask for clarification of words and ideas I do not understand				
I respect every person's right to his or her opinion, even if I do not agree with them				

Total Score:

Key:
30–40 You are a terrific listener!
20–29 You are a pretty good listener
10–19 You are not listening well to others
< 9 You are a very poor listener

Activity 10 Fact file: Communication styles

Assertive

- Assertive communicators get their point across in a direct, honest manner in order to defend their rights in a positive way while at the same time respecting the rights of others.
- Goal: Communicate with respect to understand each other and to find a solution to the problems
- Verbally
    - Speak calmly, directly and clearly
    - Objective and unemotional
- Non verbally
    - Maintain direct eye-contact
    - Sit or stand facing the person they are talking to
    - Have good posture that conveys confidence and control

Passive

- Passive communicators allow their own rights to be violated by failing to express their own feelings.
- Goal: To avoid conflict at all costs
- Also tend to be shy and inhibited in their communication
- Often believe that if they really express how they think or feel, it will upset others
- Verbally
    - Do not say exactly what is on their minds
    - Defers to others' opinions, for example, 'I don't know … whatever you think'
- Non verbally
    - Body language reveals timid nature, shoulders slumped, don't maintain eye contact
    - Quiet tone

Aggressive

- Aggressive communicators tend to employ an angry, confrontational, hostile manner in their interactions with others.
- Goal: To 'win', to get their own way at all costs
- Verbally
    - Use 'you' messages, causing the receiver to feel on the defensive immediately
    - Strong, emotive language
- Non verbally
    - Loud and belittling
    - Gestures may be strong and threatening
    - Invade the personal space
    - May use violence/verbal abuse

Activity 10 Fact file: Communication styles

Which communication style is appropriate?

Assertive is generally recommended; however, the other styles are also important.

- Aggressive
  - In an emergency
  - When there is no time for compromise
- Passive
  - For minor issues
  - When the result of pushing the issue would outweigh the benefits

What are the benefits of good communication?

- Reduced stress
  - Conflict is a source of stress
  - Good communication can help prevent and resolve conflict
- Improved self-esteem
  - Helps us define who we are to ourselves and others

How can we improve communication?

- Recognise our communication styles
- Use 'I' statements and avoid 'you' statements
- Focus on achieving compromise, not getting your own way

'I' Statements

- 'I think ... What do you think?'
- 'I feel ...'
- 'This is how I feel ...'
- 'This is the way I see it ...'
- 'In my opinion ...'
- 'This is what it means to me ...'
- 'I would like ... What would you like?'
- 'I need ...'

Avoid 'you' statements

These are demanding and blaming

- 'You make me ...'
- 'You think ...'
- 'You should/shouldn't ...'
- 'It's your fault.'
- 'Don't you think ...?'
- 'If only you would ...'

Activity 10 Fact file: Communication styles

How can we improve our listening skills?

- Stop talking. Concentrate on listening to what the other person has to say, not what you are going to say next. Wait for the listener to finish before you speak.
- Provide both verbal and non verbal feedback. Encourage the speaker with 'yes', 'I see', 'oh, OK'. Look alert.
- Paraphrase the speaker's ideas. State in your own words, what you have understood the speaker to have said. This shows that you have been listening, that you are interested, and allows for correction if you have not understood correctly.

Tips for conflict resolution

- Focus on one topic at a time.
  'I may seem angry, but I had a hard day at school, and I am worried about several major assignments that are due next week'
- Cool down.
  Recognise when things are getting too out of hand and take a break to allow collection of thoughts. Go for a walk. Do some relaxation exercises.
- Avoid saying things that are needlessly hurtful.
- Don't dredge up past events and old grudges during a fight.
- Be specific.
  Use: 'When I see your stuff all over my bedroom floor, I feel that you are not cleaning up after yourself, and I feel taken advantage of'
  Instead of 'you are a messy, lazy, slob'
- Never think in terms of winning the argument.
  Think instead of ways to prevent them from occurring, and to resolve the conflict in a way that both parties win.

Activity 10 Teacher's fact files

What is self-esteem?

- Self-esteem is the total value we put on ourselves encompassing concepts and feelings about ourselves, self-satisfaction, self-acceptance, self-confidence, self-respect and the extent to which we can identify and appreciate the diversity of abilities.
- Self-worth and self-esteem are derived from a general positive sense of self. Self-concept is defined as the sum of an individual's beliefs about his or her personal attributes, qualities, positive or negative value.
- Self-image or self-concept is comprised of the way we perceive ourselves. The many different dimensions of the self are outlined in the diagram below:

Self-Image
What is Self-image? Self-image or self-concept are made up of the many factors that contribute towards what we think of ourselves, how we see ourselves and how we feel about ourselves.
- The factors listed below are facets of a person's self-concept.

Other People's Perceptions of Us

Job Competence

Romantic Appeal

Abilities and Competencies e.g. Academic achievement, athletic competency, other skills, e.g. art, music, cooking, design, sewing

The development of self-esteem

- Self-esteem develops from birth and early childhood.
- Preschool and early primary school children mainly distinguish two aspects of self-esteem, social acceptance and competence. For example, a six year old can tell you that he/she is 'good' at doing things and that he/she has friends.
- Primary school children can further identify things they are competent at such as academic work, relationships with others, physical abilities and physical appearance.
- Adolescents and adults add three more aspects of self-esteem to their total self-concept— close friendship, romantic appeal and job competence.
- Integrating all of these aspects of self-concept results in a total, overall, 'global self-worth' or self-esteem.
- Self-esteem is largely comprised of an inner sense of self-worth and self-acceptance and should not be confused with other traits such as self-confidence, assertiveness, extroversion, ego or narcissism. These traits may be present in a child, adolescent or young adult in the absence of true self-worth.

A POSITIVE SENSE OF SELF IN CHILDREN AND ADOLESCENTS IS LINKED TO	OUTCOMES OF POOR SELF-ESTEEM	BARRIERS TO SELF-ESTEEM
Positive academic outcomes Mental wellbeing Adjustment Happiness Success Life satisfaction Overall 'health' including mental, physical, social and spiritual dimensions of health.	• Mental disorders—depression, eating disorders, anxiety, suicide • Poor social outcomes— aggression, violence, school drop out Risky health behaviour—drug use, alcohol abuse, not protecting oneself, e.g. not negotiating safe sex or feeling able to insist on using condoms, vulnerability when intoxicated, susceptibility to be in relationships, teen pregnancy.	• The real self versus the ideal self • Super critical self and the futile pursuit of perfectionism • Self comparison with others • Negative 'self talk' • Lack of opportunity to discover dimensions of the self, lack of practice, competence and autonomy.

References

Abraham S & O'Dea J (2001), 'Body mass index, menarche and perceptions of dieting among pre and post pubertal adolescent females', *International Journal of Eating Disorders, 29*(1), 23–8.

Alsaker F (1992), 'Pubertal timing, overweight and psychological adjustment', *Journal of Early Adolescence, 12*, 396–419.

Bayer AE (1984), 'Eating out of control: Anorexia and bulimia in adolescents', *Child Today*, Nov/Dec, 7–11.

Blyth D, Simmons R, Bulcroft R, Felt D, van Cleave E & Bush D (1981), 'The effects of physical development on self image and satisfaction with body image for early adolescent males', *Research in Community and Mental Health, 2*, 43–73.

Boyd KR & Hrycaiko DW (1997), 'The effect of a physical activity intervention package on the self-esteem of pre-adolescent and adolescent females', *Adolescence, 32*(127), 693–708.

Brooks-Gunn J (1984), 'The psychological significance of different pubertal events to young girls', *Journal of Early Adolescence, 4*(4), 315–27.

Button E (1990), 'Self-esteem in girls aged 11–12: Baseline findings from a planned prospective study of vulnerability to eating disorders', *Journal of Adolescence, 13*, 407–13.

Button EJ, Sonuga-Barke EJ, Davies J & Thompson M (1996), 'A prospective study of self-esteem in the prediction of eating problems in adolescent schoolgirls: Questionnaire findings', *British Journal of Clinical Psychology, 35*, 193–203.

Button EJ, Loan P, Davies J & Sonuga-Barke EJS (1997), 'Self-esteem, eating problems and psychological well being in a cohort of schoolgirls aged 15–16: A questionnaire and interview study', *International Journal of Eating Disorders, 21*, 39–47.

Collins ME (1991), 'Promoting healthy body image through the comprehensive school health program', *Journal of Health Education, 22*(5), 297–302.

Coopersmith S (1967), *The Antecedents of Self-esteem*, WH Freeman, San Franciso.

Emmanouel C, Zerevas Y & Vagenas G (1992), 'Effects of four physical education teaching methods on development of motor skill, self concept and social attitudes of fifth grade children', *Perceptual Motor Skills, 74*, 1151–67.

Felker DW (1968), 'Relationship between self-concept, body build and father's interest in sport in boys', *Research Quarterly, 39*, 513–17.

Felker DW & Kay RS (1971), 'Self-concept, sports interests, sports participation, and body type of seventh- and eighth-grade boys', *Journal of Psychology, 78*, 223–8.

Folk L, Pedersen J & Cullari S (1993), 'Body satisfaction and self concept of third and sixth grade students', *Perceptual Motor Skills, 76*, 547–53.

Frankl D (1996), 'Swimming and diving project for youth: Aquatic skills and the development of self-esteem', *Kinesiology, 28*(1), 14–19.

French SA, Story M & Perry CL (1995), 'Self-esteem and obesity in children and adolescents—a literature review [Review]', *Obesity Research, 3*(5), 479–90.

French SA, Perry CL, Leon GR & Fulkerson JA (1996), 'Self-esteem and change in body mass index over 3 years in a cohort of adolescents', *Obesity Research, 4*(1), 27–33.

Gardner RM, Friedman BN & Jackson NA (1999), 'Body size estimations, body dissatisfaction, and ideal size preferences in children six through thirteen', *Journal of Youth and Adolescence, 28*(5), 603–18.

Ghaderi A, Mårtensson M & Schwan H (2005), 'Everybody's different: A primary prevention program among fifth grade school children', *Eating Disorders, 13*(3), 245–59.

Goni A & Zulaika L (2000), 'Relationships between physical education classes and the enhancement of fifth grade pupils' self-concept', *Perceptual and Motor Skills, 91*(1), 246–50.

Gortmaker SL, Must A, Perrin JM, Sobol AM & Dietz WH (1993), 'Social and economic consequences of overweight in adolescence and young adulthood', *New England Journal of Medicine, 329*(14), 1008–12.

Harper JF & Marshall E (1991), 'Adolescents problems and their relationship to self-esteem', *Adolescence, 26*(104), 799–808.

Harter S (1982), 'The perceived competence scale for children', *Child Development, 53*(1), 87–97.

Harter S (1983), 'Developmental perspectives on the self system' in Heatherington, EM (ed.), *Handbook of Child Psychology: Socialization, personality and social development* (4th edn, 275–385), Wiley, New York.

Harter S (1988), *Manual for the Self Perception Profile for Adolescents*, University of Denver, Colorado.

Harter S & Monsour A (1992), 'Development analysis of conflict caused by opposing attributes in the adolescent self-portrait', *Der Psych, 28*(2), 251–60.

Harter S, Marold D & Whitesel N (1992), 'Model of psychosocial risk factors leading to suicidal inclination in young adolescents', *Developmental and Psycho Pathology, 4*(1), 167–88.

Hawkins DB & Gruber JJ (1982), 'Little league baseball and players' self-esteem', *Perceptual and Motor Skills*, *55*(3), 1335–40.

Heath GW, Pratt M, Warren CW & Kann L (1994), 'Physical activity patterns in American high school students: Results from the 1990 youth risk behaviour survey', *Archives of Pediatric & Adolescent Medicine*, *148*, 1131–6.

Hill AJ, Oliver S & Rogers PJ (1992), 'Eating in the adult world: The rise of dieting in childhood and adolescence', *British Journal of Clinical Psychology*, *31*(1), 95–105.

Kimm S, Sweeney C & Janosky J (1991), 'Self concept measures and childhood obesity: A descriptive analysis', *Journal of Developmental and Behavioural Paediatrics*, *12*(1), 19–24.

Kimm SY, Barton BA, Berhane K, Ross JW, Payne GH & Schreiber GB (1997), 'Self-esteem and adiposity in black and white girls: The NHLBI Growth and Health Study', *Annals of Epidemiology*, *7*(8), 550–60.

Mann M, Clemens MH, Herman PS & de Vries NK (2004), 'Self-esteem in a broad-spectrum approach for mental health promotion', *Health Education Research*, *19*(4), 357–72.

Marsh H (1989), 'Age and sex effects in multiple dimensions of self concept: Preadolescence to early adulthood', *Journal of Educational Psychology*, *81*(3), 417–30.

Marsh HW (1990), 'A multidimensional, hierarchical model of self concept: Theoretical and empirical justification', *Educational Psychology Review*, *2*(2), 77–173.

Marsh H & Peart N (1988), 'Competitive and cooperative physical fitness training programs for girls: Effects on physical fitness and multidimensional self concepts', *Journal of Sport and Exercise Psychology*, *10*(4), 390–407.

Marsh HW, Barnes J, Cairns L & Tidman M (1984), 'The Self Description Questionnaire (SDQ): Age affects in the structure and level of self concept for preadolescent children', *Journal of Educational Psychology*, *76*, 940–56.

Marsh HW, Parada RH & Ayotte V (2004), 'A multidimensional perspective of relations between self-concept (Self Description Questionnaire II) and adolescent mental health (Youth Self-Report)', *Psychological Assessment*, *16*(1), 27–41.

Marsh HW, Ellis LA & Parada RH (2006), 'A short version of the Self Description Questionnaire II: Operationalizing criteria for short-form evaluation with new applications of confirmatory factor analyses', *Psychological Assessment*, *17*(1), 81–102.

McVey GL, Pepler D, Davis R, Flett GL & Abdolell M (2002), 'Risk and protective factors associated with disordered eating during early adolescence', *Journal of Early Adolescence*, *22*(1), 75–95.

McVey GL, Lieberman M, Voorberg N, Wardrope D & Blackmore E (2003a), 'School-based peer support groups: A new approach to the prevention of disordered eating', *Eating Disorders*, *11*, 169–85.

McVey GL, Lieberman M, Voorberg N, Wardrope D, Blackmore E & Tweed S (2003b), 'Replication of a peer support program. Designed to prevent disordered eating: Is a life skills approach sufficient for all middle school students?', *Eating Disorders*, *11*, 187–95.

McVey GL, Davis R, Tweed S & Shaw F (2004), 'Evaluation of a school-based program designed to improve body image satisfaction, global self-esteem and eating attitudes and behaviours: A replication study', *International Journal of Eating Disorders*, *36*(1), 1–11.

Mellin LM (1988), 'Responding to disordered eating in children and adolescents', *Nutrition News*, *51*(2), 5–7.

Mendelson BK & White DR (1982), 'Relation between body esteem and self-esteem of obese and normal children', *Perceptual and Motor Skills*, *54*(3 Pt 1), 899–905.

Mendelson BK & White DR (1985), 'Development of self-body esteem in overweight youngsters', *Developmental Psychology*, *21*(1), 90–6.

Mendelson BK, White DR & Mendelson MJ (1995), 'Children's global self-esteem predicted by body esteem but not by weight', *Perceptual Motor Skills*, *80*(1), 97–8.

Miller R (1989), 'Effects of sports instruction on children's self concept', *Perceptual and Motor Skills*, *68*(1), 239–42.

Neumark-Sztainer D, Sherwood NE, Coller T & Hannan PJ (2000), 'Primary prevention of disordered eating among preadolescent girls: Feasibility and short-term effect of a community-based intervention', *Journal of the American Dietetic Association*, *100*(12), 1466–73.

Neumark-Sztainer D, Wall M, Guo J, Story M, Haines J & Eisenberg M (2006), 'Obesity, disordered eating, and eating disorders in a longitudinal study of adolescents: How do dieters fare five years later?', *Journal of the American Dietetic Association*, *106*, 559–68.

O'Dea J (1994), 'Food habits, body image and self-esteem of adolescent girls from disadvantaged and non-disadvantaged backgrounds', *Australian Journal of Nutrition and Dietetics*, *51*, 74–8.

O'Dea J (2003), 'Why do kids eat healthy food? Perceived benefits of and barriers to healthful eating and physical activity among children and adolescents', *Journal of the American Dietetic Association*, *103*(4), 497–501.

O'Dea JA (2006), 'Self-concept, self-esteem and body weight in adolescent females: A three-year longitudinal study', *Health Psychology, 11*(4), 599–611.

O'Dea J & Abraham S (1995), 'Should Body Mass Index be used in young adolescents?' (Letter), *The Lancet, 345*, 657.

O'Dea JA & Abraham S (1999a), 'Association between self-concept and body weight, gender, and pubertal development among male and female adolescents', *Adolescence, 34*(133), 69–79.

O'Dea JA & Abraham S (1999b), 'Onset of disordered eating attitudes and behaviours in early adolescence: Interplay of pubertal status, gender, weight, and age', *Adolescence, 34*(136), 671–79.

O'Dea J & Abraham S (2000), 'Improving the body image, eating attitudes and behaviours of young male and female adolescents: A new approach that focuses on self-esteem', *International Journal of Eating Disorders, 28*, 43–57.

O'Malley PM & Bachman JG (1983), 'Self-esteem: Change and stability between ages 13 and 23', *Developmental Psychology, 19*, 257–68.

Parishplass J & Lufi D (1997), 'Combining physical activity with a behavioural approach in the treatment of young boys with behaviour disorders', *Small Group Research, 28*(3), 357–69.

Paxton SJ (2002), *Research review of body image programs: An overview of body image dissatisfaction interventions,* Victorian Department of Health and Human Services, Melbourne, Victoria.

Phelps L, Sapia J, Nathanson D & Nelson L (2000), 'An empirically supported eating disorder prevention program', *Psychology in Schools, 37*(5), 443–52.

Piran N (2001), 'Re-inhabiting the body from the inside out: Girls transform their school environment', in Brydon-Miller D & Tolman M (eds), *From Subject to Subjectivities*, New York Press, New York, 219–38.

Radell SA, Adame DD, Johnson TC & Cole SP (1993), 'Dance experiences associated with body-image and personality among college students—a comparison of dancers and nondancers', *Perceptual and Motor Skills, 77*(2), 507–13.

Renouf A & Harter S (1990), 'Low self worth and anger as components of the depressive experience in young adolescents', *Development and Psychopathology, 2*(3), 293–310.

Richman CL & Rehberg H (1986), 'The development of self-esteem through the martial arts', *International Journal of Sport Psychology, 17*(3), 234–39.

Rosenberg M (1965), 'Measurement of self-esteem', in Rosenberg M (ed.), *Society and the Adolescent Self Image*, Princeton University, New York, 297–307.

Rosenberg M (1979), *Conceiving the Self*, Basic Books, New York.

Salokun SO (1994), 'Positive change in self-concept as a function of improved performance in sports', *Perceptual and Motor Skills, 78*(3 Pt 1), 752–4.

Savin-Williams RC & Demo DH (1984), 'Developmental change and stability in adolescent self concept', *Developmental Psychology, 20*, 1100–10.

Schime M, Cook-Cottone C, Kane L & Watson T (2006), 'Group prevention of eating disorders with fifth grade females: Impact on body dissatisfaction, drive for thinness, and media influence', *Eating Disorders, 14*, 143–55.

Shavelson RJ, Hubner JJ & Stanton GC (1976), 'Validation of construct interpretations', *Review of Educational Research, 46*, 407–41.

Sherrill C, Holguin O & Caywood AJ (1989), 'Fitness, attitude toward physical education, and self-concept of elementary school children', *Perceptual and Motor Skills, 69*(2), 411–14.

Shisslak CM & Crago M (2001), 'Risk and protective factors in the development of eating disorders', in Thompson JK & Smolak L (eds), *Body Image, Eating Disorders and Obesity in Youth*, American Psychological Association, Washington, DC, 103–25.

Shisslak CM, Crago M, Neal ME & Swain B (1987), 'Primary prevention of eating disorders', *Journal of Consulting and Clinical Psychology, 55*, 660–7.

Shisslak CM, Crago M & Neal ME (1990), 'Prevention of eating disorders among adolescents', *American Journal of Public Health, 5*(2), 100–6.

Shisslak CM, Crago M, Renger R & Clark-Wagner A (1998), 'Self esteem and the prevention of eating disorders', *Eating Disorders, 6*(2), 105–17.

Steiner-Adair C, Sjostrom L, Franko DL, Pai S, Tucker R, Becker AE & Herzog DB (2002), 'Primary prevention of risk factors for eating disorders in adolescent girls: Learning from practice', *International Journal of Eating Disorders, 32*, 401–11.

Stewart DA, Carter JC, Drinkwater J, Hainsworth J & Fairburn CG (2001), 'Modification of eating attitudes and behaviour in adolescent girls: A controlled study', *International Journal of Eating Disorders, 29*, 107–18.

Stice E (2002), 'Risk and maintenance factors for eating pathology: A meta-analytic review', *Psychological Bulletin, 128*(5), 825–48.

Stice E, Cameron RP, Hayward C, Taylor CB & Killen JD (1999), 'Naturalistic weight reduction efforts prospectively predict growth in relative weight and onset of obesity among female adolescents', *Journal of Consulting and Clinical Psychology, 67*, 967–74.

Strauss RS (2000), 'Childhood obesity and self-esteem', *Pediatrics, 105*(1). Viewed at: http://www.pediatrics.org/cgi/content/full/105/1/e15

Taylor M & Cooper P (1992), 'An experimental study of the effect of mood on body size perception', *Behavioural Research and Therapy, 30*(1), 53–8.

Teri L (1982), 'Depression in adolescence: Its relationship to assertion and various aspects of self image', *Journal of Clinical Child Psychology, 11*(2), 101–6.

Troiano RP & Flegal KM (1995), 'Overweight prevalence and trends for children and adolescents: The National Health and Nutrition Examination surveys, 1963 to 1991', *Archives of Pediatric and Adolescent Medicine, 149*(10), 1085–91.

Tsimicalis A (2002), 'Evaluation of a Health Promotion Program design to enhance body image and self-esteem in children in grades seven and eight', Queen's University, Unpublished Masters Thesis.

Wallace JR, Cunningham TF & Del Monte V (1984), 'Change and stability in self-esteem between late childhood and early adolescence', *The Journal of Early Adolescence, 4*, 253–7.

Weiss K & Wertheim EH (2005), 'An evaluation of a prevention program for disordered eating in adolescent girls: Examining responses of high and low risk girls', *Eating Disorders, 13*, 143–56.

Wylie RC (1979), *The Self Concept* (vol 2), University of Nebraska Press, Lincoln, NE.

5 Media literacy for a positive body image

Introduction

Media literacy and media advocacy interventions are effective in the promotion of a positive body image. The major aim of media literacy for body image improvement is to encourage self-acceptance and help to reduce the internalisation of the thin ideal and the pervasive body image norms which are constantly promulgated and reinforced by the media.

The media promotes a slim ideal for young females and a mesomorphic muscular ideal for young males. The impact of media literacy programs is most powerful when the final result is rejection of the thin or muscular ideals and the facilitation of self-acceptance. Participants in media literacy education derive an overall sense of self-acceptance and self-worth from the media literacy program. In this way, media literacy programs may encompass an overall self-esteem building approach.

This chapter outlines media literacy approaches and lesson activities for the improvement of body image and the prevention of eating problems.

The benefits of positive body image in boys and girls

The development of a positive body image in boys and girls is desirable because it helps to promote general mental and social health and involvement in physical activity. Children and teens who have a positive body image are likely to be positive about themselves in general and positive about their lives. A positive body image is associated with having a healthy social life and general self-esteem. Research shows that people of all ages who exercise are generally more positive about their bodies than non-exercisers. Physical activity also helps young people 'feel better' because of its stress-reducing, 'relaxing' effect.

Positive body image also protects boys and girls against dieting and weight loss attempts. Research has repeatedly shown that 'dieting' is not a harmless activity and that it is likely to lead to further body dissatisfaction, disordered eating and eating disorders. Dieting also leads to binge eating when dieters 'go off' their diet. Hence, dieting has been shown to predict weight gain in teenage girls. A positive self-image protects against eating disorders, drug and alcohol abuse, depression, youth suicide, teenage pregnancy and other risky behaviours.

What is media literacy?

The media exists in many different shapes and forms in our society and includes print and pictorial media (newspapers, magazines, billboards, posters, books) and electronic media (radio, television, videos, movies, music videos and the Internet).

The term 'media literacy' refers to a student's ability to critically analyse and decipher media messages and 'read the media'. Students of media literacy learn to identify the different types of media and media messages; the aims and purpose of media messages;

and ways of identifying and critiquing media messages. Students of media literacy become skilled in decoding and analysing media messages.

Students of media literacy learn that media messages are quite deliberately designed to achieve three major objectives. The first is to inform and educate consumers about new or existing products and their various features. Second, the media aims to entertain and attract the attention of consumers. Finally, the media aims to sell ideas and products.

Media literacy education is designed to enable students to become aware of the media's existence in our day-to-day lives and to understand how the media operates to create messages and 'sell' ideas and products.

Students of media literacy also learn how media messages can be educational and helpful to consumers as well as how they can be inaccurate, untruthful and can promote unhealthy and harmful attitudes and behaviour.

Media literacy and body image

The major aim of media literacy education is to help students understand how media messages are constructed, how the message often reflects a commercial aim, how different people interpret different media messages and how media can have powerful uses in education and social change. In regard to body image education, media literacy is helpful in teaching students how to critique the media messages and then reject the stereotypical body image ideals that are constantly promoted in the media (Berel & Irving, 1998).

Students of media literacy learn that all messages in the media are created and constructed with a very specific purpose in mind. Media do not usually reflect reality but, rather, they carefully craft and create images and messages that create a certain way of seeing things. Media literacy teaches children and teenagers how to take these media messages apart to show how they are made. Likewise, media literacy helps students understand that media messages are not necessarily 'true'.

In addition, students learn that the media construct our reality and that much of our view of life is created by what we see and hear in the media. The media constructs a 'story', complete with attitudes, interpretations and conclusions, but very few students instinctively know how to analyse these messages to get to the real story or the real truth. Media literacy helps students understand how and why media 'stories' are created.

An important lesson in media literacy is that people in the general public have to interpret the meaning of media messages. Not all people in the general public interpret media messages in exactly the same way. We all interpret media messages differently according to our personal background, our needs, worries, family and cultural background and how we are feeling at the time.

One of the most salient lessons of media literacy is that virtually all media messages are linked to marketing activities which have commercial aims. Media messages may come to us in the form of advertisements, television commercials, sales promotions, advertorials, news, current affairs and other forms of 'entertainment'. Students in media literacy learn how to discern between the different commercial aims of media messages.

All media messages convey messages about our values, beliefs and our way of life. Media messages openly or discreetly comment on all aspects of our lives including what we 'need' in order to have a 'great' life or a 'better' life; how various products can 'help' us to achieve our goals in life; how men and women are supposed to be; how we are supposed to behave or not. Media literacy education helps students understand how these social messages are created and propagated in our lives.

It is essential to convey the message to students that media can have a great degree of influence on social and political change and that this influence can be positive or negative, helpful or damaging. In the case of body image for example, students learn that media images can reflect positive or negative messages about body image. Media messages can have great influence on how people in the general public perceive an issue or a problem and how public opinion can effect social and political change. The media can educate and involve us in social and political issues that we may be otherwise unaware of or uninterested in. Public issues such as human rights and global concerns become part of our 'education' as consumers of the media. Students of media literacy learn how the media can educate us and how we can use the media to educate others.

Media influences on body image and eating problems

Several recent research studies have found a link between the negative influence of the mass media upon the body image of young people. Specifically, the impact of media messages is believed to contribute to a critical, negative body image, body dissatisfaction, a desire for the slim ideal among females and the muscular ideal among males and the onset of dieting and disordered eating (Botta, 1999; Champion & Furnham, 1999; Crouch & Degelman, 1998; King et al., 2000).

In an early study of the relationship between television viewing, magazine reading and body image, Stice (1994) found a strong association between the amount of media images that a person had viewed during the previous month and the risk of body dissatisfaction, gender role endorsement and eating disorder symptoms. Another study by Stice and Shaw (1994) found that viewing models from *Cosmopolitan* magazine was more detrimental to the body image, desire for thinness and emotional status of young women than the viewing of normal weight models.

In their recent large meta analysis of 25 studies, Groesz, Levine and Murnen (2002) analysed the effect of experimental manipulations of the thin beauty ideal, as portrayed in the mass media, on female body image.

Data from 25 studies of women were used to examine the main effect of mass media images of the slender ideal, as well as the moderating effects of pre-existing body image problems, the age of the participants, the number of stimulus presentations and the type of research design.

The results of the analysis of 25 studies found that in most studies, the body image of women was significantly more negative after viewing thin media images of women than after viewing images of average size models, plus size models, or houses or cars. This effect was stronger for young or teenaged girls less than 19 years of age, and for girls and young women who were vulnerable to develop a desire for the thin ideal.

The authors concluded by saying that the results support the sociocultural perspective that mass media promulgate a slender ideal that elicits body dissatisfaction via social comparison.

These findings are in line with many research studies that show that viewing television images or magazine images of slim women increases body image concerns and body dissatisfaction among young women, which in turn may promote their pursuit of the slim ideal via dieting and disordered eating. These findings, plus the many other studies of the effect of media images on the body image of girls, boys and young adults (Field et al., 1999; Levine & Smolak, 1996; Martin & Gentry, 1997; Shaw & Waller, 1995; Vaughan & Fouts, 2003; Williams & Thompson, 2000), reinforce the huge impact that the media has on young people and the importance of helping them make sense of, and become resistant to, media messages.

Theorists and practitioners who endorse the use of a media literacy approach for the improvement of body image and the prevention of eating problems, argue that women and men become highly self-critical after viewing impossibly 'perfect' images of other women and men in the media and this form of social comparison results in a damaging sense of failure, inadequacy and, often, a futile life-long pursuit of the unachievable ideal body (Cattarin et al., 2000).

Media literacy lessons from the 'Everybody's Different' program

The use of media literacy lessons can assist in helping students understand the role and impact that the media has upon their self-image. Intervention studies using media literacy approaches have improved the body image of the girls and boys involved.

In the 'Everybody's Different' intervention (O'Dea & Abraham, 2000) male and female students in Years 7 and 8 were involved in media literacy activities to teach them how to explore and critically analyse the portrayal of stereotypes in popular magazines. Students learned about the definition of stereotypes and, particularly, gender stereotypes, and were then set the task of finding some stereotypical images in their own magazines that they had brought into class. Students worked in small groups to identify and analyse the stereotypical messages and produce a large poster illustrating what they had discovered. An important part of the lesson was to encourage students to reject the stereotypes and reinforce the self-acceptance message that everybody is different and that self-worth is derived from many facets of the self, not just physical appearance. As mentioned previously in Chapters 2 and 3, this type of media literacy approach, combined with the overall development of student self-acceptance and self-esteem produced very positive results on the body image of both boys and girls. A similar approach using the media literacy lessons from the 'Everybody's Different' program also produced some positive results among the body image of Australian school children (Wade et al., 2003).

Other studies that utilise the media literacy approach

Studies that have included media analysis, media literacy and examination of media gender stereotypes that have resulted in various improvements in body image include the study of Neumark-Sztainer et al. (2000) which was conducted among 226 girls aged 9–11 years attending Girl Scouts in USA. This program incorporated six sessions dealing with pubertal development, positive self-assessment, self-esteem, media awareness of body image ideals, media literacy and media advocacy. The intervention was successful in improving student knowledge and reducing the desire for the slim ideal among girls.

An earlier program that had included media literacy conducted with girls nine to 10 years of age (Smolak et al., 1998) found improved knowledge of nutrition, effects of dieting and causes of body fat. Interestingly this study did show an improvement in the students' attitudes and beliefs about fat people and two years later, several of these effects were still present (Smolak & Levine, 2001).

A study of 12–13-year-old school students was conducted by Varnardo-Sullivan and her colleagues (2001) in the USA. While this program was not purely a media literacy intervention, it did incorporate sessions about body image, social and media influences and self-esteem. The results found that female and male participants improved on fear of fatness and avoidance of forbidden foods.

The study of Withers et al. (2002) was conducted among 218 Australian private school girls in Year 7 aged 12–13 years. The intervention group received a 22-minute video including information about female development, sociocultural and media influences on body image, the harmful effects of dieting and eating disorders, healthy eating and self-image enhancement. This intervention was similar to others in that it combined concepts of self-esteem development and media literacy into one program rather than purely testing the effects of programs separately. Results found that girls who watched the video made positive changes to drive for thinness and intention to diet.

Kater et al. (2002) conducted a study among 415 boys and girls aged 9–13 years in USA who received an 11-week program. Topics included pubertal changes, genetic diversity, hazards of dieting, nutrition, coping skills and media analysis. An important finding of this study was that there was a modest improvement in students' knowledge and effect of the media.

Steiner-Adair et al. (2002) conducted a study among 500 girls in 7th grade aged 12–14 years in USA. The eight weekly lessons delivered by teachers, nurses and guidance counsellors included topics about pubertal changes, weightism, positive self-assessment, self-esteem, media literacy, fad diets and nutrition and coping skills. Results found that the girls' knowledge of issues discussed in the program improved as did their body esteem. Eating behaviours did not change, but this program outcome suggests that the combined self-esteem and media literacy approach is beneficial.

McVey and Davis (2002) conducted a study among 263 girls in Grade 6 aged 10–11 years in Canada consisting of a six-session program about the dangers of the thin ideal and promotion of self-esteem, stress management and peer relation skills. The lessons were facilitated by a psychologist (Dr McVey). The results of this particular study showed no particular intervention effect, but two follow-up studies conducted later found that the program improved body image satisfaction, self-esteem and reduced dieting (McVey et al., 2003a; 2003b).

Media literacy lessons are known to be beneficial for body image improvement, but the paucity of research in this area makes it difficult to determine which factors are at play when media literacy is implemented. Sound media literacy programs improve skills, beliefs and attitudes, as well as creating self-acceptance and improving body image. Further research should focus on the role of media literacy in each of these areas of self-image improvement.

Media literacy and body image messages

The aims of media literacy education from 'Everybody's Different' are for students to:
- develop an awareness of how gender stereotypes and 'bodies' are created and portrayed in the media
- employ critical thinking skills to analyse the content and meaning of media messages
- question how media messages operate to sell products, messages and ideas
- discover how media images are created, retouched, airbrushed and made to look 'perfect'
- understand how the creation of media messages can adversely affect the self-image and self-esteem of young people
- reject inappropriate and unhealthy media messages
- reinforce the message that 'everybody is different' and to promote the idea that diversity and uniqueness is valued and respected.

Media literacy activities

Media literacy education focuses on critically analysing the way media messages and images infiltrate our way of thinking, so that we end up 'believing' the messages that we are constantly bombarded with on a daily basis. The following media literacy activities are suitable for use with primary, secondary and tertiary students and it is left to the teacher or lecturer to make the material most suitable to the age group of the class. I have used these activities with all age groups and in training workshops with teachers, health educators and health professionals.

The major objectives of the media literacy lessons are to:
- discover how media messages create social norms in our society
- examine stereotypes of males and females in our society
- understand that we do not have to conform to stereotypes
- understand that everybody is an individual, with a unique appearance.

Each lesson generally fits into one class period unless specified.

Activity 1   My 24-hour media diary
Activity 2   'Picture perfect'
Activity 3   Stereotypes in the media and 'Sending up the stereotypes' (2 lessons)
Activity 4   Stereotypes collage activity (2 lessons)
Activity 5   Talking advertisements
Activity 6   Retouching exposed (2 lessons)
Activity 7   Male magazine makeover
Activity 8   Debate, group discussion or essay topic
Activity 9   Other computer-based activities
Activity 10   Computer investigation using Adobe Photoshop
Activity 11   Critique and discussion of newspaper article 'School photos digitally "fixed"'
Activity 12   Discussion of the new Dove campaign for real beauty
Activity 13   Media literacy word puzzle

Summary

The media includes print and pictorial media (newspapers, magazines, billboards, posters, books) and electronic media (radio, television, videos, movies, music videos and the Internet).

The term 'media literacy' refers to a student's ability to 'read the media'. This means they should be able to analyse and decipher media messages and become aware of the media's existence in our day-to-day lives. The students learn to identify and critique these messages and in doing so they understand the aims and purposes behind the media. Students of media literacy become skilled in decoding and analysing media messages making them less susceptible to marketing techniques aimed at young people. In addition, media literacy helps students to identify cultural stereotypes that are used to sell ideas and products.

Students of media literacy learn how media messages are designed to inform consumers about new or existing products and their features; to entertain and attract the attention of consumers; and to sell ideas and products.

The students also learn how media messages can deliver educational and helpful information to consumers, as well as the inaccurate and untruthful messages that can promote unhealthy and harmful attitudes and behaviour.

In this chapter, I have outlined how media literacy can be employed to help students identify and reject the media-created body image stereotypes. The final component of this approach involves reiterating the acceptance of diversity and differences among people to reinforce the idea that everybody is different.

Activity 1 My 24-hour media diary

- In this lesson students become aware of the existence of different forms of media and how they are affected by the media.
- A 24-hour diary is used to help students map the influence of the media in their day-to-day lives.
- Students are each given a copy of the 'My 24-hour media diary' handout and they are instructed to start keeping the diary from the moment they wake up on the following day.
- Students finish the diary when they go to sleep the following day.
- Students must identify all the different types of media that they are exposed to in the 24-hour period, including print and electronic media.
- Students should also make an analysis of the main messages from the media each time they are exposed to the different type of media. For example, if the student is watching television, they should keep a record of each program as well as each advertisement, a description of what they saw and an explanation of the main message.
- Students should then count the total number of media messages that they saw during the 24-hour period.
- Finally, students are instructed to bring their diary to the next class as well as an example of one of the media messages that they saw. For example, they could bring in a magazine, newspaper, poster or some other print form that contains an advertisement or other media message.
- In class, the teacher pairs the students up to discuss what each of them found.
- Then a class summary of the number of media messages is tallied up to illustrate how much we are all affected by the media, every day.
- Teacher asks a few students to describe to the rest of the class what their partner found.

Activity 1 My 24-hour media diary

Time	Place	Type of media source: magazine, TV, Internet, newspaper, book, billboard, poster	Type of media image: What I saw	Main message I got from the media
Example: 7.30am	Example: Home	Magazine picture	Picture of boys and girls with surf gear—board shorts, wetsuits, rash tops, boards	Surfing is cool. Surf gear is cool. Having surf gear makes you a good surfer and makes you more popular with other boys and girls

Activity 2 'Picture perfect'

- Students use the 'Picture perfect' work sheet to explore the basic principles of media literacy.
- Students employ critical thinking skills to analyse the content and meaning of media messages.
- Students learn how to question how media messages operate to sell products, messages and ideas.
- Using the handout, the teacher prompts the students to use the example of the media message that they have brought in from home, or the teacher gives students some magazines so that they can find media images or messages.
- Students select a media image and use the 'Picture perfect' work sheet to analyse it.
- Students paste their image on the back of the 'Picture perfect' handout.
- Teacher prompts the students by asking the following questions:
  - Who created this image?
  - Why was this image created?
  - What is the main message?
  - How is the message being put across?
  - What techniques are being used to put the message across?
  - How does the message have different meaning for different people?
  - Do you like the message?
- Teacher's summary reinforces that the students have learned how to question how media messages operate to sell products, messages and ideas.

Activity 2 'Picture perfect'

Who do you think created this media message?

_____

_____

Why was this media message created?

_____

_____

What do you think is the main message?

_____

_____

How does the creator of this message put their message across?

_____

_____

How might other people understand this message differently from you?

_____

_____

Do you like this media message?

_____

_____

Why or why not?

_____

_____

Activity 3 Stereotypes in the media and 'Sending up the stereotypes'

Instructions

- Teacher divides class into small groups of three or four students and instructs them to list typical features of the male and female stereotypes on the work sheet.

For example:

Male	**Female**
Strong	Weak
Hard	Soft
Big and muscly	Small and slim
Non emotional	Very emotional

Student presentations and discussion and evaluation

- Groups read out what they came up with.
- Do you agree or disagree with the stereotypes that our society presents?
- How does advertising change the way we think about men and women?
- Can you find an example of this in a magazine? (Teacher gives each group a magazine in which they find one example of how advertising creates and perpetuates stereotypes.)
- Discussion focuses on the fact that we do not have to believe these stereotypes and we do not have to accept them.

'Sending up the stereotypes'

- Teacher presents the 'Sending up the stereotypes' example in front of the class.
- Each group of students is instructed to work on the handout 'Sending up the stereotypes'.
- They choose a picture from a magazine that represents a stereotype. For example, very thin beautiful woman in underwear, macho man with muscles, 'perfect' housewife, 'perfect' baby, 'perfect' families etc.
- The group writes a funny caption sending up or contradicting the stereotype.
- This activity is meant to be very humorous and basically 'makes fun' of the stereotypes our society perpetuates, especially the narrow gender stereotypes.
- Each group presents their picture and caption to the rest of the class, explaining its meaning.
- Teacher summarises main messages from this activity that:
  - Media creates and perpetuates stereotypes in our society.
  - Stereotypes are usually exaggerated and are usually wrong.
  - Everybody's different—and this is normal and acceptable.
  - We do not have to 'believe' stereotypes.

Activity 3 Stereotypes in the media and 'Sending up the stereotypes'

Names...

What is a stereotype?

_____

_____

_____

List the typical features of male and female stereotypes used in advertising and in our society in general.

_____

_____

_____

For example:

Male   Female

Tough   Weak

Paste your picture of a stereotype below. Write your suggested caption in the thought bubble.

'Yeah baby ...'

Activity 4 Stereotypes collage activity

Materials and equipment

- Cardboard, dictionary, glue, scissors, coloured pens, magazines (students can be instructed to bring in old copies of their own magazines as this creates personal relevance).

Instructions

- Students work in groups during class or as homework or a group project.
- Teacher asks if group can define 'stereotype'. Use a dictionary and examples of words that describe stereotype. Students explore many different stereotypes in our society. For example, stereotypes of families, gender stereotypes, racial stereotypes, employment stereotypes, age stereotypes.
- Make a collage illustrating a typical stereotype by cutting out images and pasting them onto a large piece of cardboard. (Allow at least two class periods for this activity.)
- Students work in groups producing a collage with a theme about stereotypes.
- Groups develop their theme and then present their work to the rest of the class, explaining what they have done and what their final message is.
- Posters are displayed in the school or presented at school assembly.

Activity 5 Talking advertisements

Teacher introduces the activity by asking students to brainstorm the question 'Why do ads exist?' and records all of the student answers on the board.

'Why do advertisements exist?'

- To introduce new and existing products
- To inform consumers about the characteristics, properties and benefits of products
- To encourage consumers to buy the product
- To help people choose *between* different types or brands
- To 'sell' something that goes along with the product. For example, it will help you to be:
  - sexy, strong
  - cool, attractive
  - smart
  - smooth
  - honest
  - reliable
  - trustworthy
  - successful.

Students then work individually or in pairs to further analyse the messages and images portrayed in advertisements.

Students are asked to particularly focus on any health messages, whether positive or negative, that they think the advertisement is promoting.

Activity 5 Talking advertisements

- Paste your advertisement in the space below.

- What does this picture tell you about the product?

_____

_____

- How does it inform you about the characteristics, properties or benefits of the product?

_____

_____

- How does it encourage you to buy the product?

_____

_____

- Does it also try to 'sell' something that goes along with the product?

_____

_____

Activity 6 Retouching exposed

- The purpose of this media analysis activity is to allow students to discover the many computer enhancement techniques that are used to manipulate media images.
- In addition, students are encouraged to discuss how this manipulation of images presents a false view of the world and how this practice might impact upon students' body image.
- Teacher uses the following 'Retouching exposed' handout to introduce the computer enhancement techniques used to change images in the media.
- Students work in pairs to investigate the manipulation techniques using the 'Retouching exposed' work sheet and the 'Retouch website' at http://demo.fb.se/e/girlpower/retouch/
- Students present their work back to the whole class with discussion about what they have found and what they think about the use of these computer enhancement techniques.
- Teacher questions focus on 'What did you discover?', 'Were you surprised by what you found?', 'Do you think seeing computer manipulated images like this changes how young people feel about their appearance and their bodies?'
- Students are asked to write an essay or debate to summarise their opinions on this issue.

How are computer techniques used to manipulate images?

Airbrushing

The photograph is transferred from the camera to the computer.
A computer program is then used to do any or all of the following on pictures of men and women.

- Remove 'red' eyes
- Whiten teeth
- Cover pimples, scars, bruises, freckles, hair or wrinkles
- Change eye colour, hair colour, skin colour
- Change the shape of the nose, ears, chin etc.

Cropping

A computer program is used to take out a piece of the photograph and replace it with something else. For example, the computer technician can remove someone's head and replace it with another person's head; give the person different hair or a different body; use the computer to enlarge or reduce parts of the body.

Erasing

The outline of the image is increased or reduced. For example, the outline of a person's legs can be erased to make them appear to be slimmer. The outline of a male's body can be made to look more muscular.

Merging

Two or three different photographs can be merged together to form a completely new image. For example, people can be added to the photograph and their images can be 'flipped' or rotated to be facing a different direction.

Activity 6 Retouching exposed

Names ....

Instructions

1   Choose a partner and a computer.

2   Write your names on the work sheet.

3   On the computer, type in the web address for the retouch website
    http://demo.fb.se/e/girlpower/retouch/

4   Double click your mouse on 'Reveal the bluff' which is located on the left-hand side of your screen.

5   Wait a minute or two while the web page is loading and 'unveil the fraud' pops up on the right-hand side of the screen.

6   Click on 'unveil the fraud' and click on the eyes, teeth, lips, nose, right through to shirt colour to see how this image has been manipulated to look perfect.

7   Write down three examples of airbrushing that you found.

    1   _____

    2   _____

    3   _____

8   Write down three examples of cropping that you found.

    1   _____

    2   _____

    3   _____

9   Write down three examples of erasing that you found.

    1   _____

    2   _____

    3   _____

10 Write down any examples of merging that you found.

    _____

    _____

Activity 7 Male magazine makeover

- 'Do you think images of boys and men are manipulated too?'
- 'Do you think this affects the body image of boys and young men?' 'How?'
- Investigate the computer enhancement of male images using teen or male interest magazines.
- Teacher and students bring in copies of magazines. The activity requires the comparison of the cover pictures, so the whole magazine is not required.
- Pictures of teen magazine covers can be found on the Internet.
- Be careful with the use of magazines, as some content is often unsuitable, especially for younger students. It is best to just use a picture of the cover.
- It is best if teachers can copy and laminate a set of magazine covers from magazines from a number of different months, for example, January–December.

Students examine each cover using the 'Male magazine makeover' work sheet to identify the features of the male cover models and the stereotypical 'perfect' male.

- Students can be asked to bring in other magazines aimed at young men to examine the images, but I have found that the male interest magazines almost always have cover pictures of a very stereotypical muscular male ideal of a Caucasian with short brown hair, perfect white teeth, abdominal muscularity, sun tan and wearing board shorts. Students discover the creation of this male stereotype quite easily, by simply looking at the same image on each cover, every month.
- Students work in groups of boys and girls to describe and discover the male stereotype and the ways in which the image has been computer enhanced.
- Discussion focuses on what the students discovered and their opinions about how this sort of media stereotype and media manipulation can adversely affect the body image of young males.

Activity 7 Male magazine makeover

Names ....

Instructions

1   Write your names on this work sheet.

2   Choose the three magazine covers that you would like to analyse.

3   Describe the physical features of the male on each of the three different covers.

1   _____

_____

2   _____

_____

3   _____

_____

4   What did you discover about the images of each of the three men?

_____

_____

_____

_____

_____

_____

5   Describe the ways in which you think that the images have been computer enhanced.

_____

_____

_____

_____

_____

_____

_____

Activity 8 Debate, group discussion or essay topic

'Using computer-enhanced photographs is dishonest and should be banned.'

Activity 9 Other computer-based activities

This activity can be given to students as homework, extension work or as a special project:

- Use any of the following Internet sites to discover the way media images are manipulated and write a report stating:
  - what you discovered
  - your opinion on whether or not the media should be allowed to use these 'false' images.
- http://www.girlpower.gov/girlarea/bodywise/yourbody/body.htm
- http://www.campaignforrealbeauty.ca/bblank.asp?id=6899/

Activity 10 Computer investigation using Adobe Photoshop

- Teacher uses a digital camera to take a picture of each student.
- Students are given the jpeg image of their photo and they work in pairs, using a computer program such as 'Adobe Photoshop' to demonstrate how easily an image can be changed or created.
- This is a fun activity with a serious message—that almost all of the images we see in the media today are manipulated and computer enhanced in some way.
- Students show the teacher and the class their 'Before' and 'After' pictures or alternatively, they can print their before and after picture for use as a hand-in assignment or a class display.
- In this way, the students can educate other students in the school about the impact of media manipulation on the images that we see in the media.
- Teacher reinforces the main messages from the media literacy lessons that:
  1 Media images are manipulated to be perfect.
  2 Nobody is really that perfect, not even models.
  3 Everybody is different.
  4 Students should accept themselves and others the way they are.

- Students are divided into pairs or small groups and given the newspaper article to discuss.
- Discussion questions include: What is your opinion about digitally fixing school photos? Do you agree or disagree with this practice? Why or why not?

School photos digitally 'fixed'

By Danny Buttler

August 04, 2006

THE class of 2006 will be the best lookers yet, with parents getting the option to digitally remove pimples and marks from their teenagers' school photos.

For $8, Victorian parents can buy a touch-up option for official school portraits.

Even parents of Grade one children are asking for blemishes to be airbrushed.

The company offering the service said it was popular with many parents and children.

National School Photography services state and private schools across Melbourne.

Owner Peter Gillahan said the pressure to look good was growing.

'People are very conscious of their image these days. They're bombarded with beautiful people in the media who all look fantastic and parents and students want to look like that themselves,' he said.

Mr Gillahan said many parents asked for the touch-up because they didn't want a permanent reminder of their children's pimples.

'They say "get rid of that pimple, it's not going to be there forever it's going to come and go, so it's not really part of their personality",' he said.

'One mum said in 20 years' time her son is going to be different and she didn't want to be looking at that forever.'

The digital make-over option was tested at one school last year before being offered to all students photographed by the company.

For $8, the company will remove obvious pimples, scratches or other blemishes, even going the extra mile for children suffering severe skin problems.

'It's pretty hard if you've got a young lad with acne all over his face, so the retouchers will do more than what we charge for it because we want a nice photo to go out to our customers,' Mr Gillahan said.

But teen health experts were shocked to hear of the touch-up service.

'My immediate reaction is that I'm appalled,' said Susan Sawyer, director of the Centre for Adolescent Health at the Royal Children's Hospital.

'It's suggesting that this is not normal, that you should not look like this, that no one should have pimples.

'I think it gives a very unsavoury message that you are not OK.'

Prof. Sawyer said that the pressure from media on both parents and children was behind the push for perfection.

'What we see around us is airbrushed perfection in every magazine,' she said.

'If we accept that it is fine for celebrities to cut inches off their bottoms and thighs and upper arms ... then should we be surprised about this?'

Prof. Sawyer even questioned whether the use of electronic photography aids would end at smoother skin.

'First pimples, next teeth, next ethnicity or colour of the skin—who knows?' she said.

But Mr Gillahan said more sophisticated digital alterations were too complicated to be offered on a widespread basis.

'That would become a minefield because then people would want you to whiten their teeth and remove the braces,' he said.

But digital imaging allows photographers to manipulate school portrait images like never before.

'We often open eyes by swapping eyes from one photo of a student to another photo of the same student ... if they've blinked in one we'll swap the eyes over,' Mr Gillahan said.

'It's the same in the class photos ... we'll combine a number of photos to make it the best one we can.

'Pull the socks up, plant a tree in the background if a car has pulled up when it shouldn't have.'

Mr Gillahan said no photos were retouched without consent.

'It's a parent's choice, we don't just retouch because sometimes students have a birthmark on their face ... that is part of them.'

Mr Gillahan said he expected plenty of repeat customers from the digitally perfect class of '06.

'It will only grow because if you've had Jimmy's or Jenny's photo done this year, when they go to school in following years they will have to have them done then as well,' he said.

Basic school portraits start at $18.

But some parents were taking the desire for perfection to extreme levels.

'When we get requests for a retouching on a six year old you think what can you do to a six year old?'

Article from: Herald Sun

Activity 12 Discussion of the new Dove campaign for real beauty

Let's face it.
Firming the thighs of a size 8 supermodel is no challenge.

Not retouched

Real women have real curves. To celebrate those curves we asked real women to try our new Dove Firming range. Here are the results.

NEW

☛ Intensive Cellulite Gel-Cream. After 1 week, skin around problem areas feels noticeably firmer; after 3 weeks the appearance of cellulite is noticeably reduced.*

☛ Firming Lotion. After 1 week skin is significantly smoother; after 2 weeks, skin is noticeably firmer.**

☛ Firming Bodywash. Leaves your skin feeling noticeably firmer and smoother.

New Dove Firming. For beautifully firm skin.

*Agreed by 78% of consumers with cellulite **Agreed by 82% of consumers. LEVREX0974

This advertisement is reproduced with permission from DOVE.

Activity 12 Discussion of the new Dove campaign for real beauty

Dove Firming Ad

- Observe the Dove advertisement on the page provided.
- This advertising campaign has been introduced by Dove worldwide.
- All advertisements produced by Dove contain real women whose pictures have not been airbrushed or digitally retouched in any way. The ads are stamped 'Not Retouched'.
- What do you think this advertisement is saying?

_____

- Do you think it will have a positive impact on the girls and young women who see it? Why? How?

_____

_____

- Do you think all advertisements should use not retouched images? Why or why not?

_____

_____

- Do you think ads that contain pictures of men should use 'Not retouched' images? Why or why not?

_____

_____

Dove TV Ad

- Use the Dove campaign for real beauty webpage to view their new television advertisement for self-esteem—have students write a report about the advertisement.
  http://www.campaignforrealbeauty.ca/flat2.asp?id=4801
- The campaign for real beauty aims to present healthy images of real women which have not been retouched or airbrushed or changed in any way.
- What do you think of this ad for self-esteem?

_____

- What message did you get from it?

_____

_____

- What do you think of this new Dove international advertising campaign?

_____

- Do you think it will benefit the body image of girls and women who see the ads? How? Why or why not?

_____

_____

- Do you think such an advertising campaign would be helpful for ads that advertise men's products? Why or why not?

_____

Activity 13 Media literacy word puzzle

Name   Date

Find each of the following words.

NEWSPAPER	PHOTOGRAPH	ILLUSTRATE	RADIO
INVESTIGATE	PICTURE	PHOTOGRAPHIC	DOWNLOAD
ANALYSE	TECHNOLOGY	NETWORK	PLACARD
SOFTWARE	COMMUNICATION	VIRUS	VIDEOS
INTERNET	MEDIA LITERACY	IMAGE	ADVERTISEMENT
CROPPING	STEREOTYPE	BROADCAST	MERGING
WEB SITE	ANALYSIS	MEDIA	ERASING
PICTURESQUE	BANNER	RETOUCHING	COLLAGE
GRAPHIC	BROWSER	POSTER	PRODUCTS
IMITATIVE	PORTRAIT	SCRUTINISE	SLICK MAGAZINE
VISUALISE	MANIPULATE	BILLBOARD	INFORMATION
MOVIE	ENHANCE	AIRBRUSHING	FRAMING
IDEAS			

```
G N I P P O R C I M A G E S N O R K R O W T E N R A
R G A T I A R T R O P R I O F V S M E D I A A A E E T
C I N V E S T I G A T E M E P O S T E R S A U D O V
N P I C T U R E D D E M B D Y D N R W R E S W O R B
A I O O I D A R A N A L Y I S A I N T E R N E T F D
H N O I T A M R O F N I D V R E V I M I T A T I V E
N D O I P H O T O G R A P H M O B O I M A E E O E R
E A B A N N E R E R O S F D N A E O M P T T O E S T
P O O S T E R C I H P A R G O T O H P A A W P U P I
Y L S P R O D U C T S A T L I I Z N L R T Y R Y T O
G W C E R A S I N G O H N S D G T U T E T R W N S P
O O R V N E N N A B L W B E S L P S N O I N E N I O
L D U E E R G O L L O B R S A I U G E V G M O A D N
O R T U W G N L O D E T A N N L N R E N E A D A Y W
N N I Q S N I C E W O E A A L I E T I S S E O C G E
H O N S P B H Z N T D S M I G T I M I U M L A A N O
C I I E A B C E I I S N I R S S A T R I N R N R I S
E T S R P R U S Z V O A E W B R R I C W E G P S H I
T A E U E D O I A D F M C E F E V S O T N R H W S G
E C T T R R T L G R T E W D V I I D I E H A O I U Y
Z I E C I A E A A A W G R D A S M L D S A P T E R O
Y N N I R O R U M C A E A A Y O A L R Y N H A G B O
A U R P U B O S K A R N I L T I R S A L C I G A R T
N M I E T L A I C L E T A V D F E B C A E C R L I N
A M T T C I M V I P U N E E O A O A E N A N A L A I
N O N B I B I E L G A A M E D M E S L A B Y P O E I
E C I E P L T O S O G N S I E G U P P O A E H C G L
```

References

Berel S & Irving LM (1998), 'Media and disturbed eating: An analysis of media influence and implications for prevention', *Journal of Primary Prevention, 18*, 415–30.

Botta RA (1999), 'Television images and adolescent girls' body image disturbance', *Journal of Communication, 49*, 22–41.

Cattarin JA, Thompson JK, Thomas C & Williams R (2000), 'Body image, mood, and televised images of attractiveness: The role of social comparison', *Journal of Social and Clinical Psychology, 19*, 220–39.

Champion H & Furnham A (1999), 'The effect of the media on body satisfaction in adolescent girls', *European Eating Disorders Review, 7*, 213–28.

Crouch A & Degelman D (1998), 'Influence of female body images in printed advertising on self-ratings of physical attractiveness by adolescent girls', *Perceptual and Motor Skills, 87*, 585–6.

Field AE, Carmago CA Jr, Taylor CB, Berkey CS & Colditz GA (1999), 'Relation of peer and media influences to the development of purging behaviors among preadolescent and adolescent girls', *Archives of Pediatric Adolescent Medicine, 153*, 1184–9.

Groesz LM, Levine MP & Murnen SK (2002), 'The effect of experimental presentation of thin media images on body satisfaction: A meta-analytic review', *International Journal of Eating Disorders, 31*, 1–16.

Kater KJ, Rohwer J & Londre K (2002), 'Evaluation of an upper elementary school programme to prevent body image, eating and weight concerns', *Journal of School Health, 72*, 199–204.

King N, Touyz S & Charles M (2000), 'The effect of body dissatisfaction on womens perceptions of female celebrities', *International Journal of Eating Disorders, 29*, 341–7.

Levine MR & Smolak L (1996), 'Media as a context for the development of disordered eating', in Smolak L, Levine M & Streigel Moore R (eds), *The Developmental Psychopathology of Eating Disorders: Implications for research, prevention and treatment*, Lawrence Erlbaum Associates, Mahwah, NJ, 235–57.

McVey GL & Davis R (2002), 'A program to promote positive body image: A 1-year follow-up evaluation', *Journal of Early Adolescence, 22*(1), 96–108.

McVey GL, Lieberman M, Voorberg N, Wardrope D & Blackmore E (2003a), 'School-based peer support groups: A new approach to the prevention of disordered eating', *Eating Disorders, 11*, 169–85.

McVey GL, Lieberman M, Voorberg N, Wardrope D, Blackmore E & Tweed S (2003b), 'Replication of a peer support program. Designed to prevent disordered eating: Is a life skills approach sufficient for all middle school students?', *Eating Disorders, 11*, 187–95.

Martin MC & Gentry JW (1997), 'Stuck in the model trap: The effects of beautiful models in ads on female pre-adolescents and adolescents', *Journal of Advertising, 26*, 19–33.

Neumark-Sztainer D, Sherwood N, Coller T & Hannon P (2000), 'Primary prevention of disordered eating among preadolescent girls: Feasibility and short term effect of a community based intervention', *Journal of the American Dietetic Association, 100*(12), 1466–73.

O'Dea J & Abraham S (2000), 'Improving the body image, eating attitudes and behaviours of young male and female adolescents: A new educational approach that focuses on self-esteem', *International Journal of Eating Disorders, 28*, 43–57.

Shaw J & Waller G (1995), 'The media's impact on body image: Implications for prevention and treatment', *Eating Disorders: The Journal of Treatment and Prevention, 3*, 115–23.

Smolak L & Levine MP (2001), 'A two-year followup of a primary prevention program for negative body image and unhealthy weight reduction', *Eating Disorders, 9*, 313–25.

Smolak L, Levine MP & Schermer F (1998), 'A controlled evaluation of an elementary school primary prevention program for eating problems', *Journal of Psychosomatic Research, 44*(3–4), 339–53.

Steiner-Adair C, Sjostrom L, Franko D, Pai S, Tucker R, Becker A & Herzog D (2002), 'Primary prevention of risk factors for eating disorders in adolescent girls: Learning from practice', *International Journal of Eating Disorders, 32*, 401–11.

Stice E (1994), 'Review of the evidence for a sociocultural model of bulimia nervosa: An exploration of the mechanisms of action', *Clinical Psychology Review, 14*, 633–61.

Stice E & Shaw H (1994), 'Adverse effects of the media portrayed thin-ideal on women and linkages to bulimic symptomatology', *Journal of Social and Clinical Psychology, 13*, 288–308.

Varnado-Sullivan PJ, Zucker N, Williamson DA, Reas D, Thaw J & Netemeyer SB (2001), 'Development and implementation of the Body Logic Program for adolescents: A two-stage prevention program for eating disorders', *Cognitive and Behavioural Practice, 8*, 248–59.

Vaughan KK & Fouts GT (2003), 'Changes in television and magazine exposure and eating disorder symptomatology', *Sex Roles: A Journal of Research, 49,* 313–20.

Wade TD, Davidson S & O'Dea J (2003), 'A controlled evaluation of a school-based media literacy program and self-esteem program for reducing eating disorder risk factors: A preliminary investigation', *International Journal of Eating Disorders, 3,* 71–83.

Williams RL & Thompson JK (2000), 'A laboratory study of media exposure and body image: Disentangling the role of model and product', paper presented at the 9th Academy for Eating Disorders convention, New York.

Withers GF, Twigg K, Wertheim EH & Paxton SJ (2002), 'A controlled evaluation of an eating disorders primary prevention videotape using the elaboration likelihood model of persuasion', *Journal of Psychosomatic Research, 53,* 1021–7.

6 Growth, development and puberty

Introduction

It is important to teach students about their growth, development and pubertal changes in a factual, positive and reassuring manner. Students need to learn the facts about pubertal changes, but they also have many questions and concerns about these particular topics. These questions can be answered by the teacher in many cases, but, sometimes, students have questions that are best answered by their doctor and a referral is something that teachers may like to explore.

Teaching growth and pubertal development in a positive manner is very important because the onset of the pubertal growth spurt often results in body image dissatisfaction, especially for girls. One of the facts of pubertal development for both boys and girls is that their slim, 'low fat' preadolescent body is re-formed to become covered with a layer of fat. In essence, it is true that the adolescent is 'fatter' than when they were prepubertal and this increased percentage of body fatness can present a body image problem for some teenagers.

The majority of boys and girls adjust to their pubertal growth and development with little fuss or trauma. However, some pubertal adolescents may become highly sensitive about their weight, height, body shape and size and these young people, both boys and girls, can go on to develop any of the following serious problems including poor body image, fad dieting, disordered eating, eating disorders, low self-esteem, depression and social isolation. These body concerns may develop in both boys and girls and can cause physical, emotional and psychological damage during the early teenage years.

In a study of body mass and puberty in more than 500 adolescent girls (O'Dea & Abraham, 1995), we found the post-menarcheal girls (those who were well and truly pubertally developed and had experienced their first menstrual period) were certainly heavier and fatter than their pre-menarcheal counterparts. The post-menarcheal girls were more dissatisfied with their bodies and were attempting to lose weight—even at the very young ages of 13, 14 and 15 years of age. Similar onset of body image concerns and body dissatisfaction was found in another study of nearly 500 adolescent males and females. Both the boys and the girls became more concerned about their bodies when puberty started, but this concern was not evident in their prepubertal peers of the same age (O'Dea & Abraham, 1999a; 1999b). In a study of dieting in adolescent girls, we found that the postpubertal girls had weight concerns and were dieting, but the prepubertal girls were not (Abraham & O'Dea, 2001).

Hence, when teaching about puberty, teachers need to focus on the positive outcomes of growth and development—height increase, strength, development towards adulthood—and reassure students that all the changes they are experiencing are normal and that they will soon become used to their newly developed bodies.

The activities that follow provide many different fun and interactive activities for both male and female students.

Child and adolescent growth

Child and adolescent growth and development go hand in hand with sound nutrition. A child's body needs to be provided with all of the essential nutrients to nourish every part of their rapidly growing bodies. This ensures the best start in life and allows them to grow to their full potential—both physically and mentally. Hence, sound nutrition is extremely important for children and adolescents because their bodies are growing so rapidly.

Growth rates are greatest among babies from birth to one year of age when their birth weight triples and their length increases by an average of 17 centimetres. One of the most important aspects of child nutrition is the nutrition of the growing brain, which is very important for babies, toddlers and children. The growth and development of a child's brain continues from birth right through to 16 years of age. The child's intelligence, ability to concentrate and their school performance are all dependent upon receiving the right foods and nutrients every day. The circumference of a baby's brain and head grows by six centimetres in the first three months of life and has increased by 12 centimetres from birth to the first birthday. The head circumference has increased by about 16 centimetres by the age of three years. This huge increase in the brain material and brain size will determine the child's intelligence and how well they perform at school. One factor that teachers often forget to mention to students and parents is the rapid growth of the brain in childhood and the obvious need for good nutrition.

The brain and every other part of the child's body is growing, including the skin, blood, immune cells, muscles, organs, hair, bones and teeth. Every day, these body cells are also being repaired and replaced. Any period of poor nutrition during childhood will delay the growth, development and repair of these essential body cells, leaving the child prone to growth failure, shorter height, poor immunity and poor brain function.

In a recent study of 5000 school children (O'Dea, 2003), there was a difference in height of 2.3 centimetres in the low-income children. A finding of concern is the fact that the poor bone growth (reflected in the children's lower height) may also suggest poor brain growth. If the child's diet is so poor as to result in lower bone growth, then it is likely that other parts of the body are not growing properly as well—namely, the child's brain. This sort of growth failure due to poor nutrition is common in poor, developing countries where children do not have enough food. It is also seen in cases where children are not fed the nutritious foods that promote growth. The overall result for the child is poor brain growth, lower intelligence and poor school performance. Poor academic achievement is seen in children who are hungry and distracted, such as those who go to school without any breakfast, but it is also seen in children whose brain size and function have been hampered by poor nutrition. One of the most beneficial functions of good nutrition in children is the production of full brain development, intelligence and the achievement of the child's full academic ability.

Poor physical growth and development is largely irreversible, especially in early childhood, so any deficiencies in early nutrition generally cannot be made up later on. If you measure your head circumference using a tape measure and then measure your students' you will find that your students still have a lot of growing to do, and this growth is solely dependent on good nutrition. A summary of growth patterns in babies, toddlers, children and adolescents is given below.

Facts about growth

Unlike other mammals, humans spend their first 16–18 years growing and developing. Growth among girls and boys is rapid during infancy when weight quadruples and height almost doubles in the first two years.

Growth continues, but slows down during the pre-school and primary school years, averaging a 4 centimetre growth in height and a 2 kilogram increase in weight per year up to the age of 9 or 10 years.

Interestingly, the heights and weights of boys and girls up to age 10 years are very similar with the typical girl just slightly shorter and lighter than the typical boy. In general, boys and girls have a similar physical capacity at this age.

Puberty and adolescence are marked by a sharp acceleration in height and weight and sexual maturation.

Following are some facts about growth and development in babies, toddlers, school-aged children and adolescents.

Birth to 12 months

This is the greatest period of growth in humans. The child grows faster in the first year of life, than at any other life stage. Growth directly reflects nutrient intake. Head circumference nearly doubles during the first 12 months of life. Head circumference increases by about 6 centimetres in three months, 9 centimetres in six months and 12 centimetres in 12 months. Birth weight doubles in the first five months and triples in the first year of life. Birth length increases by about 16–18 centimetres in the first six months. Birth length increases by about 25 centimetres in the first 12 months. At this stage of life, 50 per cent of the baby's food intake is used by the brain.

Toddlers 1–3 years

Growth slows down slightly from one to three years and this also explains the reduction in the child's appetite often observed by early childhood teachers and parents at this time. Head circumference increases by 3–4 centimetres from 1–3 years. Seventy per cent of adult brain size is achieved by age three years. An estimate of adult height can be made by doubling the child's height at age two years to predict their adult height.

Children 3–10 years

Growth during middle childhood is slow and steady in both boys and girls. Children average growth of 5–6 centimetres and 2–3 kilograms per year until their ninth or tenth birthday. Brain growth continues slowly and steadily until full brain development is achieved at around 16 years of age. Ninety-five per cent of adult brain size is achieved by age seven years. The total amount of body fat begins to decrease in toddlers and continues to decrease until 6–8 years of age when it begins to rise again in both boys and girls. Both boys and girls naturally start to develop a layer of body fat at about age 8–10 years, which is used as a source of energy to fuel the pubertal growth spurt that is just about to begin, especially in girls. After age 8–9, girls naturally have more body fat than boys and this gives them a rounder, more curvaceous figure. Girls begin their pubertal growth spurt at about 9–11 years, which is on average, about two years before boys. This is a noticeable phenomenon in primary school children, where the Year 5 and 6 girls are usually bigger and taller than their male peers. The trend becomes even more pronounced in Year 7 where the girls tower over the boys at the school dance! Hence, it is advisable to discuss this with students before they enter Year 7, as some tall girls and some short boys, may become quite self-conscious about these perfectly normal events. The message to begin with at an early age is that everybody is different and, in the end, we will all grow up.

Adolescents 9–16 years

Pubertal development may begin in girls as young as seven or eight years of age, including development of the breast bud, nipple, underarm and pubic hair and widening of hipbones. Boys develop more muscle (and therefore more strength) than girls at puberty and girls develop more fat.

In both boys and girls, different parts of the body grow at different rates. Fat is laid down before bone and muscle. Hands and feet enlarge first, just before dramatic height and weight spurt. Legs lengthen first, before the lengthening of the torso. The jaw in both boys and girls lengthens and thickens. An important detail to mention to adolescent boys is that the muscularity in shoulders and chest expands last of all and it is largely dependent on genetic makeup. Boys should be prepared early for the fact that they will not be fully grown and developed until after their height spurt and no amount of weight training or nutritional supplementation will change this fact. This sequence of developmental events, accounts for the 'all legs' phase of adolescent growth and the awkwardness and clumsiness that may result. Both girls and boys in the height spurt phase of their adolescence will have long, gangly arms and legs and will develop a more balanced fuller torso later on.

The growth spurt begins on average two years earlier in girls than it begins in boys. The general sequence of events in girls is marked by an increase in body fat at age 9, 10 or 11 and the beginnings of a nipple bud. The fuller breast bud development follows in sequence with the height spurt, development of pubic and underarm hair and some general rounding of the body under the influence of the female hormone oestrogen.

Once the female height spurt has slowed down and virtually finished, the onset of menstruation begins. Menstruation tends to indicate the end stages of the height spurt in girls, and a girl will not grow much more in height after menarche (the first menstrual period). Menstruation is never regular from the beginning of the menarche and this is a very important point to make with girls. The menstrual hormones take quite a few months to settle down into a regular cycle, so girls need to be reassured that their periods may take up to six months to a year to settle into a regular monthly cycle. There is a great deal of individual difference in the settling of the menstrual cycle in girls and many girls seek reassurance from their teacher about this. Girls should not seek to 'settle' their menstrual cycle by using the contraceptive pill as the pill produces an artificial menstrual period. Girls should be encouraged to relax and allow their bodies and their hormones to settle naturally.

An overview of the general age of onset of pubertal developments in girls is presented below. There is great individual variation in the events of puberty in girls and this point needs to be reiterated several times with students in Years 5 through to Year 10—it is worth repeating to students that 'everybody's different' and every individual will follow their own growth pattern at a different time.

TABLE 6.1 Summary of average pubertal development stages in girls

Girls (average ages)
• First breast bud 9–12 years
• First pubic hair 10–12 years
• Height spurt 11–13 years
• First menstrual period (menarche) 10–15 years
• Average age of menarche 12 years
• Full breast and nipple 12–18 years
• Full pubic hair 12–18 years

Pubertal Tanner Stages 1–5 in girls

The stages of pubertal development are known as Tanner Stages after the paediatrician who developed them. A representation of each stage for breast development and pubic hair development in girls is presented on the following page.

The preadolescent breast is known as Tanner Stage 1 and consists of a small elevated nipple with no significant underlying breast tissue. Stage 2 of breast development is the breast bud stage. Here, there is elevation of the breast and nipple as a small mound and the areola begins to enlarge. Milk ducts inside the breast begin to grow. In Stage 3, there is further enlargement and elevation of the breast and areola and the areola begins to darken in colour. The milk ducts give rise to milk glands that also begin to grow. In Stage 4 there is projection of the areola and nipple to form a secondary mound. The full adult breast is illustrated as Stage 5.

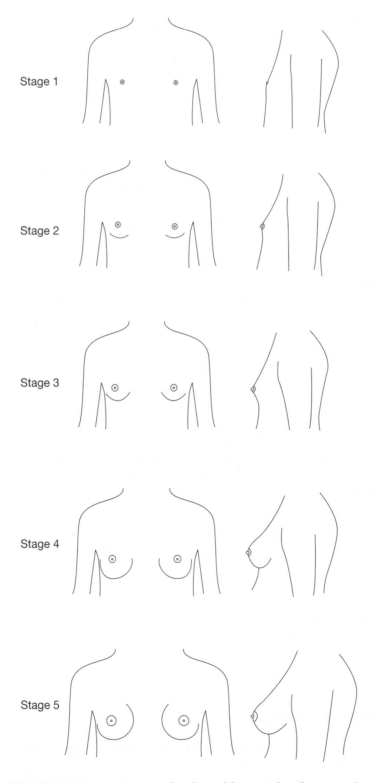

FIGURE 6.1 Tanner Stages of pubertal breast development in girls

Just as breast development is staged from Tanner Stage 1 to 5, so too is pubic hair development as outlined below.

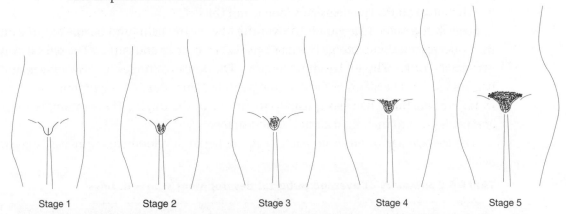

FIGURE 6.2 Tanner Stages of pubic hair development in girls

In Stage 1, the preadolescent child has no pubic hair except for the usual fine body hair.

In Stage 2, there is sparse growth of long, slightly darkened, downy hair mostly along the labia. This hair is usually straight or only slightly curled.

In Stage 3, the pubic hair becomes darker, coarser and curlier. It now grows sparsely over the mons veneris (mound of Venus) area.

In Stage 4, the hair grows more densely. It becomes as coarse and curly as in the adult, but there is not as much of it.

In Stage 5, the mature adult has the classic coarse and curly pubic hair that extends onto the inner thighs and may extend up to the lower abdomen.

The Tanner stage of breast development usually coincides with the same stage of pubic hair development. The onset of the first menstrual period, menarche, usually occurs during the late part of Stage 4.

Pubertal Tanner Stages 1–5 in boys

The first sign of puberty in boys usually occurs at around 9½ to 13½ years old and is signified by an increase in the size of the testicles. Next, pubic hair appears and the penis begins to grow in length and width. The complete change from preadolescent to adult takes between two and five years.

Tanner Stage 1 is the preadolescent. There is no pubic hair except for a fine body hair. The penis and testicles are in the same size and proportions as in childhood.

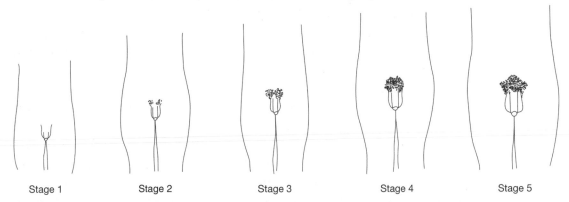

FIGURE 6.3 Tanner Stages of testicular, penis and pubic hair development in boys

In Stage 2, there is sparse growth of long, slightly darkened, pubic hair at the base of the penis. The testicles begin to get larger, and the scrotum begins to get a reddened and altered texture. The penis may grow slightly or not at all.

In Stage 3, the pubic hair gets darker, coarser and curlier. It begins to spread over the pubic bone. The testicles continue to enlarge and the scrotum texture becomes more like that of an adult. The penis gets longer and thicker.

In Stage 4, the pubic hair grows to cover the base of the penis and begins to grow on the upper part of the scrotum. The hair gets darker, coarser and curlier. The scrotal skin gets darker as the testicles continue to grow. The penis continues to grow longer, and becomes wider. The glans, or head, of the penis becomes much more prominent.

In Stage 5, the pubic hair has spread to the inside of the thighs. The scrotum, testicles and penis grow to their final adult size and shape.

The average age of onset for each of the pubertal developments in males is given below.

TABLE 6.2 Summary of average pubertal development stages in boys

Boys (average ages)
• First pubic hair 12 years
• Testes growth 12–16 years
• Penis growth 13–15 years
• Height spurt 13–15 years
• Voice change—enlargement of voice box (larynx) 13–15 years
• First ejaculation of semen (semenarche) 15 years

Factors that influence height

Students are often very interested in their height and their height potential, but they have many incorrect assumptions about height. These concerns about height can develop into a body image problem. Tall girls can slouch in order to make themselves seem shorter and short boys, or those who are late maturers, can become very self-conscious about their height. Teachers can help by not allowing any name calling or teasing about height and weight.

Following are some of the major factors that influence a child's height, with genetic potential being by far the greatest influence.

- Genetics—a child's height is determined by the biological parents' height. Children tend to be an average of their parents heights with boys being a little taller (6.5 cm) than the average of their parents' heights and girls being a little shorter (6.5 cm) than the average of their parents' heights.
- Nutrition—better nutrition for the last few generations of children has resulted in children growing taller than their parents. Children grow to their full potential when they have good nutrition, including good daily food sources of protein, calcium and zinc.
- Birthweight—birthweight can predict the overall size of a baby and whether or not he or she is 'big', 'small' or 'average'.
- Smoking—smoking causes vasoconstriction which limits the blood supply to the body. Children who smoke may stunt their growth by smoking instead of eating and reducing the supply of oxygen and nutrients to growing body tissues.
- Stage of pubertal development—children who have entered puberty will be taller and fatter than their prepubescent peers.
- Gender—girls begin the height spurt before boys and in classes of Year 5, 6, 7, 8 and 9 students, the girls tend to be taller than the boys. It is a fun activity to do a 'class average' for height as this reflects that the girls tend to be taller at this age, but that

the boys will catch up soon. Do not do a class activity for weight as this usually results in students feeling over sensitive about their weight. Any group activity should be completely anonymous so that individual students are not stigmatised.

- Childhood illnesses and prolonged lack of nutrition affect height because long-term, chronic illness often results in poor nutrient intake. The introduction of child immunisation has resulted in lower childhood illness rates and better growth in children and adolescents. General population growth rates have improved as a result of fewer childhood illnesses.

Teaching about puberty in a positive way

It is important to teach this topic in a factual, positive and reassuring manner. Students need to learn the facts about pubertal changes, and the more facts you can provide the better.

When teaching about puberty, teachers need to focus on the positive outcomes of growth and development—height increase, strength, development towards adulthood and reassure students that all the changes they are experiencing are normal and that they will soon become used to their newly developed bodies.

The activities that follow in this section provide many different fun and interactive activities for boys and girls and whole class groups of students.

Activities for teaching about growth and development

Activity 1   Match the right age group with the growth and development facts (1 lesson)
Activity 2   Pubertal development
Activity 3   Puberty, puberty, wherefore art thou, puberty?
Activity 4   Student self-assessment of pubertal stage
Activity 5   Teen species from the BBC website (1–2 lessons)
Activity 6   'And now, it's time to call a friend' (1 lesson)
Activity 7   Puberty word puzzle

Summary

This chapter outlines how teachers can adopt a positive approach when it comes to educating students about pubertal growth and development. While the majority of boys and girls adjust to their pubertal growth and development with little fuss or trauma, some students, particularly girls, become highly sensitive about their weight, height, body shape and size, and these young people can go on to develop any of the following serious problems including poor body image, fad dieting, disordered eating, eating disorders, exercise disorders, low self-esteem, depression and social isolation. Teenagers with body image concerns are less likely to participate in physical activity. These body concerns may develop in both boys and girls and can cause physical, emotional and psychological damage during the early teenage years.

This chapter provides teachers with the facts about growth and development as well as some interesting and engaging ways of helping students to learn about their bodies.

Recommended websites

The following websites are recommended but teachers should be reminded that website activities need close teacher supervision of students to prevent them accessing the wrong websites or the wrong information.

http://www.bbc.co.uk/science/humanbody/
A great site for interactive learning about the body and mind, with well set out information, games and demonstrations on muscles, organs and senses as well as a puberty demo.

http://www.afraidtoask.com
Contains information on a wide range of sensitive topics, including pubertal development, sexual health and medical conditions. Also has a section where you can 'ask a doctor' if you haven't found the information you need on the site.

References

Abraham S & O'Dea J (2001), 'Body mass index, menarche and perceptions of dieting among peri-pubertal adolescent females', *International Journal of Eating Disorders, 29*(1), 23–8.

O'Dea JA (2003), 'Differences in overweight and obesity among 4441 Australian schoolchildren of low and middle/high socioeconomic status', *Medical Journal of Australia, 179*, 63.

O'Dea J & Abraham S (1995), 'Should body mass index be used in young adolescents?', *The Lancet, 345*, 67.

O'Dea J & Abraham S (1999a), 'Association between self-concept and body weight, gender and pubertal development among male and female adolescents', *Adolescence, 34*, 69–79.

O'Dea J & Abraham S (1999b), 'Onset of disordered eating attitudes and behaviours in early adolescence: Interplay of pubertal status, gender, weight and age', *Adolescence, 34*(136), 671–80.

Activity 1 Match the right age group with the growth and development facts

- Teacher makes 10–15 copies of the grid below and cuts them into cards. It can be enlarged on the photocopier. This works very well if you are able to laminate the cards and keep 10–15 sets for students to use.
- Students work in pairs or small groups to match the picture of the age group or life cycle stage to the developmental features.
- Teacher then discusses and uses factual information to talk about growth in humans and introduces the stage of pubertal development.

Match the right age group with the growth and development facts

	Has finished physical growth. May start developing lifestyle diseases like heart disease.		Depends on mother for all oxygen and nutrition. Starts to suck thumb. Likes to kick.
	Muscles may be smaller because of lack of exercise. May have chronic disease. Likes to reminisce		Height increases rapidly. Sweat glands, body hair and foot size increase. Voice breaks.
	Eats same foods that the family eats. Has friends of the same gender. Boys and girls both grow at similar rates.		Growth slows to a steady rate. Still has all 20 baby teeth.
	Height growth slows. Full pubic hair. Periods begin. Interested in romance.		Only eats one type of food. Brain size increases rapidly.
	Weight triples in one year. Eats different foods. Begins to walk and talk.		Becomes interested in forming a family. May have young children.

Activity 1 Match the right age group with the growth and development facts

Teacher's answers

	Depends on mother for all oxygen and nutrition. Starts to suck thumb. Likes to kick.		Only eats one type of food. Brain size increases rapidly
	Weight triples in one year. Eats different foods. Begins to walk and talk.		Growth slows to a steady rate. Still has all 20 baby teeth.
	Eats same foods that the family eats. Has friends of the same gender. Boys and girls both grow at similar rates.		Becomes interested in forming a family. May have young children.
	Height increases rapidly. Sweat glands, body hair and foot size increase. Voice breaks.		Has finished physical growth. May start developing lifestyle diseases like heart disease.
	Height growth slows. Full pubic hair. Periods begin. Interested in romance.		Muscles may be smaller because of lack of exercise. May have chronic disease. Likes to reminisce.

Activity 2 Pubertal development

Puberty questions from Emma, Luke and Sam

- Students work in pairs or small groups and use the 'Facts' about puberty work sheet to investigate the questions from three fictitious teenagers, Emma, Luke and Sam.
- Students write their answers to each of the fictitious characters beginning, 'Dear Emma, 'Dear Luke' or 'Dear Sam'.
- Student responses are written on the back of the handout and the teacher can use these for marking and assessment.
- Whole group discussion focuses on the changes in puberty for girls and boys and the fact that all individuals grow and develop at different ages. Teacher reinforces that everybody is different and that averages are only estimates.

Activity 2 Puberty questions from Emma, Luke and Sam

Can you answer their questions?

Sam Is it true that girls generally begin the growth spurt before boys of the same age, because I'm the shortest kid in class? Will I always be the shortest?
Luke I heard that the first sign of puberty in boys is the voice going all funny and crackly? Is that true?
Emma Does a girl get her periods when she starts puberty? How do you know when to expect it?
Luke I have just gone up two shoe sizes in six months. Is that normal 'cause it's costing my Mum a fortune?
Sam Is it normal for boys to have a wet dream? Does it mean there might be something wrong with me like an infection or something?
Emma I heard that all girls should have developed full pubic hair by 13 years. Is that correct 'cause I'm 14 and I don't have any. Is that normal?
Sam Is it true that girls get a deeper voice in puberty? My sister's voice has become a bit deeper.
Luke Is it true that different parts of the body develop at different rates because my legs are really long, but my middle is the same size as always?
Emma Is it true that a girl needs to reach a certain level of fatness and roundness before she will get her first period?
Emma Is it true that you have reached your maximum height at age 16 for girls and 18 for boys?
Sam I heard that some girls and boys can grow by up to 12 cm and 10 kilos in one year? Is that normal?

Activity 2 Puberty questions from Emma, Luke and Sam

Teacher's answers

Sam Girls begin the growth spurt an average of two years before boys. Sam will catch up later and he will be about as tall as the average of his parents' heights.
Luke No, the first sign of puberty for boys is the facial hair, pubic hair and growth of the testicles. The voice breaks in the middle of puberty.
Emma Girls normally have their first menstrual period towards the end of their growth spurt. A girl will grow only another 2–4 cm after her first period.
Luke This is normal. During the pubertal growth spurt, the hands and feet enlarge first, then the arms and legs and then the torso.
Sam A boy will normally have his first ejaculation of semen (spermarche) as a 'wet dream' between the ages of 13–15 years. There is great individual difference in the age of spermarche. This means that everything is working properly and boys should not worry that there is anything wrong with them.
Emma There is great individual variation in the development of breasts and pubic hair in girls. The average age range is 13–16 years. Emma will start to develop soon.
Sam Yes, it is true. The voice box, or larynx (Adam's apple), grows in size in both males and females and this causes the voice to deepen. The voice 'breaks' in response to the larynx (voice box) and vocal cords growing larger and therefore being able to make different sounds.
Luke Yes, it is normal. The hands and feet grow first, then the limbs, then the trunk and torso. The 'all legs phase' is normal and may be a little more noticeable in tall boys and girls.
Emma Yes, it is true. Adult women are naturally supposed to have a round figure and this roundness reflects that she has enough body fat. The amount of body fat helps with the normal production of female hormones. Girls who lose weight or girls who stay very thin tend to delay their first menstrual period.
Emma Maximum height in most people is generally achieved by these ages. Late maturers will continue growing past these ages, especially boys. Some boys continue to grow and fill out into their early twenties.
Sam Yes, the adolescent growth spurt is a time of rapid and enormous growth for girls and boys. You can expect to grow a lot in one or two years and you can expect to be very hungry too!

Activity 2 Facts about puberty

The pubertal growth spurt

Every individual grows and develops at a different rate. The following averages represent the general teenage population.

- There is great individual variation in growth rates, age of menarche, age of spermarche and physical development—everybody is different.

- Boys and girls enter their growth spurts at varying ages.

- Girls begin before boys.

- Some people are 'early maturers', some are average and some 'late maturers'.

- Early maturers are not necessarily more emotionally mature or socially developed. These children should not be treated as 'older' by teachers.

- It is normal for girls in the early years of secondary school to be taller than boys.

- Boys will catch up later and will generally be taller than the girls.

- A girl's age of menarche will probably be similar to that of her mother's.

BOYS (Average ages)
- First pubic hair 12 years
- Testes growth 12–16 years
- Penis growth 13–15 years
- Height spurt 13–15 years
- Voice change (enlargement of voice box) 13–15 years
- First ejaculation of semen (semenarche) 15 years

GIRLS (Average ages)
- First breast bud 11–12 years
- First pubic hair 11 years
- Height spurt 11–13 years
- First menstrual period (menarche) 10–15 years
- Average age of menarche 12 years
- Full breast and nipple 12–18 years
- Full pubic hair 12–18 years

CHANGES IN YOUR BODY SHAPE AND SIZE
- Different parts of your body grow at different times.
- The general pattern is a layer of fat being laid down first in early puberty, then bone growth (height) then muscle.
- The 'filling out' with muscle comes last at the end of puberty or late adolescence.
- Your hands and feet enlarge first, just before your dramatic height and weight spurt.
- Remember, for every centimetre of height gain, you can expect a half kilo or more increase in weight.
- The first sign of puberty is often an increase in your shoe size!
- Legs lengthen first, before the lengthening of the torso.
- Jaw in both boys and girls lengthens and thickens.
- Shoulders and chest expand last. This accounts for the 'all legs' phase of adolescent growth and the awkwardness that may result.
- Growth spurt begins in girls two years before it begins in boys.
- Girls may begin their pubertal growth spurt as early as 8, 9 or 10 years of age and boys may begin at 10, 11, 12 or as late as 15 or 16—remember that everybody is different.

Activity 3 Puberty, puberty, wherefore art thou, puberty?

Females	Males
• Cartilage in hip joints is specialised to respond to the rise in female hormones (oestrogens).	• Cartilage in shoulder region specialised to respond to rise in male hormones (androgens).
• Broadening of hips relative to shoulders.	• Broadening of shoulders relative to hips.
• Height increase averages 8.3 cm per year in growth spurt.	• Height increase averages 9.5 cm per year. • Breaking of the voice generally indicates mid puberty.
• Increased heart, lung and muscle size. It is normal for girls to gain fat on the hips, thighs, buttocks, breasts, arms and upper back.	• Increased heart, lung and muscle size. Boys develop more muscle and bigger hearts and lungs than girls which result in greater strength and lung capacity among boys.
• Total body fat increases and provides female hormonal regulation. Increase from 10 per cent at beginning of growth spurt to 25–30 per cent as an adult woman.	• Bone density continues to increase in girls and boys up to the ages of 25–30 years.
• Menarche (first menstrual period) indicates late puberty.	
• Boys' and girls' height will generally be an average of their mother's and father's height.	
• Girls will be approximately 6.5 cm shorter than their parents' average heights.	• Boys will be approximately 6.5 cm taller than the average of their parents' heights.

Activity 4 Student self-assessment of pubertal stage

- 10 minutes or private activity as homework.

My pubertal stage of growth

Charts for girls

Use the pubertal stage charts below to estimate your stage of pubertal development.

Select which breast stage of development you currently match from Stage 1 to Stage 5.

| Stage 1 | Stage 2 | Stage 3 | Stage 4 | Stage 5 |

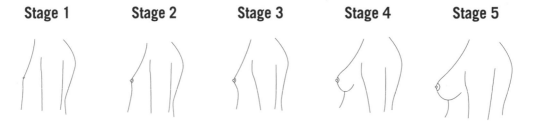

Select which pubic hair stage of development you currently match from Stage 1 to Stage 5.

| Stage 1 | Stage 2 | Stage 3 | Stage 4 | Stage 5 |

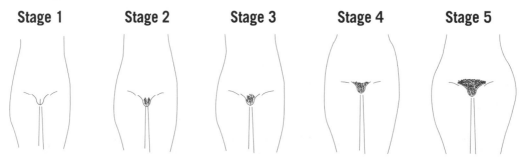

Stage 1 You are prepubescent. You have not started puberty yet, but you will soon.

Stage 2 You have just started puberty.

Stage 3 You are right in the middle of puberty.

Stage 4 You are coming to the end of puberty. You may have already had your first menstrual period or you may get it soon. Your height spurt will slow down now and you have probably reached your adult height.

Stage 5 You are fully grown now. You are an adult woman. Congratulations!

Activity 4 Student self-assessment of pubertal stage

My pubertal stage of growth

Charts for boys

Use the pubertal stage charts below to estimate your stage of pubertal development.

Select which stage of development you currently match for pubic hair, testicular development and penis development from Stage 1 to Stage 5.

| Stage 1 | Stage 2 | Stage 3 | Stage 4 | Stage 5 |

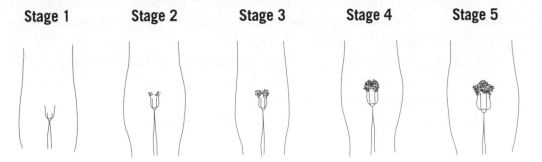

Stage 1 You are prepubescent. You have not started puberty yet, but you will soon.

Stage 2 You have just started puberty.

Stage 3 You are right in the middle of puberty. You can soon expect your voice to start changing as your voice box (larynx) begins to enlarge. You may experience ejaculation of semen during a wet dream. This is a normal part of physical development.

Stage 4 You are coming to the end of puberty. Your voice may have settled down now into a generally deeper tone. Your height spurt will slow down now and you have nearly reached your adult height. Your muscles will start to 'fill out' now.

Stage 5 You are fully grown now. You are an adult man. Congratulations!

Activity 5 Teen species from the BBC website

- This lesson utilises the resources from the BBC Science Human Body homepage
  http://www.bbc.co.uk/science/humanbody/
  This is an excellent website for interactive learning about the body and mind, with well set out information, games and demonstrations on muscles, organs and senses as well as a puberty demo.
- Students use the work sheets titled 'Teen species (That means you!)', which are designed for girls or boys.
- Students receive a copy of the work sheets and are then set up on a computer with a partner. This activity can divide students with same sex partners or mixed, depending on whether or not the teacher wants students to learn about their own pubertal development or that of the opposite sex as well.
- Students then use their work sheet to type in the website address to the male or female sections of the website that focus on pubertal development, and they are required to answer questions on the work sheets provided.
- Teacher can use the work sheets as a form of student assessment.

Activity 5 Teen species (That means you girl!)

Go to the BBC website 'Teen species'

http://www.bbc.co.uk/science/humanbody/body/interactives/lifecycle/teenagers/

- Click on the dots on the 'hot spots' on the female body to answer the following questions about female growth and development

1 The two female sex hormones are ....

 and ....

2 The female facial bones change from round to ....

3 The type of sweat changes in puberty. This type of sweat is found only in the

 armpits, belly button, ... , ... and ....

4 The female nipple and areola become larger during puberty and the colour

 becomes ....

5 The menstrual cycle lasts around .... days but this varies among

 individuals.

Now go to another section of the website to investigate pimples, acne, spots and answer the following questions

http://www.bbc.co.uk/science/humanbody/body/articles/lifecycle/teenagers/spots.shtml

1 .... per cent of teens get pimples, acne, spots.

2 Who is more likely to get pimples, boys or girls?

3 Why?

4 Pimples occur on the face, ..., upper back, ... and

 ....

5 Pimples are caused by ....

6 Are pimples caused by eating chips or chocolate? Yes or no?

Activity 5 Teen species (That means you boy!)

Go to the BBC website 'Teen Species'

http://www.bbc.co.uk/science/humanbody/body/interactives/lifecycle/teenagers/

• Click on the dots on the 'hot spots' on the male body to answer the following questions about male growth and development

1   The male sex hormone is ……………………………………..

2   The male facial bones change from round to ……………………………………

3   The type of sweat changes in puberty. This type of sweat is found only in

the armpits, belly button, …………………… , …………………………. and

………………………..

4   The male voice becomes deeper because the voice box is becoming

…………………… and the vocal cords are becoming ……………………

5   The first sign of puberty is when the ………………………….. get bigger.

6   It is normal for males to get …………… as this indicates that the body is functioning properly.

Now go to another section of the website to investigate pimples, acne, spots and answer the following questions

http://www.bbc.co.uk/science/humanbody/body/articles/lifecycle/teenagers/spots.shtml

1   ……… per cent of teens get pimples, acne, spots.

2   Who is more likely to get pimples, boys or girls?

3   Why?

4   Pimples occur on the face, ………….., upper back, ……………………… and

………………….

5   Pimples are caused by …………………………………………………………

6   Are pimples caused by eating chips or chocolate? Yes or no?

Activity 5 Teen species

Teacher's answers

Girls

1   The two female sex hormones are (oestrogen) and (progesterone).
2   The female facial bones change from round to (oval).
3   The type of sweat changes in puberty. This type of sweat is found only in the armpits, belly button, (ears), (groin) and (nipples).
4   The female nipple and areola become larger during puberty and the colour becomes (darker).
5   The menstrual cycle lasts around (28) days but this varies among individuals.

Boys

1   The male sex hormone is (testosterone).
2   The male facial bones change from round to (oval).
3   The type of sweat changes in puberty. This type of sweat is found only in the armpits, belly button, (ears), (groin) and (nipples).
4   The male voice becomes deeper because the voice box is becoming (larger) and the vocal cords are becoming (longer).
5   The first sign of puberty is when the (testicles) get bigger.
6   It is normal for males to get (erections) as this indicates that the body is functioning properly.

Answers to pimples, acne, spots

1   (80) per cent of teens get pimples, acne, spots.
2   Who is more likely to get pimples, boys or girls? (Boys)
3   Why? (Because the male hormone testosterone promotes pimples, and the female hormone oestrogen prevents them.)
4   Pimples occur on the face, (neck), upper back, (shoulders) and (chest).
5   Pimples are caused by (sebum blocking the tiny hair follicles at the base of each hair).
6   Are pimples caused by eating chips or chocolate? (No!)

Activity 6 'And now, it's time to call a friend'

- This activity is aimed at having students realise that everybody has to go through puberty and that they are not alone when it comes to having feelings of confusion or frustration about their changing bodies.
- Students are organised to work in pairs, as individuals or in small project groups.
- This activity makes an excellent group project, as students can divide the workload into activities such as conducting the interview, writing the summary notes, organising audiovisual recording materials, oral presentation skills etc.
- Students find and interview a same sex person to explore their experiences of puberty with the group of students. Student use the work sheet and groups present their work as a written assignment, a poster or an oral presentation.

Activity 6 'And now, it's time to call a friend'

- Choose a partner of the same sex.

- Choose a person to interview. They should be the same sex as you and your partner.

- Your person could be an older student, teacher, parent, family member or other adult.

- Interview the person together asking the following questions:

- How old are you?

  _____

- Do you remember at what age you started going through puberty?

  _____

- What do you remember?

  _____

  _____

- What do you think are the positive aspects of puberty?

  _____

  _____

- What do you know now about puberty that you would have liked to have known when you were going through puberty?

  _____

  _____

- What advice do you have for someone like me who is currently going through puberty?

  _____

  _____

Activity 7 Puberty word puzzle

Name   Date

Find each of the following words.

PLACENTA	SEMEN	ADOLESCENCE
ACNE	ZYGOTE	OESTROGEN
TESTES	OVULATION	ESTROGEN
HORMONES	DEVELOPMENT	PIMPLES
UMBILICAL CORD	MENARCHE	WEIGHT
MUSCLE	GROWTH SPURT	SCROTUM
FERTILISATION	LARYNX	EGG
MENSTRUATION	TESTOSTERONE	PUBERTY
HEREDITY	SPERM	HEIGHT
EMBRYO		

```
L  P  P  M  N  T  O  E  S  T  R  O  G  E  N  S  M  M  D  N
R  M  P  L  E  N  E  G  O  T  S  O  E  S  E  M  E  M  R  U
E  E  U  S  A  N  E  T  S  T  L  L  N  H  I  E  N  C  O  Y
P  W  B  S  G  C  A  G  P  P  O  E  C  E  O  C  O  G  C  F
S  Y  E  E  C  I  E  R  O  I  I  O  A  I  R  N  R  R  L  W
S  R  R  O  E  L  E  N  C  R  M  R  Y  G  C  A  E  N  A  E
E  A  T  E  T  I  E  W  T  H  P  M  H  S  C  T  O  C  I
T  L  Y  G  Z  Y  G  O  Y  A  E  S  L  T  N  S  S  I  I  A
S  G  G  E  S  E  N  O  M  R  O  H  E  E  N  E  O  T  L  R
E  R  S  C  R  O  T  U  M  Y  E  R  C  O  S  L  T  A  I  C
T  N  E  M  P  O  L  E  V  E  D  S  I  E  L  O  S  L  B  L
E  Y  E  M  B  R  Y  O  S  E  E  T  O  R  A  D  E  U  M  R
T  T  I  S  I  T  S  E  T  L  A  H  I  A  V  A  T  V  U  M
O  I  T  N  N  R  C  S  O  U  A  E  S  P  E  R  M  O  E  E
Y  D  E  L  C  U  M  D  R  P  R  R  S  N  E  T  O  G  Y  Z
Z  E  E  E  E  A  A  T  B  T  N  E  T  R  O  G  E  N  I  B
G  R  O  W  T  H  S  P  U  R  T  D  M  O  W  E  I  G  H  T
S  R  A  E  N  N  E  F  E  R  T  I  L  I  S  A  T  I  O  N
T  E  S  G  E  R  S  E  M  E  N  T  X  N  Y  R  A  L  Z  S
R  H  I  M  E  T  C  S  N  P  Y  Y  C  M  I  L  P  E  R  T
```

7 A positive approach to food and nutrition

Introduction

Sound nutrition, healthy eating and exercise have always been important for the health of young people. Nutrition is essential for growth and health in childhood and adolescence, and many of our adult eating and exercise behaviours and habits are well entrenched in childhood. Good nutrition provides energy, immunity, brain function and physical performance. Children's eating habits and attitudes are now becoming increasingly scrutinised with the exponential rise in childhood and youth obesity. It is important for teachers to teach nutrition in a positive way. Many teachers focus mainly on what students should not eat, rather than motivating them towards choosing more healthy options.

Teaching nutrition in a positive way cannot occur without some knowledge of foods and food groups, which is then followed with some information about nutrients. Also, teaching about food and nutrition in a positive way is most valuable and meaningful when it incorporates some form of food tasting or simple cookery.

This chapter outlines the many important benefits of childhood nutrition, including the promotion of growth, development, immunity, brain function, dental health, resistance to adult diseases and the development of sound eating habits for life. While weight control and the prevention of overweight and obesity are valid factors in teaching about healthy eating, they are not the only factors and they should not dominate lessons about food and nutrition. In fact, the most effective way to teach about food and nutrition is to engage the students with some sort of personal relevance and personal interest so that they learn to apply the nutrition theory to their everyday lives. This chapter therefore includes some information about the benefits of healthy eating from a large survey of 5000 school children from primary and secondary schools. This survey can also be applied as a learning activity in your school. Students learn to become motivated towards healthy eating because of the many personal advantages it may confer on them as individuals.

There is also detailed nutritional information about the content of foods and, in particular, the protein, iron, calcium and fibre content of foods. Vegetarian diets are discussed and lessons about vegetarian eating are included. A detailed account of sports nutrition is also given with several classroom activities for students of various ages. There are several quizzes, work sheets and lesson ideas to teach students about food groups, nutrients, major nutrients from foods, how to keep a food diary, what factors affect food habits, tips on how to read a food label, the content of packaged foods, fad diets and a card game called 'Nutritional pursuit'.

The eating habits and attitudes of children and adolescents

The eating habits of school children aged 6–18 years were assessed in the National Nutrition and Physical Activity Study which was conducted all around Australia from July to November 2000 (O'Dea, 2003b). The major aims of the study were to examine the importance of nutrition and physical activity; assess the eating habits of children and adolescents and the relative nutritional quality of their diets; measure the degree of overweight and obesity among school children and examine students' beliefs and attitudes about healthy eating and physical activity. In particular, the study aimed to understand which factors motivate healthy eating and exercise behaviours among Australian school students. Research data was collected from nearly 5000 students from city, regional and rural schools from every state and territory of Australia.

Students in focus groups answered the following questions about food and nutrition.

- What do you think are healthy foods and drinks?
- Is eating healthy food important to you? Why? Why not? Which of these reasons is the most important? Why? Is nutrition important? Are other things more important or less important?
- What are the benefits of eating healthy food? What can it do for you? Which is the most important benefit? Why?
- If you don't eat healthy foods can you tell me why? What do you think stops you? How? Why/Why not? What could help you to eat more healthy foods or drinks?
- Have you had breakfast today? If not, why not?
- Is there anything about food or nutrition that you would like to learn more about? Similar questions were asked about exercise and physical activity.

Following are some of the study results related to the importance of nutrition and physical activity, breakfast consumption, nutritional quality, and overweight and obesity.

Perceived benefits of healthy eating

The vast majority of students (more than 75 per cent) believed that healthy eating was important. The specific benefits of healthy eating as described by students are given in Table 7.1 with typical quotes and comments from the students involved in the study (O'Dea, 2003a).

The older students in Years 6–11 were able to describe the 'refreshing' effect of healthy foods which were identified as fruits, vegetables, juices, pasta, milk, cheese, bread, cereals, meat, chicken and water.

The students reported that they benefited from these foods because they made them feel 'clean, refreshed, feeling good and revived'. Conversely, students described less healthful, high fat foods as having deleterious effects on their bodies including 'slowing down the mind and body, draining energy, making the body feel heavy and clogging up the system'.

When asked what would help students to consume a more healthy diet, the major replies were:

- Parental support—parents were perceived as having control over the food supply and therefore controlling whether or not it is healthy. The majority of students reported that they ate what was available at home, at school and at friends' houses, so that if they wanted to eat more healthily, their parents would have to assist.
- Planning/organisation—students indicated that if they wanted to eat more healthily, they would have to employ some organisation and time management skills such as carrying these foods to school, not buying school lunches if they are not healthy, not taking money to school, reducing the availability of unhealthy foods at school, home and in the community and increase the supply of healthy foods and drinks.
- Cognitive strategies—using self-motivation strategies to remind oneself of the many benefits of healthful eating and the undesirable short-term impact of 'junk' foods

TABLE 7.1 Major themes related to the perceived benefits of healthy eating identified by children and adolescents

Most important benefits	Typical comments
Cognitive function/cognitive performance Enhanced concentration Mental alertness/mental activity Improved mental function Improved school performance	'After eating healthy it just cleans out the system and you focus better … I focus better on school work and just everything.' (Year 11 female)
Physical performance Enhanced fitness Enhanced sports performance Enhanced strength, energy, endurance	'It helps me run … it can make me do things like run … skip … jump … hop … walk a long way.' (Year 3 female) 'It keeps you fit … like I've got heaps of energy and I eat healthy foods if I want energy …' (Year 6 male)
Psychological impact Cleans, refreshes and clears mental function Self-reward—done something good for self Self-pride—sense of achievement Enhances self-esteem Enhances self-confidence Reduces guilt and anxiety Improves relationship with parents	'It's just a personal achievement … it's my personal feeling like I've done something for myself …' (Year 8 male) 'I like feeling that I've done something good for myself, feeling good about myself … not feeling guilty.' (Year 11 female)
Physical sensation Feel good physically Feel 'fresh and clean' on the inside Feel 'fresh and clean' physically Cleansing effect Not 'clogged up'	'I feel good … I feel more refreshed … lighter … cleaner … I feel cleaner on the inside.' (Year 9 female) 'Eating healthy foods is like taking a shower' (Year 8 male) 'I feel clean as well … it cleans your whole system …' (Year 11 male)
Regulation of energy Creates energy Sustains energy and endurance Regulates energy Moderates energy	'You don't feel tired and you don't feel held back and you don't feel heavy.' (Year 11 male) '… I eat a salad and I feel … just like all fresh and I feel like going out and doing stuff … but if I sit there and pig out on junk food I feel like a blob … I can't move …' (Year 9 female) 'Every time I eat fruit I feel revived … it's energising.' (Year 7 male)
Moderately important benefits	
Health protection General health enhancement Reduced sickness (colds and stomach upsets) Creates a strong immune system Maintains a strong immune system	'My immune system is a lot stronger as well … germs don't attack you …' (Year 6 male)
Somatic impact Tastes good Reduces hunger and effects of hunger Enhances satiety Enhances sleep Enhances relaxation	'I get really tired if I don't have breakfast … when I do my work I'm always really hungry … I can't concentrate without food …' (Year 5 female)
Future impact Enhances growth Prevents atherosclerosis Reduces future disease Enhances longevity	'Everything feels fresher on me … you feel better … without no zits …' (Year 11 male) 'It makes you get bigger … if you wouldn't eat your food properly you'd stay the same size forever …' (Year 3 female)
Moderate barriers	
Cultural factors Advertising/packaging of less healthy alternatives irresistible Belief that less healthy alternatives are necessary for a balanced diet Greater variety offered by less healthy alternatives	'Because unhealthy foods look more tempting in the shops … the packets … they've got sprinkles on them and all that …' (Year 4 female)
Financial limitation Healthy foods too expensive in comparison to less healthy alternatives	'When you're out … like shopping … healthy choices are so expensive' (Year 9 female)

(O'Dea, 2003a)

- Educational strategies—increasing information and education about food and nutrition; increasing advertising of healthful foods to make them more appealing; receiving personal advice from a doctor or dietitian about healthful eating habits.

Eating habits

Following is a summary of some of the students' eating patterns and food habits, particularly those relating to breakfast. Teachers may like to give students a research project on the topic of breakfast or ask them to repeat this survey in their school or local community.

Many students were consuming very little of the healthy foods such as fruit, juice, vegetables, cereals, dairy foods and protein foods.

The percentage of students consuming none of these foods at all on the three days prior to the study is outlined in Table 7.2 below.

TABLE 7.2 Percentage of children and adolescents in the National Nutrition and Physical Activity Study who reported consuming none of the foods listed in the three days prior to the study

Fruit	% consuming none
Apple	29.3
Orange	46.2
Banana	43.4
Apricot, peach, plum	72.1
Pineapple, mango	61.4
Pear	73.4
Fruit juice	22.8
Vegetables	
Green vegetables	16.2
Potatoes	18.2
Orange vegetables	28.0
Tomatoes	43.1
Lettuce, cabbage, spinach	41.8
Cereals	
Bread	4.1
Breakfast cereal	28.5
Pasta, noodles	27.2
Rice	41.2
Dairy foods	
Milk	9.6
Cheese	24.6
Yoghurt	53.1
Meat and eggs	
Red meat	17.7
Chicken	26.9
Fish	66.4
Eggs	45.1

Consumption and nutritional quality of breakfast

The consumption of breakfast was quite poor among many students. The following data summarises the major findings:

- 1 in 5 students in primary and high schools consumed nothing at all for breakfast—not even a drink of water.
- 1 in 4 students in primary schools consumed nothing at all or a non-nutritious drink such as water, cordial, coffee, tea or soft drink.
- 1 in 3 teenagers in high schools consumed nothing or water, cordial, coffee, tea or soft drink.

The nutritional quality of breakfast was ascertained by asking students to write down everything they had eaten or drunk on the morning of the survey. Below is a summary of the type of breakfast consumed on the day of the study.

TABLE 7.3 Type of breakfast consumed on the day of the study

Type of breakfast	Male %	Female %
Cereal and milk	48.6	37.8
Toast/bread	17.8	24.2
Nothing at all	19.9	19.5
Other	7.2	8.8
Juice only	1.3	3.0
Water only	1.9	2.6
Milk drink	1.5	2.2
Coffee/tea only	1.2	1.5
Soft drink/cordial	0.6	0.4
Inadequate breakfast (nothing or fluids (not milk)	**24.9**	**27.0**

As shown in Table 7.3, more than a quarter of Australian school children consume what is considered to be a nutritionally inadequate breakfast.

The function and benefits of child and adolescent nutrition

Sound child nutrition offers many varied benefits, including growth, brain function, intelligence, immunity to infections, energy regulation, better concentration and behaviour, dental health, prevention of lifestyle diseases and the development of good eating habits, many of which continue into adolescence and adulthood. An interesting point about child and adolescent nutrition is that the food habits learned at these stages of life are often carried on and taught to future generations of children. This can ensure healthy food habits for many next-generation children or the continuation of poor eating habits and the risk of adult ill health.

The following provides more details about each of these specific benefits of good nutrition for children.

Growth

As outlined in Chapter 6, a child's or adolescent's body needs to be regularly provided with all of the essential nutrients to nourish every part of their rapidly growing bodies. This ensures the best start in life and allows them to grow to their full potential—both physically and mentally. Sound nutrition is extremely important for babies, toddlers and children because their bodies are growing so rapidly. Poor nutrition can be largely tolerated by adults without dangerous consequences because their growth has finished, but babies, children and adolescents cannot get away with poor nutrition.

The overall result of poor nutrition for the child is poor brain growth, lower intelligence and poor school performance. Poor academic achievement is seen in children who are hungry and distracted, such as those who go to school without any breakfast, but is also seen in children whose brain size and function have been hampered by poor nutrition. One of the most beneficial functions of good nutrition in children is the production of full brain development, intelligence and the achievement of the child's full academic ability.

The specific details of pubertal growth and development are outlined in Chapter 6.

Energy regulation

Most children have a lot of energy, but some, especially those who do not consume a nutritious breakfast, suffer a mid morning slump in energy and concentration. Providing a regular intake of nutritious foods and drinks helps children and adolescents have a regular supply of energy throughout the day, and helps them settle at night time. In many cases that I have worked with in schools, students' behavioural problems have been largely improved by making sure that they receive a good breakfast or morning tea. This prevents them becoming irritable and distracted and helps them focus in class. Many schools have introduced breakfast programs in order to improve student behaviour.

Improved behaviour

Students of all ages are unable to behave properly when they are hungry or poorly nourished. Good nutrition, especially a good breakfast, helps children to settle at school in the mornings and regular meals, snacks and drinks help to moderate the child's behaviour over a 24-hour period.

Health protection and immunity

The human body has many ways of protecting itself from viruses, bacteria and other infective agents, but specific nutrients are required each day in order to produce these protective immune cells. A child will be healthier and more able to fight off infections and illnesses if he/she receives good nutrition every day.

Good nutrition is essential for the production of immune cells that fight infection and disease in babies and children. Breast milk, the child's first food, contains many anti-infection agents such as immunoglobulins, which are anti-viral agents and lactoferrin and anti-bacterial agents.

These immune factors in breast milk provide a constant supply of infection-fighting agents for babies and toddlers for as long as they are breastfed. Breastfed babies and toddlers are known to have fewer colds, ear infections and bouts of gastroenteritis than non-breastfed babies and the immune factors in breastmilk also help breastfed babies to fight off illnesses more quickly than babies who are not breastfed. Full breastfeeding with no other additional foods, drinks or water is recommended by the World Health Organization (WHO) until the baby is six months old.

After the age of six months, babies can start to eat foods apart from breast milk and these foods also provide the child with the ability to produce the immunoglobulins and other infection fighting agents. The size of the child's lymphatic system doubles in size by age seven years old and then doubles again up to the age of 12 years. Good daily nutrition must be provided in order for the child's body to be able to produce immune tissue and the white blood cells which engulf and destroy viruses and bacteria. The child's immune system can even fight off cancer cells and other infective agents that may enter the child's body.

Children who do not eat well or those who suffer malnutrition develop more infections than well-nourished children because they produce fewer white blood cells, immunoglobulins, antibodies and other immune cells. Poor nutrition and poor immunity becomes a nasty, vicious cycle in poorly nourished and undernourished children because infection and illness often leads to poor appetite and even poorer nutritional intake. Thus, the poorly nourished child becomes infected, eats less and becomes even more poorly nourished and prone to further infection and further malnutrition. Similarly, the sick child cannot concentrate or misses out on important schoolwork and their academic performance suffers. The key to a stable health status in children is to maintain sound nutrition every day.

Childhood is therefore a very important time for provision of the protein, iron, zinc and vitamin C, which are all required daily to build the child's immune system. Children who are lacking in any of these nutrients will be more prone to colds and viral infections and the common childhood illnesses such as earache, chicken pox and gastroenteritis. Children who have good nutrition are able to grow properly, stay well and develop to their full physical and mental ability.

Protection against adult diseases

The major diseases have their origins in genetics, but the lifestyle patterns that predispose us to adult diseases often begin in childhood and adolescence. Diseases such as heart disease, high blood pressure (hypertension), Type 2 diabetes and certain cancers can all be prevented by good nutrition in childhood, adolescence and throughout life.

Nutrition in childhood helps to fight short-term infections, but also fights against adult diseases that may start to develop in childhood and adolescence. The child's immune system fights a constant battle against infective agents and also fights and protects children from the development of cancer cells. Many substances that occur naturally in foods, particularly fruits and vegetables, protect children against cell damage and cell changes that can cause cancer. Food substances such as dietary fibre, antioxidants (beta carotene, vitamin C, vitamin E) and other phytochemicals (indoles, isothiocyanates, phytosterols, isoflavones and flavenoids) are found in fruits, vegetables, berries, garlic, onions, legumes and tea and they prevent body cells becoming abnormal or cancerous.

It is very important to note that foods contain thousands of different substances and chemicals, and much is still unknown about which substances in foods provide anti-cancer activity. Certainly, we have known for many years that fruits and vegetables reduce the risk of cancer. Many researchers believe that the anti-cancer chemicals in foods combine and act in conjunction with one another to produce an anti-cancer effect and this is why it is better to eat the foods rather than to take individual supplements. In any case, providing fruit and vegetables to babies, toddlers, children and adolescents is known to reduce their risk of cancer.

Sound child nutrition will ensure daily health but will also reduce the risk of developing illnesses and disease later in life. This is important for all children, but particularly important for children from families where parents, grandparents and other relatives suffer from nutrition related illnesses such as heart disease, high blood pressure, stroke, diabetes, certain kidney stones, gall bladder disease, osteoporosis (thin bones), diverticulitis, haemorrhoids (piles) and several cancers such as bowel, stomach, prostate cancer and breast cancer. Children can be protected from all of these diseases by sound nutrition. In addition, children will learn to develop nutritious, life-long eating habits which they will then pass on to their own children.

Protection of teeth and gums

A pleasant smile showing strong white teeth is an important part of positive self-image and body image. Healthy teeth and gums are also important for the proper development of speech and the chewing of food.

It is only within recent years that dental caries (tooth decay) has proven to be preventable in both children and adults; it is a misleading belief that some children are born with 'bad teeth' and nothing can be done to make very much difference. Teeth are completely formed in the womb and become visible when they start to 'cut' through the gums, usually between four to eight months after birth. The mother's diet may therefore affect development of a child's teeth making it important for pregnant women to receive adequate calcium, protein and fluoride from drinking water and other nutrients necessary for tooth formation. It is clear that the foods we eat contribute to the development of tooth decay and this begins at a very young age.

Tooth decay occurs when micro-organisms in the mouth convert sugars from food into acids. The acid that is produced in the mouth can dissolve the outer coating of tooth enamel resulting in a cavity. The filling of cavities, tooth extractions and expensive dental bills are an unnecessary burden on children and parents, and can be minimised by teaching good oral hygiene and healthy eating habits from a very young age. Cleaning teeth or rinsing the mouth with water can reduce the amount of sugars, micro-organisms and acids from teeth. Regular check-ups at the dentist and the use of fluoridated water and fluoridated toothpaste have been proven to reduce tooth decay enormously since the 1950s. Children these days have virtually no tooth decay compared to those of 20 to 40 years ago and this is mainly attributed to proper cleansing and the use of fluoridated water and fluoridated toothpaste.

Important foods for the development of healthy teeth are fruits, vegetables, wholegrain breads and cereals, milk, cheese and nuts; these foods have also been shown to be 'anticariogenic' or protective against tooth decay.

'Cariogenic' foods, or those that cause tooth decay, include sweet and sticky foods such as sugar, honey, jams, lollies, 'health' bars, sultanas, biscuits, cakes, sweetened drinks, ice blocks, ice creams. The naturally occurring sugars, such as those found in fruits and vegetables and milk, can be cariogenic under certain conditions such as the continual sipping of fruit juices or milk. This is a particular problem with young children who are allowed to breastfeed or bottle feed continuously throughout the night because the teeth are constantly in contact with lactose, the natural sugar in milk. This gives oral bacteria all night to produce acid from the sugar, which then attacks the teeth. Fruit, vegetables and milk are excellent foods for children and should be included in the diet, but the mouth should be properly cleansed or rinsed when children clean their teeth after meals and snacks at home and at school. Teachers can suggest that students rinse with water at school or when they are out. A very effective method of preventing tooth decay is for teachers to allow a bottle of water on each student's desk, as sipping on water will clean their teeth. Sugar-free chewing gum also serves to produce extra saliva, which naturally cleans the teeth. Once established in early childhood, and reinforced throughout the teenage years, these good habits will help to ensure healthy teeth and an attractive smile throughout life.

Development of good eating habits for life

Children develop their eating habits right from birth and many of these habits stay with the child for a lifetime. Encouraging nutritional eating habits helps the child to develop physically, and also helps them to develop an interest in cookery as well as cooking skills that they will keep for life.

Nutrition needs of children and adolescents

Nutrition is the science of food and how our bodies use that food. Children and adolescents need food to provide the nutrients required for energy, growth, repair of old tissues, regulation of body processes and protection against disease.

The five food groups

The five food groups changed in 1992 to incorporate the different nutritional requirements of humans. The original five food groups used to be defined as fruits and vegetables; breads and cereals; milk and dairy foods; meats and meat substitutes; and fats and oils. With more advanced nutritional analysis techniques, researchers were able to detect the presence of many different types of fats and oils in various foods including all of the other food groups, so the fats and oils group was deemed unnecessary as we can obtain essential fats and fat soluble vitamins from many other foods. For this reason, the fats and oils group was considered to be incorporated into the other food groups and it was deleted as a separate food group. Similarly, different features of fruits and vegetables resulted in these two food groups being identified separately. The five food groups now consist of breads and cereals; vegetables; fruits; meat and meat substitutes; and milk and dairy foods.

Cereals and bread for energy, vitamins, minerals and fibre. Includes all products made from flour, grain, rice, oats and rye including bread, cereals, spaghetti, crisp bread, scones and pasta. Wholegrain varieties should be included to provide dietary fibre. Children need at least four serves daily and adolescents need more, depending on their level of physical activity. Teenage sports people need a lot of foods from this food group, and may eat anywhere up to 10 servings daily to fuel their high energy requirements. An example of one serving from this group would be 2 slices of bread, 1 scone or 1 cup cereal, rice or pasta.

Vegetables for energy, vitamins, minerals and fibre. Vegetables also provide protective substances such as antioxidants and phytochemicals. The most brightly coloured vegetables contain the most protective substances. Children and adolescents should aim to eat five servings of vegetables each day. One piece of broccoli or potato can supply enough vitamin C; one or two serves of green, yellow or orange vegetables will supply vitamin A; and two serves of other vegetables will supply B group vitamins, fibre and other protective agents (fresh, raw, tinned and frozen are all suitable for this).

Fruits provide carbohydrates, dietary fibre, vitamins and minerals. Like the brightly coloured vegetables, the most colourful fruits appear to be the most protective against diseases such as cancer. Tomatoes, citrus fruits and tropical fruits are all very high in vitamin C, as are their juices. The whole fruit contains dietary fibre, whereas fruit juices do not, unless they are completely pulped, not strained and all parts of the fruit are consumed. Two servings of fruit or juice per day are recommended. Children and adolescents should avoid drinking more than two servings of fruit juice per day as the high fructose content may result in diarrhoea in toddlers and weight gain in older children and teenagers.

Fish, meat, eggs, nuts, seeds and legumes provide protein, vitamins and minerals and are particularly good sources of iron. This group includes all meats, poultry, fish, egg dishes, dried beans, peas, lentils and nuts. One or two servings daily will provide sufficient protein for children and adolescents. Some people, especially teenage girls, have an aversion to red meat which may be related to ethical issues or animal protection and this form of vegetarianism will be discussed in more detail later in this chapter. Lean red meat is a very nutritious food and can supply a rich source of protein, thiamin (vitamin B), iron, zinc and vitamin B12. Small amounts of red meat can certainly be part of a nutritious, healthy diet for children as young as eight months old. Likewise, foods like fish, chicken, other meats and eggs are very nutritious sources of protein, iron and zinc.

Milk and dairy products supply protein, vitamins, zinc and calcium. This category includes regular milks, skim milk, milk powder, evaporated milk, fat-reduced milks, cheese, yoghurt and buttermilk. Children need 600 millilitres (mL) daily and pubertal adolescents need about a litre! This may sound like a lot of milk at first, but just imagine how much calcium children need to build strong bones and teeth. One cup of milk (250 mL) supplies approximately the same amount of calcium and protein as one cup of yoghurt or 40 grams of cheese, so dairy foods can provide variety as well as calcium.

The food groups chart below illustrates how many servings of each food group children and adolescents need. Appropriate serving sizes are also given.

TABLE 7.4 Daily food servings from the five food groups for children and adolescents aged 7–18 years

Food group	Serving Sizes	Daily servings
Breads and cereals	2 slices of bread 1 bread roll 1 cup cooked rice, noodles, pasta 1 cup breakfast cereal 1 cup cooked porridge ½ cup natural muesli 4 crispbread or 6 water crackers	5–9 servings
Milk and dairy foods	1 cup (250 mL) milk or custard 1 tub (200 g) yoghurt 1 square (40 g) cheese 2 slices cheese, ½ cup grated cheese 2 scoops ice cream	3–4 servings
Vegetables	All vegetables (raw, frozen, canned, dried) ½ cup cooked, 1 medium potato, ½ cup grated carrot, 1 cup lettuce/salad Legumes and beans (e.g. baked beans) ¼ cup Tofu (made from soya beans) ½ cup	5 servings
Fruits	1 piece fruit (e.g. apple, orange, banana) 2 pieces small fruit (e.g. plums, kiwi, apricot) ½ cup of 100 per cent fruit juice 8 strawberries, 20 grapes ¼–½ cup cooked fruit ¼ cup grapes, berries, tomato 4 pieces dried fruit (e.g. apricots) 1½ tablespoon dried fruit (e.g. sultanas)	2 servings
Meat and meat substitutes	100 g cooked (2 slices) lean meat, fish, chicken ½ cup cooked mince, 2 small chops ½ cup tuna or salmon 2 eggs Peanut butter (2 tablespoons) ⅓ cup nuts or seeds ½ cup baked beans	1–2 servings

New dietary guidelines for children and adolescents

The new dietary guidelines for children and adolescents were introduced in 2003 and they are quite different in structure to the earlier dietary guidelines. The content, however, has not changed very much at all, with the same nutrition guidelines being given consistently across the past five decades. The new guidelines are outlined below with some explanation as to their importance and how to explain them to students.

- Encourage and support breastfeeding—breast milk is the best form of nutrition for babies up until the age of six months. Discuss the advantages of breastfeeding with your male and female students as the attitude of the father is one of the strongest factors in whether or not a baby will be breastfed. If fathers support breastfeeding, then it makes it easier for mothers to choose to breastfeed.
- Children and adolescents need sufficient nutritious foods to grow and develop normally
- Growth should be checked regularly in young children
- Physical activity is important for all children and adolescents
- Enjoy a wide variety of nutritious foods—children and adolescents should be encouraged to:
    - eat plenty of vegetables, legumes and fruits
    - eat plenty of cereals (including breads, rice, pasta and noodles), preferably wholegrain
    - include lean meat, fish, poultry and/or alternatives
    - include milks, yoghurts, cheeses and/or alternatives (reduced fat milks are not suitable for young children under two years because of their high energy needs, but reduced fat varieties should be encouraged for older children and adolescents)
    - choose water as a drink.
- Care should be taken to:
    - limit saturated fat and moderate total fat intake
    - avoid low-fat diets that are not suitable for infants or toddlers
    - choose foods low in salt
    - consume only moderate amounts of sugars and foods containing added sugar
    - prepare and store your child's food safely.

FIGURE 7.1
The healthy eating pyramid

Reproduced with the permission of The Australian Nutrition Foundation Inc.

The healthy eating pyramid

Use the healthy eating pyramid for nutrition education and as a guide to planning meals and shopping. The pyramid encompasses all of the five food groups in the right proportions, as well as indicating 'extra' foods which should be limited and only eaten occasionally. The main part of a healthy diet should come from bread and cereals such as pasta, rice, breakfast cereals and other grain and flour products, together with plenty of vegetables and fruits. One or two daily servings of lean meat, poultry, fish, dried beans, peas, lentils, nuts or eggs should be included as well as milk, cheese or yoghurt. Children require only small amounts of butter, margarine, oils, cream and other fats. The healthy eating pyramid is a concept that even small children can understand.

Nutrient requirements of babies, toddlers, children and adolescents

The major nutrients children and adolescents require are given in the following table:

TABLE 7.5 Major recommended dietary intakes for young people

	Babies		Toddlers	Children			Teens	
	0–6 months[a]	7–12 months[a]	1–3 years[b]	4–8 years[b]	9–13 years[b]		14–18 years[b]	
					Boys	Girls	Boys	Girls
Protein (g/day)	10 (1.43 g/kg)	14 (1.6 g/kg)	14 (1.08 g/kg)	20 (0.91 g/kg)	40 (0.94 g/kg)	35 (0.87 g/kg)	65 (0.99 g/kg)	45 (0.77 g/kg)
Calcium (mg/day)	210	270	500	700	9–11 yrs 1000 12–13 yrs 1300	9–11 yrs 1000 12–13 yrs 1300	1300	1300
Iron (mg/day)[c]	0.2	7	9	10	8	8	11	15
Vitamin C (mg/day)	25	30	35	35	40	40	40	40
Sodium (mg/day)[d]	120	170	200–400	300–600	400–800	400–800	460–920	460–920
Fibre (g/day)	None set	None set	14	18	24	20	28	22
Energy (kJ/day)[e]	1800–2700	2500–3500	3200–6300	6100–8200	8800–11200	8200–10000	11900–14000	10300–10900
Water (mL/day)[f]	Total 700	Total 700	Total 1400 Fluids 1000	Total 1600 Fluids 1200	Total 2200 Fluids 1600	Total 1900 Fluids 1400	Total 2700 Fluids 1900	Total 2200 Fluids 1600

(a) Figures refer to an Adequate Intake (AI) value, except for energy.

(b) Figures refer to a Recommended Dietary Intake (RDI), except for energy.

(c) Absorption of iron is lower from vegetarian diets so intakes will need to be up to 80 per cent higher.

(d) For sodium, figures refer to an Adequate Intake (AI) value.

(e) Estimated Energy Requirements (EER) have been set for a range of activity levels for individuals of a specific age, gender and body size. The values here are for those who are moderately active.

(f) Fluid needs are general estimates and are increased in hot or humid weather and when the child is vomiting or has diarrhoea. Total water includes water from foods as well as fluids. 'Fluids' refers to the non-food component only.

Reference: National Health and Medical Research Council (2006) Executive Summary of Nutrient Reference Values for Australia and New Zealand including Recommended Dietary Intakes. Commonwealth Department of Health and Ageing, Australia, and Ministry of Health, New Zealand. Available at: http://www.nhmrc.gov.au/publications/synopses/n35syn.htm

Macro nutrients

Protein for growth, tissue repair and energy: meat, fish, poultry, eggs, milk, cheese, yoghurt, dried beans, peas and lentils and nuts, peanut butter, seeds, tofu.

Carbohydrates for energy and fibre: bread, cereals, pasta, rice, oats, wheat, fruits and vegetables all provide carbohydrates. Wholegrain breads and cereals and fruits and vegetables provide the fibre to help keep bowel movements regular.

Fats for energy and to provide the fat-soluble vitamins A, E, D and K: butter, margarine, oils and cream. Fats are also found in fruits, vegetables, meats, cereal and dairy foods.

Water is vital for all life. Our kidneys need water to make the urine in which we get rid of body wastes. Children and adolescents need water to prevent dehydration, especially in hot weather.

Micro nutrients

Vitamins are required in tiny amounts from food to help us grow and to burn up food for energy. Important vitamins for children are vitamin C (fruits and vegetables), vitamin A (yellow, green and orange fruits and vegetables) and B group vitamins thiamine (B1), riboflavin (B2), niacin (B3), (breads, cereals, meats, milk and eggs).

Minerals are needed for growth and for regulation of body functions. Important minerals for children are calcium for bones and teeth (milk, cheese and yoghurt); iron (meat, fish, poultry, bread, cereals, green vegetables and legumes) and zinc (flesh foods, nuts). Iron is necessary for production of haemoglobin which is the protein component of red blood cells and the production of myoglobin which is a component of muscle tissue. Zinc is required for growth.

Each day we can combine these nutrients in the right amounts by eating a variety of foods—different foods contain different nutrients. No single food is essential in a child's diet—if they have a variety of foods from the five food groups they will obtain enough nutrients.

Protein: Growing babies and toddlers need nearly two grams of protein for each kilogram of body weight and this is roughly double the amount needed by fully grown adults. Children and teenagers need about one gram of protein per kilogram of body weight. Obtaining this amount of protein is not usually a major problem in developed countries. Most children receive more than enough protein from food. For example, 1 cup of milk, 1 egg, 1 lamb chop, 2 slices of sandwich cheese and 1 cup of baked beans all provide 6–10 grams of protein. However, poor diets, dominated by non-nutritious foods and drinks such as biscuits, snack foods, chips, 2-minute noodles, lollies, soft drinks and cordial will not supply the child with enough protein to promote growth.

I have termed this type of feeding pattern, 'Western Malnutrition' where the child or teenager becomes poorly nourished, malnourished or undernourished, not because of lack of food or poverty, but because of poor food choices. The child or adolescent can be surrounded by a more than plentiful supply of foods and drinks, but they are not of good enough nutritional quality to promote proper growth and development.

Some vegetarian children are at risk of nutritional deficiency because vegetarian foods tend to be very filling and the child may be 'full' before nutritional needs have been met. This is the case in the vast majority of malnutrition cases around the world, where the child becomes malnourished because there is a lack of food or a lack of the most nutritious foods that promote child growth. These are usually the protein foods which tend to be the most difficult to obtain or the most expensive around the world. It is easier to meet the protein, energy and vitamin and mineral needs of vegetarian children if they also have milk foods and eggs and this is outlined later in this chapter under the heading of vegetarian diets.

Table 7.6 outlines good sources of dietary protein.

TABLE 7.6 Good food sources of dietary protein

Food	Serving size	Protein (grams)
Chicken, lean, breast	100 g, 2 slices	28.0
Chicken, lean, leg	100 g, 1 drumstick	27.0
Meat, lean, cooked	100 g, 2 small chops	27.0
Tuna/salmon, tinned, brine or oil	100 g, ½ cup cooked	22.1
Fish, average, cooked	100 g, ½ cup cooked	22.0
Lobster, prawn, cooked	100 g, ½ cup cooked	22.0
Mussels	12 cooked	20.0
Scallops, cooked	6	13.0
Crab, cooked	100 g, ½ cup cooked	12.6
Yoghurt, natural	1 tub (200 g)	11.6
Pasta, egg, boiled	1 cup cooked	10.5
Tofu (soybean curd)	½ cup	10.0
Peanuts	½ cup	9.8
Milk	1 cup, 250 mL	9.0
Soy drink	1 cup, 250 mL	8.9
Yoghurt, fruit flavoured	1 tub (200 g)	8.6
Soya beans, canned, drained	½ cup cooked	8.6
Mixed nuts	½ cup	8.1
Pasta, white, cooked	1 cup cooked	7.2
Peanut butter	1 tablespoon	6.8
Baked beans	½ cup	6.4
Red kidney beans, lentils, mixed beans (canned)	½ cup, drained, cooked	6.4
Egg, boiled	1 medium	6.3
Avocado	½ pear	6.0
Oysters, raw	6	6.0
Rice, brown, boiled	1 cup	5.7
Rolled oats, raw (e.g. muesli)	½ cup	5.0
Cheese, processed, cheddar	1 slice (21 g)	4.5
Rice, white, boiled	1 cup	4.4
Tahini (sesame seed paste)	1 tablespoon	4.3
Cheese, cheddar	1 cube (2.5 cm cube)	4.1
Rolled oats, porridge, cooked	1 cup	4.1
Sunflower seeds	1 tablespoon	3.4
Breakfast biscuits, whole wheat	2 biscuits	3.4
Bread, wholemeal	1 slice	3.0
Hummus, chick pea and tahini mix	½ cup	3.0
Peas, green, boiled	½ cup	2.6
Bread, white	1 slice	2.4
Carrots, zucchini, broccoli	½ cup	1.6
Fruit—banana, apple, orange	1 piece	1.0

Calcium is essential, yet all too often children receive inadequate supplies of this important nutrient. Calcium is necessary for growth of teeth and bones, and is found in milk, cheese, yoghurt, powdered milk and the bones of tinned fish. Growing children need nearly twice as much calcium as adults and should be drinking at least 600–750 mL of milk or the equivalent from other foods each day.

This milk can be consumed in the form of cheese, yoghurt, custard, milk powder or milk puddings.

TABLE 7.7 Good food sources of dietary calcium

Food	Serving size	Calcium (mg)
Milk (skim)	1 cup (250 mL)	375
Yoghurt (low fat, natural)	1 small tub (200 g)	360
Yoghurt (low fat, fruit)	1 small tub (200 g)	320
Milk (low fat)	1 cup	310
Soya drink (fortified with calcium)	1 cup	290
Yoghurt (whole, plain, natural)	1 small tub (200 g)	290
Salmon (canned, solids and liquids—bones included)	½ cup with bones	280
Milk (whole)	1 cup	275
Cheddar cheese	2.5 cm cube (30–40 g)	240
Sardines (canned and drained—bones included)	¼ cup, with bones	175
Fruche (low fat)	200 g tub	160
Tofu—firm (made with calcium coagulant)	½ cup (100 g)	160
Custard, whole milk	½ cup	150
Prawns	100 g, ½ cup, peeled	150
Figs, dried	5 figs	150
Ice cream	2 scoops	130
Milk chocolate	50 g	125
Hummus	1 cup (246 g)	124
Milo	2 tablespoons	110
Ricotta cheese	3 tablespoons	100
Baked beans	1 cup	90
Tahini paste (sesame seed paste)	1 tablespoon	90
Chocolate bar (Mars, Milky Way, Snickers)	1 regular sized bar	80
Tofu—soft (with calcium coagulant)	½ cup (100 g)	80
Almonds (dry roasted)	¼ cup	73
Potato (mashed with milk)	1 cup (210 g)	55
Cottage cheese	3 tablespoons	30
Broccoli (cooked)	1 cup	30
Dark chocolate	50 g	25
Peanut butter	2 tablespoons	20
Mineral water	1 cup	4–18

Iron is required to make red blood cells which carry oxygen throughout the body. Children who do not eat enough iron will become tired, faint, pale, uninterested in play and may complain of headaches. Children who do not eat enough iron will also be susceptible to colds, flu and other infections, as daily iron is required to build the immune system. Iron is an essential building block for brain tissue and iron deficiency can result in poor mental development and lower intelligence. A doctor can supply iron supplements when a child or adolescent is anaemic, but otherwise it is best to keep up a good iron intake to prevent any deficiency. The best sources of iron are haem iron from meat, fish and chicken. Vitamin C helps non-haem iron to be 'taken up' by the body, so make sure the child has a serve of fruit, vegetables or juices to supply vitamin C. The food source of vitamin C should be eaten at the same time as the food containing non-haem iron so that the iron and the vitamin C can combine in the stomach to produce the better-absorbed haem iron. Examples of this include combining fruit juice with breakfast cereal or bread, pasta or rice with tomato sauce, baked beans with juice or salad, and peanut butter with juice. This is another reason why eating a variety of different foods is important for your child. If the child does not like meat or is a vegetarian, try serving other foods that contain iron, such as wheatgerm, wholegrain bread and cereals; peas, beans, lentils, baked beans or leafy green vegetables. Lentils or kidney beans, meat or fish paste spread made in a blender, and salmon and tuna patties or dips are other alternatives.

TABLE 7.8 Good food sources of dietary haem and non-haem iron

Foods containing haem iron	Iron (mg)	Foods containing non-haem iron	Iron (mg)
Liver (100 g)	11.1	Bran breakfast cereal (30 g)	5.4
Kidney (50 g)	5.7	Pasta boiled (1 cup)—wholemeal	3.1
Beef (120 g)	3.6	Corn Flakes (30 g)	2.8
Lamb (120 g)	3.0	Milo/Ovaltine (2 tablespoons)	2.8
Salmon/Tuna (150 g)	2.6	Breakfast wheat biscuits (2 biscuits)	2.6
Pork (1 chop)	1.8	Baked beans, lentils (½ cup cooked)	2.2
Chicken (120 g)	0.8	Spinach (½ cup, boiled)	2.2
Fish (120 g)	0.5	Dried apricots (10 apricot halves)	2.2
		Bread (2 slices)—wholemeal	1.4
		Broccoli (⅔ cup, boiled)	1.0
		Peanut butter (2 tablespoons)	1.0
		Egg (1 whole)	0.9
		Rice boiled (1 cup)—brown	0.8
		Pasta boiled (1 cup)—white	0.7
		Rice boiled (1 cup)—white	0.6
		Nuts (15 g)	0.6
		Bread (2 slices)—white	0.6

Fibre is required to keep bowel movements regular and soft. The estimate for dietary fibre is based on the formula that a child needs at least '5 grams plus age' (see explanation, Table 7.5)

TABLE 7.9 Good food sources of dietary fibre

Food	Serving Size	Fibre (g)
Muesli, natural, uncooked	½ cup	7.0
Beans (baked beans, kidney, mixed beans, cooked lentils)	½ cup, cooked	6.0
Passionfruit	2	5.6
Peas, green	½ cup, cooked	4.6
Pasta, wholemeal, cooked	½ cup, cooked	4.6
Wheat biscuits	2 biscuits	4.1
Sweet corn	1 medium cob	4.0
Bran cereals	½ cup	3.8
Prunes	6	3.5
Porridge, cooked	1 cup	3.4
Apple (with skin), banana, pear, orange	1 medium piece	3.0
Kiwi fruit	2 medium	3.0
Strawberries	½ cup, sliced	2.8
Broccoli, cooked	½ cup	2.5
Carrot, cooked	1 medium, ½ cup	2.5
Bread—mixed grain	1 slice	2.3
Apricots	2 fresh	2.1
Bread—wholemeal	1 slice	2.0
Beans, green, sliced, cooked or raw	½ cup	2.0
Cabbage, cauliflower, cooked or raw	½ cup	2.0
Melon (rockmelon, watermelon, honeydew)	1 cup chopped	2.0
Avocado	½ medium	1.9
Apricots	4 dried	1.8
Potato, peeled, baked	1 medium	1.8
Bread, white (high fibre)	1 slice	1.8
Lettuce	2 medium leaves	1.7
Sultanas	1 tablespoon	1.7
Rice, brown, cooked	½ cup	1.6
Bean sprouts, raw	½ cup	1.5
Bread, white	1 slice	1.4
Crumpets, wholemeal	1	1.4
Pasta, white, cooked	½ cup	1.3
Corn Flakes, Rice Bubbles	1 cup	1.0
Mushrooms, raw, sliced	½ cup	1.0
Cherries	7 large	1.0
Zucchini, cooked	½ cup	0.9
Crumpets, white	1	0.9
Pumpkin, cooked	½ cup	0.8
Rice, white, cooked	½ cup	0.8
Tomato	½ medium	0.7
Tofu	¼ cup	0.7
Celery	1 full stalk	0.5
Cucumber (unpeeled)	5 slices	0.4
Fruit juice	200 mL	0.0

Nutritional problems in children and adolescents

Constipation

'Normal' bowel patterns can cover a wide range of frequency in children as well as adults. Some children who have 'lazy bowels' can go for two or three days without a bowel movement while their brother or sister may have two or three bowel movements per day. Parents often worry if their child seems to have too few or too many bowel movements within sensible limits but the fact is that every child is different. More regular bowel movements can be produced by giving children foods such as wholemeal bread, wholegrain cereals, bran, brown rice, wholegrain spaghetti and noodles which are high in dietary fibre. Wholegrain crisp breads, cakes and biscuits, nuts, fruits, vegetables and juices are also good sources of fibre as are dried beans and lentils such as soya beans, red kidney beans and baked beans. Children must be given plenty of water or fluids with fibrous foods, as the fibre acts by absorbing water and stimulating bowel movements. Constipation in babies and toddlers is often related to dehydration, especially when the child is too young to ask for a drink.

Bowel movements can also be regulated by encouraging children to settle into a routine in the morning. Just eating breakfast can improve bowel movements and constipated children will often be those who do not eat breakfast. The presence of food or liquid in the stomach in the morning can 'signal' a bowel movement, so it is desirable to eat breakfast at around the same time each morning and allow at least 15 minutes to half an hour afterwards to wait for the 'signal' to go the toilet. Rushing children from the table to the car or school bus can interfere with bowel movements and thereby worsen constipation. Bowel movements should not be forced as this causes haemorrhoids or 'piles'. Children should be taught not to 'push' with difficult bowel movements. A child should take no longer than two or three minutes to pass a bowel movement. Sitting on the toilet for a long time or reading should not be allowed as this places strain on the muscles surrounding the bowel, rectum and anus and this may contribute to haemorrhoids.

Children need physical exercise to keep them fit and healthy. Lack of exercise can lead to constipation, so parents should encourage daily exercise such as walking to school. There are plenty of old wives' tales about constipation. You will probably remember being told about certain foods that cause constipation. Myths abound about cheese and milk in particular as being 'binding foods' which prevent bowel movements—this is an old wives' tale and is completely untrue. The only reason these foods could be at all 'constipating' is because they contain no dietary fibre and therefore do not stimulate bowel movement. Children will not become constipated by eating milk, cheese or any other food claimed to have a 'binding' effect and these foods should not be restricted from a child's diet.

How much dietary fibre should a child eat each day? Current nutritional recommendations suggest the '5 plus age' estimate for daily grams of dietary fibre in children older than two years (see information about dietary fibre in Tables 7.5 and 7.9). It is likely that this recommendation will be revised soon to a '10 plus age' recommendation, so the current '5 plus age' recommendation is considered to be a minimum. Children who meet the dietary fibre recommendations tend to have one or more soft bowel movements each day. Children who have less tend to become constipated or have bowel movements every second or third day. Regular, soft bowel movements prevent haemorrhoids (piles) in childhood and prevent diverticulitis (painful inflammation of the bowel) and bowel cancer later in life. To prevent constipation, children and teenagers need at least five servings of fruit or vegetables each day (including legumes such as baked beans) and 4–5 servings of breads and cereals such as wholemeal bread, breakfast cereal, porridge, or wholemeal pasta or rice.

Choking

All infants, children and even adolescents put objects into their mouths which can cause choking if swallowed or inhaled, and one of the most common things to cause choking is food. Students also commonly choke at school on apple, sausage skins, chewing gum, plastic pen lids and pieces of plastic. For these reasons, it is a useful rule for teachers to enforce no 'chewing' in class.

Children under five years of age are at particular risk of choking and should never be given nuts, particularly peanuts, unless they are finely chopped. Small children and toddlers can also choke on foods like whole peas by 'inhaling' them, so it is a good idea to mash peas for very small children. Always have children and adolescents seated when they are eating or drinking. Never allow them to 'graze' or eat or drink while running or playing as this contributes to irregular breathing patterns and increases the risk of inhaling food pieces.

In years gone by, teachers were taught how to implement the Heimlich manoeuvre; however, this technique is no longer recommended because it may result in food being regurgitated into the trachea (windpipe) causing a worsening of the choking. The current technique to apply when a child is choking is outlined below.

If one of your students is choking, follow these steps:

- If the student is making noises, breathing or crying, they are not choking seriously and they may be able to move the food themselves. Try to settle the student and allow them to clear the food themselves.
- Pull the food out yourself if it is stringy but do not push it further down the child's throat.
- If the student is not breathing, bend the child over to allow the food to come out of the child's throat.
- Give four sharp blows to the child's upper back between the shoulder blades to dislodge the food.

If the child is still not breathing call an ambulance on 000 (111 in New Zealand) and they will tell you what to do next.

Do not squeeze the child's stomach or apply the Heimlich manoeuvre as this method is no longer considered safe and it may contribute to further choking.

Remember to supervise your students when they are eating or drinking.

Dehydration

The human body is approximately 60 per cent water and any fluid losses from sweat, breath, urine and faeces needs to be replaced daily. Dehydration can occur very quickly and easily in children and adolescents, and this is usually caused by vomiting, diarrhoea, sweating or excessive heat. Students who are participating in sports carnivals or swimming carnivals are at increased risk of dehydration. To avoid heat stroke students should be kept in the shade, should wear hats and should be regularly encouraged to drink water. Students will not become thirsty enough to drink until they are already dehydrated, so students need to be instructed to sip water regularly.

To avoid heat stroke, athletic events and carnivals can be held during the early morning hours before the sun becomes too intense. Likewise cross-country and other long distance events can be scheduled for morning time slots.

Severe dehydration is life threatening and shows up with drowsiness, lethargy, sunken eyes, lack of urination and severe weight loss. Slight dehydration can be managed by giving the child a drink of water, keeping them relatively cool and waiting until they produce urine which is mostly clear and not yellow. Severe dehydration is a medical emergency and the child must be taken to hospital or a doctor's surgery as soon as possible. Treatment may require insertion of a drip to restore the child's fluid balance or the prescription of an electrolyte solution. Children who have been vomiting or those who have diarrhoea should *never* be given full strength lemonade, cordial, juice or other soft drinks because these can cause sudden 'osmotic' diarrhoea which further dehydrates the child. Appropriate fluids for children with diarrhoea include electrolyte solutions made up exactly as per the directions or juice, flat soft drinks (no bubbles) made up to 1 part juice or soft drink to 4 parts cooled, boiled water. Children should slowly sip the fluid until they feel better and they are producing normal urine.

Caffeine consumption in children and adolescents

Studies of school children have found that many frequently drink caffeinated drinks. A study conducted among 381 primary and high school children in 2000 found around a quarter of students regularly consume high caffeine energy drinks such as Red Bull, 'V' and Lift Plus (O'Dea & Rawstorne, 2000). Students also reported consuming high caffeine supplements such as guarana. In a later study, male adolescents reported their reasons for consumption of energy drinks, with improved sports performance as the main one (O'Dea, 2003c). In fact, caffeine is likely to create adverse effects for sports people as it results in dehydration, jitteriness, stomach upsets and frequent urination. Many students who consume energy drinks before sports events report having to take time out of the game to go to the toilet!

The caffeine content of energy drinks is the equivalent of drinking a cup of strong coffee. See Table 7.10 for the caffeine content of foods and drinks. Caffeine is a natural stimulant found in many common foods and drinks including tea, coffee, cocoa, cola soft drinks, energy drinks and chocolate. Some 'natural' remedies and herbal products may contain caffeine especially guarana, which has seven times the concentration of caffeine as coffee. Over the counter drugs such as cold and flu tablets and cough mixtures may also contain caffeine. Side effects include wakefulness, diuresis (production of extra urine); stomach upsets (for example, diarrhoea), nervousness, headaches, trembling and

TABLE 7.10 Caffeine content of some common foods and drinks

Foods and drinks	Size of serving	Average milligrams (mg) of caffeine
Coffee, brewed, drip, percolated (e.g. cappuccino, espresso)	1 cup	130
Coffee, brewed, plunger	1 cup	94
Energy drinks	250 mL	80
Coffee, instant	1 cup	74
Tea, iced tea	375 mL	60
Leaf tea or tea bags	1 cup	45
Green tea	1 cup	45
Soft drink, cola	375 mL	45
Diet cola	375 mL	30
Chocolate, bakers chocolate	30 g	25
Dark chocolate	30 g	20
Milk chocolate	30 g	10
Cocoa	1 cup	10
Chocolate sauce syrup	1 tbs	4
Coffee, decaf, instant or brewed	1 cup	3
Tea, herbal teas	1 cup	3
Soft drink, caffeine free	375 mL	0

rapid heart beats. Caffeine can cause sleeping problems and bed wetting in children and some studies show a rise in blood pressure and blood fats in children who have had more than 140 milligrams of caffeine per day. Other studies have shown that children who consume more than 95 milligrams of caffeine can show signs of increased anxiety (worrying, uneasiness) and may suffer nightmares. Children under the age of 12 years should not consume any caffeine. Senior students who are using caffeinated drinks or tablets to stay awake for study report disturbed sleeping patterns due to the night time consumption of caffeine. This inability to get to sleep often results in lack of sleep and a poor school or athletic performance the next day. Students who snack or drink caffeinated drinks late at night are also more likely to miss breakfast the following morning, and this too is related to low energy levels and poor concentration at school the following day.

Caffeine consumption is a feature of the diet that should be investigated in students. Students' study routines should not become dependent on caffeine. A better management of study patterns could be taught to students via the use of frequent breaks with some form of physical activity to increase mental alertness rather than a dependence on caffeine. This topic is covered later in this chapter by involving students in the analysis of their diets for caffeine content.

How to read food labels

Students and adults alike are fascinated to know what is in their food. Helping them to read food labels helps children to understand the ingredient content of packaged foods but also helps them to understand the value for money. The following is a brief guide to reading and understanding food labels.

A description or name of the food Each label describes or 'names' the specific food.

Ingredient list All of the ingredients are listed in order by weight. Generally, the first three ingredients are the major components of the food. For example, the ingredients of sweet biscuits are flour, vegetable shortening, sugar, wheatmeal, brown sugar, golden syrup, raising agents (503, 500, 450), salt, flavour. You can see from this list that the main three ingredients are flour, fat and sugar. When other sugars are listed on a product ingredient label (sucrose, glucose, maltose, fructose syrup, honey, corn syrup, molasses, invert sugar), they can all add up to make sugar the overall main ingredient.

Food additives are all checked for safety by the government before they are allowed to be added to foods. Additives such as preservatives, colours and flavours are added to foods to improve the taste, appearance, quality, stability and shelf life of a food. Rather than printing the whole name of the additive, manufacturers usually print the type of additive (for example, thickener, humectant, anti-caking agent, antioxidant) and then the specific number for example, thickener (440). Some manufacturers list the name of the additive and all of the additional information for example, pectin (thickener, 440). Some people are allergic to certain foods (for example, eggs, milk, nuts) or are sensitive to certain additives so all of this information is printed on the food label to allow consumers to make informed choices about their foods and drinks.

Net weight The weight of the food without the weight of the packaging. Teach your students to read the net weight and compare net weight on large packages versus small packages. Sometimes, large and small packages can both be 500 grams net weight! Teach your students to compare the price of similar weight products and to understand value for money. The price of advertising, fancy packaging and other marketing activities is eventually passed on to the consumer via the price of the product. This explains why some generic brands are significantly less expensive than the branded products.

Nutrition panel Gives the energy (kilojoules), protein, fat (total fat and how much of the total is saturated fat), carbohydrate (total carbohydrate and how much of that is sugar or starch), dietary fibre and sodium. Nutrients are shown per average serving and per 100 grams. If, for example, a muesli bar is listed as 35 grams of sugar per 100 grams, you know that it is 35 per cent sugar. This will also be obvious from the ingredient list.

Similarly, you can see how much fat is in the food by checking the amount of fat per serving and the per cent of fat (per 100 grams). Anything below 3 per cent is a low fat food, anything from 7–15 per cent tends to be moderate and above 15 per cent fat is high.

Use by or **Best before** date. On foods with a shelf life of less than two years 'Best before' date refers to the suggested time limit on the food before it begins to spoil or go stale. It does not necessarily mean that the food will have 'gone off'. It is illegal to sell food which has gone past its date marking.

Country of origin Country or countries where the food was made or the country from where the ingredients came. (This is not required in New Zealand.)

Product of Australia, Product of New Zealand The vast majority of ingredients are from, and production has occurred in, Australia or New Zealand.

Name and address of manufacturer or distributor This information must be put on the label so that consumers can contact the manufacturer if required.

Allergy warning Ingredients that cause common allergies are listed. Examples are gluten (for people who suffer coeliac disease), nuts, eggs, bee pollen etc.

Storage instructions The manufacturer has tested the food product and provides storage and cooking instructions based on these quality tests—follow these instructions.

Bar code The identification number for the food which is electronically scanned at the cash register.

Dietary claims

No added sugar No sucrose (table sugar) or glucose, honey, dextrose, maltose or fructose has been added to the food. Natural sugars, such as the fructose naturally occurring in fruit juices are not 'added'.

Fat free Less than 0.15 per cent fat.

Low fat Less than 3 per cent fat in a solid food and less than 1.5 per cent fat in a liquid food.

97 per cent fat free About 3 per cent or less fat.

98 per cent fat free About 2 per cent or less fat.

Reduced fat At least 25 per cent less fat than the regular product. This means that it has been made with less fat than normal, but it is not necessarily low in fat.

Low salt No more than 120 mg sodium per 100 grams of food or less than half the amount of sodium than the normal food product.

Reduced salt At least 25 per cent less sodium than the regular food. This means that it is made with less salt than usual, but it is still not necessarily low in salt.

Low joule A liquid or drink is low joule if it has less than 80 kilojoules per 100 mL and a solid food is low joule if it has less than 170 kilojoules per 100 grams.

Cholesterol free, **No cholesterol** The food contains no cholesterol but may still contain significant amounts of fat, for example, avocados. Cholesterol only comes from animal foods.

High in fibre At least 3 grams of fibre per serve of the food.

Very high in fibre At least 6 grams of fibre per serve of the food.

No artificial colourings or flavourings No added, synthetic colours or flavours but naturally occurring colours and flavours are permitted and often used, for example, betacarotene (160).

No preservatives No added chemical preservatives.

No MSG No added monosodium glutamate, although MSG is found naturally in tomatoes, mushrooms and some cheeses.

Other food label claims:

Lite or **Light** This has no strict definition and can refer to flavour (for example, light olive oil) or less fat, or lower in alcohol (for example, light beer) or a thinner (for example, lite cream) or lighter product (for example, lighter potato chips).

Natural this word has no strict definition and is used in a variety of ways on food labels.

Vegetarian diets

Vegetarian eating is not new or unusual. In fact, many of the world's most ancient cultures have survived and flourished on a traditionally vegetarian diet. Vegetarian eating has become more popular in Australia since the 1950s, with many people regularly choosing vegetarian or semi vegetarian meals. The reasons for vegetarian eating are many and varied and may include religious (Hindus, Buddhists, Seventh Day Adventists), cultural (for example, Asian or Mexican food), environmental (land use, animal rights), ethical (world hunger issues, animal welfare, killing of animals), economic (vegetarian foods are inexpensive), and health reasons. Studies of vegetarian populations, such as the well-known Seventh Day Adventist studies, have reported lower rates of coronary heart disease, blood cholesterol, lower blood pressure, as well as less obesity and fewer cases of cancer, particularly colon cancer and non-insulin dependent diabetes.

TABLE 7.11 Types of vegetarian diets

Type of vegetarian diet	Nutritional risk to children
Lacto-ovo vegetarians The most common type of vegetarian diet. These people avoid flesh foods, but include eggs, milk, dairy foods, fruit, vegetables, breads and cereals.	Very little nutritional risk. Need attention to good sources of absorbable dietary iron.
Lacto-vegetarians Do not eat flesh foods or eggs, but include milk, yoghurt, other dairy foods and most other foods.	Little nutritional risk. Children need attention to total kilojoules, good source of protein and absorbable dietary iron.
Semi-vegetarians Don't eat red meats, but may occasionally include fish or other 'white' meats. Include most other foods.	Low nutrition risk. Nutritionally adequate if the child's diet is mixed with good source of protein (milk, cheese, yoghurt, eggs, fish, chicken, nuts, peanut butter).
'New-Age' vegetarians May eat a traditional diet and simply remove the meat from meals, e.g. eat a plateful of vegetables or rice.	May be high nutritional risk. Nutritional adequacy depends on quality of protein. Diet will be adequate if it includes milk, dairy foods, eggs, vegetables, fruit, bread and cereals. This type of 'vegetarian' diet is often associated with eating disorders in adolescents.
Vegans Don't eat any animal products and may avoid food which contains animal products such as butter, milk and honey, cosmetics which contain animal products, wearing animal fibres such as leather and wool.	High nutritional risk, particularly in babies, children, adolescents, pregnant and lactating women. Likely to be low in kilojoules, iron, calcium, zinc, vitamin B12, protein.
Fruitarians Don't eat anything other than raw fruit, berries and some nuts. Misinformed belief in a 'natural' diet from which humans evolved.	Very high nutritional risk. Unlike some primates, humans cannot survive on this diet. Extremely low in calories, protein, fat, iron, zinc, calcium, vitamin B12.
Zen macrobiotic vegetarians Very restricted dietary regimen based on the teachings of George Ohsawa. Large amounts of brown rice, small amounts of fruit, vegetables, legumes.	Very high nutritional risk. Inadequate calories, protein, zinc, iron, calcium, vitamin B12. Several deaths have been recorded from this extreme diet.

Health benefits

The known nutritional benefits of vegetarian eating include the preventive effects of a low fat, low cholesterol content of most vegetarian diets, combined with the protective effects of a high fruit, vegetable, dietary fibre and antioxidant content. In addition, recent research shows that the phytoestrogens found in soy products such as soya drinks and tofu may have special benefits for women such as reducing hot flushes. Naturally, many vegetarians are also likely to be health conscious people who do not smoke, drink alcohol, consume excessive caffeine and who generally partake in a healthy lifestyle, and these factors combined may contribute to the better health status of vegetarians.

Types of vegetarian diets

Vegetarian eating patterns vary according to the reasons for becoming vegetarian, income, nutritional knowledge and availability of foods. The different types of vegetarian diets are outlined in the table on the previous page. The most common type of vegetarian diet is a lacto-ovo diet which usually contains mixed and balanced amounts of breads, cereals, rice, pasta, legumes (beans, baked beans, dried peas, seeds, lentils), nuts, vegetables, fruits, peanut butter, milk, cheese, margarine, sugar, and oils.

The healthy eating pyramid for vegetarians

A nutritious lacto-ovo vegetarian diet is illustrated below in the healthy eating pyramid for vegetarians.

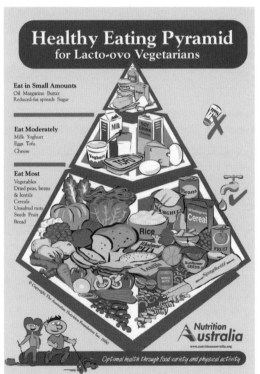

FIGURE 7.2
The healthy eating pyramid for vegetarians

Reproduced with the permission of The Australian Nutrition Foundation Inc.

Growth of vegetarian children and adolescents

A varied vegetarian diet providing adequate energy, protein, vitamins and minerals will meet all of the requirements of the growing child. Several cases of severe protein-energy malnutrition and deficiencies of iron and vitamins B12 and D have been reported in infants and children who were fed inappropriate, strict vegetarian diets. Growth in vegan or strict vegetarian children may be compromised, but growth in Seventh Day Adventist children (lacto-ovo vegetarians) has been shown to be similar to omnivorous children. Catch-up growth by age 10 has been found to be possible in vegan children but vegetarian children still tend to be lighter than those on a mixed diet. Older vegan children and adolescents can obtain the same energy and protein intakes as those on an omnivorous mixed diet, provided the energy intake is adequate to prevent protein being used as an energy source and that the protein sources are of good quality. A later age of menarche has been reported among leaner Seventh Day Adventist vegetarian girls and this has also been found in some studies of British and Chinese girls.

Nutritional risk in adolescent vegetarians

A vegetarian diet containing a variety of different foods will usually provide children and adolescents with enough energy, protein, vitamins and minerals to promote normal growth and development. Problems arise when the diet becomes too limited in the amount of food and kilojoules, the variety of different food groups (for example, fruitarians, vegans, semi-vegetarians, 'New Age' vegetarians) or when the diet is restricted to only a few different foods (fruitarians, vegans, zen macrobiotic diets, some 'New Age' vegetarians). Children and adolescents have high energy and nutrient needs to meet the demands of the growth spurt as well as physical activity. In fact, the nutrient needs of adolescents are usually far greater than those of fully grown adults, a point which is largely missed by parents who may be concerned about the large appetites and food intakes of their teenagers.

Energy and protein

The high energy needs of children and adolescents demand that they eat large amounts of foods. The type of food eaten needs to be of high nutrient density to provide calories, protein and other nutrients. Diets high in dietary fibre such as vegan diets, are unsuitable for children because they tend to 'fill up' before they have consumed enough energy, protein and nutrients. This is one reason why vegetarian diets are advantageous for overweight adults, because the foods are filling and quickly satisfying. Unfortunately, high intakes of breads, cereals, rice, pasta, fruits and vegetables provide low intakes of energy and are poor sources of protein and are therefore unlikely to meet the energy, protein and nutrient needs of children. In addition, a vegetarian diet contains a higher percentage of dietary fibre and the phytic acid in dietary fibre has the potential to interfere with micronutrient absorption by binding minerals such as iron and zinc.

Good sources of protein include milk, eggs, cheese, yoghurt, soy drink, tofu, peanut butter, nuts, seeds, dried peas, beans, baked beans and lentils. Children may choose low-fat milk and dairy foods after two years of age, but these foods are unsuitable for younger children because they need the extra energy and fat soluble vitamins provided by whole milk and dairy foods.

Fats

Humans can manufacture all but two of the fatty acids—linoleic acid (omega-6 fatty acid) and linolenic acid (omega-3 fatty acid). These fatty acids are known as essential fatty acids because they must be supplied in the diet. Essential fatty acids are required to build cell membranes, and to maintain normal growth and development. A varied and nutritious vegetarian diet containing grains, seeds, nuts, leafy green vegetables, beans (especially soya beans) and lentils, vegetable oils and margarine will provide enough of the essential fatty acids to maintain health and growth.

Iron

The non-haem iron in plant foods (ferric iron) is not as well absorbed as the haem iron (ferrous iron) from animal meats. Vegetarian children need to obtain large amounts of iron (see Table 7.5 for list of nutrient needs) to ensure growth, and females need iron to offset the losses from menstruation. The vitamin C in vegetables, juices and fruits improves the absorption of non-haem iron by reducing it to its ferrous source. Therefore, eating a variety of foods at the same meal will enhance the absorption of dietary iron in vegetarian diets. Foods such as breakfast cereals, baked beans, dried peas and beans, legumes, nuts, seeds, leafy green vegetables, dried fruits and peanut butter and tahini (sesame seed paste) are good vegetarian sources of iron.

Calcium

Dietary calcium is often deficient in strict vegetarian diets such as vegan diets and fad vegetarian diets such as fruitarian and 'New Age' vegetarian diets. Calcium is well supplied by milk, hard cheeses (not soft cheeses like cottage or ricotta), yoghurt, ice cream, custard, calcium fortified soy drinks, almonds, tahini, bok choy and broccoli.

Zinc

Zinc is important for the function of many enzymes and for growth and development. Clinical signs of zinc deficiency include poor wound healing and impaired immune response. Zinc is supplied by meats, eggs, milk, dairy foods and other foods previously mentioned as good sources of protein.

Vitamin B12 (cyanocobalamin)

Vitamin B12 deficiency has been found among strict vegetarians, vegans and their children and young breastfed babies of vegans. Even though the recommended dietary intake for vitamin B12 is minute and deficiency takes years to develop, vitamin B12 deficiency may still result from diets which do not contain any animal products or in patients with atrophic gastritis or severe ileal malabsorption. Vitamin B12 deficiency is characterised by large cell anaemia (megaloblastic anaemia) and a smooth, sore tongue. These deficiency symptoms are accompanied by fatigue, skin hypersensitivity and nerve disorders such as tremors. Vegetarians who eat milk, dairy foods or eggs will receive enough vitamin B12, but vegans and other strict vegetarians must pay strict attention to this vitamin. Vegans should take vitamin B12 supplements and should not rely on spirulina, seaweed, tempeh (fermented soya beans) or other fermented foods as a source of B12 because these sources are of variable vitamin B12 content and 80–94 per cent of the vitamin B12 content of these foods is inactive.

Vitamin D

Children who follow a vegan diet may be low in dietary vitamin D, but they will be able to produce vitamin D from the cholesterol on their skin if they are exposed to direct UV sunlight. Vegans or poor eaters who are indoors or bedridden will need vitamin D supplementation. Muslim women and girls who are fully veiled are likely to develop a vitamin D deficiency if they do not receive enough exposure to direct sunlight. This situation is becoming more common and more women are being diagnosed with vitamin D deficiency. Women and girls who are veiled need to be encouraged to sit in the sun without their veils every day and get 10 minutes of direct sunlight on their face, arms and shoulders. This protects them from deficiency and ensures that vitamin D is present in breast milk if women are breastfeeding. This also ensures that their breastfed baby will get enough vitamin D.

Fad weight loss diets

Fad diets are popular among teenagers and adults alike, despite a wealth of scientific information about the many pitfalls of fad weight loss plans and the commercial nature of most people who are 'selling' weight loss. Fad diets are also becoming popular

TABLE 7.12 Example of a healthy eating plan for lacto-ovo vegetarian adolescents aged 13–18 years

Food	Kilojoules	Protein (g)	Iron (mg)	Calcium (mg)
Breakfast				
Breakfast cereal (30 g)	398	3.4	2.6	10.0
Milk (½ cup) (Low fat)	585	10.8	0.1	375
Toast (wholemeal, 1 slice)	282	3.0	0.7	16.0
Butter/margarine (1 teaspoon)	269	0	0	0
Fruit juice (200 mL)	300	1.0	0	11.0
Morning snack				
Banana	501	2.0	0.7	7.0
Flavoured milk, 300 mL	813	9.6	0.3	360
Lunch				
Bread (wholemeal, 2 slices)	564	6.0	1.4	32.0
Peanut butter (2 tablespoons)	1238	13.6	1.0	24.0
Cheese slice	291	4.5	0	131
Water	0	0	0	0
Milo (2 tablespoons with 200 mL milk)	852	10.0	4.0	368
Afternoon snack				
Apple	230	0.3	0.2	5
Water				
Evening meal				
Baked potato (2 medium)	612	5.8	1.2	6
Baked beans (½ cup)	393	6.4	2.2	47
Cheese, 1 cube 2.5 cm	270	4.0	0	124
Salad, lettuce, tomato, cucumber	98	1.0	1.0	8
2 scoops ice cream	394	1.2	0.05	65
Serve of tinned fruit salad (½ cup)	102	0.2	0.2	3
TOTAL	8116	82.8	15.7	1592
Average Recommended Dietary Intake for an adolescent aged 13–18 years—depending on stage of growth, menstrual status and physical activity levels. Extra kilojoules should come from fruit, vegetables, bread and cereals.	8000–14 000	0.77–0.99 grams per kilo body weight	8–15 mg girls 8–11 mg boys	1300 mg

among boys and young men who may be more susceptible in many ways because their knowledge of food and nutrition may not be as good as that of their female peers. Boys are particularly susceptible to fad weight gain diets and weight gain products. Fad diets are usually easy to identify. The most common feature of a fad diet is the offer of quick, easy and massive weight loss or weight gain. Fad diets are also likely to be unbalanced and usually do not contain foods from all of the five foods groups. In addition to a low intake of foods, low kilojoules or an unbalanced intake of foods, fad diets may also have a very unbalanced intake of macro nutrients such as low carbohydrate, high protein or high fat. Another feature of fad diets is the requirement that the consumer buy something—a book, a potion, formulas, products, equipment, foods etc. The spruiker of the fad diet usually has fake or meaningless credentials, often from a mail order university and they provide equally fake testimonials from people who claim amazing results from the use of the fad diet or product.

The following list outlines the features of a fad diet and these criteria can be used in classes to help students identify and critique common fad diets.

Common features of a fad diet

- Does not contain foods from all of the five groups. Often only contains a few foods. For example, the diet may be called the 'grapefruit diet' where the main dietary component is grapefruit.

- Does not contain lots of cereal, rice, pasta, bread, breakfast cereal, vegetables and fruits as recommended by the healthy eating pyramid. For example, the diet may focus on one food or one food group to the exclusion of others. Many diets simply induce a state of ketosis (where the body is required to burn up glycogen stores, body protein, muscle and some fat in order to function) by only allowing consumption of meats, fats and protein foods. Low carbohydrate diets cause the body to go into ketosis, examples of this are the Atkins diet, the Israeli Army diet and the Scarsdale diet.
- Does not recommend sensible dietary practices such as cutting the fat off meats and the skin from chicken.
- Does not recommend sensible cooking methods such as foods cooked without added fat (butter, oil, margarine, mayonnaise and cream) and salt.
- Does not include regular meals such as breakfast, lunch, dinner, morning tea and afternoon tea. Fad diets will often have the person eat nothing substantial until the evening meal. This form of meal replacement fad diet often has some drink as a substitute for normal meals.
- Lacks a variety of different foods and drinks—often includes only a few foods.
- Requires 'additional' support with pills or other supplements which are often very expensive.
- Promises rapid weight loss or weight gain. The human body can only burn up about half to one kilo of fat per week and any further weight loss is likely to be glycogen stored in the liver and muscles (800 g of glycogen plus 2000 g of water stored with glycogen), and muscle. For example, a low carbohydrate diet can quickly and easily result in a 3 kg 'weight loss' in around 24 hours, but none of this weight loss is fat and it is all replaced quickly when a normal carbohydrate intake is resumed.
- Makes exaggerated claims, for example, curing cancer, melting away fat, increasing the metabolism to burn fat, improving libido, providing limitless energy. Many fad diets, pills, herbs, formulas and potions promise a boost in energy. The 'lift' that some of these products seems to supply is often attributable to caffeine or guarana, a caffeine-containing berry native to South America, in the product. The other form of any perceived energy boost is believed to be nothing more than a very expensive placebo effect.
- Contains expensive ingredients. Many fad products, meal replacement formulas, drinks, soups and various other fad potions contain simple, common ingredients that are sold at an exorbitant price. Fine examples of this common practice are the slimming milkshakes and the body building formulas in which the main product is usually powdered milk. Students can easily learn to recognise such fad products by simply reading the list of ingredients on the food label.

The lessons that follow later in this chapter help students to brainstorm criteria for identifying and deciphering fad diets.

Sports nutrition

The major nutritional consideration for athletes and people involved in training or sport is to maximise performance and minimise adverse effects. The major issues in sports nutrition include the following: obtaining enough carbohydrate to provide energy and to prevent 'hitting the wall'; prevention of dehydration and heat stroke; obtaining adequate iron to prevent anaemia and maximise aerobic performance; obtaining enough calcium to protect bone density; bulking up for power sports; and weight control for many endurance sports.

Carbohydrates (CHO)

All of our body cells prefer glucose as a source of fuel. Carbohydrates are composed of sugars and starch which are digested quickly and provide a quick source of energy. The body cells, particularly those of the exercising muscle, can metabolise carbohydrates quickly and efficiently in order to provide energy. Foods high in carbohydrates are those at the base of the healthy eating pyramid (see Figure 7.1) and include breads, cereals, pasta, rice, fruits and starchy vegetables. The recommendations for peak sports nutrition diets during training and competition are as follows. The diet should be:

- 65–75% of total kilojoules from carbohydrate
- 10–20% of total kilojoules from protein
- 20–25% of total kilojoules from fat.

The amount of carbohydrate required by individuals can be estimated by combining the effects of your body weight, training levels, type of sport, gender and your appetite. The level of carbohydrate required for different levels of physical activity is outlined in the following table.

TABLE 7.13 Levels of energy expenditure and carbohydrate requirements

Carbohydrate/activity level	Physical activity level
Level 1	Low carbohydrate diet—less than 50 grams per day
Level 2	Very low activity level, sleeping, resting, sitting, almost completely sedentary
Level 3	Very light physical activity, generally inactive, but moves around house, school
Level 4	Light physical activity—stands, walks about 30 minutes per day
Level 5	Walks, does moderate exercise, may play sport or dance a few times per week, exercises for 2–4 hours per week
Level 6	Amateur sports person or athlete, exercises most week days for about an hour, 5–10 hours per week
Level 7	Serious professional athlete, exercises every day for an hour or two, 10–15 hours per week
Level 8–9	Serious professional endurance athlete, exercises and trains for 20 or more hours per week
Level 10	Full time athletes, ultra endurance, iron man, iron woman, Olympic athlete

(Table re-worked with permission from Glenn Cardwell (2006), *Gold Medal Nutrition* (4th ed), Human Kinetics Publishers, p. 33)

Carbohydrate needs are calculated by using the following formula:
Weight (kg) × Activity level 1–10 = Amount of carbohydrates needed each day
For example, a 58 kilogram 16-year-old girl who swims two hours every day will need 58 × 7 = 406 grams of carbohydrate daily

Glycaemic index

Glycaemic index or GI is a measure of how quickly a carbohydrate food is digested and released as blood glucose. The quicker the release into the bloodstream, the higher the GI. Calculation of a GI for each food is done by comparing it to the effect of a 50 gram load of pure glucose. The score given to pure glucose is a GI of 100 and then every other food is compared in reference to that. A high GI is quite advantageous for some athletes during training or during an event because these foods produce a quick amount of glucose to replenish blood glucose without causing any stomach upsets. At other times, such as after training or before training, low GI foods are useful as a slow and steady source of blood glucose. People with diabetes (high blood sugar that results from not having enough insulin) are encouraged to eat low to moderate GI foods in order to keep their blood glucose levels steady.

TABLE 7.14 Major sources of carbohydrates in foods

Food	CHO (grams)	Food	CHO (grams)	Food	CHO (grams)
Bread, 1 slice	15	Fruit, 1 piece, apple, orange, pear (medium), banana (small)	15	Potato, boiled, 1 medium	16
Bread roll	27	Fruit, cooked, canned, ½ cup	15	Potato, mashed, 1 cup	30
English muffin	28	Dried apricot, ½ cup	30	Sweet potato, cooked, 1 cup	40
Crispbread, 2	8	Sultanas, ¼ cup	35	Corn kernels, cooked, 1 cup	30
Water crackers, 6	18	Grapes, 1 cup	25	Baked beans, kidney beans, bean mix, ½ cup	25
Crumpet, 1	20	Banana, medium	22	Breakfast biscuits, 2	20
Lebanese bread, 1 whole circle	57	Fruit juice, 1 cup	25	Breakfast cereal flakes, 1 cup	33
Scone or rock cake	25	Cherries, 10	5	Muesli, natural, 1 cup	65
Plain biscuit, sweet, 1	7	Mandarin, 2, medium	15	Porridge, 1 cup, cooked	20
Fruit cake, 1 slice, 50 g	28	Melon, 1 cup	11	Weeties, 1 cup	65
Raisin bread, 1 slice	15	Strawberries, 1 cup	4	Milk, 1 cup	15
Rice cake, 1	10	Sports drink, 1 cup	15	Flavoured milk, 300 mL	25
Rice, pasta, boiled, 1 cup	50	Soft drink, 1 cup	28	Yoghurt, plain, 1 tub, 200 mL	10
Sugar, lollies, glucose, 1 teaspoon, 5 g	4	Cordial, made up with water, 1 cup	17	Yoghurt, flavoured, 1 tub	25
Jam, 1 teaspoon, 5 g	7	Fruit drinks, 1 cup	30	Sustagen drinks, 1 cup, 250 mL	30
Honey, 1 teaspoon	11	Ice cream, 2 scoops	20	Lucozade, 1 cup, 250 mL	46
Chocolate, small bar, 50 g	30–40	Pizza, 1 slice	35	Meat pie, sausage roll (large)	33

Endurance

The basic principles of endurance sports such as long distance running, orienteering, swimming and games that take an hour or more is the reliance on a slow and steady release of blood glucose. The glucose used for endurance events mostly comes from a glucose store in the liver and muscles called glycogen. Glycogen molecules are made from glucose and stored with water. At full glycogen capacity, the liver contains about 600–800 grams of glycogen each stored with 3 grams of water. This store is a ready release form of glucose that goes directly from the liver into the bloodstream when blood glucose declines. Glycogen fuels the body's energy systems and keeps a ready supply of glucose and this prevents 'hitting the wall'. Many athletes report a complete physical collapse, dizziness, shaking, sweating, hunger and lack of energy during endurance events or training. This is a classic situation where blood glycogen stores have run out and the blood glucose level drops below normal. This low blood glucose or hypoglycaemia is common among athletes or sports people who have not eaten enough carbohydrate before training or before an endurance event. Some athletes train in the mornings or afternoons without having had a snack or drink and some train without breakfast. This sort of meal and snack skipping is a common cause of 'hitting the wall'. For this reason, sports people are advised to eat a high carbohydrate diet all the time in order to keep liver and muscle glycogen stores as full as possible. During endurance events, competitors are advised to eat or drink a practical, easy to consume source of glucose such as lollies, sports drinks or bananas.

Constant replenishment of carbohydrate will keep glycogen storage high and will prevent low blood glucose fatigue.

TABLE 7.15 Outline of some low, moderate and high GI foods

Low GI foods	GI	Moderate GI foods	GI	High GI foods	GI
Rye bread	50	Potato, mashed	70	Maltose	105
Porridge, cooked oats	49	Bread, wholemeal	70	Glucodin	102
Carrots, cooked	49	Bread, white	70	Glucose	100
Baked beans	48	Soft drinks	68	Sports drinks	95
Cake	47	Cordial, diluted	66	Honey, lamington	87
Fruit/raisin bread	47	Breakfast cereal, most types, e.g. Vita Brits, Nutri-Grain, Sustain	66–61	Rice cakes, jelly beans	82
Mixed grain bread	45	Table sugar, sucrose	65	Water crackers	78
Custard	43	Raisins	64	Weetbix, Coco Pops, Corn Flakes	75–77
Apricot, dried, orange, grapes	43	Potato, boiled Mars bar	62	Doughnut	76
Snickers bar	41	Icecream	61	Pumpkin	75
Pasta, white	41	Rice, white	59	Swede	72
Pasta, wholemeal	37	Muesli, natural	56	Watermelon	72
Apple, pear	36	Sweet corn kernels	55		
Milk, flavoured	34	Rice, brown	55		
Kidney beans, lentils	27	Sweet potato, potato chips, orange juice, banana	54		
Yoghurt, low fat	14				
Peanuts	14				

Weight control

Some sports such as rowing, dancing, gymnastics, wrestling and long distance running require a low body weight to create less of a load for the athlete to move. Weight control is generally important for all athletes, but weight control should not come at the expense of proper nutrition and carbohydrate intakes. Athletic performance is reduced when athletes try to lose weight by restrictive dieting. Many athletes lose weight and lose strength and endurance because they are not getting enough nutrition. Athletes should be encouraged to eat well in order to get enough carbohydrate and enough vitamins and minerals. In general, athletes who eat mostly carbohydrates and less fat, maintain an appropriate weight. Eating less fat, more carbohydrate and maintaining a regular training regimen is usually all that is required to keep at a healthy weight, although some athletes become very tired after a long day's training and fall asleep before they have eaten enough dinner. Weight loss and fatigue is common in this situation, where athletes don't get enough replenishing nutrition and enough rest and recovery.

Dehydration

Dehydration is the most common cause of poor sports performance and low endurance among all types of athletes and sports people. Dehydration is officially defined as the loss of 10 per cent or more of total body weight, and this may be easily monitored and detected by weighing participants before and after their training and endurance events. If they have lost 1–2 kilograms of total body weight, then they need to replenish this amount of water and glycogen stores. Unfortunately, once any level of dehydration has occurred, the poor performance has more than likely already occurred. Poor performance declines before the level of dehydration, so prevention of any degree of dehydration is one of the most important aspects of sports nutrition.

Loss of body fluid can be noticed in the symptoms of nausea, vomiting, headache, fainting, dizziness, cramps, profuse sweating or in later stages, reduced sweating culminating in shock. Dehydration is seriously life threatening, especially for children and most cases should be treated by giving intravenous solutions at a hospital or straight after long distance events. The best form of prevention for any degree of dehydration is to make students drink whether they are thirsty or not, because thirst follows dehydration. In other words, if your students are thirsty, then they are already dehydrated to some extent. To focus on the prevention of any level of dehydration for the purpose of improving sports performance, teachers and coaches should help students plan for morning or evening training sessions, away from the midday sun and heat.

Students need to plan to lose 500–1000 mL of water as sweat and breath per hour and this needs to be quickly replaced. Interestingly, the fittest people sweat more and their sweat is more dilute, indicating a training effect. In hot, humid climates, there will be greater sweat losses of around 1000–1200 mL per hour and again, these water losses need to be almost instantly replaced in order to prevent any level of dehydration or overheating. Intake of fluids needs to be enforced, as students will not take time out to drink unless they are told to do so. Participants should always drink 1–2 cups of water or sports drink before training or before long distance events. This first rehydrating drink should be followed by a half to 1 cup every 15 minutes during training or during the event. Finally, participants should drink at least 2 cups after training or after the event.

Students should be taught to monitor their production of urine after training and after endurance events to keep track of how much urine they produce and the colour of it. Students should produce some urine in the half hour following an event, and if not, they may be dehydrated. If the urine is dark yellow, rather than clear, then the student is dehydrated and needs to drink until their urine is clear. One of the B Group vitamins, riboflavin (B2) is bright yellow in colour, so this effect on urine should be excluded when trying to determine dehydration. In general, students should be taught to drink to a level that keeps their urine clear at all times. Sports drinks are suitable for the purpose of rehydrating students and preventing dehydration, and they are particularly useful because they taste good and students like to drink them more than plain water. Energy drinks and alcohol will only serve to further dehydrate sports people and athletes because alcohol and caffeine are diuretics. Alcohol worsens any sort of sports injury because it has a vasodilating effect, which increases the impact of any swelling after injury.

Bulking up

The type of muscle gain required in some sports, such as rugby, will only occur under the influence of testosterone and this point is an important one to make with adolescent boys. No amount of weight lifting or dietary supplementation will result in muscle gain without the male hormones. In fact the excess protein that is often consumed by boys in their attempts to gain weight is either used as fuel or stored as body fat, resulting in many boys overeating but gaining weight as fat rather than the desired muscle. Similarly, the amount of muscularity is mostly genetically determined, so some boys will simply never be able to bulk up if their male relatives are not naturally muscular. Protein supplementation is not required by athletes who are eating a good, mixed diet, because they only need about 0.75 grams of dietary protein per kilo of body weight. Very muscular men such as weightlifters and some endurance athletes need up to 1.2 grams per kilo of body weight, but again, this amount of protein can be easily obtained via a general Western diet. It is best for all types of athletes and sports people to choose low fat sources of protein such as low fat milk, lean meat, chicken and fish.

In those young men who are pubertally developed, whose voices have broken and whose testosterone levels are increased, moderate weight training and natural androgens (testosterone) will increase muscle size and bulk, but fads such as amino acids, protein formulas or creatine will not. Boys need to be kept away from heavy weights which are likely to cause shoulder injuries, knee injuries and hernias.

Fad diets for athletes

Low carbohydrate diets are the worst for athletes because they cause weight loss via the depletion of glycogen stores which, in conjunction with the three grams of water that each gram of glycogen is attached to, causes a weight loss of 2 kilograms or more almost overnight. This sort of extreme weight loss is attractive to some athletes who need to 'make weight' quickly, but it results in low blood glucose and hence, poor performance. In addition to lowering blood glucose levels and depletion of glycogen stores, low carbohydrate diets result in the body using muscle as a source of glucose, effectively causing the body to 'eat' its own muscle. This reduces 'weight' because muscle contains a lot of water and is heavy, but none of the weight loss is actually fat and the loss of carbohydrate and muscle mass significantly reduces sports performance. The Atkins diet, the Israeli Army diet and the Scarsdale diet are examples of these fad low carbohydrate diets.

Other diets and fads cause weight loss by inducing dehydration. Fad pills and potions often contain caffeine which causes weight loss via diuresis and increased urination. In some sports, caffeine is still a banned substance, so competitors need to be very careful about the consumption of this common ingredient in so-called weight loss formulas.

Fad diet products like fat metabolisers do not exist and are just exploitative marketing tactics. Other fad products or herbal products may contain banned substances so athletes need to be warned about taking any sort of supplement.

Weight control is an important issue for most sports people, and one phenomenon that needs attention is the sort of huge weight gain that can occur when athletes are injured or inactive during the non-competitive off season. Athletes do not need their usual intake of food when they are not burning it off during training sessions, so they need to monitor their intake in order to avoid this common form of weight gain. Another very important issue for weight control is the use of alcohol, which can be very fattening.

Important nutrients for athletes

Iron is an extremely important mineral for sports people because it is required to form the structure of haemoglobin, the oxygen-carrying protein in red blood cells. Iron is particularly important in the diets of women athletes and girls, as they lose iron regularly during the menstrual cycle. The high impact sports such as road running and gymnastics may cause damage and injury to red blood cells and this may explain the iron losses and the high iron needs of some athletes. Vegetarian athletes need special dietary attention to iron and calcium and some may need iron injections.

Calcium is another important mineral for athletes and sports people, as this mineral is required to replenish bone density. Growing teenagers need huge amounts of calcium (see Table 7.5 and Table 7.7) because their bones are growing in length as well as in density. Female athletes often develop osteoporosis because of poor dietary calcium intakes combined with the bone weakening effects of low oestrogen caused by loss of too much body fat. This set of conditions is known as the 'female athlete triad' where there is a combination of low body weight or low body fat (causing low oestrogen and amenorrhoea), eating disorders and osteoporosis in females. Teachers and coaches need to watch out for any sort of weight loss in girls or women athletes and body image concerns or eating disorders need early intervention from a dietitian, doctor or counsellor. The loss of bone density resulting from the female athlete triad is largely irreplaceable in young women, making them susceptible to bone fractures and osteoporosis for life.

Another important issue for teachers and coaches to stay aware of is that of steroid abuse in males. The effect of steroids in growing adolescents is disastrous. Steroid intake stops the growth of bone plates in adolescents that causes height stunting. It also causes aggression ('roid rage'), results in very bad acne (especially on the back) and causes testicular shrinkage, cancer, kidney damage, very high blood pressure and high blood cholesterol. Steroids are illegal drugs that are far too dangerous for teenagers and young men to play around with and teachers and coaches need to make this clear.

Sound sports nutrition and adequate rehydration have a huge impact on sports performance and endurance and this has been known for many decades. Sports enhancing activities are based on two main nutrition principles: obtaining large amounts of carbohydrates for the production of energy from glucose as well as the prevention of any level of dehydration. Nutrition and rehydration account for huge gains in sports performance and endurance and the fad diets, fad pills and potions account for minute gains if any at all. Most fads have adverse effects such as inadvertent dehydration.

Teaching nutrition in a positive way

Food and nutrition are very interesting and relevant topics for students of all ages, but all too often this material is taught in a very negative way. Teachers often focus on telling students what *not* to eat rather than encouraging them to enjoy healthy options. This sort of approach is a very negative and unnecessarily narrow approach to nutrition education because the key components of human nutrition are balance, variety and moderation. In this regard, there is no one food that cannot be included in a balanced diet. Teachers need to approach the topic of nutrition education using the 'balance, variety, moderation' messages in a consistent manner.

When talking about the many benefits of food and nutrition for children and adolescents, teachers should first ask their students what benefits they actually derive from healthy eating. Questions similar to those asked in my national survey mentioned earlier in this chapter are highly suitable for this purpose. For example, ask your students, what do you think healthy eating can do for you? How does eating healthy make you feel? Physically? Mentally? How do you feel when you eat healthy foods compared to when you choose not so healthy options?

The list of student answers will surprise you, as it did me in my research focus groups (O'Dea, 2003a). Students in Year 6 and above are likely to be able to clearly articulate the many varied benefits of healthy eating and the teacher can use this in class to establish personal relevance and student interest in the topic. These survey questions also make a useful guide for teachers who want to approach this topic by having students undertake a school research survey. Results can then be compared with the national study of school children conducted all around Australia in 2000.

The message about food, nutrition, growth and health is that these issues go hand in hand among growing children and adolescents. We need nutritious foods and drinks in order to grow to our full potential. When teaching about growth and development, take every opportunity to reinforce healthy eating messages and vice versa. Students then learn that general health covers many different aspects. It is important to focus on the positive aspects of growth and development and the positive outcomes of healthy eating. For example students can monitor changes in their height to learn about their own growth, but not necessarily focus on their weight, especially if students are sensitive. A very important message for teachers to give to students of all ages is that weight and height are expected to increase with growth. Similarly, teachers can reinforce the message that everybody is different and that children with a muscular body build are likely to have a heavier weight and BMI, particularly if they also tend to be short. Explain that these students are not overweight, but that their weight is composed of more muscle than others.

A prime target for nutrition education is to always keep the focus of food and nutrition lessons positive rather than negative, critical or blaming. I encourage teachers not to use the term 'junk' food as it simply creates blame and guilt.

I especially encourage teachers to shy away from lessons that are simply based on the so called 'bad' components of food, without presenting a more balanced argument for the inclusion of all foods in a healthy, balanced and enjoyable diet. For example, avoid lessons that simply focus on the 'bad' sugar and fat content of food.

Teachers can educate students, as well as promote the nutritional benefits and enjoyment of healthy foods. For example, have students enjoy tasting low fat flavoured milks, yoghurts and custards rather than focus on the fat content of whole milk. Involve real foods as much as possible by simply getting children and adolescents to try new foods as this is often the greatest barrier to getting them eating healthy options. Having regular 'taste tests' is a fun and enjoyable way to teach about food and nutrition.

Probably the most important point to note in the implementation of a positive approach to teaching food and nutrition is for teachers to avoid reference to 'good' or 'bad' foods. It is no coincidence that young women and men secretly 'pig out' on 'bad' or forbidden foods like cakes, biscuits, ice cream and chocolates when they have been repeatedly told to deny themselves these 'evil' indulgences. Teachers can do much to help students enjoy and respect their food intake with a healthy attitude to foods. Teachers should never miss an opportunity to reinforce the sound nutrition themes of variety, balance and moderation.

Teaching nutrition with some sort of practical food-oriented approach is vital to helping students learn sound eating habits. Teachers can encourage the preparation and enjoyment of quick and simple healthy foods and snacks. Talking about food is often much more meaningful and realistic than talking about nutrients, especially if you are only going to be able to spend a few lessons on this topic.

Another aspect of teaching nutrition in a positive way is educating students about food in other cultures and celebrating and reinforcing the diversity of foods and recipes in Australia. Teachers can implement a unit of work about multicultural food habits in many different ways. These food and nutrition activities can include recipes from families, visits to supermarkets or shopping trips to specialist food stores such as Asian grocery stores. Visits to restaurants or food processing plants are always very popular with students and parents. Having school food days is a popular way to educate students about the positive aspects of human diversity and diversity of cultures. This is a great way to involve students, teachers, parents and the local community.

When planning programs and units of work, try coupling lessons with inter school departments or try combining the related topics of growth, development, food, nutrition, health, culture and practicalities of managing your lifestyle. For example, teachers can design cross-curricular activities on growth and development with self-esteem building lessons about students' diversity, uniqueness, individual differences, individual interests and talents, self-acceptance and tolerance of others.

When discussing body image issues and eating habits, student discussion can focus on the basic issue of prejudices and why prejudice is unacceptable in our society.

Following is a summary list of teaching tips about how to combine curricula, involve other teaching departments and implement a positive, holistic approach to teaching about health issues.

Some tips for teaching food, nutrition, growth and health in a positive, non blaming, non shaming way:

- Keep the focus of food and nutrition lessons positive rather than negative, critical or blaming.
- Remember to talk about food as well as nutrients. Discuss the practical and relevant aspects of foods as well as the theoretical aspects of nutrients.
- Do not use the term 'junk' food—it simply creates blame and guilt.
- Avoid focusing on the sugar and fat content of food; focus on the positive benefits of healthy food choices instead.
- Promote the nutritional benefits of foods and the enjoyment of healthy foods. For example, have students enjoy tasting healthy foods rather than focus on the fat content of 'unhealthy' foods.
- Taste tests of fruits and vegetables are a fun way to introduce students to healthy eating.
- Never refer to 'good' or 'bad' foods. Reinforce the major nutrition themes of variety, balance and moderation.
- Don't make negative comments about your own weight, your diet or your poor eating habits. Try to be a sensible role model.
- Try to be seen choosing and enjoying healthy options from your school canteen.
- Encourage students to become involved in the preparation and enjoyment of healthy foods and snacks at school and home.
- Focus on what students can enjoy rather than what they should avoid.
- Couple lessons or design cross-curricular activities on growth and development, food and nutrition with body image and self-esteem building lessons about students' diversity, uniqueness, individual differences, individual interests and talents, self-acceptance and tolerance of others.
- Focus on positive messages such as expected body changes, enjoyment of foods and the benefits of physical growth and development for both boys and girls; for example, strength, skills development, abilities.
- Focus on the positive aspects of growth and development, for example, monitor changes in height but not necessarily weight.
- Explain that weight and height and appetite are expected to increase with growth. Growing, pubertal adolescents will have voracious appetites and they need to know that this is normal.
- Encourage some non competitive, collaborative physical activity using various games and skill development.
- Focus on self-competence and personal achievements rather than competitive results.
- Children with a muscular body build are likely to have a heavier weight and BMI, particularly if they also tend to be short. Explain that these students are not overweight, but that their weight is composed of more muscle than others.

- Reinforce that being physically active is healthy at any size or shape and that movement can be undertaken in many different types of activities.
- Reinforce the idea that students should enjoy their physical activities so that they can continue to enjoy some aspect of fitness and movement for life.
- Encourage students to enjoy cooking.
- Don't forget to include the boys—they are interested in nutrition, cookery and body image and they are sensitive about their bodies too!

Food and nutrition lessons and activities

Activity 1	Introduction to the five food groups
Activity 2	Introduction to the healthy eating pyramid
Activity 3	Blindfold taste tests
Activity 4	Introduction to nutrients—the nutrient matching game
Activity 5	Food diary and self-assessment of food group servings using food charts of dietary fibre, protein, calcium and iron
Activity 6	What are the factors that affect food habits?
Activity 7	How to read a food or drink label. What's in packaged foods?
Activity 8	Vegetarian diets—plan a menu for a vegetarian teenager
Activity 9	Fad diet detective
Activity 10	Evaluating fad diets
Activity 11	Design a fad diet
Activity 12	Nutritional pursuit
Activity 13	Sports nutrition case studies
Activity 14	Sports nutrition word puzzle
Activity 15	Foods and nutrition word puzzle

Summary

Food and nutrition are very interesting and relevant topics for students of all ages, but all too often this material is taught in a very negative way. Teachers often focus on telling students what *not* to eat rather than encouraging them to enjoy healthy options. This sort of approach is a very negative and unnecessarily narrow approach to nutrition education because the key components of human nutrition are balance, variety and moderation. In this regard, there is no one food that cannot be included in a balanced diet. Teachers need to approach the topic of nutrition education using the 'balance, variety, moderation' messages in a consistent manner.

This chapter has outlined how teachers can include facts about growth and development and also reinforce healthy eating messages and vice versa so that students learn that general health covers many different aspects. It is important to focus on the positive aspects of growth and development and the positive outcomes of healthy eating. For example students can monitor changes in their height to learn about their own growth, but not necessarily focus on their weight, especially if students are sensitive. A very important message for teachers to give to students of all ages is that weight and height are expected to increase with growth. Similarly, teachers can reinforce the message that everybody is different.

A prime target for nutrition education is to always keep the focus of food and nutrition lessons positive rather than negative, critical or blaming. In this chapter, I have outlined why I encourage teachers not to use the term 'junk' food or emphasise the 'bad' components of food, without presenting a more balanced argument for the inclusion of all foods in a healthy, balanced and enjoyable diet.

Teachers can educate students as well as promote and reinforce the nutritional benefits of foods and the enjoyment of healthy foods using practical applications such as taste tests, basic cookery, investigations of foods from different cultures, label reading and product analyses.

Recommended websites

http://www.nutritionaustralia.org

Nutrition Australia (formerly the Australian Nutrition Foundation) is a non-government, non-profit, community-based organisation. Nutrition Australia is an independent body that aims to promote the health and wellbeing of all Australians. The website provides lots of nutrition information, resources and recipes and is an excellent resource for students and teachers.

http://www.healthinsite.gov.au/topics/Food_and_Nutrition

This is the website for the Australian Commonwealth Government information service and it contains a lot of sound and reliable nutrition information.

http://www.csiro.au/csiro/channel/ich2k.htmL

This CSIRO website provides information about food, nutrition, research, diets, events, resources, fact sheets and the latest diet and nutrition news.

http://www.daa.asn.au/index.asp?pageID=2145841683

This is the website for the Dietitians Association of Australia. The website contains information about food, nutrition and health as well as information about careers in food and nutrition and it is an excellent resource for students and teachers.

http://info.library.unsw.edu.au/biomed/guides/foodpol/foodpolpol.htmL

This is the website of the University of NSW Food Technology Library and it provides information about food and nutrition, food policy guidelines and other useful food and nutrition related documents.

References

National Health and Medical Research Council (2006), Executive Summary of Nutrient Reference Values for Australia and New Zealand Including Recommended Dietary Intakes. Commonwealth Department of Health and Ageing, Australia and Ministry of Health, New Zealand. Available at: http://www.nhmrc.gov.au/publications/synopses/n35syn.htm

O'Dea J (2003a), 'Why do kids eat healthful food? Perceived benefits of and barriers to healthful eating and physical activity among children and adolescents', *Journal of the American Dietetic Association, 103*, 497–501.

O'Dea J (2003b), 'Differences in overweight and obesity among Australian schoolchildren of low and middle/high socioeconomic status', *The Medical Journal of Australia 179*(1), 63.

O'Dea JA (2003c), 'Consumption of nutritional supplements among adolescents: usage and perceived benefits', *Health Education Research, 18*(1), 98–107.

O'Dea J & Rawstorne P (2000), 'Consumption of dietary supplements and energy drinks by schoolchildren', (Letter) *Medical Journal of Australia, 173*, 389.

Activity 1 Introduction to the five food groups

- In this lesson students expand their knowledge of many different foods, including foods from different cultures and different ethnic foods.
- Students are asked to name the five food groups.
- Students are then divided into five groups representing each food group.
- Each group is given a large piece of cardboard and coloured pens on which they write as many foods from their food group as they can think of. The group task is to think of more foods than any other of the groups.
- Encourage students to include foods from different cultures and ethnic cuisines. Students should count the number of different foods they come up with at the end of the brainstorming session.
- Each group presents their food group poster to the rest of the class.
- End this lesson with a tasting of some unusual fruits or vegetables such as starfruit, pomegranate, persimmon, tangelo, tamarillo, custard apple, capsicum, broccolini or snow peas. Encourage students to try new foods from different cultures or ethnic groups.
- Follow up this activity with students bringing in different foods to taste, especially foods from different cultural cuisines and different ethnic groups.
- Students can also report on how the food is grown and how it is prepared and cooked.
- Some parents may be pleased to be invited to participate in helping with this activity.
- Students can also be given homework or a personal research project investigating foods and recipes from different culture or ethnic cuisines.
- Another excellent research project is to have students investigate foods for religious days or religious/cultural festivals.
- Students learn that our food choices are influenced by many different social, cultural, psychological and physical factors.

Activity 1 Introduction to the five food groups

- Teacher uses the list of foods below to prompt students.

Fruits	Meats and meat substitutes	Milk and dairy	Bread and cereals	Vegetables
Blueberry	Beef	Milk	Breads	Artichoke
Mulberry	Lamb	Powdered milk	Bread roll	Asparagus
Raspberry	Pork	Evaporated	Lebanese bread	Avocado
Strawberry	Veal	milk	Pita bread	Beans, legumes
Grapefruit	Fish	Condensed	Crumpet	Bean sprouts
Lemon	Chicken/turkey	milk	English muffin	Bamboo shoots
Mandarin	Duck/quail	Cheese—	Crackers	Broccoli
Orange	Rabbit	(Different	Naan	Brussels sprout
Tangelo	Lobster, yabbies	types can be	Crispbread	Cabbages
Apricot	Bacon/ham	listed, e.g.	Chapatti	Capsicums
Cherry	Sausages	brie, cheddar,	Pancakes	Carrot
Date	Liver	cottage, ricotta,	Lasagne	Cassava
Nectarine	Kidneys	edam, swiss,	Noodles	Cauliflower
Peach	Brains	romano, feta,	Scones	Celery
Apple	Tripe	mozzarella,	Cereals	Turnips
Plum	Tongue	quark,	Weetbix	Champignon
Grapes	Corned beef	jarlsberg,	Vita brits	Chilli
Banana	Frankfurt	camembert,	Muesli	Choko
Currants	Venison	blue vein,	Barley	Cucumber
Sultanas	Eggs	parmesan,	Wheat bran	Eggplant
Figs	Salami	Cheshire,	Oats	Marrow
Guava	Mortadella	gouda, etc.)	Porridge	Bok choy
Melons	Brawn	Yoghurt	Rice	Mushrooms
Pomegranate	Nuts/seeds	Custard	Pasta	Onions
Pear	Devon	Buttermilk	Bulgur	Peas, lentils
Pineapple	Fritz	Cream cheese	Polenta	Potatoes
Quince	Kabana	Ice cream	Wheatgerm	Parsley
Lychee	Polish sausage	Mousse	Semolina	Herbs
Rhubarb	Liverwurst	Fruche	Couscous	Pumpkins
Passionfruit	Pate	Ricecream	Arrowroot	Shallots
Pawpaw	Spam	Junket	Corn flour	Spinach
Mango	Shellfish, crab	Milo	Rice flour	Yams
Loquat	Fish paste	Ovaltine	Rye flour	Zucchini
Cumquat	Sardines	Hot chocolate	Pappadums	Corn
Kiwifruit	Oysters			Taro
Jackfruit	Squid			Tomatoes
Honeydew	Prawns			Parsnips
Starfruit	Tofu			Tapioca
	Peanut butter			

Activity 2 Introduction to the healthy eating pyramid

Teacher's notes

- This lesson is designed to build upon the previous lesson about food groups and show students how the healthy eating pyramid consists of all of the five food groups (fruit; vegetables; milk and dairy; meats, eggs and nuts; breads and cereals) in the correct proportions.

- It is important to note that foods from all different cultures and ethnic cuisines will fit into the healthy eating pyramid.

- Students are reminded of their five food groups posters, which are put up on the wall as a reference.

- Each pair of students draws a blank copy of the pyramid on paper with blank ✗ and ✓ boxes.

- Students guess where each food group fits on the pyramid.

- Students are asked to report why the food groups are placed where they are.

- Students are asked to write on their pyramid examples of the 'extras' or 'eat in small amounts' foods such as lollies, chips, soft drinks, chocolates, butter, ghee, lard, margarines, oils, cream, sugar, alcohol (for adults), biscuits, snack foods, snack biscuits, cakes, muesli bars, pastries, cordial, etc.

- The message in this lesson is that all foods can have a place in a healthy and enjoyable diet, but some are needed every day and some are only occasional foods. Too much of any one food or drink is also unhealthy.

- I prefer not to use the term 'junk' food as it is a very negative term with great potential to inaccurately label some perfectly nutritious foods as 'junk' just because they come in a package or they contain sugar.

- Examples of some foods that are mistakenly labelled as 'junk' are custards, ice cream, milk desserts, flavoured milks and yoghurts. These foods are nutritious for children and adolescents who are growing and need a lot of kilojoules and high intakes of calcium.

- I prefer to call the 'eat least' foods 'extras' or 'sometimes foods' or 'occasional foods' and I think this is a more positive, sensible and accurate message to give students.

- Remind students about where salt and water fit in a healthy diet and remind them about the need for daily physical activity!

Reproduced with the permission of
the Australian Nutrition Foundation Inc.

Activity 2 Five food groups and healthy eating pyramid

Names ....

- Work in pairs to complete the pyramid puzzle

- List the five food groups ....

- Where does each food group go in the healthy eating pyramid?

_____

_____

_____

- List as many foods and drinks as possible that go in the 'eat in small amounts' section of the pyramid.

_____

_____

- List five reasons why these foods and drinks are to be only eaten sometimes in small amounts and not every day.

1 _____

2 _____

3 _____

4 _____

5 _____

- Which food or drink goes in the ✗ box and why?

_____

_____

- Which food or drink goes in the ✓ box and why?

_____

_____

Activity 2 Five food groups and healthy eating pyramid

Teacher's answers

- List the five food groups

  Fruit; vegetables; milk and dairy; meats, eggs and nuts; breads and cereals

- Where does each food group go in the healthy eating pyramid?
  See Figure 7.1.

- List as many foods and drinks as possible that go in the 'eat in small amounts' section of the pyramid.
  Lollies, cakes, biscuits, chocolate bars, chips, soft drinks, energy drinks, sports drinks, cordial, corn chips, chocolates, butter, ghee, lard, margarines, oils, cream, sugar, alcohol (for adults), snack foods, snack biscuits, muesli bars, energy bars, fruit and nut bars, pastries.

- List five reasons why these foods and drinks are to be only eaten sometimes in small amounts and not every day.
  1 They usually contain sugar which causes tooth decay.
  2 They can contain a lot of sodium which contributes to high blood pressure.
  3 They do not contain significant amounts of protein, vitamins, minerals.
  4 They may reduce the appetite and displace more nutritious foods.
  5 They provide extra kilojoules which can add to weight gain.
  6 They train our taste buds to like only sugary or salty flavours.
  7 They can be expensive compared to more nutritious snacks.
  8 They are occasional foods, but not every day foods!

- Which food or drink goes in the ✗ box and why?
  Salt (sodium chloride), because it may promote high blood pressure, especially among people with a family history of high blood pressure (hypertension).

- Which food or drink goes in the ✓ box and why?
  Water because it is an essential nutrient; we need about 2 litres per day; in many places it contains fluoride which prevents tooth decay; it is free.

Activity 3 Blindfold taste tests

- This activity involves students in tasting different foods in a fun way.
- Teacher and students need to wash their hands or use anti-bacterial hand wipes.
- The teacher prepares for the lesson by cutting up small pieces of different fruits and vegetables. Suitable choices are grapes, oranges, mandarins, carrot, celery and different coloured capsicums (bell peppers).
- It may be advisable to check up on any student allergies first.
- The food pieces are kept in separate containers, well hidden and secret from the students.
- You will also need some paper towels and two or three sets of food tongs.
- A student volunteers to be the first to try the blindfold taste test and after being given a blindfold, the student is given a piece or fruit or vegetable to taste. The teacher demonstrates using food tongs as this is most hygienic.
- Teacher asks—Is it a fruit or vegetable? Is it cooked or raw?
- Do you like it? Do you know what colour it is?
- Can you tell us what it is?
- This activity works well with the three different coloured capsicums (green, red and yellow) as blindfolded students often identify the green capsicum as red and vice versa.
- Students are now divided into pairs and each is given a blindfold. This can be made out of strips of cloth or an old tie. Any type of blindfold will do.
- When the first of the student pairs is blindfolded, the teacher brings out the first set of foods for tasting and the other student collects two pieces of fruit or vegetable from the teacher's collection using food tongs and a piece of clean paper towel.
- When it is the other student's turn to do the blindfold taste test, the teacher lets them choose from a different collection of foods.
- Students take it in turns to taste and guess the different types of food.
- Lesson ends by all students having a taste of some other type of fruit or vegetable such as those from different cultural or ethnic groups.
- Good choices for this would be some of the unusual tropical fruits and vegetables such as papaya, starfruit, custard apples, yams, cassava.
- An extension of this activity would be a visit to a local farm or market to allow students to identify different types of fruits and vegetables and learn about where they are produced, how they are grown and how they are cooked and prepared.
- The focus of this activity is to encourage students to overcome their 'food neo-phobia' (fear of new foods) in a fun activity.

Activity 4 Introduction to nutrients—the nutrient matching game

Nutrients in human nutrition

- This activity helps students to identify major macronutrients (protein, fats, carbohydrates, water); micronutrients (vitamins and minerals) and their functions.

- The teacher will need to photocopy 12 sets of the 'Nutrient matching game' cards on coloured pieces of paper, cut them up into nutrients cards, clue cards and food group cards and place all of the pieces in an envelope. They will need to be enlarged.

- The same preparation is done for the 'Food groups and nutrients puzzle'.

- Students are divided into pairs and are given an envelope.

- They are instructed to match the correct nutrient with its description and function and then match it with the foods in which it is found.

- Teacher goes through correct answers using the answer sheet and reinforces that different food groups are required because they provide different nutrients.

- Students are asked to place the nutrients which are provided by this food group.

- Final message is that we need to eat from all five food groups every day in order to get a variety of all nutrients.

- Also, point out that alcohol provides no nutrients at all, but it does provide kilojoules and it is fattening.

- All foods and drinks provide some water.

- If the teacher chooses not to use the 'Food groups and nutrients puzzle' in class, students can investigate for homework, as a project, or as a group quick quiz in class, the other scientific names of the vitamins, e.g. vitamin C is ascorbic acid.

- Answers are given on the game and puzzle pages (before the photcopies are cut up).

Activity 4 Nutrient matching game

Fibre	I am not found in any animal foods. If you eat me and drink lots of fluids, I can help prevent constipation.	Wholemeal bread, breakfast cereals, fruit and vegetables
Protein	Builds and repairs all of your body tissues. Essential for growth.	Meats, cereals, eggs, nuts and milk
Carbohydrate	Gives you energy. I can be simple or complex (nobody understands me!)	Breads and cereals, vegetables (complex), fruits (sugars (simple))
Fats	Provides energy. Essential in the diet yet most people eat too much of me.	Just about everywhere, especially in chips, pies, fried and fast foods
Alcohol	Provides energy, but no nutrients. Dangerous in large amounts. Have too much of me and I can help you to embarrass yourself!	Beer, wine, spirits
Vitamin A	Soluble in fats. Helps you to see in the dark. Also called carotene.	Green and orange fruits and vegetables
B group vitamins	Soluble in water. Helps you to use the energy from your food.	Bread, cereals, fruits and Vegemite
Iron	Helps to transport oxygen in your blood. Prevents anaemia. I am required for muscle growth in girls and boys.	Red meat, eggs, green leafy vegetables
Calcium	Building block of your bones and teeth.	Milk, dairy products, dark green vegetables
Vitamin C	Soluble in water. Helps iron absorption. Sailors were very grateful when I was discovered in lemons and limes.	Fruits and vegetables, particularly citrus fruits
Vitamin D	Soluble in fats. Manufactured in the body from cholesterol and sunlight. Helps bone strength.	Milk and dairy foods
Vitamin E	Soluble in fats. Required for cell reproduction and I am often called the 'anti sterility factor'. I am an antioxidant which means I stop body cells being damaged.	Wholegrain breads and cereals, vegetables, fruits and oils
Vitamin K	Soluble in fats. Can be made inside the intestines. I help blood to clot so that you don't bleed to death.	Fruits and vegetables
Water	The most vital nutrient of all. You cannot survive for longer than three days without me.	Fruits, vegetables, drinks
Zinc	I am mostly found in animal foods. Vegetarians find it hard to get enough of me. I am required for wound healing and growth.	Meats, eggs, milk, nuts

Activity 4 Food groups and nutrients puzzle

Fruits	Vegetables	Breads and Cereals	Meat, eggs, nuts	Milk and dairy
Vitamin C (also called ascorbic acid)	Vitamin C	B Group vitamins (Thiamin B1, Riboflavin B2, Niacin B3)	Protein	Protein
Vitamin A in orange fruits and orange juices	Vitamin A (also called carotene) in orange vegies and leafy green vegies	Iron	Iron	Calcium
Folic acid (also called folate, folacin)	Folic acid (also called folate, folacin)	Carbohydrates	Zinc	Zinc
Dietary fibre	Dietary fibre	Dietary fibre, mainly in wholemeal bread or wholegrain cereals like brown rice	Fats—a mixture of fats, but can contain saturated fats	Vitamin A (also called retinol) Vitamin D (also called calciferol)
Carbohydrates as 'fruit sugar' also called fructose	Carbohydrates as starch such as potato, sweet potato, pumpkin	Fats—mostly healthy polyunsaturated fats	Water (H_2O)	Riboflavin (vitamin B2)
Water (H_2O)	Vitamin E (also called tocopherol) in leafy greens	Vitamin E (also called tocopherol) in wholegrains		Water (H_2O)
	Vitamin K (also called menadione or menaquinone)	Water (H_2O)		
	Water (H_2O)			

Activity 5 Food diary and self-assessment of food group servings using food charts of dietary fibre, protein, calcium and iron

Examination of factors affecting food choices

- This lesson can be delivered as two or three periods or given as an assignment or personal research study.
- Students are each given a copy of the food diary and asked to write their name on it and today's date.
- They begin the diary from the time they woke up this morning.
- They write down everything they eat and drink today and stop recording when they go to sleep tonight.
- Do not allow students to focus on how much they eat as this may be a negative way of approaching this lesson.
- The food diary is a useful tool in helping students to observe their own eating habits, how their eating habits are influenced by where they were, who they were with, when they were eating and their emotions at the time.
- Teacher makes copies of the food charts for dietary fibre, protein, calcium and iron in Tables 7.6, 7.7, 7.8 and 7.9. It is a good idea to make several class sets of these information charts and have them laminated if possible. Otherwise, paste them onto cardboard so that you can use them again in Activity 7 where students will need to use the food charts to plan a menu for a vegetarian teenager.
- Students assess whether or not they have consumed enough from the five food groups and enough from each of the nutrient groups—fibre, protein, calcium and iron.

Activity 5 My food diary

Name   Day   Date

Time	Place	What I ate or drank	How much I ate or drank	What I was doing	How I was feeling
Example: 7.30 am	Example: home at kitchen table	Example: Toast	Example: 1 slice	Example: watching TV	Example: tired, bored, angry, happy etc
Example	" "	Example: Butter	Example: 1 teaspoon	" "	" "
Example	" "	Example: Jam, strawberry	Example: 2 teaspoons	" "	" "
Example	" "	Example: Milk, Lite White	Example: 1 cup	" "	" "
Example	" "	Example: Milo	Example: 2 teaspoons	" "	" "
Example	" "	Example: Sugar	Example: 1 teaspoon	" "	" "

Activity 5 My food diary

Name   Day   Date

Time	Place	What I ate or drank	How much I ate or drank	What I was doing	How I was feeling

Activity 6 What are the factors that affect food habits?

- Students refer to their diaries and comment on how different cultural foods or cultural food habits may have affected their food choices.
- Students are also asked to comment on the different factors that influenced their eating habits on the day they kept their diary.
- Teacher asks 'Do you think where you were and who you were with influenced what you ate or drank?'
- 'How did your feelings affect what you ate or drank?'
- 'Did you eat more (or less) when you were bored, tired, upset, lonely, angry or stressed?'
- Students brainstorm all of the factors affecting food choices and food habits on the board.
- Teacher summarises all of the factors affecting food habits using the summary chart as an overhead or handout. What are the factors that affect food habits?
- Students comment on how their diet could be made more nutritious as well as more delicious.
- **Social factors**—time, work requirements, convenience, who you live with, who cooks and shops for you, what other people like to eat and drink, peer pressure, where you meet your friends, what is available, prestige, e.g. drinking only Perrier, obligation—someone wants you to eat it, advertising, marketing, lifestyle.
- **Cultural factors**—cultural norms and cultural food patterns, availability of different foods and different cuisines from different cultures, e.g. Thai food is commonly available in Australia. Different imported foods are available.
- **Physiological factors**—hunger, thirst, taste, individual likes and dislikes, allergies, adverse reactions to certain foods, past experience with certain foods, e.g. 'I always feel bad after eating ...'
- **Psychological factors**—mood, boredom, eating or drinking in response to stress, curiosity, body image concerns, rewarding yourself with food or drink, eating to please others, food beliefs and attitudes, bad past experiences with certain foods or drinks. We are all susceptible to media and food advertising.
- **Economic factors**—price, available income to spend on food, time costs, price of food is influenced by marketing costs, packaging costs, transport and distribution costs—the price of petrol is passed on to the consumer. Some governments tax foods quite highly.
- **Religious factors**—some religions require a vegetarian diet, e.g. Seventh Day Adventists recommend a lacto-ovo diet, Buddhists and Hindus are vegetarian. Judaism, Islam and other religions have food rules, taboo foods and special foods on religious holidays. Festivals include Christmas, Ramadan, Hannukah, Chinese New Year.
- **Environmental**—availability in certain areas may be low if transport is not available, refrigeration may not be available, crops may be destroyed by fire, flood, cyclones, drought, pests (e.g. locust plagues).
- **Political**—food production practices may encourage production of cash crops rather than food, e.g. coffee, sugar, tobacco, opium. War reduces the production, availability and distribution of foods. Food is often redirected to the army. Aid agencies may provide food or emergency relief.

Activity 7 How to read a food or drink label. What's in packaged foods?

- In this activity students learn to identify the information on a food or drink label and they learn how to interpret the information. The information is outlined on pages 169–171.
- Students are asked to bring in empty food packages, cans, drink bottles, wrappers or any kind of food or drink label.
- Teacher can also collect a box full of empty packages and food labels to keep as teaching resources for this lesson.
- Teacher uses an overhead or handout of the blank 'How to read a food or drink label' diagram.
- Teacher gives students a copy of the blank diagram and asks the class, pairs or groups to fill in the gaps in the diagram and answer the questions.
- Students may do this in pairs or small groups using the food packages to get clues about the required information on a food label.
- Questions for the students include: What are some common names for sugar that are used on a food label? What are some common names for fat? What are some common names for salt?
- Students report back to the whole group with information about their food label and the product contained in it.
- An extension of this lesson, especially suited to senior students or assignment work, is to take students on a supermarket tour where they practise reading different food labels.
- The label reading activity can be ended with the class participating in a food tasting of a new food product such as a fruit bread with different types of margarine or spread.
- A 'mini supermarket' taste test can be set up in class with groups of students each given responsibility for bringing in different types of foods for tasting, e.g. dairy foods, biscuits, crackers, cakes, cereals etc.

Activity 7 How to read a food or drink label

Yummy
Scrummy
Food

1 What are the three major ingredients in your food product?

2 Can you identify some other names for sugar, fat or salt on your label?

3 What percentage of your product is carbohydrate, protein and fat?

Activity 7 How to read a food or drink label

Teacher's answer sheet

Other claim, e.g. 'lite' or natural

Allergy warning

Dietary claims, e.g. low fat

Ingredient list

Storage instructions

Barcode

Product of Australia, NZ or other country

Name and address of manufacturer

Net weight

Description or name of food

Yummy Scrummy Food

Country of origin

Use by or Best before date

Nutrition panel

1	What are the three major ingredients in your food product?	The three ingredients listed first are the major components of the food or drink. Ingredients are listed in order by weight, so the first three ingredients are the heaviest and form the major part of the product.
2	Can you identify some other names for sugar, fat or salt on your label?	**Sugar**—sucrose, glucose, maltose, dextrose, fructose, honey, syrup, lactose, high fructose corn syrup, maltodextrin, molasses, invert sugar. **Fat**—lipids, oil, vegetable oil, lard, dripping, tallow, margarine, shortening, hydrogenated vegetable oil. **Salt**—sodium chloride, sodium bicarbonate, seasoning.
3	What percentage of your product is carbohydrate, protein and fat?	The proportion of carbohydrate (sugars and complex), protein and fats are listed as a percentage of grams per 100 g of food by weight. Fats may be divided into saturated, monounsaturated, polyunsaturated or trans fatty acids.

Activity 8 Vegetarian diets—plan a menu for a vegetarian teenager

- Each pair or group of students is given a copy of the vegetarian diets handout (Tables 7.11 and 7.12), the calcium, iron, fibre and protein food tables (Tables 7.6, 7.7, 7.8 and 7.9) and a copy of the 'Advise a teen vego' case studies.
- Class sets of the food tables and case studies are laminated or pasted onto cardboard.
- Students work in pairs or small groups and are asked to give advice to one of the following vegetarian teenagers, Zac, Melanie or Max.
- Students finish this activity by planning a day's menu for him or her. The menu should be varied, interesting, nutritious and delicious!

Activity 8 Advise a teen vego

Each of these teenage vegetarians is in need of dietary advice. Can you advise them?

- **Zac**—is a 13-year-old boy who plays soccer three afternoons a week and competes in matches on a Saturday. Zac dislikes tomatoes, strawberries, milk and peanut butter. He is a lacto-ovo vegetarian as are the rest of his family. Zac has just started getting facial and underarm hair. Zac is tired of the sausage sizzle at soccer every weekend (mainly because he doesn't eat sausages so he has to eat a boring old bun with sauce and onions!) and he is trying to think of new things to take instead—can you advise him?

- **Melanie**—is a 15-year-old lacto-ovo vegetarian who likes to dance, swim and go horse riding. She has just decided to be vegetarian after she saw a documentary about how raising animals can affect the environment. She was particularly opposed to the idea that large areas of land are required to be cleared in order to farm beef cattle and sheep and that this land clearing promotes soil erosion and the destruction of forests. Melanie has had no professional advice about vegetarian eating so her diet is pretty crazy and unbalanced at the moment. She is thinking of becoming fruitarian. Her doctor noticed that Melanie was pale, tired and lacking energy so she asked Melanie to try to eat more foods with iron. Melanie has been living on salad, vegetables and cheese and she is getting pretty tired of that! What can you do to help Melanie spice up her life?

- **Max**—is nearly 18 years old and a vegetarian. He eats eggs, nuts and other vegetarian foods but he doesn't like to drink milk. He can tolerate milk sauces in recipes such as pasta, mashed potato or vegetable lasagna and he loves different cheeses. He has been vegetarian for a while, ever since his girlfriend introduced him to the idea of health and nutrition in Year 10, but they have since broken up and Max is not sure how to keep being vegetarian without her help as she did a lot of the cooking. Max now prepares snacks and meals at home for himself and his family, but he is looking for some new recipe ideas. Can you help Max?

Activity 9 Fad diet detective

- Students brainstorm and develop a list of criteria for examining a fad diet.
- Brainstorm what makes up a fad diet.
- Teacher can write this on the board or ask students to work in pairs or small groups to come up with some criteria for identifying a fad diet.
- The final criteria are outlined below.
- Then students work in pairs or small groups to solve the diet detective case studies of 'Worried Wendy', 'Skinny Sarah', 'No Bread Becky', 'Buff Billy' or 'Confused Carl'.

How do I spot a fad diet?

- A fad diet usually contains some or all of the following criteria:
  - It provides a very low kilojoule intake.
  - It aims to sell something to you—a book, diet food, formula, pill, special foods, supplements, equipment, a costly group program. It is usually expensive.
  - It promises extreme results like fast weight loss, huge weight loss, huge weight gain, muscle gain and it makes it all sound very simple, quick and easy.
  - It does not contain all of the five food groups.
  - It does not look like the healthy eating pyramid. It does not contain mostly fruits, vegetables, cereals, pasta, rice, breads and other grains.
  - It does not contain regular meals with morning and afternoon snacks. It often recommends skipping meals or replacing meals with formula drinks, or other 'meal replacements'.
  - It contains only a few foods.
  - It is being sold by someone with no proper nutritional qualifications.
  - It is not supported by any scientific research.
  - It provides testimonials or photos from people who claim to have succeeded on the diet plan, but there is no way of knowing whether this is true or whether pictures have been computer enhanced.
  - It promises impossible things like sexual attractiveness, extreme sexual performance, vitality, virility, curing diseases.

Activity 9 Fad diet detective

The following are letters to the diet detective—it is your job to analyse the diet of the case you have been given, and give some helpful advice. To do this, read the case you have been assigned, then do some research to find out more about it. To help, go through the 'How do I spot a fad diet?'. Then reply to the person with some helpful advice.

To: The Diet Detective
From: Worried Wendy
Re: My friend Jane

We have our school formal in a few weeks and my friend Jane has started acting really weird at lunch times. She says she is on a 'health kick' to try and fit into her dress, but she is skipping breakfast, and has told me that she has been throwing up some of her meals and using some laxatives she found at home in order to try and lose weight. I am worried about her, as she has gone really quiet all of the time, and says she doesn't even have the energy to hang out, or even go shopping for accessories!

To: The Diet Detective
From: Confused Carl
Re: I don't get it

I am trying to lose a bit of my stomach for footy training, and so I thought I would cut back on how much food I have each day. Mum still packs my lunch, so I usually just eat one devon and mayo sandwich instead of three, and I only have a small packet of chips instead of a family-sized one. Even after footy, I only have one meat pie for a snack instead of two. I have also started doing lots of sit-ups every day, 'cos I only want to lose weight from my gut, so I thought I would exercise there. After all this, I still have my gut! I don't get it—what am I doing wrong?

To: The Diet Detective
From: No bread Becky
Re: Low carb diets

I found this diet in one of my Mum's magazines, and I'm thinking about trying it. It's one of those low-carbohydrate diets that I've read about celebrities using. There are also three women that are quoted as saying it worked for them—they lost 15 kilograms in three weeks! All I have to do is not eat any carbs (no bread, cereal, rice, potatoes, pasta, lollies etc) for a few weeks. Do you think this will work?

To: The Diet Detective
From: Buff Billy
Re: Protein powders

At the gym where I workout there are all these posters advertising protein powders and supplements to help with weight gain. I have also started going to the sauna for half an hour after my workout, as I have heard that this helps to melt fat. I want to get real buff to impress all the girls at school—do you think these things will help?

To: The Diet Detective
From: Skinny Sarah
Re: Too thin?

Can girls be too thin? I eat lots of healthy foods and I do a lot of exercise, but I just can't seem to gain weight! Some girls call me names, or ask if I have an eating disorder. Some say they are so jealous of me because I can eat whatever I want. I feel bad, but I don't know what to tell them. Is it possible that I am just naturally thin like this?

Activity 9 Fad diet detective

Teacher's answers

No bread **Becky** **Low carb diets**	• Bread, potatoes and other high carbohydrate foods are NOT fattening! They provide energy for the body, and are necessary in a healthy balanced diet. • Low carbohydrate diets cause 'ketosis', a condition where the body is forced to burn body muscle as a form of energy. • Any weight lost will be water, stored in carbohydrate (glycogen) and muscle. • This weight is regained when the body goes back to normal. • Low carb diets can lead to low energy levels, and very bad breath.
Buff Billy **Protein** **powders**	• Body building powders and drinks are usually made up of very expensive milk powder, flavouring, vitamins and minerals. They are fad diet products. • They contain a very high amount of calories, and will cause you to gain fat or muscle. • Taking vitamin and mineral supplements does not provide any benefits except when clearly deficient. • Creatine has not been proven to be safe or effective. • These drinks and pills are also often expensive! • Saunas, spas and plastic wraps do not 'burn' fat. They simply cause loss of weight from water loss, which the body quickly replaces. • Regular exercise and small weights will tone and build muscles in most people. • Girls generally do not go for muscle men—they choose a boyfriend on the basis of character, friendship and being able to communicate well with each other.
Worried **Wendy** **My friend Jane**	• Fad diets don't work because they only result in loss of glycogen stores, fluids and make you feel terrible! • Skipping meals slows down the body's metabolism, and will therefore result in poor nutrition, low energy levels, and less calories burned during the day. All of these things actually slow down weight loss rather than help it.
Skinny Sarah **Too thin?**	• Everybody is different and people come in all shapes and sizes. • Body weight and shape is largely determined by genetics, so if you have a look at your parents and grandparents, you should see the body type that you have inherited. • Being teased for being underweight can be very upsetting. You can tell these people to stop teasing and that you live a very healthy lifestyle—but that you have inherited your body size and shape. Teasing and bullying about weight and shape is just another form of prejudice—just like racism, religious intolerance and sexism. • Girls and women can be too thin. If they lose too much weight, they upset their hormone levels (particularly oestrogen) and this causes irregular menstrual cycles. This is a sign that the woman is too thin and she should try to gain weight, until she is in the healthy weight range.
Confused Carl **I don't get it**	• His diet is quite high in fat, even though he only has 'small packets' of chips. • It is not possible to lose weight ('spot reduce') from one particular area of the body. • He could ask his mum to include a healthier and more balanced school lunch, with a filling chicken and salad sandwich, and some fruit. He could also choose low fat snacks, diet soft drinks and exercise.

Activity 10 Evaluating fad diets

- Using the information provided on the following pages on three amazing new diets—the Cabbage Soup Diet, the Israeli Army Diet or the Noxious Weeds Diet. Students use the fad diet detective's criteria to evaluate the diets.
- This is a fun activity that helps students realise how ridiculous fad diets can be!

Activity 10 Evaluating fad diets

Using the information that you have on the Cabbage Soup Diet, the Israeli Army Diet or the Noxious Weeds Diet, go through the following steps to see if it meets the fad diet detective's standards!

The tick boxes shaded with grey show what a healthy diet should contain. For each box that you tick outside of these grey boxes, the more likely that the diet is a fad diet, and, therefore, the lower the score that it will get at the end.

Does the diet contain … (Tick if yes)

1   Foods from all food groups?

Breads and cereals	Fruit	Milk and dairy	Vegetables	Meat and meat substitutes
☐	☐	☐	☐	☐

2   Does it contain …

Breakfast?	Lunch?	Dinner?	Snacks?
☐	☐	☐	☐

3   Does it contain …

	YES	NO
Lots of cereals (rice, pasta), bread, breakfast cereal, vegetables and fruits?	☐	☐

4   Does it contain …

	YES	NO
Nutritious but lean foods such as lean meats, chicken without skin, fat-reduced milk and dairy products?	☐	☐

5   Does it contain …

	YES	NO
Foods cooked without added fat (butter, oil, margarine, mayonnaise and cream) and salt?	☐	☐

Activity 10 Evaluating fad diets

6   Does it contain …

	YES	NO
Pills or other supplements?	☐	☐

7   Does it contain …

	YES	NO
Promises of rapid weight loss or weight gain?	☐	☐

8   Does it contain …

	YES	NO
Variety of different foods and drinks?	☐	☐

9   Does it contain …

	YES	NO
Exaggerated claims, e.g. Losing or gaining huge amounts of weight in a very short period of time?	☐	☐

10 Does it contain …

	YES	NO
Expensive ingredients or ingredients that are difficult to find?	☐	☐

The Verdict …

Have a look at how many of the grey shaded boxes you have ticked for the diet. The more, the better! Also have a look at how credible the promoter of the diet is and their qualifications, as well as where the information about the diet was published.

Use all of this information to give the diet a score out of 17
This diet scores ?/17

I would grade this diet as (Circle one):

FAIL   D   C   B   A   A+

Activity 10 Evaluating fad diets

Cabbage Soup Diet

Created by: The authors of the 'Cabbage Soup Diet' book. Only $79.95 at a bookstore near you!
This amazing new book will reveal the discovery of new and exciting ways to lose lots of weight in a very easy way. You can lose 10 kilos in one week by eating cabbage which acts as a 'fat metaboliser'. The cabbage causes your body fat to melt away—even while you are asleep! There is no need for you to do any exercise, just sit back, relax and let the cabbage do all the work for you!

The Cabbage Soup Diet is based on a fat-burning soup that contains no calories! The more of the soup that you eat, the more calories you will burn and the more weight you will lose. Dieters are allowed all the water and cabbage soup they want, plus some delicious other foods—all of which have fat burning qualities. Just eat your way to a slim, sexy body and better health!

The Seven Day Diet Plan

Eat as much soup as you desire for seven days and you can lose 10 kilos in only one week! The recipes in this scientifically tested diet vary slightly, but they include a variety of low-calorie vegetables such as cabbage, onions, and tomatoes, flavoured with delicious stock cubes, onion soup mix, and tomato juice.

Each day of the seven-day program has specific foods that must be eaten, including potatoes, fruit juice, many vegetables and, on one day, even a delicious beef steak!

Day 1

Eat only fruit, all the fruit you want except banana. You must flush all of the unwanted, poisonous toxins from your body to allow the magic components of the cabbage to infiltrate your body cells and start to burn away the fat. To do this you must only supply your body with unsweetened tea, black coffee, cranberry juice or water. Eat as much soup as you like.

Day 2

All you want—fresh, raw, or cooked vegetables of your choice. By now, the secret magical components of the cabbage will have started eating away and dissolving your body fat. Some of the body fat will disappear into the air around you, so be careful not to breathe in the air that you have expired.

Stay away from dry beans, peas and sweet corn. Reward yourself with a big baked potato with butter for dinner. Eat as much soup as you like but no fruit for today.

Day 3

Combine Day 1 and 2, eat as much fruit, vegetables and soup as you like, but no baked potato.

Day 4

Eat as many as eight bananas and drink as many glasses of skim milk as you would like on this day, along with your soup. This day is supposed to lessen your desire for sweets.

Day 5

You may have a big, juicy steak (300–500 grams) and a large tin of tomatoes or up to six fresh tomatoes. Drink at least six to eight glasses of water this day to wash the poisonous body toxins that cause fat to be made from your body. Eat your soup at least once today. You may eat chicken (skinless) instead of beef.

Day 6

Eat beef and vegetables today. You can even have two or three steaks if you like, with fresh vegetables or salad. No baked potato. Eat your soup at least once.

Day 7

Start again with Day 1—Soup, soup and more soup! Remember the more you eat of this magical soup, the more body fat will simply melt away.

You will be slim and beautiful with an endless supply of energy in no time at all!

Activity 10 Evaluating fad diets

THE NOXIOUS WEEDS ONE WEEK DIET!

Buy your Noxious Weeds One Week Diet pills from us online for a special one-off limited offer of only $99.99 for one week's supply.

Noxious weeds have previously been known only as useless garden plants or weeds, but new and exciting scientific research has discovered that these noxious weeds are really important and powerful herbs that have been known to contain magical qualities throughout history. It is believed that Julius Caesar obtained his amazing strength and vitality by consuming a potion of noxious herbs every morning before he got out of bed. Even Cleopatra had a private collection of noxious herbs as part of her beauty routine as these magical plants produced great health and sexual attraction.

You can now benefit from years of research into how to lose weight by eating only noxious weeds which have been carefully cultivated in the jungles of South America by scientists. We at the Noxious But Therapeutic Weeds Institute have spent 25 years researching the benefits of South American noxious weeds for fast, simple and easy weight loss or weight gain.

All you have to do is take a course of our scientifically proven noxious weeds weight loss pills or the Noxious Weeds weight gain pills and you will be looking slimmer or more muscular or both as soon as you can say cash or credit!

Also subscribe now to our 'Perfect Body With Noxious Weeds' new monthly magazine which is full of new scientific research and tips about having a better life and a perfect body by simply popping our special brand of magic pills. It's easy, it's scientific and it requires absolutely no effort or lifestyle change on your behalf! You don't need to engage in any sweaty or unsightly physical activity—you don't even have to leave the safety and comfort of your own home! All you have to do is send us your credit card details online and we will ship our amazing new products right to your door.

Eat nothing but our magical noxious weeds for only one week and you will have the body and the lifestyle you have always desired!

Activity 10 Evaluating fad diets

The Israeli Army diet

This amazing and unique new diet has been created by a team of secret agent specialist scientific doctors and nutritionists who were paid millions of dollars to design the very best scientific diet for the Israeli Army.

The diet that these doctors came up with will amaze and delight you and your loved ones, who will praise and embrace the new you! Your friends will envy you and you will become irresistible to the opposite sex! All in just seven days!

Just follow this simple, scientifically proven diet for only one week and you will lose all of the weight you want—quickly, easily and without ever feeling hungry!

Day 1 and Day 2:   Apples (black tea/coffee allowed)

Day 3 and Day 4:   Cheese (black tea/coffee allowed)

Day 5 and Day 6:   Chicken (black tea/coffee allowed)

Day 7:   Salad (black tea/coffee allowed)

Activity 11 Design a fad diet

- Using everything they have learned about fad diets, students work in pairs to design a new fad diet.
- The 'Noxious Weed Diet' outlined on page 212 is a particularly useful example of a fad diet. I made this diet up to demonstrate how easy it is to create a fad diet and how gullible people can be when it comes to fad diets that make outrageous and usually very expensive claims.
- Students can use the noxious weeds diet or they are instructed to create and present their new diet as a brochure or a television advertisement.
- Students are encouraged to exaggerate as much as possible and demonstrate how claims for fad diet products can be easily detected by identifying the language and messages used by the marketers of such products.
- Students make presentations to the rest of the class and the class votes on who the winner is.
- One way of presenting this activity to students is to tell them to imagine themselves as sleazy, shady, seedy marketers and sales people who need to make a fast buck. They can imagine themselves as the 'Dodgy Brothers' who need to sell something to make quick money.
- Students are asked to take on the role and milk it for all it's worth!
- The more unscientific and unachievable the fad diet is the better!

Activity 12 Nutritional pursuit

- This game is used to evaluate student learning in the areas of food and nutrition; growth and development; and general health.
- Students play in pairs or teams using the game cards and the one-page score board.
- Teacher can conduct this game on the overhead projector by dividing the class into two teams and colouring in the spaces on the overhead game sheet in different colours when each team answers a question correctly.

Activity 12 Nutritional pursuit

How to play

1 Play in pairs or teams; each student or team has a different coloured highlighter pen.

2 Player 1 picks a starting square from food and nutrition, health or growth and development.

3 Player 2 reads a question from food and nutrition, health or growth and development cards.

4 If your answer is correct, colour in that square.

5 Player 2 then picks a square and player 1 reads the question for them.

6 Play until the board is filled or time runs out.

7 At the end, add up your correct squares. The player with the most squares wins!

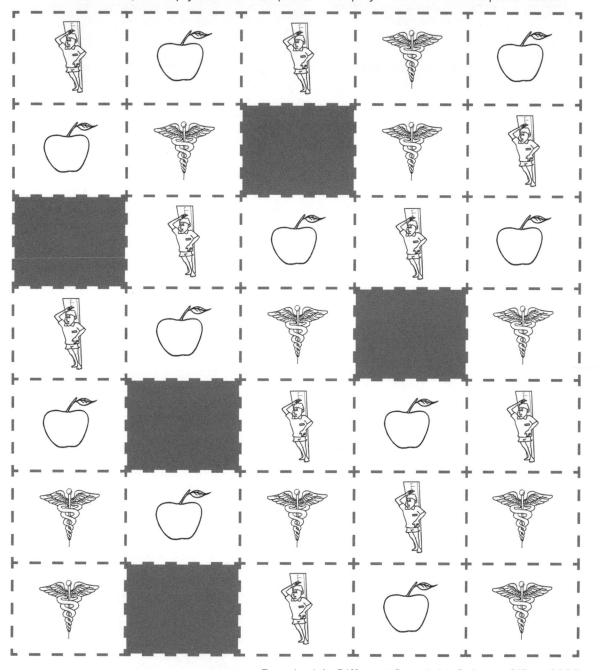

Activity 12 Nutritional pursuit

How much do you know about food, nutrition, growth, development and general health?

Test your skills in food and nutrition

Q: Strawberries, broccoli and potato are all high in which nutrient?
A: Vitamin C

Q: What do we normally call sodium chloride?
A: Salt, table salt

Q: Which food is best for babies up to six months of age?
A: Breast milk

Q: What is the common name for ascorbic acid?
A: Vitamin C

Q: Do avocados contain cholesterol?
A: No, only animal sources of fats contain cholesterol

Q: Give one other name for sugar.
A: Glucose, lactose, maltose, galactose, sucrose, fructose

Q: Which mineral is essential for forming red blood cells?
A: Iron

Q: Wholegrain breakfast foods such as cereals provide which nutrients?
A: Fibre, carbohydrates, B group vitamins, vitamin E and minerals such as iron

Q: Which nutrient is required for growth and immunity?
A: Protein

Q: Give another name for fats.
A: Lipids, oils, fatty acids, triglycerides

Q: What does RDI stand for?
A: Recommended dietary intake

Q: Which nutrient is the most essential for humans on a day to day basis?
A: Water, humans can only survive for about three days without any water

Q: How many servings of fruit should you eat per day?
A: Two servings

Q: True or False:
   Honey has the same amount of kilojoules as sugar.
A: True

Q: How many servings of vegetables should you eat per day?
A: Five servings

Q: What sorts of foods can be substituted for meat?
A: Beans, lentils, eggs and nuts (they contain iron and protein)

Q: What is used to measure the energy content of foods?
A: Kilojoules or calories (1 calorie = 4.2 kilojoules)

Q: What do the B group vitamins do?
A: Help to burn energy from food

Q: Which food group is the most important?
A: None, they are all important in a balanced diet

Q: Which foods are the main source of calcium in the diet?
A: Milk and milk products

Activity 12 Nutritional pursuit

Q: Which contains the most kilojoules per gram, fat or alcohol?
A: Fat: 37 kilojoules (9 calories per gram); Alcohol: 29 kilojoules (7 calories per gram)

Q: Name the three macronutrients.
A: Protein, carbohydrates, fats

Q: Name two micro nutrients.
A: Vitamins, minerals—vitamins A, B, C, D, E, K or minerals iron, calcium, zinc, sodium, magnesium, potassium

Q: Can eating fruits and vegetables help to prevent cancer?
A: Yes, especially the very brightly coloured fruits and vegetables like berries, oranges and leafy greens

Q: What does pasteurisation do to milk?
A: It heats milk very briefly to destroy any harmful bacteria

Test your skills in general health

Q: What is osteoporosis?
A: Thinning of the bones. Bones become very porous with lots of tiny holes in them and they are likely to break (fracture). The most common sites of bone fracture in osteoporosis are wrist, forearm and pelvis.

Q: Are people that are very overweight more likely to develop Type 2 diabetes?
A: Yes and so are people who are inactive

Q: Which gender is most at risk of developing osteoporosis?
A: Females, especially those who smoke, are too thin or women after menopause when oestrogen levels naturally decrease

Q: What does iron (haemoglobin) transport in the body?
A: Oxygen

Q: What is the maximum daily alcohol limit for fully grown adult women?
A: Two standard drinks. More than that can cause liver damage and other adverse effects on the body.

Q: List three unhealthy ways of dealing with stress.
A: Eating; drinking; bottling up emotions; taking drugs, alcohol; keeping to yourself; getting violent

Q: Will smoking one cigarette harm your health?
A: Yes, each cigarette contains over 4000 poisonous chemicals (and it gives you very bad breath)

Q: Name two foods that can prevent constipation.
A: Fruit, vegetables, beans, wholemeal bread, wholegrain cereal, wholemeal pasta, brown rice

Q: Heart disease is a major cause of death in Australia. List three things that you can do to avoid getting heart disease?
A: Don't smoke, reduce salt, check blood pressure, check blood cholesterol, get some daily exercise, reduce fat in the diet

Q: Do boys have a greater lung capacity than girls?
A: Yes, they generally have bigger lungs, but fitness and training are the major factors

Q: True or False: Too much sugar in the diet can lead to diabetes?
A: False, too much sugar can cause dental decay, but diabetes is caused by lack of insulin

Q: How much water do you need each day?
A: About 2 litres (2000 mL). Some of that will come from foods but most of it comes from drinks.

Activity 12 Nutritional pursuit

 Q: What is the maximum daily alcohol limit for fully grown adult men?
A: Four standard drinks. More than that can cause damage to body cells.

 Q: When diuretics (fluid pills) are taken, what is lost from the body?
A: Water

 Q: List three healthy ways of reducing stress.
A: Physical activity; talking to someone; relaxation; letting emotions out

 Q: True or False: Girls can't exercise or swim when they are menstruating.
A: False, girls can do any form of exercise or swimming when they are menstruating as long as they are using reliable pads or tampons. It is a myth that exercising when you have your periods will make you sick.

 Q: True or False: Sweating is unhealthy.
A: False, sweating is the natural way that the body cools itself. We can maintain a normal body temperature of 37°C by sweating and allowing the sweat to evaporate and cool.

 Q: True or False: Deaths in Australia are mostly caused by infectious diseases like influenza.
A: False, deaths in Australia are mostly caused by lifestyle-related diseases like heart disease, stroke and cancer

 Q: True or False: Mental activity such as studying or sitting an exam burns lots of energy.
A: False. Energy is only required to keep the organs functioning and to move the body. Extra brain activity uses no extra energy.

 Q: True or False: The diet of Australians is related to nearly two-thirds of deaths.
A: True, because diet is related to heart disease, high blood pressure and cancer. Alcohol is also a problematic component of the Australian diet.

 Q: True or False: Mental health, like feeling satisfied with yourself, is an important part of general health.
A: True. Our overall health is not just about our bodies, it is about having mental health, social health and a sense of belonging. We need to be happy and healthy!

 Q: True or False: Deaths from heart disease in Australia are rising.
A: False, deaths from heart disease have been declining since the 1970s. This is mainly due to people quitting smoking, better medical care, heart surgery and cholesterol lowering drugs.

 Q: True or False: Shopping is exercise.
A: True! Walking around a shopping mall for hours will move the body and burn extra energy (and cash!).

 Q: True or False: The brightly coloured fruits and vegetables play an important role in the prevention of cancer.
A: True. Components of brightly coloured fruits and vegetables, including berries, orange fruits and vegetables, purple cabbage, leafy greens etc. protect our body cells against cancer.

Activity 12 Nutritional pursuit

Q: True or False. Fit people sweat more than unfit people.
A: False. Sweating is a natural adaptation to exercise and the need to cool the body—the more you sweat, the better your body is at maintaining a cooler body temperature. The sweat of fit people is more dilute and has less salt than the sweat of unfit people.

Q: True or False: Vitamin supplements are essential for good health.
A: False, all vitamins and minerals can be obtained in a balanced diet

Test your skills in growth and development

Q: True or False: Humans are growing for the first 16–18 years of life, and therefore should be gaining weight.
A: True

Q: True or False: The breaking of the voice is the first sign of puberty in boys.
A: False. A boy's voice will start to break in the middle of puberty. The first sign of puberty in boys is pubic hair, facial hair, enlargement of the testicles and growth of the hands and feet.

Q: True or False: Females with very low body fat delay the onset of menstruation.
A: Yes, girls need a certain amount of body fat to maintain a normal menstrual cycle

Q: True or False: Eating breakfast is a good way to maintain a normal weight.
A: True. Teenagers who eat breakfast, morning tea and lunch are less likely to binge eat or overeat after school. Dieting or starving yourself is likely to make you want to overeat.

Q: Do all adolescents grow at the same rate?
A: No, every individual person is different

Q: List three things that can tell you what your adult height will be.
A: The height of your parents (you will be an average of your parents' heights—boys will be a little taller than the average of parents' heights, girls may be a little shorter); whether you get good nutrition; whether or not you smoke (smoking can reduce nutrient distribution and oxygen to growing tissues and stunt height); illnesses during your growing years (if you get sick a lot and don't eat, then your growth is affected)

Q: Which part of the body grows first, second and last in pubertal teenagers—arms and legs; hands and feet; torso.
A: Hands and feet grow first, then arms and legs, then torso last of all

Q: Is body shape and size inherited from the parents?
A: Yes, this is the major influence on body shape and size. If your parents or grandparents are tall, muscular, round, or slim, then your body shape will probably be similar.

Q: True or False: Some adolescents can grow up to 12 cm per year.
A: True. The adolescent growth spurt can result in very large changes in height and weight over a relatively short amount of time.

Q: True or False: Males who do not eat enough or those who diet severely, can delay their pubertal development.
A: True.

Activity 12 Nutritional pursuit

Q: True or False: A girl will not grow much taller after her first menstrual period.

A: True. The first menstrual period (menarche) indicates the end of puberty and the end of the growth spurt for most girls. A girl will grow no more than 2–4 cm after her first menstrual period.

Q: True or False: During puberty the voice box (larynx) becomes larger only in boys.

A: False. The voice box becomes larger in both boys and girls during puberty and their voices become deeper.

Q: True or False: Adults need more energy from food than teenagers.

A: False, growing, active teens need more energy than adults

Q: True or False: A developing foetus can suck its thumb in utero.

A: True, this begins at about 36 weeks gestation

Q: True or False: Fad diets are a good way of losing weight.

A: False, only water is lost

Q: True or False: The teenage brain keeps developing up until the age of 23 years.

A: True. The brain size is complete by around age 16 years, but the hard wiring of the brain and the neurological patterns of the brain continue to develop until the early twenties. This is why drug use is best avoided in the teen years and early twenties, because the brain is still developing and drug use may interfere with normal brain development.

Q: True or False: Anaemia is common in teenage girls.

A: True. Anaemia is caused by a dietary deficiency of iron. When there is not enough iron the body cannot receive enough oxygen. Teenage girls and boys both need iron for growth, but girls tend to need more iron because they lose iron in the monthly menstrual cycle.

Q: True or False: Human breast milk provides immunisation to diseases like measles, mumps and rubella (German measles).

A: False. Breast milk provides a great deal of protection from colds, flu and viruses, but babies need to be immunised for other major childhood diseases like measles, mumps, rubella, tetanus, diphtheria, polio and chicken pox.

Q: True or False: The human brain does not finish growing in size until age 12 years.

A: False. The human brain continues to grow in size until 16 years of age.

Q: True or False: A baby's brain size doubles in the first year of life.

A: True

Activity 13 Sports nutrition case study

- Teacher uses overhead of 'Healthy diets for sport' or lists on the board an outline of the major nutritional requirements for athletes.
- Students use the case study of Jessie to explore the many different nutritional requirements of teens who are involved in sports.
- Jessie can be male or female—let the students decide!
- Teacher supplies students with copies of the information on sports nutrition (Tables 7.5, 7.13, 7.14 and 7.15) for them to analyse Jessie's diet, calculate how much carbohydrate and fluids Jessie needs and choose foods and drinks with more carbohydrates.
- An extension for more advanced students would include consideration of the glycaemic index with students choosing low to moderate GI foods for the majority of Jessie's carbohydrate intake. The GI chart is Table 7.15.

Activity 13 Healthy diets for sport

Glycaemic Index to provide a constant supply of blood glucose during training and a quick supply of glucose during competition

Carbohydrates for energy and endurance

Calculate CHO needs based on appropriate activity level

Make sure that vegetarian diets are balanced and able to promote growth and health

Make certain that adolescent athletes obtain enough protein, CHO, fats, vitamins and minerals to ensure pubertal growth as well as energy output

Hydration and the need for fluids. Avoid any degree of dehydration.

Avoid fad weight loss and fad weight gain diets

Maximise glycogen stores with regular carbohydrates during training, competition and recovery

Iron to prevent anaemia and to increase oxygen uptake by muscles

Calcium for bone growth and bone density to prevent fractures

Balance of protein, carbohydrates and fats

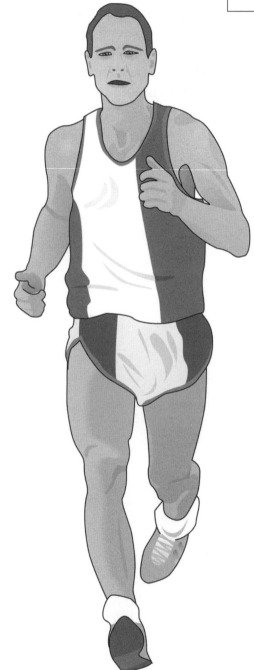

Activity 13 Healthy diets for sport

Jessie

Jessie is a member of a rowing squad. She is 14 years old and in Year 8. She is training for the Australian Championships next year. Recently, Jessie has started worrying about what she is eating as her weight had increased by 2 kilograms over the past six months. She started weighing herself every morning before training, which only made her more confused as her weight changed from day to day.

She thought skipping breakfast before training might help decrease her weight. The only problem was that this tended to make her very hungry after school and then she would overeat on the way home from school or afterwards.

Jessie's coach asked her to keep a diary of her daily food intake which is outlined below.

6 am	Water.
6.30–8 am	Training—water.
8–8.45 am	Get ready for school, 200 mL juice on the way to school.
9–10.30 am	Morning classes at school.
10.30–11 am	Recess: morning snack of juice, potato chips.
11 am–1 pm	Classes.
1–1.45 pm	Lunch: soft drink (1 can), 6 water crackers, Mars bar.
1.45–3 pm	Afternoon classes.
3–5 pm	Snacking on way home from school or at home—Twisties, soft drink, cereal and milk, biscuits, whatever is in the house.
6.30 pm	Dinner, whatever Mum cooks—mostly meat and three vegetables—usually I'm too tired to eat much—I'm always tired.
8–10 pm	Homework, ice cream, energy drink to stay awake.

What is your general advice to Jessie?

_____

_____

What dietary advice can you suggest?

_____

_____

Is Jessie getting enough carbohydrate for her activity level?

_____

_____

Can you create a new, yummy food plan for Jessie for one of her training days?

_____

_____

Activity 13 Healthy diets for sport

Teacher's answers—Jessie

- Jessie is not thinking about what she eats and she is not paying attention to her nutritional intake.
- In general, she is probably not eating enough to maintain her training schedule and she needs more carbohydrates.
- Her weight gain probably reflects normal growth for a 14-year-old girl, so she need not worry about it and she should certainly not be skipping breakfast before training.
- She needs to focus on eating a more nutritious diet, spread more evenly throughout the whole day to enable her to meet her training and study requirements. She is tired because she has not eaten enough carbohydrates and she will notice a huge difference in endurance and general energy levels when she starts to eat properly and more regularly.
- Her tiredness may also be related to iron deficiency anaemia, so it is advisable for her to have a blood test. She should go to her doctor for a checkup.
- She needs to eat more dairy foods for protein, calcium and zinc—students should add three serves of milk, yoghurt, custard, ice cream or cheese to her new food plan.
- She needs to include two fruits and five vegetables each day with starchy, high carbohydrates being the best choice.
- She needs to focus on high carbohydrate snacks like bread, toast, crumpets, cereal and milk, pasta, rice etc., rather than salty snacks like potato chips; she could have these foods occasionally but not every day.
- She needs to choose a more interesting drink during training and especially something with a little carbohydrate in it like a sports drink, juice or cordial.
- Students should create a food plan that is both nutritious and delicious.

Activity 14 Sports nutrition word puzzle

Name   Date

Find each of the following words.

FOOD	NUTRIENT	TRAINING
DEHYDRATION	CALCIUM	CARBOHYDRATES
GLUCOSE	EXERCISE	GLYCAEMIC
MUSCLE	TRAIN	SUGAR
DIET	GLYCOGEN	FAT
PROTEINS	REST	SPORTS DRINK
METABOLISM	NUTRITION	ANAEMIA
LIPID	PROTEIN	DIGESTION
SWEAT	NUTRIENTS	MINERAL
MINERALS	FRUIT	CARBOHYDRATE
WATER	ENERGY	OXYGEN
IRON	VITAMIN	VITAMINS
FATS	ACTIVITY	CALORIE
BONES		

```
G N I N I A R T A I D T P E F N I R D S T R O P S D
T U E I M C A I S M O I T R T A A W T G I L E E D M
A I I O L A S W E A T C E N O T S Y A I I E E N D Y
E R E A O L E E R T S S S T R T A T E G A E E R K N
T F T I B C B T R N T A R E N D E T D N L I D N N G
T I O M A I I N I N U T R E I N T N A W R U I A C Y
R I R E T U E E E A A G R E R U A U S O B R C R R F
A Y P A E M T I M C O D T A O E E S L E D U B L E G
I S E N M O R I B N N A G S V S X A C S C S I E X V
N P N A R T W A T E R U I C O A C L T I N T Y A E S
E L E P U D G I C D S N R C I M A R T C I F A T S G
I T R N E S E R Y S T T U N I M O D T R M S O E E S
I M G Y I A N H E I N L A I A P E A O E G L A I N L
E I Y F F D O E Y N G E O M S O V A G X N L I P E D
B N A E A B E S M D I R A A E I I R C E G L Y C O E
A E N S R H G E E A R M E T B R T E F Y A R E N I M
T R S A A N I T A T T A T I T O A A N A L R E I R C
E A C Y T I V I T C A I T V L T M R Y A N G S O M E
O L A N N L I U O V S R V I T A T M I N E R A L S N
W C A C I N A S N O R I D N O W D N K U N M D M C E
S N L L D M A T T M N N E Y K N I D I P I L A L T A
L R R T T G E L T A W I P I H R C A L O R A Y I E M
N E M I A L S T D F R U I T I O N O I T I R U N M D
S O N E F Y D N I T O R P O P T B I G R E N E G N C
C I O E T C E D U V E O X Y G E N R T R A I N I N T
N T I T E A I N N I E T O R P D T T A D E R Y L N N
C I T S N E B C G N I M A T I V N D E C O F O O D I
E R S E E M E O F R U I R G L U C O S I T M U S C N
L T I R G G L M L O A M R I I S N I M A T I V G O A
C U G B O R C F U I D I G E S T I O N O X Y E N I Y
I N I E C I S D A S S T N U T R I T I O N N U T R I
U B D A Y R U O O E C M A I N I A R T M N B O N E S
M N O N L V M A M I N L D T S L A R N I M P R O T S
S I F O G N N E N Y S E I T N T E G R E C E N R N D
```

Activity 15 Food and nutrition word puzzle

Name   Date

Find each of the following words.

CHOLESTEROL	BREAD STICK	STARCH	VEGETABLE
GRAPEFRUIT	ORANGE	BANANA	FARINA
FOOD	CALORIES	ENERGY	MINERAL
MINERALS	MEAT	CORN	CHEESE
SODA	MILK	POTATOES	FRUITS
CALCIUM	DRY CEREAL	BALANCED DIET	VITAMINS
CHICKEN	VEGETABLES	CARBOHYDRATES	FOOD GUIDE PYRAMID
PASTA	GLUCOSE	PROTEIN	BREAD
PIZZA	VITAMIN	GRAVY	NUTRIENT
SUGAR	DIET	APPLES	POULTRY
FRUIT	CALORIE	COFFEE	PYRAMID
NUTRITION	DAIRY FOODS	CARROTS	WATER

```
E Y F O O D G U I D E P Y R A M I D R Y C E R E A S
A B P I Z Z A E V N C A L O R I E R O G R A V Y E E
M I N E R A L S A E T L C F E R C O F F E F R U I T
M A Y C Y R S D N N G I E H I Y O G U E S I L L I M
K C H I C G L O M R A E U E I F M I L K O N A P I C
C F A R N A R T D C O B T R F C H O L E S T E R O L
I I C H E E S E E E A C R A F F K F R U T I R T D N
T A L S E P I N N S T R O T B E O I P N N U E B F T
S T A P O N C I D E O N B S A L P C N S I R C A N L
D G L U C O S I O O E C E O R T E E R E A F Y T I S
A D N N H I A A F R D V U I H S T N R B N E R R M M
E U E V A T P Y G A I B I L R Y U A I G A P D U A I
R E T A W I O L S N E P I T G T D G E I N A S G T R
B R P A E R B T A G T C I S A E U R A M N R A O I O
I N R A C T I O L E P E O M U M A N A S A G S Y V S
M O S C R U F Y R C S O I V I G I P F T B A N O R T
A Y E T R N V I O E A M T D E N A N I O E S I U M N
D A L F E U A E L O N L U A D S E R S R S S M A L E
I G P T R N D B E R U G C K T E E R I A R R E S A E
M I A G A E A T E G E V E I B O C H D N E P T N R E
A R I N O T U N E O T I R T U N E N C T Z R I C E O
R T A S E I R O L A C E O C A M S S A C A R V A N T
Y B D G T T S T A R N E K C I H C A R L A A P R I E
P D E A S Y R T L U O P A P Y R W L R F A C R R M S
A V N A D O S R L A R E N N I M A L O M A B O O A N
I W S D O O F Y R I A D S C E R A F T Y N E T O M L
I A S E L P P A O R D A I R Y F O A S O C T E T A P
D C A L C A I M Y S T A R C H I Y C E H C C I S T R
E Z Z I P P A S T A F O O D A E R B I T D A N S I M
D A S R R I E A E T T T D A C U G R Z O A I F E V R
```

8 Weight issues and child obesity prevention

Introduction

Studies in a number of different countries have shown increases in the prevalence of overweight and obesity among children over the past three decades. These increases have given rise to concern about children's health and wellbeing, particularly in regard to the risk of Type 2 diabetes. The terminology used in these studies varies, but no matter what terminology is used, such studies are generally based on weight expressed as body mass index (BMI), a measure of weight for height, calculated as weight in kilograms divided by metres squared, and not on body fatness.

There are many different BMI methods that can be used to estimate child overweight or obesity. In this chapter, the measurement of overweight and obesity is discussed as well as the many limitations of using the BMI among growing children and adolescents. The prevalence of obesity among Australian school children is currently at around 6–8 per cent of the 6–18-year-old population. These children and adolescents are possibly 'too fat' and some may be at risk of illness later in life, especially if there is a family history of Type 2 diabetes. But the assumption that a child or adolescent is 'too fat' or at risk of ill health due to increased weight cannot be made unless they are examined by a doctor or trained health professional.

There are many issues for teachers and school administrators to consider before they embark on any obesity prevention activities. An important consideration is the potential to inadvertently create or worsen body image concerns among students, particularly among overweight students or those who perceive themselves as overweight. Several case studies of real students in real life situations are outlined in this chapter to illustrate how, despite our very best intentions, teachers can sometimes do more harm than good when attempting to deal with issues in child obesity prevention. Similarly, some true case studies of positive student experiences are also given. Finally, the holistic approach to teaching about these health issues is outlined and some suggested activities and classroom lessons are presented including activities to teach about health in a multidimensional way, a quick quiz about overall health status, a discussion of health statements, a school health survey and lessons about bullying and harassment, including an activity about cyber bullying.

Concurrent prevention of eating problems, body image improvement and obesity

The prevention of eating disturbances and body image concerns is vital today, as is the concurrent prevention of child obesity. Because overweight, perceived overweight and weight concerns are known to precede dieting, hazardous weight loss behaviours and eating disturbances, the current trend towards the co-occurrence of increasing eating disorders and increasing child overweight is of concern. It is probable that the increasing rates of child overweight may be one of the factors that have resulted in more dieting and weight loss attempts among young people. Hence, the two trends could be expected to continue in tandem and prevention of both is required.

Further to the intricate relationship between disordered eating and child obesity is the relationship between weight control behaviours and further weight gain. Recent research supports the thesis that children and adolescents who use extreme weight loss attempts only serve to perpetuate the futile cycle of dieting, purging, binge eating and further weight gain. The phenomenon of weight rebound following dietary restriction has been observed in a study of adolescent girls. In their recent large, well-designed, longitudinal study spanning four years, Stice and his colleagues (1999) found that among high school girls of various weights, those who tried extreme methods to lose weight were the most likely to gain weight over time and were therefore at greater risk for obesity. Girls who used more extreme weight loss methods such as laxatives, appetite suppressants, vomiting and fasting gained more weight than those who were not involved in extreme weight loss attempts. Among girls who dieted, the risk of obesity onset was greater than for non-dieters, irrespective of their actual weight at the beginning of the study.

Similar results were found by Neumark-Sztainer and her colleagues (2006) in a large longitudinal study of teenage girls. The girls who dieted the most and used fad methods of weight control were the ones most at risk of overweight and obesity at the end of the study.

One of the major aims of prevention programs to improve body image, eating problems and child obesity is to encourage healthy eating and physical activity among children and adolescents without promoting weight loss attempts and the diet-binge cycle. For this reason, a positive, healthy approach such as the self-esteem approach is a relevant and appropriate approach to take in both the prevention of body image and eating problems and the prevention of child obesity, because the two issues are inextricably entwined.

Measurement of 'overweight' and 'obesity' in children and adolescents

Children are defined as overweight for population surveillance purposes using a variety of BMI cut-off points. The important thing to remember about BMI is that it does not measure body composition and thus, it does not measure fatness or over-fatness. Body weight and body composition can consist of water, muscle, fat, bone, minerals (such as 4 kilograms of calcium) and organs. BMI measures weight but does not differentiate between the type of weight and therefore does not measure fat. Thus, BMI is only a limited screening tool, not a diagnostic tool and a child or adolescent will always need to be individually assessed by a doctor in order to make a judgement about their weight status, their degree of actual fatness and their health status.

Children with a BMI over the stated cut-points are not necessarily 'over fat' and do not necessarily have clinical complications or health risks related to over-fatness. A more in-depth assessment of individual children is required to ascertain health status and this is best done by a doctor who can measure body fatness, waist circumference, blood pressure, blood glucose, insulin, blood cholesterol and family history. The definitions of overweight generally used are working definitions that are valuable for general public health surveillance, screening and similar purposes, but they do not accurately assess individuals or their health risk.

The terminology regarding weight and overweight used in studies varies with some studies reporting 'overweight', some to 'obesity' and some to 'at risk for overweight'. Even when the same term is used (for example, 'overweight') the meaning of that term is often not the same in different countries or across studies. However, whatever the terminology used, such studies are generally based on weight and not on body fatness.

In practice, measurement of body composition and body fat is difficult both in clinical applications and in population studies. In addition, there are no well-accepted standards for body fatness for children (or for adults). Thus, in general, weight, adjusted for height, is used rather than a more direct measure of body fat. A variety of methods has been used to adjust weight for height, but currently the most common, both for children and for adults, is the body mass index (BMI), defined as weight in kilograms divided by height in metres squared. For children, BMI increases and varies with age, height and growth, so the BMI of a child or adolescent is compared on BMI charts with the BMI of a reference population of children or adolescents of the same sex and age. Adult BMI ranges should never be used to try to estimate overweight or obesity among children because children are still growing.

In adults, the cut-offs to define obesity or overweight are based on fixed BMI values related to health risk. Health risks and mortality increase at very low or very high BMI and these have been found independent of cigarette smoking. In children there are no risk-based fixed values of BMI used to determine overweight, because it is unclear what risk-related criteria to use. The time between childhood and adulthood may involve a lot of change in a young person's weight, height, growth and lifestyle, so it may take a long time for any adverse outcomes to appear—if any appear at all.

A statistical definition of overweight based on the 85th and 95th percentiles of BMI-for-age in a specified reference population is often used in childhood and adolescence and a variety of reference data sets for BMI in childhood exist. If the child is greater than the 85th percentile for weight or height or BMI, then the health practitioner can assume that the child is bigger than 85 per cent of the population—they are in the top 15 per cent. Similarly, if a child is greater than the 95th percentile, then they can be considered to be in the top 5 per cent of weight or height or BMI, depending on which chart is being used. In the past few decades more children have been found to have weight or BMI in these top percentiles and this appears to be because more children are becoming overweight or obese.

In many countries, BMI reference data are used or recommended as part of monitoring of children's growth so that the longitudinal pattern of growth can be observed from infancy to adolescence. This is a very useful way to observe a child's individual growth pattern and weight pattern over time and they are intended for clinical use in monitoring children's growth. The use of selected percentiles of such charts to define overweight and obesity is a secondary purpose.

In 2000, Cole and colleagues published a set of BMI cut-off values based on the combination of six nationally representative data sets from Brazil, Great Britain, Hong Kong, the Netherlands, Singapore and the USA (Cole et al., 2000).

These values, often referred to as the International Obesity Task Force (IOTF) cut-off values, represent cut-off points chosen as the percentiles that matched the adult cut-offs of a BMI of 25 and 30 at age 18 years.

The Cole (IOTF) reference grew out of a workshop held by the International Obesity Task Force and was developed to provide a suggested common basis for prevalence estimates internationally. The goal was to develop BMI criteria that could be used for international comparisons of prevalence without depending on using solely US or UK reference data and without using a specified percentile, such as the 85th or 95th percentile, of a specific population.

IOTF cut-offs were not intended as clinical definitions and were not intended to replace national reference data, but rather to provide a common set of definitions that researchers and policy makers in different countries could use for descriptive and comparative purposes internationally.

Limitations of using the BMI

In order to assess exactly how many children are at risk of developing weight problems, most researchers use the international comparison method developed by Cole et al. (2000) to estimate how many students are on a trajectory for being overweight as an adult (BMI >25) and how many were on a trajectory for being obese as an adult (BMI >30).

This use of the BMI charts is an extrapolation that is merely an estimate based on the assumption that weight status stays on a similar pattern from childhood to adolescence to adulthood and, of course, this is not always the case.

In addition to the limitations in extrapolating child BMI to assumed pattern of adult BMI, other limitations with the assessment of a child's body mass index (BMI) include the following weaknesses:

- BMI does not take muscularity or body composition into account. This is a rather large weakness in the methodology because some students can be very muscular and their 'weight' is certainly not a sound reflection of 'fatness'.
- BMI does not measure 'fatness'; although BMI correlates with fatness in adulthood, it does not correlate particularly well with fatness in childhood or adolescence. BMI is not necessarily a very good measure of body fatness, particularly for children. Body mass index is simply a form of weight adjusted for height, and as such cannot measure body composition any more than weight can measure body composition. For children, the changes in BMI with age make the picture more complex. It is likely that even at a given age taller children may well have higher BMI values. Although at the highest BMI levels, children are likely to be over-fat as well, the very highest percentiles of BMI perform fairly well to identify the fattest children but slightly lower percentiles of BMI perform poorly. In particular, BMI from the 85th to the 95th percentile may be a poor predictor of excess body fat (Mast et al., 2002).
- BMI does not take stage of pubertal development into account. In a 1995 study of nearly 500 11–15-year-old girls, we found the post-pubertal girls, who had reached menarche, had a BMI on average two points greater than the pre-menarcheal girls (O'Dea & Abraham, 1995). In other words, among girls of the same age, post-menarcheal girls can expect to have an average BMI of 21 whereas pre-menarcheal girls of the same age can expect an average BMI of 19. This pubertal effect is similar for boys, but pubertal boys can often be relatively thinner than pre-pubertal boys because of the rapid height spurt. This can make some teenage boys appear to be underweight on BMI charts. Obviously, the individual stage of pubertal development is going to have a huge impact on an adolescent's BMI status.
- BMI does not take ethnicity into account. This is a particularly important issue when trying to assess children from tall, muscular ethnic backgrounds, such as Maori, Fijian, Samoan or Tongan children who may appear to be overweight or obese on regular BMI charts. These BMI charts have been derived from mainly Caucasian, middle class children from the USA and the UK, so the lack of ethnic representation is a large limitation of the data. Some studies now suggest a higher BMI cut-off to indicate 'overweight' in some ethnic groups. For example, some research suggests a BMI of 28 for overweight in African Americans and Pacific Islanders. Children and adolescents from Asian backgrounds may have a lower BMI than their same age counterparts from other ethnic groups.
- BMI does not measure or correlate with markers of health such as blood pressure, blood cholesterol or blood sugar in children and adolescents. While BMI tends to correlate with these measures of 'health' and 'risk of illness' in adults, particularly at the obese level of BMI, it does not correlate well among children or adolescents. It

is reasonable to estimate that true obesity at levels corresponding with an adult BMI of 30 or greater is a health risk for Type 2 diabetes among children and adolescents but a BMI lower than that does not necessarily indicate a health risk for children. The assumed risk is projected to when they become adults.

- When used as a one-off measure at one time in a child's stage of development, BMI is a very weak measure of true weight status and how the child is growing and developing. That is why growth patterns need to be monitored by a child's doctor over several months or years in order to reveal the true pattern of growth and weight risk in that individual child. A one-off measure of BMI says very little about an individual child's weight status or health status.

- BMI cut-offs that categorise children and adolescents as 'overweight' or 'obese' are statistically derived definitions and not actual clinical measures. These two categories are often lumped together in a combined category of 'overweight or obese' which inflates the impact of the figures and exaggerates the health risk. Numbers such as 'one quarter or one third of young people are overweight or obese' are often used in media reports about the issue. In fact, both of the categories are merely estimates of body composition and both are a very poor measure of actual fatness. The overweight category is a particularly poor measure of actual fatness or health risk in growing children and it is really quite different to the obese category. Teachers should understand the many limitations of using these BMI data and they should beware of exaggerated and emotive media claims about our children's weight status.

Assessment of weight status among Australian school children

In 2000, I conducted a national study in which I surveyed nearly 4500 primary and secondary school children from every state and territory of Australia (O'Dea, 2003; O'Dea & Wilson, 2006). Students completed a survey about their knowledge, beliefs, attitudes and behaviours related to food, nutrition, body image and physical activity and each student had their height and weight measured. In order to assess exactly how many children were at risk of developing weight issues, I used the international comparison method developed by Cole et al. (2000) to estimate how many students were on a trajectory for being overweight as an adult (BMI >25) and how many were on a trajectory for being obese as an adult (BMI >30).

The following table summarises the findings about overweight (a body mass index equivalent to ≥25 in adulthood) and obesity (a body mass index equivalent to ≥30 in adulthood). See the full research paper by Cole et al. (2000) for a complete explanation of these BMI cut-offs for child overweight and obesity.

TABLE 8.1 Overweight and obesity in 4441 Australian school children

		Males % (n = 2232)	Female % (n = 2209)
Primary school students	Overweight Obese	17.0 5.7	19.0 5.9
High school students	Overweight Obese	16.7 6.8	16.8 6.7

In total, 17.3 per cent of students were in the overweight category of BMI and 6.4 per cent were in the obese category. An interpretation of these percentages indicates that all around Australia, about 7 per cent of school children are probably carrying a level of body fat that may be detrimental to their health, especially if they have a family history of Type 2 diabetes or high blood pressure.

Likewise, the 17 per cent of students in the 'overweight' category indicates that these children are big and certainly bigger than their peers, but not necessarily 'too fat' or at risk of imminent illness due to their weight. This percentage of students, around 17 per cent, may be approaching a level of body weight that puts them at risk of becoming obese.

It is misleading and incorrect, but very common in the media, to include all of the overweight and obese students together in the same category. This is because some of the students classified as 'overweight' may be more muscular than their peers and this trend appears to occur in children from some ethnic groups, especially Pacific Islanders. Similarly, some students in the 'overweight' category may have been just about to go into their adolescent height spurt, thereby growing 'into' their weight. There may be no health risk at all among the vast majority of students in the overweight category.

In the 2000 study (O'Dea & Wilson, 2006) there was a modest trend towards overweight and obesity being slightly more common among children from low-income areas. Students from low-income areas also tended to be, on average, 2 centimetres shorter than children from middle- or high-income areas. These findings suggest a type of 'Western malnutrition' where the students' height deficit may be due to consumption of poor growth foods which may be making children shorter and therefore 'too short for their weight'. This finding is new and of concern and needs to be further examined to test whether it is a real trend. We are currently investigating the association between the very important factors of social class and ethnicity on height and weight in children and adolescents.

Prevalence of overweight and obesity over the past three decades

In 2001, Magarey and her colleagues conducted a study to compare the prevalence of overweight and obesity in Australian children and adolescents in two national samples, 10 years apart, using the new standard international definitions of the International Obesity Task Force Childhood Obesity Working Group (Cole et al., 2000).

The study participants were 8492 school children aged 7–15 years who had participated in the Australian Health and Fitness Survey in 1985 and 2962 children aged 2–18 years who had participated in the National Nutrition Survey in 1995 (Magarey et al., 2001). The review measured the prevalence of BMI categories of overweight and obesity in both samples of school children using the international standard definition. In the 1985 sample, 9.3 per cent of boys and 10.6 per cent of girls were in the overweight BMI category and a further 1.4 per cent of boys and 1.2 per cent of girls were in the obese BMI category. In the 1995 sample, overall 15 per cent of boys (varied with age from 10.4 per cent to 20 per cent) and 15.8 per cent of girls (varied with age from 14.5 per cent to 17.2 per cent) were categorised as overweight, and a further 4.5 per cent of boys (2.4–6.8 per cent) and 5.3 per cent of girls (4.2–6.3 per cent) were categorised as obese. The prevalence of overweight and obesity in the 1995 sample peaked at 12–15 years in boys and 7–11 years in girls. In school children aged 7–15 years, the rates represent a relative risk of overweight in 1995 compared with 1985 of 1.79 (10 per cent overweight in 1985 versus 15 per cent in 1995) and of obesity of 3.28 (1.3 per cent obese in 1985 versus 5 per cent in 1995) suggesting that overweight had nearly doubled and obesity had tripled between the two surveys.

In my national study of 4441 school children aged 6–18 years conducted in 2000 (O'Dea, 2003) I found overweight to be around 17.3 per cent and obesity to be 6.3 per cent. Roughly speaking, when comparing my findings with those of Magarey, there appears to have been a slight increase of around 2 per cent in overweight and 1 per cent in obesity between 1995 and 2000 but it was not a huge increase and it may suggest that the rise in weight among Australian children and adolescents may be slowing down.

In the recent NSW study of 5400 school children in kindergarten to Year 10 conducted in 2004, Booth and his colleagues (2006) reported an average of 18.4 per cent of students as overweight and 7.7 per cent obese. Again, it is difficult to compare these study results without employing precise statistical tests because some of the studies include children from national samples and the Booth study includes NSW students only, but it is reasonable to suggest that the number of children in the overweight category increased by about 1 per cent from 2000 to 2004 (6.3 per cent to 7.7 per cent) and the number in the overweight category also increased by 1 per cent (17.3 per cent to 18.4 per cent). Further research is currently underway to examine whether the greatest increase in weight among children and adolescents may have occurred between 1985 and 1995 as shown in the study by Magarey and her colleagues in their 2001 paper, and therefore, whether weight gain in Australian children may have already peaked.

At present, the national study conducted in 2000 is being repeated in a large research study of the same schools all around Australia (Probyn & O'Dea, 2005), so an estimate in any national change in overweight and obesity between 2000 and 2006 will be able to be analysed soon.

Prevalence of overweight and obesity in international studies

The prevalence of obesity among school-age children and teens in the USA has more than tripled, from five to over 16 per cent in the last three decades (Hedley et al., 2004; Ogden et al., 2002; Troiano & Flegal, 1998). Similar increases have been reported in the UK (Chinn & Rona, 2001), Finland (Kautiainen et al., 2002), China (Luo & Hu, 2002), Chile (Kain et al., 2002), Portugal (Padez et al., 2004), Brazil (Wang et al., 2002), Germany (Kalies et al., 2002), France (Heude et al., 2003; Romon et al., 2005) and Russia (Wang et al., 2002).

BMI and risk of Type 2 diabetes

The increases in child overweight and obesity have given rise to considerable concern about children's health and wellbeing, particularly in relation to the risk of development of Type 2 diabetes which is more common in people who are overweight or inactive or both.

Children and adolescents who are obese, inactive, have a family history of Type 2 diabetes or are Aboriginal or Torres Strait Islander, South Pacific Islander, Indian/ Pakistani, Native American, African American, Hispanic American are at an increased risk for Type 2 diabetes.

The first reported cases of Type 2 diabetes among children were eight girls in the UK, aged 9–16 years and all were of Pakistani, Indian or Arabic origin (Ehtisham et al., 2000). They were all obese and all had a strong family history of diabetes in at least two generations. Type 2 diabetes was also observed among four very obese Caucasian children in the UK (Drake et al., 2002). Type 2 diabetes in obese Caucasian children has also been reported from elsewhere (Wabitsch et al., 2004; Wiegand et al., 2004). Many of these cases occurred in children with very high BMIs, often in the range of 35 to 40, as well as a family history of Type 2 diabetes. Family history seems to play a strong role in the development of Type 2 diabetes among obese or inactive youth. Keeping young people physically active and promoting growth in height are two very important ways of preventing Type 2 diabetes. These two roles are highly relevant issues for teachers.

Issues for teachers to consider before initiating obesity prevention

'First, do no harm'

The prevalence of child obesity has steadily increased in Western and developing countries over the last two decades and child obesity prevention is now firmly on the agendas of nearly all major governments. We are now confronted with the challenge of what to do about the problem and the general consensus among various academics, researchers, practitioners and administrators worldwide is that prevention needs to begin. Before governments, schools and other agencies leap into actions that they assume to be beneficial in the battle against child obesity, we must remember to employ one of the most important principles of modern medicine and prevention science, 'First, do no harm'.

An examination of potentially unhelpful or dangerous outcomes of child obesity prevention efforts is required before prevention activities begin. There are many examples of perfectly reasonable and well-intentioned health messages being partially misconstrued or misunderstood by members of the general public, resulting in the inadvertent production of undesirable effects in the implementation of supposedly health-promoting activities.

The early 'control your weight' messages of the past, and those of today, identified people who were overweight as failures, deviants or moral outcasts who needed some sort of 'treatment', most of which, when undertaken by the overweight person, resulted in further failure, defeat and humiliation, leaving us with the current prevalence of obesity of today. Is our message to overweight people and obese children any different today? Are our current preventive strategies any different or any more likely to succeed? At whom is child obesity prevention targeted? Before we begin any sort of preventive activity, we must make certain that our preventive efforts are well conceived and based on a sound knowledge of prevention principles.

The first step in approaching any health education problem or planning any prevention program is to know what it is that we are trying to achieve and to have a clear definition of what we are trying to prevent. In the case of child obesity, we need to be aware that our role as health educators and prevention specialists is not in the diagnosis or treatment of child obesity.

Prevention versus treatment

Health educators and teachers involved in the prevention of child obesity need to understand the difference between treatment and prevention. The treatment of child obesity should only occur in a supervised clinical setting after a thorough and appropriate clinical assessment. Prescription of weight control programs, dietary advice or other individual interventions for the obese child should remain the role of the paediatrician, general practitioner, dietitian or other clinically trained staff. Community-based professionals such as teachers, health educators, nutritionists, nurses, youth workers, sports coaches and others working with children and youth must understand the difference between child obesity treatment and prevention and must act accordingly using appropriate referrals without confusing their clinical and educational roles.

Teachers should also be acutely aware of the fact that a child's health status encompasses several different dimensions including physical, mental, social, cultural and spiritual health, not merely the absence of disease, and we must be very careful to 'do no harm' to any of these essential dimensions of health in our efforts to treat or prevent child obesity.

Inadvertent suggestion of dieting and other weight loss techniques

Health and education professionals who work in the treatment and prevention of child obesity also need to be aware of the fact that their best intentions may have the potential to inadvertently do more harm than good. The unintentional creation of body image and weight concerns, dieting, disordered eating and eating disorders is a probable outcome of child obesity prevention programs that focus on the 'problem' of overweight and refer to issues of weight control. Overweight children and adolescents are already known to have poor body image and a fear of food (Neumark-Sztainer et al., 2002; O'Dea et al., 1996), as do many normal weight youth who incorrectly perceive themselves to be 'too fat' (Croll et al., 2002).

It is a common myth that overweight children and adolescents make little effort to try to control their weight. Health education messages about overweight and weight control are likely to make young people feel worse about their bodies and themselves in general. Preventive activities must be examined for their unintended negative outcomes such as those known to result from unsupervised weight control attempts among children and adolescents and that can include growth failure (Brook et al., 1974; Davis et al., 1978; Lifshitz & Moses, 1988; Mallick, 1983), height stunting (Lifshitz & Moses, 1989; Pugliese et al., 1983), delayed puberty and menarche (Frisch et al., 1980; Kulin et al., 1982; Lev-Ran, 1974), delayed bone age, bone length and reduced bone density (Bonjour et al., 1991; Dhuper et al., 1990; Ott, 1991; Theintz et al., 1993).

Health education for child obesity prevention may also result in the iatrogenesis of inappropriate weight control techniques whereby the health education program generates unplanned, undesirable and health damaging effects (Garner, 1985; O'Dea, 2000). Unintended effects of weight education programs include unhealthy behaviours such as starvation, vomiting, laxative abuse, diuretic and slimming pill usage and cigarette smoking to suppress appetite and as a substitute for eating (Ikeda & Mitchell, 2001; Strauss & Mir, 2001). The risk of obese children and their parents adopting fad weight loss regimens is something that health educators and teachers need to be certain to avoid.

Avoid further stigmatisation, prejudice and discrimination

Child obesity prevention programs and untested health education messages have the potential to further stigmatise fat children (Latner & Stunkard, 2003) and perpetuate the current prejudicial beliefs well documented among physicians and likely to exist among other health and education professionals, that fat people are 'weak-willed, ugly and awkward' (Foster et al., 2003; Young & Powell, 1985) and 'gluttonous, lazy, bad, weak, stupid, worthless and lacking in self control' (Schwartz et al., 2003). Obese people are well aware that they are fat, and that health care professionals are biased against them (Maddox & Liederman, 1969; Young & Powell, 1985).

In addition to obese children of both sexes being well aware of their weight problems, they also have low self-esteem (Strauss, 2000) and are currently known to exhibit high rates of extreme dieting, disordered eating and skipping breakfast (Croll et al., 2002) as well as greater levels of emotional distress and lower expectations of their educational futures (Mellin et al., 2002). Heavy girls take on the 'fat, stupid, lazy, hopeless' label from a young age (O'Dea, 2006) and it becomes worse as they become older teenagers. The last thing that obese children need is a reminder of their undesirable weight status.

In addition to the further stigmatisation of overweight children by focusing on the dangers of obesity and other negatively focused health messages, health educators may also inadvertently discriminate against overweight children by excluding them from general participation in certain events such as school games and sports teams. This type of discrimination is known to affect overweight and obese adults who suffer discrimination in employment, salary, promotion, education, marriage and healthcare (Gortmaker et al., 1993). Conversely, forcing unwilling participation in sports and physical activities is likely to have the undesirable outcome of making overweight children avoid physical activity.

Transference and misinformation

Teachers and health professionals may need to examine their own beliefs and attitudes towards fat people and fat children before embarking on any child obesity prevention activities and they may need specific training in order to undertake any role in child obesity prevention. The potential for inadvertent transference of misinformation, inappropriate advice and prejudice from educator to child needs to be examined during the design of health education and health promotion strategies for the prevention of child overweight.

In a recent study of the teachers most likely to be involved in school-based obesity prevention activities, we found a low level of nutrition knowledge, a poor level of knowledge about weight control, a great deal of dietary misinformation being conveyed from teacher to students and a very high level of body dissatisfaction and self-reported eating disorders, particularly among the young women teachers (O'Dea & Abraham, 2001).

One of the findings of most concern in the study was that 85 per cent of the teachers reported recommending strict calorie-controlled diets to their overweight students, many of whom were in the middle of their adolescent growth spurt. The potential for transference of the teacher's own beliefs, attitudes and prejudice as well as the delivery of ill-informed health education messages is clearly undesirable and dangerous in the prevention of child obesity.

Undesirable outcomes of unplanned approaches

Of similar potential danger in the prevention of child obesity is the dissemination of messages, whether intentioned or not, that have not been properly designed, pre-tested and evaluated. In an evaluation of two posters aimed at improving the body image of teenaged girls and young women (O'Dea, 2002), up to 30 per cent of 15–18-year-old girls reported that the posters were not helpful to them because they made them feel more self-critical of their bodies; 35 per cent reported not liking the posters; 69 per cent did not want their own copy; 8 per cent did not know what message the posters were meant to portray and another 8 per cent perceived an incorrect or harmful message from the posters.

Health education programs should, ideally, have no adverse outcomes, and this research clearly demonstrates that well-meaning health education initiatives and health messages may elude the target audience and may have subsequent negative effects. Planning of child obesity prevention programs should involve the program recipients, and all health education materials should be pre-tested to clearly identify the messages perceived among the target audience and to prevent unintended and potentially harmful outcomes.

Avoidance of health services and preventive screening tests

As a consequence of weight prejudice and discrimination, overweight adults, particularly women, are less likely to visit health professionals for preventive health screening examinations such as mammograms, pap smear tests and gynaecologic examinations (Fontaine et al., 1998; Wee et al., 2000). Overweight adults are also more likely than normal weight patients to cancel medical appointments (Olson et al., 1994). Health educators involved in the treatment or prevention of child obesity need to be acutely aware that focusing on children's weight in a negative or critical manner is also likely to produce a similar avoidance of health professionals, health services and preventive activities by children and their parents.

Further promoting the avoidance of physical activity

Highlighting the problem of overweight in prevention programs aimed at children and adolescents is likely to produce the adverse effect of making overweight children more sensitive about their weight and their self-perceived lack of athletic ability (O'Dea & Abraham, 1999) and therefore making them less likely to participate in physical activity, physical education and sport (Shaw & Kemeny, 1989). Studies of barriers to physical activity among adolescents (O'Dea, 2003; Shaw & Kemeny, 1989) clearly identify body consciousness, lack of privacy in change rooms and physically revealing sports uniforms as major barriers, particularly among girls. Coercing unwilling, body conscious, overweight children into sport or physical activity is likely to exacerbate these problems and further reduce their participation in physical activity, serving only to fuel the rise in child obesity. Conversely, involving children in physical activities that they enjoy is likely to boost their self-esteem, social interactions, friendships (Strauss & Pollack, 2003) and promote the very important idea that fat people can be fit and healthy (Blair, 2003). Blair studied thousands of men and their risk of having a heart attack. He found that physical activity was a very strong predictor of heart attack with overweight active men having a significantly lower risk of heart attack than slim, inactive men. The involvement of our overweight and obese students in physical activity is crucial but it will only be achieved in an enjoyable, welcoming and accepting PE environment.

Blaming the victim

The current panic about child obesity is largely fuelled by media reports that focus on the rising prevalence of child overweight and its potential health problems. The problem-based, negatively and individually focused, victim-blaming approach is something that teachers ought to avoid, as it is likely to result in nothing more than the apportioning of more blame, guilt, shame and hopelessness on fat children and their parents. As these negative reinforcing factors have not been previously associated with any degree of long term success in the past treatment or prevention of overweight in children or adults (Garner & Wooley, 1991), an evidence-based approach to current child obesity prevention efforts would do well to avoid them.

A probable outcome of the negative 'guilt, blame, shame' individual victim blaming approach to obesity treatment and prevention is the unfortunate adverse outcome of having overweight and obese people deliberately avoiding the problem because they do not want to be lectured about their weight, humiliated or made to feel guilty. Child obesity prevention messages must avoid this negative, problem-based approach.

Further marginalising low SES people

The prevalence of overweight is greater among socially and economically disadvantaged people and the association between lower socioeconomic status (SES) and obesity is well documented (Booth et al., 2006; Goodman, 2003; O'Dea, 2003; Sobal & Stunkard, 1989). Overweight adolescents are more likely than their normal weight peers to be socially marginalised (Strauss & Pollack, 2003). As health educators, we must be careful not to further 'blame the victim' by taking a judgemental, moralistic approach and inadvertently make overweight, low SES children and their parents feel even more marginalised, disadvantaged and hopeless.

Obesity or fatness as a 'sick role'

As effective teachers and health educators, we also need to be aware of promoting child obesity or any degree of fatness as a 'sick role' that needs 'medical treatment'. Having some body fat is quite normal and the idea that a healthy person has a minimum of body fat is a myth. Likewise, children of all shapes and sizes can be fit and active and healthy by participation in physical activity. Sound nutrition and physical activity are essential components for overall child health as they convey many wide ranging benefits for growth, development, brain development and cognition, immunity, socialisation and disease prevention—not just child obesity prevention. All children need good nutrition and physical activity, not just obese children.

The medicalisation of child obesity will do little to reduce it, as the failure of dietary treatments for overweight have already demonstrated many times (Garner & Wooley, 1991). The prescription of drug treatments for obese children is increasing, lending further credibility to the myth that obesity can be 'cured' with a quick fix drug treatment. At least one professional organisation, of which the author is aware, has suggested that participants and groups involved in child obesity prevention should disclose all special interests such as financial affiliations with pharmaceutical companies or the weight loss industry (Berg, 2000; Society for Nutrition Education, 2002). It is of serious concern that preventive activities among children could be influenced by those aiming to make profits out of child obesity treatment or prevention.

The need for a positive approach

A different paradigm to the individual, dieting, weight loss approach for the treatment and prevention of obesity in adults has been proposed (Robison et al., 1995; Society for Nutrition Education, 2002) with a central focus on redefining success away from the current focus on weight loss, towards an active healthy lifestyle and long-term amelioration of medical problems and improved quality of life.

Other signs of 'success' in helping overweight or obese children and adults is the short-term change in health behaviours such as decreased reliance on medications, increased physical activity and healthy eating and improved psychological functioning. The 'health at any size' movement has been successful in helping health professionals and overweight people focus on health improvement rather than weight loss. This sort of broad focus, which recognises the importance of all of the physical, psychological, social and spiritual dimensions of child health in child obesity prevention is more likely to produce positive rather than negative outcomes.

Certainly, these aims, as well as improved self-esteem are important goals to strive for among obese children and adolescents (Strauss, 2000) and this may have the additional desired impact of helping obese children and adolescents enjoy more physical activity. Dealing with larger environmental issues such as bullying and teasing are similarly likely to impact on the barriers to physical activity identified by youth and result in motivating and enabling healthy behaviours.

Finally, we urgently need a positive health education approach, grounded in sound health education theory in order to properly plan, design, implement and evaluate the most appropriate, relevant and effective child obesity prevention strategies. Much is currently known about the factors that motivate healthy eating and physical activity among children and adolescents (O'Dea, 2003) and, similarly, much is known about the barriers to healthy behaviours (Gracey et al., 1996; Neumark-Sztainer et al., 1999). Ecological, environmental and holistic approaches have been successfully employed in eating disorder prevention and body image improvement programs (O'Dea & Maloney, 2001; Piran, 1999) and child obesity prevention experts would benefit from adopting some of these large systems approaches to prevention. These whole school factors are addressed in Chapter 10.

Families who live in 'obesogenic environments' such as those living in isolated or poorly serviced neighbourhoods may not have easy access to healthy food and they may feel that their children are unable to safely engage in physical activity in their local environment. A socioecologic, environmental model to increasing physical activity therefore suggests that focusing on changing the physical environment, urban planning and transportation is likely to produce the greatest benefits in obesity prevention (Powell et al., 2002).

Barriers to physical activity in local environments need to be addressed. This includes ways of making environments less 'obesogenic', ways of inadvertently encouraging incidental exercise and ways of providing safe, enjoyable and inexpensive physical activity opportunities for children and adolescents.

TABLE 8.2 A summary of potentially undesirable and unhelpful outcomes of obesity prevention programs in schools

Inadvertent and undesirable outcomes of obesity prevention activities	Potentially harmful and unhelpful consequences among children and adolescents
Implementation of treatment rather than prevention—measuring and 'diagnosing' student overweight or obesity; giving weight loss advice to students, 'prescribing' diets or weight loss activities.	• Legal liability of diagnosing a condition rather than leaving that to medically trained staff • Encouraging weight loss diets in growing students • Labelling child with a medical 'condition' that is based only upon a one-off measure of BMI at one point in time • Lack of student privacy
Inadvertent suggestion of dieting and other weight loss techniques—discussing weight loss rather than weight maintenance or a healthy lifestyle; inadvertent promotion of dieting and disordered eating among growing children; inadvertent suggestion that dieting is normal and desirable.	• Suggestion and introduction of weight loss diets in students who may not have been susceptible to dieting or body image concerns • Introduction of dieting methods that are not suitable for growing children • Normalisation of fad diets
Creation of stigmatisation, prejudice and discrimination—weighing students and having them plot their BMI on a chart; inadvertently encouraging weight and BMI comparisons; labelling of students as overweight or obese; focus on weight in growth lessons rather than growth as evidenced by height; focus on weight issues rather than fitness and overall health markers.	• Identification, labelling, shaming of overweight or obese students • Stigmatisation of overweight or obese students as having a 'problem' and being a 'failure' • Promoting the idea that students will never be healthy or fit unless they lose weight • Lack of focus on fitness, physical activity, better markers of health (e.g. heart rate, blood pressure, daily physical activity, social, mental, cultural, spiritual health)
Undesirable outcomes of unplanned approaches—inadvertently creating weight concerns that lead to weight loss attempts and unhealthy behaviours such as smoking for weight control and appetite control, vomiting, laxatives, avoidance of exercise, social isolation, shame of body and depression.	• Students focus on weight loss rather than overall health development • Suggestion of weight loss at any cost—smoking, fad diets, dangerous weight loss attempts, development of diet–binge cycle; disordered eating, eating disorders; exercise disorders
Avoidance of health services; preventive screening tests; sport and PE—increasing a person's sensitivity about their weight is likely to make them want to avoid health screenings and physical activity.	• Likely to make students less willing to participate in health check ups because of 'lecture' about their weight • Reduced visits to doctors, mammography • Avoidance of health education, sport, PE, swimming etc.
Promotion of fatness as a 'sick role'—focusing on 'illness' rather than focusing on health and wellbeing; giving the message that fatness equates with illness; giving the idea that slimness equates with health and fitness; missing out on the message that healthy eating and daily physical activity promote health and fitness in students of all shapes and sizes.	• Giving students the narrow, prejudiced and incorrect message that 'health' is all about weight rather than the balanced message that fat people can be active, eat well and be fit and healthy • Inadvertently suggesting that slim people are healthy, irrespective of their diet, physical activity, smoking status etc.

Child obesity prevention is an important contemporary health education topic that is not going to subside for a very long time. As teachers involved in child obesity prevention, we need to question our current health education approaches and to investigate the possibility that some of our most well meaning preventive intentions may be potentially hazardous and more likely to be harmful to the overweight child than beneficial. As health education experts, we are obliged to approach the issue of child obesity prevention with a broad perspective and a thorough preventive focus, and we initially need to ensure that our preventive efforts must be certain to do no harm.

A summary of potentially undesirable and unhelpful outcomes of obesity prevention programs in schools is outlined in the table on the previous page.

Some of the adverse effects of well meaning obesity prevention activities are illustrated in the recent case studies below. All of these case studies are true stories about real students and teachers.

Case studies

Amira

Amira is a 15-year-old girl of Middle Eastern descent who attends a public, coeducational high school. Amira's high school took part in some fitness testing conducted by some expert fitness testers who came to her school. During the fitness test, students' measurements were taken for height, weight and arm circumference and they participated in a vertical jump to test for lower body power, 40 m sprint to test for speed and a shuttle run to test for aerobic endurance.

Amira was quite pleased to be part of the 'health testing' because although she knew she was overweight, she had recently undertaken some health promoting activities that included changing her diet and increasing exercise. Amira was brave to have undertaken these activities as her cultural background does not encourage women to become involved in exercise or sport. Amira was feeling pretty good about her personal achievements as she felt that she was doing something towards becoming more fit and healthy. After the fitness testing, each student was given a certificate with their results and a comparison with national percentiles. Although Amira's test results were all below the class average for vertical jump, sprint and shuttle run, Amira didn't mind too much because she knew that her personal physical fitness had recently improved and that she was working towards becoming even fitter. What caused Amira the most anguish, heartbreak and trauma was the results for her weight which was shown to be on the 100th percentile. She couldn't have been more of a failure if she tried. This left Amira with no positive feedback at all, no recognition of her personal achievements and a sense of failure and despair. Amira became very self-conscious and depressed and she did not attend school for two weeks. She has not participated in PE classes since the fitness test.

Alison, aged 14, Year 8

Alison attends a girls' school in the outer northern suburbs of Sydney. She is tall and has developed many years ahead of the other girls. She is fully grown and is a generous size 14.

Mr Hedland is Alison's PE teacher. He is in his late 40s, doesn't smoke or drink alcohol and is slim and fit.

At the start of the school year, all students were made to get on the scales, to check how much they weighed so it could be compared to their weight at the end of the year. As it was an all girls class, he thought nothing of announcing their weights to the rest of the class.

When students were slim, he would state 'Ah, Shelley you tiny little thing, let's see how much you don't weigh'. If a girl refused to get on the scales he would threaten them with after school detentions or failing the class, thus forcing them onto the scale.

If the girl was bigger than what he considered an 'acceptable weight' his tone of voice would sharpen as he commented 'OK, now it is Maria's turn, listen up girls, let's see how big she is' or 'Hmmm, Dana, my how heavy you are, no matter, I will get you skinny by the end of the year!'

Eventually it was Alison's turn to get onto the scale. She had waited as long as she could, hoping the bell would go, and it hadn't. Mr Hedland knew that she was hoping to get away with the weigh in, so he called her over 'Alison, come over here, I am very interested in the amount you weigh, perhaps we should have bets on how heavy you are? Five kilos over, perhaps 10?' Thankfully, no other students said anything to add to her shame and embarrassment.

As Alison stepped onto the scales, Mr Hedland was beaming from ear to ear, just waiting to announce her weight. Alison looked away, she didn't want to know her weight, but she didn't want anyone else to either. Mr Hedland smirked at her and announced 'Oh my, that is not good, I don't think I should say how much you are' and left it at that.

If only Alison had known that she had weighed well within the healthy weight range for her height and development level. If she had known that, perhaps she wouldn't have gone on to begin the diet, binge, purge cycle and many months of suffering from bulimia.

Matthew, aged 15, Year 9

To those around him, Matt appears to be a happy, talkative, chubby boy. To his small and close group of friends, Matt is a great kid but highly sensitive about his weight.

Matt attends a well-known, private boys' school. When he was in Year 9 as part of a compulsory subject his class had to complete a unit of home economics, with Ms Sweany, an older woman around 55 and a bit of a grump.

Half way through the first double period of the class, she announced 'I will only teach you how to cook decent food, nothing full of sugar or fat. If you eat fattening foods, chips, burgers, chocolate, you will end up the size of a house. Look around you, notice the boys who eat such food.' Then she looked towards Matt. 'You there,' she said looking at Matt, 'You must eat a lot of nasty food, look at the size of you!' Matt was horrified, his friends were shocked at Ms Sweany, but no one said a word.

Throughout the rest of the term, Ms Sweany continually harassed the bigger boys about their weight. At the end of the term of cooking 'decent food', the only lesson the boys had learned was that the fat kids and slightly chubby kids were unhealthy, unattractive, bad and looking forward to an early death!

These boys did not tell their parents, not one told another teacher. However, they were all hurt. Some went on to try and lose some weight, one went on to stop eating all meals but breakfast. But Matt became aggressive towards people who looked at his weight and he started eating more food. By the beginning of Year 10, he had put on over 10 kilograms and refused to talk to anyone about the foods he ate. No one bullied him because of his size, but his negative self-image encouraged his emotional eating. Matt is now in Year 11 and he weighs over 150 kilograms.

Positive case studies from schools

The following true case studies illustrate how a positive, health promoting approach can help students develop a positive sense of self that in turn, encourages healthy balanced attitudes and behaviours.

Clara, aged 16, Year 11

Clara was 16 and in Year 11. She attended a private, Catholic girls' school in the central suburbs of Melbourne. She appeared to be a reserved girl to most, but a roar to her friends.

Being highly creative, she and her best friend loved to participate in the yearly creative arts festival.

For the Year 11 production, Clara and her friend decided to do an underwater, 'Jaws' inspired piece. However, Clara was concerned about costumes, as her friend insisted that they should be dressed in wetsuits.

Now Clara began developing in primary school. She wore a D cup bra and was incredibly curvy. She saw no attractiveness in her body shape and was horrified at the thought of showing her 'fat' to the parents, teachers and mostly, the other girls.

However, Clara's skinny friend won out, gaining the support of several teachers and parents, who insisted wetsuits were the only appropriate garments to wear.

So, Clara and her friend performed, dressed in figure-hugging wetsuits in front of hundreds.

The next morning in class, one of Clara's teachers, Mrs Sanders commented on the performance. She told her 'you needn't have worried about the wetsuit – you looked lovely, I never knew how womanly you were under that baggy uniform.' She concluded the chat by stating that Clara had all the curves in all the right spots.

For Clara the quick comment meant a lot. She had never thought of herself as womanly. She had never considered that a woman was supposed to have curves. This comment meant the world; she finally looked at herself, not as fat and grotesque but womanly. By the end of Year 10, she was a curvaceous, happy and self-assured young woman.

Justin, aged 17, Year 11

Justin is in Year 11 at the local co-educational high school. It is a low-income area, but the kids are nice enough and so were the teachers.

Justin is a tall boy, lean and lanky. He is part of the soccer team and competes in the school squash tournaments.

Monday morning started with a double of PE. That morning, his PE teacher, Mr Papas introduced the class to their new sport for the next four weeks—gym workouts. Most of the class groaned, they would much prefer something more exciting. Mr Papas led them around the gym room, explaining the equipment.

Soon, Mr Papas separated the students into genders, and then he separated them into which half of the body they wished to work on first of all—upper or lower body. When all groups had been divided he spoke generally about fitness and how each student 'will feel that they wish to concentrate on their own individual area' and how each person is different. Mr Papas told the class that 'each body is beautiful, no matter the size or shape or colour and we should embrace our appearance'. He finished with 'never bully someone about their weight, or their muscles, we all have areas we do not like, but some people are sensitive about their body shape, and you will never know it before you open your trap'.

For a serious, sporty man, Justin and his class were surprised at his emphasis. Each group of students worked out together, with the supervision of Mr Papas. Mr Papas put on some fun music and the class really started getting into their first gym workout.

Justin was determined to add muscle; he hated being so skinny. But Mr Papas refused to suggest diets, pills and potions to help Justin, he told him 'be thankful for what you have, you are still growing, you will gather strength and muscles soon, don't rush it and don't hamper it by trying to make it come quicker'.

Justin took the advice of his teacher and continued along with his own pace. Towards the end of Year 11, Justin started to put on weight and began to grow outwards rather than upwards, much to his surprise and delight.

Factors affecting child growth and overweight

Children are individuals, and their height and weight depend not only on nutrition but also on genetics, family trends, race and their weight at birth. The child of two very tall parents will tend to be tall also, and likewise a seemingly small child may come from a family of smaller relatives.

If a child or adolescent is overweight in relation to their height and age, it may indicate prepuberty in that the child is just about to have a height spurt. Overweight is also likely to be caused by underactivity rather than overeating. Doctors and dietitians agree that kilojoule restriction diets for overweight children are undesirable because they can compromise growth and bone density. Most overweight children and teenagers become more slender as they grow in height and parents, teachers and school staff can help by encouraging healthy food choices, fewer sugary and fatty foods, more exercise and emotional support and encouragement.

Parents and teachers can help to bolster the child's self-esteem by fostering regular daily exercise, in which the child's size is not much of a disadvantage, for example, playing games, playing in the swimming pool, walking the dog, walking to school, play time during school breaks, walking to do the shopping. By joining in play and exercise with children, parents and teachers will be setting a good example as well as making it more fun.

Factors influencing a child's weight

Many factors influence a child's weight and height. Body weight is not just affected by what we eat. The following is an outline of the main factors that affect weight.

Height Tall children tend to be heavier and have greater BMIs than shorter children. As a child or adolescent grows in height he/she will also increase their weight. Girls, in particular, need to understand that as their height increases, then so too will their weight. Many students like to hear of a height increase, but they are disappointed to learn of a concurrent weight increase. The message about growth and development for students is clear—if you increase in height, then there will need to be an increase in weight. The adolescent height spurt is usually followed by a weight increase, but some boys and girls may grow in height very quickly and this can make them appear to be very thin for a while. Any inappropriate use of adult BMI charts will worsen this effect of height.

Eating habits There is no doubt that a child's eating habits influence their height and their weight. Children who do not consume enough protein, calcium and zinc (largely from milk, cheese, yoghurt and other dairy foods) will not reach their full height potential and their bones will not be as strong as they could be. Research shows that children who do not reach their full height potential may become overweight more easily. Similarly, children who constantly graze on foods and drinks will consume too many kilojoules and this will be stored by the body as fat. Sipping constantly on drinks and juices is a very efficient way to gain weight by consuming too many kilojoules.

Physical activity Being physically active is natural for most children. Children are naturally active, fidgety and full of energy and they love to move and play. The problem is that children become distracted by other activities such as television, computer games, homework and mobile phones and they lose the opportunity to play and be active. These children are at risk of becoming overweight and unfit.

Metabolic rate Everyone burns up energy at a different rate and this is known as the metabolic rate. Children tend to inherit their metabolic rate from their parents, so some children will have a fast metabolic rate and will burn their food up as energy very quickly while others will have a slower rate of metabolism. Everybody's metabolic rate can be increased by physical activity and muscle mass, so encouraging children and adolescents to play and be active will help increase their metabolism and reduce the risk of overweight.

Stage of growth Children at different growth stages put on varying amounts of weight. The weight gain tends to be rapid in babies, slow and steady in toddlers and school-aged children and then rapid again during puberty and adolescence. Girls will lay down a storage layer of body fat at about age 9–10 years and this energy store will be used to fuel the rapid growth and height spurt that most girls experience between 11–14 years of age. The 'puppy fat' stage is normal and should not be confused with overweight. Boys experience the same stage of prepubertal puppy fat storage at a later age, around 12–14 years. During their teenage growth spurt girls put on about 4–5 kilograms a year between the age of 11–14 years and about 6–10 centimetres per year. Boys can gain up to 12 centimetres and 5–8 kilograms per year between the ages of 13–16 years of age. Remember, every child begins puberty at a different age, so every child's weight and height spurt will be different. The order of body composition change in puberty is first, a prepubertal layer of fat, followed by bone length growth (hands and feet first, then long limbs and finally, torso) then muscle, then a layer of fat for protection, warmth, store of energy, femininity and hormonal regulation.

Family patterns Children's body shape, size, weight and height are largely determined by genetics. Some children take after their mother or father and some take after their grandparents. Height is largely determined by the height of parents and you can estimate a child's adult height by following the guidelines below:

- Measure the mother's height and the father's height in centimetres (for example, Mum is 155 cm and Dad is 173 cm)
- Average the two heights (155 + 173 = 328/2 = 164 cm)
- Add 6.5 cm to the average for boys (for example, 164 + 6.5 = 170.5 cm)
- Take away 6.5 cm from the average for girls (for example, 164 – 6.5 = 157.5 cm)

This method does not always work accurately for every child, but it is a reliable estimate. It is a fun and positive activity to do with students because it helps to educate them about the many factors that affect growth, weight, shape and health. I recommend a whole class lesson with height where a class average of height (not weight!) is created. Female students in Years 6, 7 and 8 are likely to be taller on average than the males and this illustrates the earlier onset of puberty among girls. This pattern is likely to reverse in Years 9, 10 and 11 when boys finish their growth spurt. The important message for students is that body shape and size is largely influenced by genetic background and everybody is different.

Emotional eating

Some children (and many adults!) eat for comfort. Children learn from a very young age that food and comfort and love often come hand in hand, and this is especially true among babies who quickly learn how pleasant it is to receive a warm milk feed and a cuddle from mum or dad! Unfortunately, some children grow into the habit of seeking emotional comfort from food and some children often eat in response to some emotional stimuli. Some children and adolescents eat because they are bored, lonely, sad, depressed or feeling neglected and unloved. This is known as non-hungry or emotional eating where the child or adolescent becomes an emotional eater who seeks emotional satisfaction from food. If you think this is happening with your students, you can teach them to explore the many factors that influence their food habits by using the food diary in Chapter 7. This activity helps students to observe their eating habits and identify the many factors that affect them. Some students may be able to observe and link their eating or drinking to feelings of sadness, anger, fear, happiness, loneliness or boredom. Students can then learn how to address their real emotional concerns and deal with their stress in more healthy ways. Eating and drinking are not effective ways of dealing with stress.

Ways of fostering a healthy weight among children and adolescents

- Schools can provide healthy food options every day for students to be able to learn to make healthy choices.
- Encourage students to become aware of their eating patterns and suggest that they learn to know for themselves when to stop eating.
- Encourage students to observe any 'grazing' activity as this is associated with poor dietary intakes and weight gain.
- Encourage students to stop eating when they have had enough. If a child doesn't eat everything that they are served, then they have probably been given too much food.
- Teach students to eat three meals and two or three snacks per day. This will satisfy the appetite of most children and prevent overeating. Eating breakfast, morning tea and lunch prevents students from binge eating later in the day.
- Be a good role model for your students. Teachers need to be seen eating well and eating appropriate amounts because your students will model many of their attitudes and their behaviours on yours.
- Do not allow your students to eat in class or 'graze' on snacks or drinks all day long. This 'grazing' behaviour is unnecessary and contributes to overweight and tooth decay. Advise your students that they can sip water in class, but do not tolerate any other type of food or drink in class.
- Do not allow students to store food or drinks other than water in their school bags or desks. Children do not need to be constantly eating and drinking all day long and they do not need to feel fearful of missing out on foods and drinks.
- Encourage your students to eat breakfast as this helps to regulate their food intake over the whole day and prevents 'snack attacks' and food binges. Breakfast consumption is also strongly related to school performance and student behaviour.

Self-esteem and weight

As acknowledged in earlier chapters, self-esteem and weight are linked among children and adolescents of all ages and both genders. Children who have low self-esteem may become overweight because they tend to isolate themselves from other children, not participate in sport or PE and may eat because of boredom, loneliness and as a way to help themselves feel better. Likewise, overweight children may have low self-esteem because they feel less worthy than other children or because they get left out of games and sport or because they get teased about their weight.

Self-esteem is important for all children, but it is particularly important for overweight students as they are known to suffer lower self-esteem. In my 2006 study of young teenage girls aged 11–14 years (O'Dea, 2006), I found that the heaviest girls had very poor self-esteem and that this persisted for the three years of the study. The heavy girls felt less attractive, less popular, had fewer friendships, reported being less socially acceptable, romantically attractive and athletically competent than lower weight girls of the same age, but of most concern was that the heavy girls also felt less intelligent, scholastically competent and less competent in general. The heavy girls in this three year study felt generally worthless and useless, just because they saw themselves as fat.

Teachers can do a lot to foster self-esteem or a sense of self-worth and self-respect in their students, especially among their overweight students or those whose self-image is largely influenced by their body image or their perceived weight status.

Here are a few tips for fostering self-esteem in your students.

Provide unconditional support and respect Try to respect and accept your students the way they are. Every child is different. Accept that each of your students is a separate individual. Remember, it is often the most difficult of our students that need our tolerance, patience and equal treatment the most. It is our most unhealthy and unfit students who really need to be gently encouraged to participate in physical education classes and learn how to enjoy some form of physical activity for life.

Identify your students' uniqueness Help your students to explore the different facets of their self-image by identifying the many varied aspects of themselves that make them unique. Start by identifying different physical features such as eye colour, hair, skin and other unique features. Then explore other features of the child that make them different such as likes and dislikes, hobbies, special talents and abilities. Then delve into their personal features such as their generosity, friendliness, honesty, compassion, sense of humour, positive outlook, patience, determination etc.

Reinforce the idea that everybody is different Teach your students to accept the fact that every person on the planet is unique and help them to respect others and be tolerant of other people's differences.

Help your students to experience success Children need opportunities to succeed at something in life. Give your students some easy tasks to complete so that they can feel competent and helpful. Remember to thank your students for their help.

Praise your students' positive features and behaviours Make certain that you notice your students' positive features and praise them for it. When your students are helpful, considerate, thoughtful, generous, determined, kind, funny or respectful, let them know that you have noticed that special aspect of themselves.

Kate

Kate was always a big child. She was a big baby and her height and weight were always on the top line of her growth charts when her mother took her to the baby health clinic. Despite the nurse reassuring the parents that their daughter was perfectly healthy and that she was just bigger than other girls of her age, the young parents continued to fret about Kate being too big and they feared that she would become very overweight. The family received the same advice from a paediatrician, who checked Kate's blood pressure, hormones, blood cholesterol, blood glucose and bone growth and reported that she was normal, healthy, happy, and that she would always be bigger than the other girls the same age. The family was advised by the hospital dietitian that Kate was in the overweight category, but growing well and that what they needed to focus on was to avoid her becoming obese. It was obvious that Kate took after her grandfather who was a very big, solid man with a tendency to put on weight easily. Kate had a build almost identical to him but her younger brother Chris was slim like his mother. In fact, the whole extended family was slim except for Kate! Kate's father remained slim by chain smoking and not eating properly. The family followed the guidelines outlined below with Kate to promote her growth, her physical health and her self-esteem.

- The parents provided healthy meals, snacks and water as the preferred drink. This meant having to placate young Chris's whining for treats and soft drinks but the parents explained firmly to the whole family that these were 'sometimes foods' and that for the most part, the family was going to focus on healthy foods and drinks.
- The mother provided a constant 'taxi' for Kate's physical activities which included swimming, physical culture and soccer. The family and school teachers encouraged Kate

to continue with these activities and they made sure that she spent after-school time and weekends doing some sort of physical activity. Kate always remained active, healthy and physically fit despite being heavy.

- The parents explained to Kate that she was bigger than other girls and that this was not going to change—her body build was large and solid and that was just the way she was made.

- The whole family, including grandparents, aunts, uncles, cousins and family friends (all of whom are slim!) and the teachers were asked to help Kate accept herself the way she was so that she would avoid developing body image problems or low self-esteem as a result of being self-conscious about her weight. Kate went to a public girls' high school where these issues of weight and body image were taken very seriously by the principal. It was one of the first schools in the country to deal with weight-related teasing and the school staff worked very hard to help bigger girls to become involved in sport and physical activity.

Kate grew and developed over the years from being a tall and solid little toddler to a tubby primary school student to a tall, solid teenager who was certainly much bigger than her teenage girlfriends. She grew up healthy and happy with much love and support from her family and school teachers and she has the sweetest and most helpful and generous nature. She is now a bigger than average, size 16–18 university student with a strong sense of self-worth and a balanced life, which can largely be put down to the love and acceptance that was provided by her parents, school, family and friends. Kate was guided into a healthy lifestyle by her school and family. She never took up smoking, binge drinking or drug taking and she learned to live an active, balanced life. Kate is lucky to have escaped the dieting merry-go-round that most big children and teenagers get trapped in when trying to change their naturally determined body shape and size. Thank goodness that Kate's parents and school teachers had the good sense to realise that her physical fitness, physical health and her mental and emotional state were more important than simply focusing on her weight.

Promoting physical activity in a positive way

Daily physical activity is the key to good health among children and adolescents. Students of all ages, shapes and sizes can benefit from the many health effects of physical activity, irrespective of their weight, and this is an extremely important message for your students.

It is much more effective to teach about physical fitness than to focus on weight. The heart rate activity lesson is an excellent way to take the focus away from weight and put the emphasis on physical activity. Encourage physical fitness by using a heart rate diary; in this way, your most unfit students have the most to gain. This is a highly beneficial activity because instead of being the fat, unfit kids in the class, students can now be given the opportunity to easily succeed at something. The heart rate of students who do not normally participate in physical activity will therefore improve the most.

Rather than presenting physical activity, PE and sport as a mandatory requirement for students, many teachers motivate their students to participate by deliberately focusing on the benefits of physical activity as perceived by the actual students themselves.

In my large national survey of children and adolescents aged 7–17 years (O'Dea, 2003) I asked 213 students in 38 focus groups to tell me why they *do* participate in sports, physical activity, exercise and movement. This was a very important question to have answered because our knowledge to date is largely based on why students *do not* participate. The following table summarises the students' reasons for participation and the benefits they feel they derive from physical activities.

TABLE 8.3 Major themes related to the perceived benefits of physical activity among children and adolescents

Most important benefits	Typical comments from students
Social benefits Fun/enjoyment Develop friendships Socialising with peers Enjoyment of teamwork Fitness aids other areas of life Potential career paths Development of sportsmanship Preparation for life's challenges Development of life skills Team identity Parental approval	'It's fun … just playing with your friends.' (Year 4 male) 'At physical culture … I just have all these friends that I've known for a long time and to have a social group outside of school … it just makes me feel better.' (Year 9 female) 'It's the social part of it that's most important … having friends in the team is really important so that you have fun and you learn to get on with people … and the life skills help with the social side.' (Year 11 male)
Psychological enhancement Sense of achievement Sense of pride Self-esteem Enhanced mood Emotional 'cleansing' Improved confidence Develop discipline Sense of balance in life Reduces guilt Enjoyment of challenges and goals	'You feel better physically and it increases your self-esteem … because you know you're doing something good for your body …' (Year 11 female) 'Feelings about yourself … in the mind … the feeling that you've done something good for yourself … feeling good about yourself … not feeling guilty …' (Year 9 female)
Physical sensation Feel refreshed, 'cleansed' Enjoy sensation of movement Energy creation Energy regulation Reduced fatigue Sensation of wellbeing, strength and fitness Enhanced sleep	'Like you're dancing … you're sweaty but you don't care … you just keep on going and then when you go out you feel so good … you feel so healthy …' (Year 11 male) 'It makes me feel good … afterwards my body just feels better …' (Year 9 female) 'It uses my energy so I'm not restless in the night and I get a good sleep.' (Year 6 male)
Sports performance Improved sports performance Skill development Improved coordination, agility, flexibility and reflexes Improved fitness, strength and endurance	'It keeps you being able to play well for the whole game …' (Year 6 male) 'Being able to run and breathe after you run …' (Year 10 female)
Cognitive benefits Clears mind/clears thinking 'Cleanses' brain Enhances concentration Strengthens brain	'It clears my mind for studying … if I go for a run I can come back and be sharper … better concentration …' (Year 11 male)
Coping strategy Stress relief Mood enhancement Outlet for aggression, frustration and anger Distraction from worries Relaxation Mental break Physical break	'Well … you get your mind off school, like all the pressures of school … you just forget about it … so that's a relief.' (Year 9 male) 'If I'm really, really angry I can go outside and go for a big walk …' (Year 11 female) 'Sometimes I just need to go and punch the punching bag and kick it and stuff and it makes me feel heaps better …' (Year 8 female)

TABLE 8.3 (Continued) Major themes related to the perceived benefits of physical activity among children and adolescents

Moderately important benefits	Typical comments from students
Specific physiological benefits Enhances heart health Enhances bone strength Enhances growth Enhances muscle growth and strength **Health benefits** Prevents minor illnesses Repairs bruises and injuries Balances body functions 'Cleanses' skin 'Cleanses' body	'It burns a bit of fat … if you don't do sports then you'd be fat.' (Year 6 male) 'This is my first year without soccer … I can feel the difference, like I'm not as fit and I can feel the muscles in my legs are skinny compared to last year …' (Year 10 male) 'You end up feeling trim and taut.' (Year 10 male) 'It just balances everything out in your body … everything is fresher and cleaner … your skin … everything …' (Year 9 female)
Excitement Enjoy excitement of competition Creates 'natural high' Enjoy adrenaline rush	'It's enjoyment … like you get this big adrenaline rush …' (Year 9 male)
Aesthetics Enjoy outdoors/fresh air	'I just like being out in the fresh air.' (Year 3 female)

These research findings indicate that students of all ages and both genders are motivated to participate in physical activities because of social and psychological reasons rather than health promotion or disease prevention reasons. Enjoyment of physical activity is therefore the strongest influence on students' participation in sport and physical activities.

The vast majority of students (around 85 per cent) reported that physical activity and exercise were important or very important to them.

The major barriers to physical activities given by the students are outlined in Table 8.4. When asked what would have to happen to help students to engage in more physical activity (What would help you to become more physically active?'), the students reported that they would have to address the following:

Planning/organisation Making arrangements to play with friends, becoming involved in a team, prioritising physical activity as important and fun; increased variety and excitement of physical activity—participants, particularly teenagers, indicated boredom with existing physical education programs and expressed interest in new and unusual activities such as aerobics, martial arts, Tai Bo, yoga, archery, hiking, rock climbing and outdoor water sports.

Parental and school support and involvement Participants of all ages indicated that they would like to do outdoor games and activities with parents and they would like their parents to encourage them to become involved in various physical activities. Students reported that they would like their school to offer different kinds of PE and sports options.

Time management Participants of all ages indicated that they needed to rearrange the amount of time spent on homework, chores, part-time work and family activities to make time for physical activities.

Restructure physical environment Female adolescents indicated that they would like female-oriented sports and activities taught in same sex groups by female teachers in private facilities. They suggested having doors on private showers and change rooms and self-selected physical education uniforms.

Children of all ages expressed the need for parents and teachers to help with these strategies. These reports about factors that motivate physical activity are very valuable data because they are the perceptions of the students themselves. These benefits of healthy behaviours can be maximised to promote the benefits of physical activity to students.

TABLE 8.4 Major barriers to physical activities as given by students in Years 4–12

Major barriers	Typical comments
Preference for indoor activities Prefer to watch TV, videos, play on computer Prefer to play with toys indoors Indoors more private Favourite toys, games, music are indoors	'I'm stuck to the television sometimes ... lots of movies ...' (Year 3 female)
Low energy level Feeling tired, lazy and sluggish 'Junk' food snacks drain energy Lack of energy	'I just can't move ... I just don't feel like moving ... I feel tired or I feel lazy ...' (Year 6 male) 'Junk food makes you slow down ... like really lazy ... you don't feel like doing anything ...' (Year 3 female)
Time constraints Homework consumes spare time Other plans, commitments consume time Part-time work consumes time	'Sometimes I just don't have time 'cause I've got school on and I've got homework or I've got to go to work ...' (Year 11 female)
Social factors Peer pressure—friends are involved in sedentary activities Parental control/preferences Lack of parental support Lack of playmates or suitable playmates Teasing/bullying from peers Criticism from others (peers, teachers)	'... it's like my social life as well ... I just like to go and hang around with friends ... sit and talk ...' (Year 9 female)
Motivation Low level of self-motivation Low level of motivation from others Low perceived rewards	'I'd do more stuff if I had someone to do it with me ... because you'd motivate each other ...' (Year 10 male)
Moderate barriers	**Typical comments**
Dislike physical activities Dislike/disinterest in school sport and school PE activities Boredom with some activities Lack of new activities	'I just get so bored with the same thing over and over ... if you've been doing the same thing for years, it gets a bit boring ... ' (Year 11 female)
Psychological factors Fear of failure Self-consciousness about appearance, uniform, skill, opposite sex Embarrassment in change rooms/showers	'You get tested ... you get a C or D in PE if you can't do a flip on the vault ... like everyone's watching ... you feel bad ...' (Year 9 female)
Access and availability Lack of transport to activities Cost of organised activities Lack of equipment	'When dad's working, I can't get down to the beach ... I'm not allowed to go because I'm too young ...' (Year 6 male)
Weather/outdoor conditions Weather extremes Lack of daylight Neighbourhood safety	'The biggest thing that stops me is the heat ... the midday heat ...' (Year 9 female)
Physical discomfort Injury or perceived risk of injury Dislike physical movement Dislike sensation of being hot and sweaty Discomfort during menstruation	'I don't like being hot and sweaty ... its nicer to be inside ...' (Year 3 female)

A particularly important factor to promote to students is the use of physical activity as a form of stress control. Many students in my research studies, particularly senior students involved in preparation for exams, reported using physical activity as an important way to release stress, re-energise for study and aid in promoting sleep. These are very important and relevant health messages for students and parents.

Unhelpful and undesirable approaches to obesity prevention in schools

Rather than applying well-considered, positively focused and research-based approaches to child obesity prevention, many schools have jumped in rather quickly to implement all sorts of kneejerk strategies to help in the prevention of overweight and obesity. Unfortunately, some of these perfectly well-meaning approaches implemented by truly caring teachers have resulted in many of the adverse outcomes outlined previously in this chapter in Table 8.2.

The following case studies have been reported from various schools. All of these case studies are based on true, real-life school situations and all of them are completely inappropriate as child obesity prevention initiatives.

Case study 1

Setting: local high school

An English teacher at the high school noticed that there were a lot of overweight girls at the school. She decided to start a weight loss group as she had a history of overweight herself and she wanted to help the overweight girls.

The teacher advertised the group by putting fliers up around the school. She did not involve members from any other school faculty.

Once the group was established they met at lunchtime and the teacher provided dieting tips, support and advice for the girls to follow.

They were encouraged to lose weight and gain support by seeking sponsorship from family, relatives, community members and friends. Money was given to students according to how much weight was lost. The money raised was then sent to starving children in Ethiopia.

Case study 2

Setting: local primary school

It was noticed that a number of the children at the primary school were overweight. A committee at the school formed to tackle the problem. The committee recommended starting a 'No fat' club.

Students were selected based on strict criteria of being a certain amount overweight. Children were identified by staff as potential members. These children were then approached and encouraged to join. The children had their weight and height measured, and were excluded if they did not meet the criteria.

The group met at lunchtimes and ate their lunch separately to the rest of the children, supervised by staff involved in the program. They were engaged in a range of physical activities and training regimens.

As part of a parent evening, the group did a performance which was a dance and they wore bandannas across their forehead which had the words 'No fat' written across them.

Case study 3

Setting: local high school

A local high school was concerned about the growing obesity problem at their school. The PE staff designed a unit of study to look at this issue.

In this unit the PE staff set tasks which get the students to:

- record a food diary
- calculate the number of calories in the diet
- calculate the grams of fat
- ask students how they could reduce their calorie intake to lose weight.

Case study 4

Setting: local high school

The community health educator received a call from her local high school principal who advised that there had been four cases of anorexia nervosa at the school in the past two years and she wanted someone to come and give a stern talk to the students.

The principal wanted the health educator to give a talk to all of the senior girls (not the boys) to specifically point out the dangers of eating disorders and the inappropriateness of weight loss methods such as dieting, vomiting and laxative abuse.

The principal also advised that in preparation for the visit, the students would be doing the following research projects:

- a research project on eating disorders and the harmfulness of eating disorder methods for losing weight
- a case study of a celebrity with an eating disorder.

Luckily, the health educator in this instance could advise the principal about more positive ways to handle the current situation. She met with the principal, teachers, parents and student representatives and discussed the broader school issues of what was being taught in the curriculum and how it was being presented to students. She provided some more positive ways of dealing with weight issues including healthy nutrition messages and ways of promoting physical activity and self-esteem. Most importantly, the health educator was able to collaborate with the school counsellor to provide some counselling and medical treatment for the girls who had eating disorders.

Activities for prevention of overweight and obesity in schools

Following in Table 8.5 are some positive approaches for activities that foster health, physical activity and wellbeing in schools while simultaneously contributing to the prevention of child overweight and eating disorders. A more detailed description of the health promoting school approach will be outlined later in Chapter 10.

Activities for teaching about health and weight in a holistic and positive way

Activity 1	'What is health?' Fact files on the many different dimensions of health
Activity 2	Native American poem about spiritual, social, cultural and environmental health
Activity 3	Quick quiz—How 'healthy' are you?
Activity 4	Health statements—'So, what's your opinion?'
Activity 5	Measuring fitness—my heart rate diary
Activity 6	Debate, group discussion and group presentation or essay topic
Activity 7	School health survey
Activity 8	Fact file—bullying
Activity 9	Michael's bad day
Activity 10	What is cyber bullying?
Activity 11	Health word puzzle

TABLE 8.5 Positive approaches for activities that foster health, physical activity and wellbeing in schools

Anti-teasing activities
- Have your school announce zero tolerance of any weight or shape based teasing or harassment including exclusion, name calling, threats, sarcasm, physical teasing such as tripping, gossip and damaging possessions.
- An excellent activity for classroom lessons on this topic is to have students investigate different types of prejudice—racial vilification, gender discrimination, religious intolerance, homophobia and then discuss how weight prejudice is just like any other form of prejudice or intolerance.
- Another activity is to have students define bullying and harassment and then design an anti-teasing policy or set of guidelines for their classroom or their school.

Peer support
- Peer support has many wide and varied benefits and providing support and guidance for students with body image issues is an appropriate focus for peer support students.
- Involving older students in the supervision and motivation of younger students in physical activities is a positive way to motivate physical activity in both groups of students.

Promotion of the many benefits of healthy eating and physical activity
- Reinforce 'whole' health that includes physical, mental, social, spiritual and cultural aspects of health.
- Avoid promoting the narrow and incorrect assumption that slimness equates with health or happiness or success.
- Likewise avoid promoting the assumption that fatness equates with illness, unhappiness or failure.
- Focus on the positive benefits of healthy behaviours rather than the negative consequences of unhealthy behaviours.
- Conduct a survey about the benefits of healthy eating and physical activity using the research surveys outlined in Chapters 7 and 8.
- Include students, parents, teachers and school staff in the survey.
- Use the survey results to promote and support a healthy school canteen and physical activities at school.

Redesign sports, PE and swimming uniforms
- Involve students in a survey to consider the redesign of clothes for physical education, sport and swimming.
- A particular focus of this research is to encourage more students to participate in PE, sport and swimming by allowing them to wear more comfortable, modest, desirable or suitable clothing.
- Design students can become involved in the actual design of the uniforms and various school classes can become involved in the research, planning, promotion etc.

Make the physical environment more suitable for participation in physical activity
- Provide privacy in change rooms and showers or allow sensitive students to change in private.
- Offer students some same sex PE activities or sports activities—especially swimming.
- Modify the sports uniform or swimwear to encourage participation in physical activity.
- Ask parents to become involved in supervision if extra staff are required.
- Offer a variety of non-competitive physical activities such as dance, yoga, rock climbing, outdoor education, walking, martial arts, tabloid games etc.

Change the school timetable to allow for more play time
- Have students first go out to play at lunchtime and then allow time for them to come inside to eat lunch at their desks. This increases play time and increases the likelihood that students will take time to eat their lunch.
- Explore different ways of students utilising play equipment and playgrounds before or after hours at school. Even if this activity was only available on one day for one hour a week, it would provide some beneficial physical activity for some children.
- Collaborate with local council, community organisations and volunteers to assist with these after-hours activities.

Encourage walking or riding to school
- Involve parent volunteers to walk to school with small groups of students.
- In many states this is known as 'the walking school bus' with parents organising small neighbourhood groups of students to walk to and from school with a parent guide.
- Encourage bike riding by having a safe lock up area so that students' bikes, scooters or skate boards do not get stolen.
- Give students personal health promotion contracts or pedometers to motivate their positive health behaviours. Have walking to school as part of their healthy criteria.

Summary

A student's weight, height and shape are both genetically and environmentally determined. The prevention of child obesity should focus on providing and promoting sensible eating habits and daily physical activity in schools and communities while simultaneously avoiding the inadvertent creation of adverse outcomes such as weight stigmatisation, weight concerns among students, poor body image and reduced physical activity because of self-consciousness, fad dieting, demoralisation of students and gateways to weight teasing and bullying.

There are many issues for teachers and school administrators to consider before they embark on any obesity prevention activities. An important consideration is the potential to inadvertently create or worsen body image concerns among students, particularly among overweight students or those who perceive themselves as overweight. Several case studies of real students in real life situations have been presented in this chapter to illustrate how, despite our very best intentions, teachers can sometimes do more harm than good when attempting to deal with issues in child obesity prevention. Similarly, some true case studies of positive student experiences are also given. Finally, the holistic approach to teaching about these health issues has been outlined and some suggested activities and classroom lessons have been presented.

Creating a safe and supportive school environment for overweight and obese students is a very important aim for schools involved in child obesity prevention. Schools can certainly make the physical environment healthier and more likely to promote physical activity among students, but one of our top priorities should also be to make certain that our bigger students do not suffer any unintentional humiliation or sense of failure. The topic of creating a health promoting whole school environment is presented in Chapter 10. It focuses in greater detail on the issues for teachers in dealing with our own body image and eating issues and how our personal weight issues may impact upon our approaches to overweight and obesity in schools. Chapter 10 also deals with teacher training issues for the prevention of body image problems and weight issues in schools.

Activity 1 'What is health?' Fact files on the many different dimensions of health

What is health?

Our health encompasses so much more than just physical health and physical fitness. While these facets of overall health are important, other dimensions also come into play when developing a framework to encourage and support health for all. The World Health Organization defines health as 'a state of complete physical, mental and social wellbeing and not merely the absence of disease of infirmity'. The following provides an overview and explanation of the many dimensions of health and wellbeing.

Physical health

Physical health often dominates our perceptions of overall health. The idea that health means 'not being sick' or 'not being fat' are common viewpoints, but these are very limited. Physical health encompasses immunity, physical growth, maintenance, recovery from injury, overall function of the senses, susceptibility to disease and disorders, body functioning, stress management and recuperative ability. It also means maintaining normal growth in childhood and adolescence.

Mental/psychological health

Mental or psychological health includes a person's mental status and their mental functioning. Again, the dimensions of mental health encompass not just being mentally ill, but also a sense of psychological wellbeing. Children and adolescents have sound mental health when they feel loved, respected, safe, secure and when they have a responsible adult taking care of them. Psychosocial health in children and adolescents is also characterised by a sense of self-worth, self-esteem, self-satisfaction and optimism about their place in the world and their future. Mental health also refers to a sense of resilience where people can develop the ability to learn from their mistakes and failures and are able to grow from experience. Decision making is a vital component of mental health.

Social health and cultural health

We all need to have social interactions and relationships with others in order to lead satisfying lives and buffer the effects of stress and anxiety. Being able to talk to someone about various issues and problems is essential for health. A strong and stable social or cultural network structure promotes overall health. Social health refers to our ability to have satisfying interpersonal relationships, to be able to interact effectively with others, to communicate our needs in an appropriate manner and to adapt to various social or cultural situations. People who have poor social interactions and poor social skills are likely to be lonely, socially isolated and susceptible to mental illness as well as drug and alcohol abuse and other unhealthy forms of stress control.

Activity 1 'What is health?' Fact files on the many different dimensions of health

Emotional health

Emotional health refers to our ability to identify and express our emotions and to have our emotional needs met. Some people grow up in a home or school environment where the four basic emotions—happiness, sadness, fear and anger—are denied, neglected, ignored, exaggerated or have become dysfunctional. In order to be emotionally healthy, we need to be able to identify and express emotions when appropriate. This means the control of expressing emotions either when it is inappropriate to do so or if it is in an inappropriate manner. Feelings of self-esteem, self-confidence, self-efficacy, trust, love and many other emotional reactions and responses are all part of our emotional health.

Spiritual health

Spiritual health refers to our sense of belonging to the world. A person who is spiritually healthy feels that they have a place in the world, that life is important and valuable, with meaning and purpose and that their destiny will also be meaningful and fruitful. Spiritual health may involve a belief in a supreme being or a specified way of living prescribed by a particular religion but this is certainly not necessary for spiritual health. Spiritual health may also include a feeling of unity with the environment—a feeling of oneness with others and with nature—and a guiding sense of meaning of value in life. It also may include an ability to understand and express our purpose in life; to feel a part of a greater spectrum of existence; to experience human emotions and various human life experiences and to acknowledge and respect all living things.

Activity 1 Teaching about health

When teaching about 'health' it is important to help students to recognise and value all of the different aspects of health and how obtaining a balance between all of the dimensions of health is important for achieving a healthy, happy lifestyle.

Lucky Dip 'Health' activities for the school classroom or university setting

- Ask the class to write their own personal definition of 'health' on a piece of paper and after asking all students to fold it in the same way (to maintain anonymity and to avoid identification), place it in the centre of the classroom in a hat or a small box. Ask students to write about what health means to them and which factors in their lives most affect their health.

- If time permits, ask students to write a few comments about how their health could be improved.

- Each student takes a piece of paper from the hat but chooses a different one if they have selected their own definition of health.

- Each student takes turns in reading the definition of health and comments on what factors were affecting the person's definition of health.

- Teacher or student scribe lists all of the different facets of health on the board and all of the factors influencing health.

- Class discussion focuses on the dimensions of health—physical, social, mental/ psychological, emotional, spiritual—and the teacher reiterates the importance of a balanced life for overall health.

- This activity almost always results in students identifying many physical health related factors such as diet, nutrition, physical activity, sleep, not smoking or using drugs and alcohol. Students often forget or fail to identify the various healthy aspects of having a social network, emotional support, someone to talk to, a belief in themselves and a sense of meaning in their life. The teacher needs to remind students of these many important factors in developing and maintaining overall health throughout life.

- Discussion also focuses on how health can be improved and how life events can change our lives and can affect our overall health.

Activity 2 Native American poem about spiritual, social, cultural and environmental health

Native American Poem

O Great Spirit,
Whose voice I hear in the winds,
And whose breath gives life to all the world, hear me!
I need your strength and wisdom.

Let me walk in beauty,
And make my eyes ever behold the red and purple sunset.
Make my hands,
Respect the things you have made and my ears sharp to hear your voice.

Make me wise,
So that I may understand the things you have taught my people.
Let me learn
The lessons you have hidden in every leaf and rock.

I seek strength,
Not to be greater than my brother
But to fight my greatest enemy—myself.

Make me always ready,
To come to you with clean hands and straight eyes.
So when life fades, as the fading sunset
My spirit may come to you without shame.

Student instructions

- Read the poem in pairs

- What do you think the poem is saying about spiritual health?

  _____

  _____

- What is it saying about social, mental and cultural health?

  _____

  _____

- What is it saying about environmental health?

  _____

  _____

Activity 2 Student health assignment— community interview activity

- Explore the different meanings of health among different people in your school, university campus, home, family or local community.

- Work in pairs or small groups to interview a person about their definition of health and the factors affecting their health.

- This activity works best if students seek a person who is in a different age group, a different gender or ethnic group or of a different cultural or religious background.

- Interviews can be written up as a descriptive case study or tape-recorded or video taped.

- Present your interviews or case studies to the whole class.

- Discuss how different people perceive 'health' and how the broad view of health encompasses physical, mental, social, cultural, emotional and spiritual health.

- Further discuss how this definition of health applies to everyone.

Activity 3 Quick quiz—How 'healthy' are you?

- Use the following quick quiz to help students of all ages to explore the different dimensions of their overall health status.
- This activity can be given as a private homework activity, an online activity or in class as a handout.
- Reiterate the many different dimensions of 'health' and the fact that all aspects of health are important.

'Holistic health' activity

- In this activity students learn about the holistic nature of health and the many different dimensions required for good health.
- Students learn that overall health cannot be achieved without attention to all aspects of health and that their weight status does not independently affect health.
- They learn that healthy behaviours such as eating fruits and vegetables, engaging in some form of relaxation or stress control and having some daily physical activity promote health.
- Students learn that health is certainly not all about weight.
- Students are given a copy of the 'Quick quiz—How "healthy" are you?'
- Students work in pairs, discussing the many factors that affect their own personal health status.
- Final discussion focuses on how students can better promote all aspects of their overall health.
- An interesting discussion at this stage of the lesson is to ask students to suggest ways of making their school more 'healthy'.

Activity 3 Quick quiz—How 'healthy' are you?

Physical health	Rarely or never	Some-times	Most of the time	Always
I get at least eight hours of sleep each night	1	2	3	4
I get colds, flu or infections	4	3	2	1
I get at least 30 minutes of walking, playing or other exercise every day	1	2	3	4
I eat fruits and vegetables every day	1	2	3	4
I do some form of relaxation and stress release daily	1	2	3	4
Social and cultural health				
I get along with the members of my family	1	2	3	4
I have someone that I can talk to about my feelings	1	2	3	4
I have a friend or friends of my own age group	1	2	3	4
I consider how what I say might affect others	1	2	3	4
I consider what I say before I speak	1	2	3	4
Emotional health				
I manage to 'bounce back' after difficult things happen in my life	1	2	3	4
I can express my feelings of happiness, sadness, fear or anger without feeling silly	1	2	3	4
I am an extreme worrier	4	3	2	1
I am able to adjust to changes in my life	1	2	3	4
When I am angry or annoyed with someone, I can let them know in a calm, respectful way	1	2	3	4
Spiritual health				
I believe that my life is worthwhile	1	2	3	4
I feel that I have my place in the world	1	2	3	4
I look forward to the things my life may offer now and in the future	1	2	3	4
I think that all people and living things have an important place on this earth	1	2	3	4
I believe that everyone has something to offer in life	1	2	3	4

Activity 3 Quick quiz—How 'healthy' are you?

Scores for 'How "healthy" are you?' quick quiz

Physical health score

- **13–17 points** You have excellent physical health—add five more points if you don't smoke! A perfect score for you will be 22.

- **10–12 points** You are moderately healthy and you can add five more points if you don't smoke! You need to take more care of yourself. Think of ways that you can look after your physical self.

- **5–9 points** You are in relatively poor physical health—but you can add five more points if you don't smoke! You need to work on all aspects of your physical health. Even small changes will help you to become healthier.

Social and cultural health score

- **15–20 points** You have excellent social health. You have people who care about you and support you and you take care with the feelings of others. You might be a bit of a social butterfly!

- **10–14 points** You are moderately healthy from a social point of view—you need to focus a little more on developing friendships and social relationships.

- **5–9 points** You are in relatively poor social health—you need to work on all aspects of your social health, relationships and social networks.

Emotional health score

- **13–17 points** You have excellent emotional and mental health. You manage your emotions very well and you adjust to upsets and changes in your life very well.

- **10–12 points** You are moderately healthy—you need to take more care of your emotional needs, expressing your feelings and talking things through with others.

- **5–9 points** You are in relatively poor emotional health—you need to work on all aspects of your emotional health.

Spiritual health score

- **15–20 points** You have excellent spiritual health.

- **10–14 points** You are moderately healthy—you need to take more care to recognise your spiritual beliefs and the meaning of your life.

- **5–9 points** You are in relatively poor spiritual health—you need to work on all aspects of your spiritual health and the meaning and satisfaction of your life.

Total health score

- **79–61 points** You have excellent overall health and you score well on all of the different health scales. Keep it up and you can look forward to a healthy life!

- **60–45 points** You are moderately healthy—you need to take more care of yourself on some scales. You may be doing quite well at some aspects of your health and neglecting other areas. Remember to take care of your 'whole' self and not just some aspects of your overall health!

- **44–20 points** You need to work on all aspects of your health. Ask someone to help you to think of ways of becoming a more 'Healthy' person.

Activity 4 Health statements— 'So, what's your opinion?'

- This activity helps students to explore various aspects of health.
- Teacher uses statements about health to elicit students' opinions about health, nutrition, physical fitness and other dimensions of health.
- Teacher enlarges copies of the opinion cards, cuts them out, sticks them on pieces of cardboard or laminates them and sticks them around the classroom using tape or Blu-Tak.
- Students are instructed to stand up.
- Teacher reads each statement and students have to give their opinion by moving to the section of the room with the opinion card—Strongly Agree, Agree, Undecided, Disagree, or Strongly Disagree.
- Students are asked to give a reason for their opinion.
- After each student has given their reason, students are given the opportunity to change their opinion and move to a different opinion card.

Statements

Physical fitness is the most important aspect of health

Wearing helmets when riding bicycles should be voluntary

Sports uniforms should be voluntary

Slimness is required for health

Good health is a matter of luck

Males should be muscly

Most Australians need to get more exercise rather than trying to lose weight

Teasing someone about their weight is just as bad as teasing someone about their religion

A good breakfast is important for teenagers

Smoking should be banned in Australia

Sporting ability is mostly inherited

Boys are naturally good at sport whereas girls are naturally good at literacy

Advertising should be strongly censored

Activity 4 Health statements—
'So, what's your opinion?'

STRONGLY DISAGREE

STRONGLY AGREE

AGREE

DISAGREE

UNDECIDED

Activity 5 Measuring fitness—my heart rate diary

1　Measure your Resting Heart Rate [RHR]

2　Move around for a few minutes

3　Measure your heart rate again

4　Sit down and rest for three minutes

5　Now measure your recovery heart rate

How do I measure my heart rate?

- Place your index and middle fingers under your jaw bone, and about halfway between your chin and ear—so that you can feel your pulse.

- Looking at your watch/clock, count how many times your heart beats in 15 seconds.

- Multiply by four and you have your heart rate in beats per minute (BPM).

Your heart rate

Record your results in beats per minute (BPM)

Resting HR	Activity HR	Recovery HR

Improving cardiovascular fitness

Each time you move around, or do any activity that increases your heart rate and makes you breathe harder, it makes your heart and lungs work hard to become more efficient at delivering oxygen to your working muscles.

By increasing the efficiency of your heart and lungs, you are increasing your cardiovascular fitness.

As you become fitter, your heart muscle can beat slower because its contractions are stronger and slower. A slow resting heart rate indicates physical fitness.

Each time you plan to do an activity, measure and record your heart rate in BPM using the 'My activity diary' hand out.

We will check to see your improvement at the end of term.

Activity 5 Measuring fitness—my heart rate diary

My activity diary

Date	Activity	Resting HR	Activity HR	Recovery HR
Example: 12/4/07	Playing with soccer ball for two minutes	85	160	95

Post test results

Resting HR	Activity HR	Recovery HR				

Activity 6 Debate, group discussion and group presentation or essay topic

Students discuss, debate or write a response to the statement 'Good health is a matter of luck', keeping in mind the full definition of health, wellbeing and all of its dimensions.

Activity 7 School health survey

- Use the following questions from my 2000 national health, nutrition and physical activity survey (O'Dea, 2003) to repeat this research project in your own classroom or in your whole school. Compare your findings with those of the 2000 survey.
- Have students work in pairs or groups to interview each other, other students, teachers, parents or community members about the many benefits of healthy eating and physical activity.

Questions about food and nutrition

Benefits of healthy eating

- What are healthy foods and drinks?
- What is healthy eating?
- Is healthy eating important to you? Why? Why not?
- What are the benefits of healthy eating to you?
- What does healthy eating do for you? How?
- Which benefits are the most important to you? Why?
- Can you vote on which benefit of healthy eating is most important to you?

Barriers to healthy eating

- If you sometimes don't have healthy foods and drinks, can you tell me why?
- What stops you having healthy foods and drinks? How? Why?
- Can you vote on which barrier has the greatest effect on you? How? Why?

Strategies to motivate more healthy eating

- What do you think would help you to have more healthy foods and drinks? How? Why?

Questions about physical activity

Benefits of physical activity

- What is physical activity?
- Is physical activity important to you? Why? Why not?
- What are the benefits of physical activity to you?
- What does physical activity do for you? How?
- Which benefits of physical activity are most important to you? Why?
- Can you vote on which benefit of physical activity is most important to you?

Barriers to physical activity

- If you are sometimes not physically active, can you tell me why?
- What stops you from being physically active? How? Why?
- Can you vote on which barrier has the greatest effect on your physical activity? How? Why?

Strategies to motivate more physical activity

- What would help you to be more physically active? How? Why?

Activity 8 Fact file—bullying

Definition

Bullying is:

- a repetitive attack causing distress not only at the time of the attack, but also by the threat of future attacks
- the imbalance of power

Types of bullying

Verbal—name-calling, put-downs, threatening

Physical—hitting, tripping, poking, punching, kicking, throwing objects, stealing

Social—ignoring, hiding, ostracising

Psychological—stalking, dirty looks, spreading rumours, hiding and/or damaging possessions, nasty anonymous text or SMS messages, nasty anonymous emails.

Prejudice

- Teasing can often be related to the general intolerance of others, simply because they are different in some way.
- Examples of this sort of prejudice are racism, sexism, religious or ethnic intolerance, homophobia, and prejudice about how people look—weight, shape, physical appearance.
- Prejudice is never correct or OK because bullying and teasing aim to make others feel controlled or intimidated and less worthy.

Reasons why people engage in bullying and teasing

There are many reasons why people may engage in bullying:

- for entertainment or revenge
- to experience power, to prove themselves or impress others
- to compensate for perceived failure or lack of friends
- to fit in with what others are doing
- because it is seen as an acceptable, funny or smart thing to do.

Students who bully often tend to have:

- high energy levels
- good verbal skills and an ability to talk themselves out of trouble
- a high estimation of their own ability
- an ability to manipulate individuals or groups
- an enjoyment of conflict and aggression
- a delight in getting their own way
- the appearance of being popular, but are often actually disliked.

Activity 8 Fact file—bullying

Teachers' tips for fostering a classroom and school environment that does not tolerate bullying

- Tell students what bullying is and outline your class rules or school rules, that is, zero tolerance.
- Include the topic of bullying in your classroom lessons and activities as well as in your rules for outside of the classroom. This is especially important for physical education teachers to clarify and enforce on the sporting field and elsewhere in outdoor activities.
- Keep your own level of teasing and name calling in check. Many teachers participate in light hearted jesting with students, but we all need to make certain that this sort of teasing is appropriate.
- Teachers need to evaluate their own history of verbal bullying, sarcasm, intimidation and public humiliation. It is sometimes tempting to publicly berate certain students, but we all need to remember that this is actually a form of power imbalance and bullying.
- Never gloss over remarks from students that are based on prejudice such as racism, sexism, religious intolerance, homophobia or weight prejudice. It is not OK to tease someone about their race, ethnicity, skin colour, religion, sexual preference or their weight and shape.
- Foster a climate of social justice in your classroom, in your outside PE areas, on the sporting field and in your general school environment.
- Foster a climate of anti bullying and anti teasing in your department and in your whole school.
- Model respectful behaviour to all of your students.
- Resist labelling your students in your mind or outwardly.
- Reinforce your guidelines on bullying regularly.
- Resist the temptation to bully the bully as this just perpetuates the whole cycle.

Bullying and harassment

- Bullying is more than physical violence like pushing, shoving, hitting, tripping etc. (see fact file on bullying developed from http://cms.curriculum.edu.au/mindmatters/)
- Research shows that bullying not only causes problems for the victims, whose self-esteem is undermined, but for bullies, who continue to misuse their power and become 35–40 per cent more likely to have criminal convictions as adults.
- http://www.cyh.com/Default.aspx?p=1
- http://www.education.unisa.edu.au/bullying/
- http://cms.curriculum.edu.au/mindmatters/

Classroom activity—zero tolerance of bullying and teasing:
- Teacher asks students to work in pairs or small groups to define and describe 'bullying'.
- Students are asked to give examples of bullying in a verbal form, physical sense, social sense and psychological sense.
- Students use the 'What is a bully?' discussion group work sheet.

Activity 8 'What is a bully?'

- What do you think bullying is?

  _____

  _____

- How does bullying occur in the following ways?

  1 Verbally

  _____

  _____

  2 Physically

  _____

  _____

  3 Socially

  _____

  _____

  4 Psychologically

  _____

  _____

- Who are the three main 'players' involved when someone is being bullied?

  1 _____

  _____

  2 _____

  _____

  3 _____

  _____

- What are some other different types of prejudice or bullying?

  _____

  _____

  _____

  _____

  _____

  _____

  _____

Activity 8 'What is a bully?'

Teacher's answers

What do you think bullying is?

Bullying is a repetitive attack causing distress not only at the time of the attack but also by the threat of future attacks. Bullying is a form of unacceptable behaviour but is also a form of hurtful, abusive behaviour.

How does bullying occur in the following ways?

1 Verbally—teasing, name calling, use of unsuitable nick names, put downs, laughing at someone, whispering, sarcasm, threats, yelling at someone, aggressive threats and taunts
2 Physically—hitting, inappropriate touching, poking, punching, shoving, pushing, kicking, throwing objects, stealing, taking possessions
3 Socially—ignoring, hiding, ostracising, leaving people out of a group
4 Psychologically—stalking, dirty looks, giggling, spreading rumours, hiding and/or damaging someone's possessions

Who are the three main 'players' involved when someone is being bullied?

1 The person being bullied—the victim
2 The person doing the bullying—the bully or bullies
3 The people who watch and do or say nothing—the bystanders

What are some other different types of prejudice or bullying?

• Racism—judging or teasing someone on the colour of their skin or their ethnic or cultural background.
• Sexism—judging or teasing someone on their gender, making assumptions about a person just because they are male or female.
• Religious persecution—judging someone on their religion.
• Homophobia—judging or teasing a person on their sexual preference.
• Weightism—judging or teasing a person on their physical appearance, their weight or their shape.

Activity 9 Michael's bad day

'I AM OK'

Teacher reads the script while holding a page that says 'I am OK' near his/her heart and tears off strips of the piece of paper. Tearing the strips illustrates how others bullying and teasing can tear us all to shreds and damage our self-image and our self-esteem.

- Students use 'Michael's bad day' to illustrate the impact of a school culture of bullying on the school experience of a student. The activity also shows how students can damage the self-esteem of others by engaging in teasing or bullying.
- Students use 'I am OK' scripts to illustrate their own experience of bullying or the experiences of others. This activity can be humorous and the message still gets across, so do not worry if your class goes crazy with this activity, the message will still get through.

Script for Michael's bad day

Michael woke up thinking he was OK. The first lesson is maths. The teacher says to take out last night's homework. Michael did the homework, but left it at home. The teacher says sarcastically, 'Michael, don't give me your weak excuses to make up for your laziness'.

RIP (Teacher tears a big strip off the page)

The next lesson is history and Michael thinks 'Oh well, at least I've got my homework for this class'. The teacher asks a question and Michael gives the wrong answer. Lots of students laugh at him.

RIP

Michael is feeling pretty low by now, but he thinks, 'At least I've got my delicious roast lamb sandwiches for lunch'. He goes to his bag to find that someone has taken his lunch and trashed his bag.

RIP

Two older boys are standing nearby and they laugh as they say 'Don't worry Michael, you need to lose weight anyway!'

RIP

After school, Michael sees the girl he likes at the bus stop. He starts to go up to talk to her, but the girls she is with start to giggle and whisper behind their hands. The girl laughs too.

RIP

Discussion

- How do you think Michael felt after this day?
- How would you feel if people treated you like this?
- How would others feel if you behaved like this?
- Practise taking care of other people's self-image.
- Teasing and bullying are never OK.
- Standing by and watching someone being bullied is also not OK.

Bully stories

- Work in pairs to create your own stories of bullying situations.
- Present your story to the class, ripping a strip off your 'I am OK' piece of paper with each incident of bullying or teasing.
- Discuss how any sort of bullying and teasing cannot be tolerated in your class or your school.
- Focus on how the bully, the victim and the bystanders can change in order to make your school a zero tolerance to teasing and bullying school.
- Give a revised presentation of the story with a more positive outcome.

Activity 10 What is cyber bullying?

Student discussion of a newspaper article about the different forms of bullying online.

Read the following article and discuss the questions below.

- What is cyber bullying?

  _____

  _____

- What is your experience of cyber bullying?

  _____

  _____

- Do you know of someone who was bullied in this way?

  _____

  _____

- What is the best way to deal with this sort of bullying?

  _____

  _____

Magazine's research reveals cyber bullying problem

By Stan Beer　　　　　　　　　　　　　　**Monday, 24 April 2006**

Teen magazine Girlfriend has conducted a survey to definitively expose the prevalence of cyber bullying and the impact that it is having on young girls, as part of a 12-month campaign to ban bullying. According to the magazine the results are more alarming than anticipated. Almost half (42 per cent) of the 13 300 teens surveyed have been cyber bullied by a student at their school.

Cyber bullying involves the use of information and communication technologies such as email, mobile phone and pager text messages, instant messaging, defamatory personal web sites and defamatory online personal polling web sites to support deliberate, repeated and hostile behaviour by an individual or group that is intended to harm others. Because kids spend so much time on mobile phones and the Internet, they are easy targets for cyber-abuse.

'There is a belief that cyber bullying isn't a big deal, but Girlfriend's survey confirms it's much more widespread than first thought. Cyber bullying needs to be seen as a significant public health issue that needs more attention,' said Dr Michael Carr-Gregg, Girlfriend and Explode magazines' resident adolescent psychologist.

'Young people today are so technologically experienced that it can be intimidating for adults to keep up, but parents and educators need to be aware of young people's on-line activities. We need to change public perception of the seriousness of the issue. It's an uphill battle because parents are often in the dark about what goes on in their children's world of Internet and text messaging communication and often don't realise that the capacity for harm in the cyber world can be much faster, more widespread and, just as damaging, as in the playground,' he added.

The Internet has taken on a central role in teenage culture, creating a new landscape for social interaction. 97 per cent of the 13 300 girls who participated in Girlfriend's survey have access to the Internet at home, and 69 per cent use their mobile phones at school so it's no surprise that cyberspace has supplemented or replaced lunchroom and after-school cliques. The new school yard now consisting of:

on-line chat rooms

instant messaging (IM)

bulletin boards

email

mobile phone text messages

personal web sites

blogs (web logs or personal diaries on a web site)

The survey reveals that flaming, online harassment, online denigration, online masquerading and exclusion from an online group are common forms of cyber bullying, with online harassment and exclusion being the two most common.

(Reproduced with permission from http://www.itwire.com.au retreived 14 September 2006)

Activity 11 Health word puzzle

Name   Date

Find each of the following words.

SICKNESS	FUN	NOURISHMENT	ENDURANCE
EXERCISE	GROWTH	DIET	VALUES
APPETITE	PHYSICAL	IDENTIFY	RELAXATION
TALKING	PROTEINS	HOLISTIC	PROTEIN
COMMUNICATION	RESPECT	BALANCE	PEER PRESSURE
FAMILY	HEART	MENTAL	FRUIT
REST	MUSCULAR	FITNESS	VEGETABLES
FOOD	CROSS-TRAINING	BULLY	MENTAL HEALTH
SELF-ESTEEM	NUTRITION	FRIENDS	HARMONY
VITAMINS	ILLNESS	CONSUMPTION	LUNGS
CONSIDERATION	WALKING	DISEASE	VEGETABLE
RELATIVES	MUSCLE	WORKOUT	SLEEP
RESPIRATORY			

```
V U T H T W O R G P A L U C S U M R A L U C S U M N
A N E L R C M P Y R O T A R I P S E R K T O S T B L
L Y O H E C N A R U D N E N A M T N S D V L E E S L
U I K I N I K L A T L T O N H S I S F I A L V X C L
E E C U T I S M N T L I S T E E E E M C L I I E Y C
S E K E A A K S M S T N L R T N E A E B U A T R F L
I E T L H D C I E P I A A O L C T T N U E L A C I N
I R T C W G M I M N E T R L N N T E T L T A L I T A
S U R S U S N U N H K P I A N N P T A L C B E S N R
E S A U I G S I L U U C L P E U L H I Y T U R E E S
L S E M A N I A K L M A I M U S P V Y U I R L A D L
B E H X O I T O T L B M H S U H E I R S R I E C I O
A R N C F N T P T S A S O A A I E T N S I F O L R P
T P L S E A M N G H I T U C Y U L A S E U C S N N E
E R A M U U M N E R E S P E C T S M O A L F A O U Y
G E N P S N U I U D S E R L E P H I K M I A O L F D
E E C N P L U O L I I S O I I C F N I N I E T O R P
V P O B A E N G M Y I I D I C O N S I D E R A T D T
R C C E C R T E W A L K I N G R E S P I R A T E H E
S S E N T I F I M M N C O N S I D E R A T I O N S N
E G N I N I A R T - S S O R C A V E G E T A B L E I
S E L F - E S T E E M G S L I L R S D N E I R F I I
M E N T A L V E G E T A B T O N E T E S A E S I D Y
N U T R I T I O N F C H O L I S T I C E I M A T I V
W A L K I N O T P R O T E I N S O W O R K O U T T A
L C R O R E L A X A T I O N N D R H A R M O N Y I W
L M S M A I D R C N E I M - A O P E N L S N R R M L
```

References

Berg F (2000), *Women Afraid to Eat: Breaking free in today's weight-obsessed world*, Healthy Weight Network, Hettinger, ND.

Blair SN (2003), 'Revisiting fitness and fatness as predictors of mortality', *Clinical Journal of Sport Medicine*, *13*(5), 319–20.

Bonjour J, Theintz G, Buchs SB, Slosman D & Rizzoli R (1991), 'Critical years and stage of puberty for spinal and femoral bone mass accumulation during adolescence', *Journal of Clinical Endocrinological Metabolism*, *73*, 555–63.

Booth M, Okely AD, Denney-Wilson E, Hardy L, Yang B & Dobbins T (2006), *NSW Schools Physical Activity and Nutrition Survey (SPANS) 2004: Full report,* NSW Department of Health, Sydney.

Brook C, Lloyd J & Wolff O (1974), 'Rapid weight loss in children', *British Medical Journal*, *3*(5922), 44–5.

Chinn S & Rona RJ (2001), 'Prevalence and trends in overweight and obesity in three cross sectional studies of British children, 1974–94', *British Medical Journal*, *322*(7277), 24–6.

Cole TJ, Bellizi MC, Flegal KM & Dietz WH (2000), 'Establishing a standard definition for child overweight and obesity worldwide: International survey', *British Medical Journal*, *320*, 1240–5.

Croll J, Neumark-Sztainer D, Story M & Ireland M (2002), 'Prevalence and risk and protective factors related to disordered eating behaviours among adolescents: Relationship to gender and ethnicity', *Journal of Adolescent Health, 31*(2),166–75.

Davis D, Apley G, Fill G & Grimaldi C (1978), 'Diet and retarded growth—medical cases of 36 British children', *British Medical Journal*, *1*(6112), 539–42.

Dhuper S, Warren MP, Brooks-Gunn J & Fox R (1990), 'Effects of hormonal status on bone density in adolescent girls', *Journal of Clinical Endocrinological Metabolism*, *71*, 1083–8.

Drake AJ, Smith A, Betts PR, Crowne EC & Shield JP (2002), 'Type 2 diabetes in obese white children', *Archives of Diseases in Children*, *86*, 207–8.

Ehtisham S, Barrett TG & Shaw NJ (2000), 'Type 2 diabetes mellitus in UK children—an emerging problem', *Diabetic Medicine, 17*, 867–71.

Fontaine KR, Faith MS, Allison DB & Cheskin LJ (1998), 'Body weight and health care among women in the general population', *Archives of Family Medicine*, *7*(4), 381–4.

Foster GD, Wadden TA, Makris AP, Davidson D, Sanderson RS, Allison DB & Kessler A (2003), 'Primary care physicians' attitudes about obesity and its treatment', *Obesity Research*, *10*, 1168–77.

Frisch RE, Wyshak G & Vincent L (1980), 'Delayed menarche and amenorrhoea of ballet dancers', *New England Journal of Medicine*, *303*, 17–19.

Garner DM (1985), 'Intragenesis in anorexia nervosa and bulimia nervosa', *International Journal of Eating Disorders*, *4*, 701–26.

Garner DM & Wooley SC (1991), 'Confronting the failure of behavioural and dietary treatments for obesity', *Clinical Psychology Review*, *11*, 729–80.

Goodman E (2003), 'Letting the 'gini' out of the bottle: Social causation and the obesity epidemic', *Journal of Pediatrics*, *142*, 228–30.

Gortmaker SL, Must A, Perrin JM, Sobal AM & Dietz WH (1993), 'Social and economic consequences of overweight in adolescence and young adulthood', *New England Journal of Medicine*, *329*, 1008–12.

Gracey D, Stanley N, Burke V, Corti B & Bellin LJ (1996), 'Nutritional knowledge, beliefs and behaviours in teenage school students', *Health Education Research*, *11*, 187–204.

Hedley AA, Ogden CL, Johnson CL, Carroll MD, Curtin LR & Flegal KM (2004), 'Prevalence of overweight and obesity among US children, adolescents, and adults, 1999–2002', *Journal of the American Medical Association*, *291*, 2847–50.

Heude B, Lafay L, Borys JM, Thibult N, Lommez A, Romon M, Ducimetiere P & Charles MA (2003), 'Time trend in height, weight, and obesity prevalence in school children from Northern France, 1992–2000', *Diabetes Metabolism*, *29*, 235–40.

Ikeda JP & Mitchell RA (2001), 'Dietary approaches to the treatment of the overweight pediatric patient', *Pediatric Clinics of North America*, *48*, 955–68.

Kain J, Uauy R, Vio F & Albala C (2002), 'Trends in overweight and obesity prevalence in Chilean children: Comparison of three definitions', *European Journal Clinical Nutrition*, *56*, 200–4.

Kalies H, Lenz J & von Kries R (2002), 'Prevalence of overweight and obesity and trends in body mass index in German pre-school children, 1982–1997', *International Journal of Obesity Related Metabolic Disorders*, *26*, 1211–7.

Kautiainen S, Rimpela A, Vikat A & Virtanen SM (2002), 'Secular trends in overweight and obesity among Finnish adolescents in 1977–1999', *International Journal of Obesity Related Metabolic Disorders*, *26*, 544–52.

Kulin H, Bwibo N, Mutie D & Santner S (1982), 'The effects of chronic childhood malnutrition on pubertal growth and development', *American Journal of Clinical Nutrition*, *35*, 527–36.

Latner JD & Stunkard A (2003), 'Getting worse: Stigmatization of obese children', *Obesity Research*, *11*, 452–56.

Lev-Ran A (1974), 'Secondary amenorrhoea resulting from uncontrolled weight reduction diets', *Fertility and Sterility*, *25*, 459–62.

Lifshitz F & Moses N (1988), 'Nutritional dwarfing: Growth, dieting and fear of obesity', *Journal of American College Nutrition, 7*, 367–76.

Lifshitz F & Moses N (1989), 'A complication of dietary treatment of hypercholesterolemia', *American Journal of Diseases in Children, 143*, 537–42.

Luo J & Hu FB (2002), 'Time trends of obesity in pre-school children in China from 1989 to 1997', *International Journal of Obesity Related Metabolic Disorders, 26*, 553–8.

Maddox GL & Liederman V (1969), 'Overweight as a social disability with medical implications', *Journal of Medical Education, 44*, 214–20.

Magarey AM, Daniels LA & Boulton TJC (2001), 'Prevalence of overweight and obesity in Australian children and adolescents: Reassessment of 1985 and 1995 data against new standard international definitions', *Medical Journal of Australia, 174*, 561–64.

Mallick MJ (1983), 'Health hazards of obesity and weight control in children: A review of the literature', *American Journal of Public Health, 73*, 78–82.

Mast M, Langnase K, Labitzke K, Bruse U, Preuss U & Muller MJ (2002), 'Use of BMI as a measure of overweight and obesity in a field study on 5–7 year old children', *European Journal of Nutrition, 41*(2), 61–7.

Mellin AE, Neumark-Sztainer D, Story M, Ireland M & Resnick MD (2002), 'Unhealthy behaviours and psychosocial difficulties among overweight adolescents: The potential impact of familial factors', *Journal of Adolescent Health, 31*, 145–53.

Neumark-Sztainer D, Story M & Perry CL (1999), 'Factors influencing food choices of adolescents: Findings from focus groups discussions with adolescents', *Journal of the American Dietetic Association, 99*, 929–34.

Neumark-Sztainer D, Story M, Hannan PJ, Perry CL & Irving LM (2002), 'Weight related concerns and behaviours among overweight and nonoverweight adolescents', *Archives of Pediatric and Adolescent Medicine, 156*, 171–8.

Neumark-Sztainer D, Wall M, Guo J, Story M, Haines J & Eisenberg M (2006), 'Obesity, disordered eating, and eating disorders in a longitudinal study of adolescents: How do dieters fare 5 years later?', *Journal of the American Dietetic Association, 106*(4), 559–68.

O'Dea J (2000), 'School-based interventions to prevent eating problems: First do no harm', *Eating Disorders, 8*(1), 123–30.

O'Dea J (2002), 'Can body image education be harmful to adolescent females?', *Eating Disorders, 10*, 1–13.

O'Dea JA (2003), 'Why do kids eat healthful food? Perceived benefits of and barriers to healthful eating and physical activity among children and adolescents', *Journal of the American Dietetic Association, 103*, 497–501.

O'Dea JA (2006), 'Self-concept, self esteem and body weight in adolescent females: A three-year longitudinal study', *Health Psychology, 11*(4), 599–611.

O'Dea J & Abraham S (1995), 'Should body mass index be used in young adolescents?', *The Lancet, 345*, 367.

O'Dea J & Abraham S (1999), 'Association between self-concept and body weight, gender and pubertal development among male and female adolescents', *Adolescence, 34*, 69–79.

O'Dea J & Abraham S (2001), 'Knowledge, beliefs, attitudes, and behaviours related to weight control, eating disorders, and body image in Australian trainee home economics and physical education teachers', *Journal of Nutrition Education, 33*, 332–40.

O'Dea J, Abraham S & Heard R (1996), 'Food habits, body image and weight control practices of young male and female adolescents', *Australian Journal of Nutrition and Dietetics, 53*, 32–8.

O'Dea J & Maloney D (2001), 'Preventing eating and body image problems in children and adolescents using the Health Promoting Schools Framework', *Journal of School Health, 70*(1), 18–21.

O'Dea JA & Wilson R (2006), 'Socio-cognitive and nutritional factors associated with Body Mass Index in children and adolescents: Possibilities for childhood obesity prevention', *Health Education Research: Theory and practice, 21*(6), 796–806.

Ogden CL, Flegal KM, Carroll MD & Johnson CL (2002), 'Prevalence and trends in overweight among US children and adolescents, 1999-2000', *Journal of the American Medical Association, 288*, 1728–32.

Olson CL, Schumaker HD & Yawn BP (1994), 'Overweight women delay medical care', *Archives of Family Medicine, 3*(10), 888–92.

Ott SM (1991), 'Bone density in adolescents', *New England Journal of Medicine, 325*, 1646–7.

Padez C, Fernandes T, Mourao I, Moreira P & Rosado V (2004) 'Prevalence of overweight and obesity in 7–9-year-old Portuguese children: Trends in body mass index from 1970–2002', *American Journal of Human Biology, 16*, 670–8.

Piran N (1999), 'Prevention in a high-risk environment: An intervention in a ballet school', in Piran N, Levine ML & Steiner-Adair C (eds), *Preventing Eating Disorders: A handbook of interventions and special challenges*, Brunner/Mazel, New York, 148–59.

Powell KE, Bricker SK & Blair SN (2002), 'Treating inactivity', *American Journal of Preventive Medicine, 23*(2), 1–2.

Probyn E & O'Dea JA (2005), 'Youth cultures of eating: A cultural analysis of youth obesity, gender, class, ethnicity and generation', *Australian Research Council Discovery Project 2005–07*.

Pugliese M, Lifshitz F, Grad G, Fort P & Marks-Katz M (1983), 'Fear of obesity: A cause of short stature and delayed puberty', *New England Journal of Medicine, 309,* 513–18.

Robison JI, Hoerr SL, Petersmarck KA & Anderson JV (1995), 'Redefining success in obesity intervention: The new paradigm', *Journal of the American Dietetic Association, 95*(4), 422–3.

Romon M, Duhamel A, Collinet N & Weill J (2005), 'Influence of social class on time trends in BMI distribution in 5-year-old French children from 1989 to 1999', *International Journal of Obesity, 29*(1), 54–9.

Schwartz M, O'Neal Chambliss H, Brownell K, Blair S & Billington C (2003), 'Weight bias among health professionals specializing in obesity', *Obesity Research, 11,* 1033–9.

Shaw SM & Kemeny L (1989), 'Fitness promotion for adolescent girls: The impact and effectiveness of promotional material which emphasises the slim ideal', *Adolescence, 24,* 677–87.

Sobal J & Stunkard AJ (1989), 'Socioeconomic status and obesity: A review of the literature', *Psychological Bulletin, 105,* 260–275.

Society for Nutrition Education (2002), 'Guidelines for childhood obesity prevention programs: Promoting healthy weight in children'. Viewed 17 January 2007 at: http://www.sne.org/Chi_Obesity.pdf

Stice E, Cameron R, Killen JD, Hayward C & Taylor CB (1999), 'Naturalistic weight reduction efforts prospectively predict growth in relative weight and onset of obesity among female adolescents', *Journal of Consulting and Clinical Psychology, 67,* 967–74.

Strauss RS (2000), 'Childhood obesity and self-esteem', *Pediatrics, 105*(1).

Strauss RS & Mir HM (2001), 'Smoking and weight loss attempts in overweight and normal-weight adolescents', *International Journal of Obesity and Related Metabolic Disorders, 25*(9), 1381–5.

Strauss RS & Pollack HA (2003), 'Social marginalization of overweight children', *Archives of Pediatrics and Adolescent Medicine, 157*(8), 746–52.

Theintz GE, Howald H, Weiss U & Sizonenko C (1993), 'Evidence for a reduction of growth potential in adolescent female gymnasts', *Journal of Pediatrics, 122*(2), 306–13.

Troiano RP & Flegal KM (1998), 'Overweight children and adolescents: Description, epidemiology, and demographics', *Pediatrics, 101*(3), 497–504.

Wabitsch M, Hauner H, Hertrampf M, Muche R, Hay B, Mayer H, Kratzer W, Debatin KM & Heinze E (2004), 'Type II diabetes mellitus and impaired glucose regulation in Caucasian children and adolescents with obesity living in Germany', *International Journal of Obesity Related Metabolic Disorders, 28,* 307–13.

Wang Y, Monteiro C & Popkin BM (2002), 'Trends of obesity and underweight in older children and adolescents in the United States, Brazil, China, and Russia', *American Journal of Clinical Nutrition, 75,* 971–7.

Wee CC, McCarthy EP, Davis RB & Phillips RS (2000), 'Screening for cervical and breast cancer: Is obestiy an unrecognized barrier to preventive care?', *Annals of Internal Medicine, 132*(9), 697–704.

Wiegand S, Maikowski U, Blankenstein O, Biebermann H, Tarnow P & Gruters A (2004), 'Type 2 diabetes and impaired glucose tolerance in European children and adolescents with obesity—a problem that is no longer restricted to minority groups', *European Journal of Endocrinology, 151*(2), 199–206.

Young LM & Powell B (1985), 'The effects of obesity on the clinical judgements of health care professionals', *Journal of Health Sociology and Behaviour, 26,* 233–46.

9 The role of teachers in body image development and prevention of obesity

Introduction

This chapter examines the important contribution that teachers, health educators, school nurses, school counsellors, school psychologists, dietitians and sports coaches have to offer in the prevention of eating disorders and child obesity.

It is important to recognise that while school staff have an extremely important role in health promotion and prevention of body image concerns and obesity, there is also a current need to specifically examine how teachers and school personnel may be best trained and prepared for such a preventive role. It needs to be determined whether teachers currently feel willing and able to undertake such a role and whether some groups of teachers may be personally susceptible to body image and eating problems themselves.

It is vital to understand the knowledge, behaviours, attitudes and expectations of teachers and other educators who will be implementing any child obesity or eating disorder prevention programs in order to ensure that they are personally and professionally capable of carrying out such prevention initiatives in schools.

Research shows that individuals involved in food and exercise-related careers have been identified as being at risk for body image and eating problems, and it may be possible that they chose their career path due to their own personal experience with eating disorders or weight issues. In such cases specific training or assistance may be required in order to enable the educators to conduct effective preventive activities.

Discussion in this chapter focuses on what may need to be done so teachers and other school-based educators can perform most effectively in the implementation of school-based eating disorder and child obesity prevention programs.

An outline of my course outline and training program for trainee health education, home economics and physical education teachers is also presented.

Schools as appropriate sites for prevention of body image problems and obesity

Schools have been recognised as appropriate settings for the prevention of eating disorders and child obesity due to the continual and concentrated access to a large number of individuals at a developmentally appropriate age (Neumark-Sztainer, 1996; O'Dea, 2000; O'Dea & Abraham, 2000; Piran, 2004; Smolak et al., 2001). In addition to providing access to children and adolescents, school-based programs offer the opportunity for curriculum support and reinforcement using a whole-school approach to health promotion (O'Dea & Maloney, 2000; Smolak et al., 1998). Although much emphasis and evaluation has been directed towards the theoretical grounding and content of prevention programs, few studies have investigated the nutrition and weight control knowledge, attitudes and behaviours of those who are delivering them (O'Dea & Abraham, 2001; Smolak et al., 2001).

Many school and health professionals are perfectly positioned and have the potential to become involved in the prevention or treatment of eating disorders and child obesity. Physical education, home economics and health education teachers have formal and informal access to a large number of young people in an environment that stimulates discussion and allows for lessons about body image, nutrition and weight control (O'Dea & Abraham, 2001; Smolak et al., 2001). These teachers also have the chance to initiate the reinforcement of prevention programs using the whole-school approach (Neumark-Sztainer, 1996; O'Dea & Maloney, 2000). Home economics, science, dance and English teachers have opportunities to become involved in preventive activities within their appropriate curriculum areas as well as through involvement in pastoral care roles such as year advisers, student welfare coordinators and head teachers. Healthcare workers in schools, such as school counsellors and school nurses, also have many opportunities to present information to students and implement prevention programs (Neumark-Sztainer, Story & Harris, 1999).

At present, schools do not make the most of these potential opportunities for the prevention of eating disorders and child obesity. School teachers and school personnel receive minimal or no training in nutrition or prevention techniques, and they consistently report a lack of knowledge as a barrier to implementing prevention programs (Neumark-Sztainer, Story & Coller, 1999; Stang et al., 1997). The knowledge, attitudes and willingness of school professionals must be considered before deeming them prepared and capable of implementing prevention or treatment programs. In addition, such intervention would also serve to protect the personal wellbeing of the professionals and the students and promote the likely success of prevention initiatives.

It is important to examine the role of teachers and other school professionals (such as health educators, school nurses, school counsellors, school psychologists and sports coaches) in the prevention of eating disorders and child obesity with specific examination of whether:

1 teachers and school professionals are adequately trained and prepared to undertake a preventive role
2 this training is likely to affect their attitudes
3 the teachers and other school education professionals are susceptible to body image and eating problems themselves.

Prevention versus treatment

In Chapter 8, the teacher's role in prevention was outlined and clarified, with their role in treatment being clearly limited. It is not our role as teachers to become involved in the treatment of eating disorders or the prescription of diets or exercise programs for overweight students. These students need to be referred to the school counsellor, nurse, local doctor or other suitable health professional.

Different types of prevention

The different types of prevention are outlined below. There are three levels of prevention:

Primary Directed at people before a health problem occurs, they show no signs of ill health and the aim of primary prevention programs is to prevent the onset of any disease. Examples of primary prevention programs are mass immunisation programs, drug education in schools and sex education in schools.

Secondary Directed at people who are at risk, but have not yet developed any ill health. For example, HIV/AIDS education programs, immunisation for rubella for teenage girls, Quit smoking programs.

Tertiary Directed at people who have a health problem. For example, exercise/nutrition programs for people with heart disease, asthma education programs for people with asthma.

Issues of professional training and preparedness

Knowledge of eating disorders, nutrition and obesity is assumed, but not guaranteed, among professionals who are likely to be involved in the prevention of eating disorders and obesity. Teachers and school professionals receive little training in nutrition and techniques used in prevention, and this lack of knowledge is reported as a barrier to the implementation of prevention initiatives (Neumark-Sztainer, Story & Coller, 1999; Stang et al., 1997). In her study of 114 school professionals in the USA, Neumark-Sztainer, Story and Coller (1999) found that no participant was currently involved in staff training to learn prevention tools, yet 72 per cent indicated a high or very high interest in the area. An additional problem is that school professionals are becoming confused about their role in the prevention of eating disorders and child obesity with many believing that they should be providing treatment. This lack of knowledge and properly defined role may be linked to the current low level of teacher involvement in preventive efforts and the modest impact of school-based prevention initiatives.

The nutrition training that school professionals receive is limited and is largely dependent upon the subject in which they are trained, the university that they attend and the teacher's personal interest in the topic. Teachers (Neumark-Sztainer, Story & Coller, 1999), school nurses (Price, Desmond, Ruppert & Stelzer, 1987) and elementary school principals (Price, Desmond & Stelzer, 1987) have a poor knowledge of the causes of obesity; with the majority holding largely outdated and simplistic views about obesity being exclusively related to excessive calorie consumption and lack of physical activity while ignoring biological or genetic factors. In a recent study O'Dea & Abraham (2001) found that 87 per cent of trainee physical education and home economics teachers reported giving strict and unsuitable dietary advice to overweight young adolescent students, such as recommending that they go on a 1200-calorie controlled diet. The teachers also had a poor knowledge and many misconceptions about the aetiology and effects of eating disorders. School professionals have been shown to both require and demand further training to assist them in the prevention of eating and weight-related problems in schools.

A study of coaches and trainers of high school athletics teams in the USA (Graves et al., 1991) found considerable variance in the amount and nature of professional training the school sports staff had received. The study also found that coaches and trainers scored poorly on a test of nutrition knowledge (59 per cent and 64 per cent respectively); and did not feel that it was their responsibility to disseminate nutrition information, despite the nature of their exposure to the students offering many opportunities for them to do so (Graves et al., 1991). In another US study, Price and colleagues (1990) found that 40 per cent of school counsellors did not feel competent in helping students with eating disorders and 49 per cent reported that they felt only moderately competent. Half of the school counsellors also reported using the mass media as a source of information about nutrition and eating disorders (Price et al., 1990). Similarly, the knowledge and skills of school nurses has been emphasised as crucial in their role of detection of eating disorders, yet the nutrition and weight-related training of this important group of health professionals is known to be inadequate (Connolly & Corbett-Dick, 1990).

High proportions (70 per cent) of high school science, physical education, health and home economics teachers have shown interest in staff training to improve their knowledge and skills in the prevention of weight-related disorders (Neumark-Sztainer, Story & Coller, 1999; Stang et al., 1997). Lack of training (53 per cent) and lack of educational materials (42 per cent) have been identified as major barriers to the implementation of weight management information in schools (Stang et al., 1997).

School professionals attending an Australian conference about the prevention of eating disorders, also requested increased staff training in preference to other resources to enable them to implement prevention activities in schools (Yager, 2003). Although this evidence may indicate a low level of current knowledge and skills, it is promising in that it suggests that school professionals would be dedicated to the school-based prevention of obesity and eating disorders provided they were adequately trained.

Prepared for prevention or treatment?

The role of teachers and school personnel in the prevention or treatment of child obesity and eating disorders needs to be clearly defined. The clinical treatment of such disorders should remain the realm of trained professionals who are capable of implementing an appropriate treatment regimen. Teachers should not be expected to become involved in activities that encroach on clinical treatment or any activity that may inadvertently delay appropriate referral or treatment of individuals. Such inappropriate activities would include attempts to counsel the child or the prescription of diets or weight control regimens.

The separation of clinical treatment and prevention of eating disorders and child obesity should be made very clear to school personnel. School professionals have a variety of formal and informal opportunities for the prevention of child obesity and eating disorders. However, at present, many seem to believe that they are responsible for the treatment of weight-related disorders; a role that is better left to professionals who are more appropriately trained. Surveys have reported that teachers and school health workers (Neumark-Sztainer, Story & Coller, 1999), elementary school principals (Price, Desmond & Stelzer, 1987), and school nurses (Price, Desmond, Rupert & Stelzer, 1987) believe that the school should play a role in the treatment of obesity, but the majority of respondents believed that they were currently not competent in doing so. Elementary school principals named the school nurse (77 per cent), the school counsellor (69 per cent) and the physical education teacher (59 per cent) as the school professionals who should play a major role in the treatment of child obesity in schools (Price, Desmond & Stelzer, 1987). One quarter of school counsellors believed that it was their responsibility to treat students for eating disorders (Price et al., 1990).

It is vital that the distinction between the school's role in the prevention and treatment of eating disorders and obesity be highlighted in future teacher training programs. School professionals must be reminded of the prospect of informal and formal opportunities for prevention, and of their important role in the early detection of eating disorders and obesity. They must be advised about appropriate and inappropriate treatments for weight-related disorders, and, most importantly, teachers need to be trained to establish and follow proper processes of referral for at-risk students. Schools do not need to be burdened by the responsibility of providing treatment for these problems, or to possess the resources or suitably trained professionals to do so.

Issues of referral

In the research literature to date, school professionals report referring at-risk students to general practitioners, counsellors and dietitians (Graves et al., 1991; Price et al., 1990). However, medical professionals such as dietitians (Story et al., 2002), paediatricians (Story et al., 2002), and general practitioners (Gurney & Halmi, 2001) report that their own lack of knowledge is a barrier in the treatment of obesity and eating disorders. In particular, dietitians and paediatricians report limited knowledge about behavioural management and providing guidance on parenting techniques (Story et al., 2002). In addition, 90 per cent of doctors did not feel that their knowledge of nutrition was adequate enough for them to feel confident in providing nutritional counselling (Kushner, 1995). It may seem that the medical profession is also unprepared for the proliferation of weight-related disorders with a lack of specialised professionals to treat obesity and eating disorders in young people.

Attitudes towards obesity and eating disorders

Reports of negative attitudes towards individuals who are obese in employment, medical and education settings dominate the literature (Puhl & Brownell, 2001). This has been linked to the stigma attached to overweight, the pervasive dominance of the thin ideal, and the perception that individual factors are the main causes of obesity. Health professionals presumed to be most knowledgeable about obesity, and who work closely with obese people in research or treatment, are not immune to bias, prejudice and discrimination towards their overweight patients. Research studies have utilised implicit attitude tests that enable the measurement of automatic associations that exist beyond conscious control and which people may be unaware of, or unwilling to report. These measures have consistently shown professionals and the general public to have implicit negative attitudes towards obesity and obese people (Schwartz et al., 2003; Teachman & Brownell, 2001). One study found medical students characterise obese individuals as lazy (57 per cent), sloppy (52 per cent) and lacking in self-control (62 per cent). Negative attitudes and bias towards obese individuals were particularly prevalent among those professionals who were young and female (Schwartz et al., 2003).

School professionals often incorrectly identify individual behaviours such as over consumption and inactivity as the major or only causes of obesity (Neumark-Sztainer, Story & Haris, 1999; Price, Desmond, Rupert & Stelzer, 1987). This has been suggested to lead to a negative, 'victim blaming' attitude towards obese people (Neumark-Sztainer, Story & Coller, 1999; Schwartz et al., 2003). Teachers have also been shown to associate thinness with intelligence, motivation and willpower (Piran, 1998). The development of appropriate attitudes towards obesity among teachers and other school professionals is crucial in the effectiveness of prevention programs (O'Dea, 2000; O'Dea & Abraham, 2001; Piran, 1998; Stewart, 1998).

The relatively low clinical prevalence, covert behaviour of individuals with eating disorders, and considerable media interest in the conditions has led to a variety of attitudes towards sufferers. While dieting and body dissatisfaction are generally accepted as a type of 'normative discontent' for women (Rodin et al., 1985), eating disorders still tend to carry a stigma different to the majority of mental illnesses (Mond et al., 2004). Research regarding the attitudes of the lay public in Britain reported that one third of respondents believed that people with eating disorders could 'pull themselves together' and had only themselves to blame for the development of their disorder (Crisp et al., 2000). School professionals have been shown to have misperceptions about the causes and development of eating disorders which could perpetuate negative attitudes by passing them on to students (O'Dea & Abraham, 2001).

Eating and exercise behaviours of school professionals

School professionals are expected to implement prevention programs for eating disorders and obesity, yet there has been no prior investigation of their personal and professional capability in these roles. Evaluations of prevention programs for eating disorders and obesity have articulated the importance of the personal body image and eating behaviours of those presenting the programs (Bassler, 2001; Piran, 1998; Piran, 2004; Rutz, 1993; Stewart, 1998). School professionals are likely to be influenced by the same sociocultural factors as other adults. There is also the possibility that home economics and physical education teachers may be more susceptible to body image and eating problems due to a personal preoccupation with, or interest in, food, exercise and weight control which has led them into that professional field of study (O'Dea & Abraham, 2001).

There is a paucity of research into the body image, dieting and eating behaviours of teachers and school professionals. One report of junior and senior high school teachers and health workers in the USA found that 76.6 per cent were practising some form of weight control, with 48.6 per cent trying to lose weight and 28 per cent trying to keep from gaining weight (Neumark-Sztainer, Story & Coller, 1999). High numbers of Australian female trainee physical education and home economics teachers reported they were currently dieting to lose weight (47 per cent), and a further 14 per cent believed that they currently had an eating disorder (O'Dea & Abraham, 2001). Both male and female teachers reported engaging in dangerous dieting behaviours such as excessive exercise, trying to induce vomiting, starvation and using laxatives. These findings were particularly significant as the majority of participants were in the normal or under weight ranges (O'Dea & Abraham, 2001). The potential for teachers to transfer these unhealthy and undesirable behaviours to their students needs to be ascertained and acknowledged.

Issues of our own susceptibility to eating problems as teachers

Dieting, body dissatisfaction, weight preoccupation, disordered eating and exercise behaviours are documented among normal weight, non-clinical populations of women (Crawford & Worsley, 1988; Hill, 2002; Kenardy et al., 2001), men (Drummond, 2002; O'Dea & Abraham, 2002) and university students worldwide. Body image and weight control issues affect the majority of young adults in some way and to some degree. Research is yet to conclude if those in food and exercise related careers are more susceptible to these problems and if food, body and weight related attitudes and behaviours of professionals may be modelled and transferred to their students and clients.

Some studies have found individuals in food and exercise related career paths to be at risk for engaging in disturbed dieting and exercise behaviours to the same or higher extent than the general population (Kinzl et al., 1999; McArthur & Howard, 2001; O'Dea & Abraham, 2001; Palmquist-Fredenberg et al., 1996; Worobey & Schoenfeld, 1999). They are exposed to similar sociocultural pressures as other adults, yet their career path is highly involved with food, eating and weight control. A preoccupation with food and exercise is known to be characteristic of some individuals with eating disorders (Larson, 1989; Worobey & Schoenfeld, 1999) and it has been suggested that this may cause them to gravitate towards careers that are food and exercise related (Crockett & Littrell, 1985; Reinstein et al., 1992; Sours, 1980). Kinzl and colleagues (1999) reported that 14 per cent of the Austrian dietitians studied had chosen their career path partly due to their own preoccupation with food and exercise.

There is evidence supporting the premise that professionals in food and exercise related career paths are susceptible to eating and weight control problems. The personal lifetime prevalence of eating disorders among eating disorder treatment professionals has been self-reported to range from 27.3 per cent to 31 per cent (Barbarich, 2002; Bloomgarden et al., 2003). This proportion reflects prevalence significantly higher than that of the general population. These findings were accompanied by evidence that not all professionals had received treatment and that 24 per cent had experienced a relapse after entering the field (Barbarich, 2002).

Anecdotal and empirical evidence have revealed disordered eating pathology, behaviours and symptoms among students enrolled in dietetics majors (Crockett & Littrell, 1985; Drake, 1989; Johnston & Christopher, 1991; Joseph et al., 1982; Kinzl et al., 1999; McArthur & Howard, 2001; Palmquist-Fredenberg et al., 1996; Reinstein et al., 1992; Worobey & Schoenfeld, 1999). Approximately 24 per cent of dietetics majors in the USA (Drake, 1989) and 25 per cent in Austria (Drake, 1989; Kinzl et al., 1999) were found to exhibit characteristics of anorexia nervosa. Dangerous weight loss techniques such as fasting, vomiting, laxatives and skipping meals were also reported to be used by trainee dietitians even though they would not recommend these techniques to clients, and some dietitians reported that they continued to use the techniques even though they did not find them useful (McArthur & Howard, 2001).

Personal trainers and aerobics instructors are often perceived as more approachable and credible sources of nutrition and weight control information than doctors due to their lean, muscular appearance, despite most receiving no formal training in nutrition (Barr, 1986; Kirk & Tinning, 1994; Soper et al., 1992; Vertinsky, 1985). Employment in the health and fitness industry is unique in that the knowledge and competence of staff is intentionally or subconsciously judged by their appearance. A recent study of male fitness leaders in Australia revealed comments such as:

> In this industry you have to look the part. I mean, there's no point in having someone who's overweight as a fitness leader. It's not the right image. You've got to look fit (Phillips & Drummond, 2001, p. 99).

Health and fitness professionals are therefore subjected to myriad intrinsic and external pressures to achieve the coveted lean, muscular appearance. This may lead them to engage in excessive exercise behaviours and other dangerous weight loss techniques (Brownell et al., 1992; Phillips & Drummond, 2001).

Physical education teachers are also presumed and expected to be slim, physically fit, and to embody the lean, muscular ideal body shape (Clark et al., 1988; Davis, 1999; Jenkins & Olsen, 1994; Kirk & Tinning, 1994; Melville & Cardinal, 1997; Melville & Maddalozzo, 1988). In order to adhere to this ideal and often unattainable goal, extreme forms of dieting and weight control may be employed. In a large study of female undergraduates in Australia, many of whom were trainee teachers, O'Dea (1999) found that almost half were currently dieting, including 42 per cent of those with a body mass index (BMI) below 18 and classified as clinically underweight (O'Dea, 1999). In another study of young female teachers, 29 per cent reported using excessive exercise, 19 per cent used starvation, 22 per cent inducing vomiting, 19 per cent used laxatives and 7 per cent used smoking to control their weight (O'Dea & Abraham, 2001). Among male PE teachers, 29 per cent desired weight gain to 'bulk up' their muscles and some reported disordered eating behaviours (O'Dea & Abraham, 2001).

The susceptibility of professionals involved in the prevention and treatment of eating disorders and obesity to eating and weight issues themselves may present serious issues in terms of their own health. Furthermore, attitudes and behaviours may be inadvertently modelled or intentionally transferred to students, patients or clients (O'Dea, 2000; Rutz, 1993). On a more positive note, teachers and school personnel who have been treated for and recovered from eating disorders or who have had a personal history of weight problems may be more empathetic and sensitive to students with similar issues.

First, do no harm

To date, the majority of eating disorder prevention programs have produced moderate results in terms of affecting attitudinal and behavioural change. Programs aimed at the treatment and prevention of childhood obesity have had similarly disappointing results, with most failing to achieve significant change of target behaviours (Campbell et al., 2004; Donelly et al., 1996; Epstein et al., 2001; Gortmaker et al., 2000; Mo-Suwan et al., 1998; Muller et al., 2001). It is crucial that program developers and implementers recognise the potentially negative effects of programs designed to prevent eating disorders and child obesity (Garner, 1985; O'Dea, 2000; O'Dea, 2005). While research into eating disorder programs confirms that planned interventions to date have not been iatrogenic (Stice & Shaw, 2004) the potential for adverse effects from unplanned, unsupervised and unproven programs is still a matter of concern. For example, the authors are aware of several schools in the USA and Australia where teachers have set up weight loss groups for overweight female adolescent students. One of the schools in question used a weight-loss sponsoring program as a fund-raising activity wherein girls who lost the most weight raised the most money. This sort of intervention is obviously unhelpful, inappropriate and dangerous.

School professionals' knowledge of nutrition, weight control and preventive techniques is known to be poor (Graves et al., 1991; O'Dea & Abraham, 2001; Price et al., 1990) and studies have reported that school professionals intentionally give students weight control advice that is inappropriate and dangerous (O'Dea & Abraham, 2001; Price, Desmond, Rupert & Stelzer, 1987; Price, Desmond & Stelzer, 1987). This may result in the content of lessons about child obesity and eating disorders providing misinformation, inappropriate advice, transference of attitudes and behaviours, and perpetuation of the thin ideal as well as increasing weight concerns and weight loss attempts among all children and adolescents, even those who are of normal weight status (O'Dea, 2000; Parcel et al., 1988). In other words, such educational approaches may 'suggest to students that they could or should be trying to lose weight, and to inform them of new ways to do so' (O'Dea, 2000).

It has been suggested that programs featuring recovered peers and celebrities may glamorise eating disorders, normalise dieting and disordered eating and have the potential to introduce students to dangerous dieting and disordered eating behaviours such as vomiting and cigarette smoking (Garner, 1985; O'Dea, 2000; Tomeo et al., 1999). School-based obesity prevention programs have the potential to endorse negative labelling of fat children and to promote excessive food restrictions. It is imperative that those developing and implementing eating disorder or child obesity prevention programs take note of previous ineffective and negative approaches and deliberately aim to develop new educational programs that do no harm (O'Dea, 2000; O'Dea, 2005).

Modelling and transference of attitudes and behaviours

The influence of the teacher or program presenter on the success of programs aimed at preventing child obesity and eating disorders is largely unexplored. There is the possibility that teachers and school professionals, who have been shown to have low perceived competence (Price et al., 1990; Price, Desmond, Rupert & Stelzer, 1987); misconceptions of (Graves et al., 1991; O'Dea & Abraham, 2001); and susceptibility to (O'Dea & Abraham, 2001; Reinstein et al., 1992; Worobey & Schoenfeld, 1999) nutrition, body image and weight control problems have the potential to model and transfer these attitudes to their students.

Bandura's social learning theory (1986) recognises the significant opportunity of teachers to vicariously influence student behaviour by role modelling, normative practices and social support. Interestingly, applied studies also confirm that role modelling plays a significant part in the success of school physical education programs (Clark et al., 1988; Davis, 1999; Jenkins & Olsen, 1994), and that the students' observation of their teacher's behaviour has a greater influence on their learning than their verbal communication (Bryan & Walbek, 1970; Spencer, 1988; Westcott, 1979). Although teachers have little control over whether their students perceive them as role models, the possibility of vicarious learning in and outside of the classroom always exists (Bandura, 1986; Davis, 1999).

Much research has investigated the potential for modelling of positive health behaviours such as participation in physical activity (Cardinal, 2001); however, little has been done to investigate the modelling of undesirable and inappropriate behaviours which may cause harm. Bulimic symptoms in adolescents have been reported to be increased due to the social reinforcement of the thin ideal and direct modelling of unhealthy attitudes from peers, family and the media (Stice, 1998). Physical education teachers are known to be under social (McCarthy, 1990; Mishkind et al., 1996), personal (Phillips & Drummond, 2001), and employment related (Melville & Cardinal, 1997) pressure to be slim and physically fit, and they use dangerous dieting and weight control practices (O'Dea & Abraham, 2001). There is anecdotal and empirical evidence to show that some physical education teachers are likely to be transferring their own negative body image, as well as their inadequate knowledge and inappropriate beliefs and attitudes about food, exercise and weight control to students (O'Dea, 2002; O'Dea & Abraham, 2001; Rutz, 1993; Stewart, 1998).

Due to the complex nature of eating disorders and child obesity, and the strong emotional and psychological connections between food, exercise, weight control and body image, it is dangerous to place individuals who have little knowledge about nutrition and prevention science and who are susceptible to, and dealing with body image and weight control problems themselves in positions to teach about these sensitive topics in schools. There is potential for inadvertent harm through misinformation, simplification of weight control attitudes, glamorisation and normalisation of eating disorders and perpetuation of the thin ideal. In order to 'do no harm' and implement effective school-based prevention for obesity and eating disorders, the personal and professional ability of those implementing any aspects of these programs must be evaluated. To address this potential problem appropriate training or retraining must be provided in the substance of any preventive package or as an early part of any preventive activity. These important issues will be outlined in more detail below.

Implications for teacher training and retraining

The apparent lack of knowledge and susceptibility to body image and eating problems in professionals dealing with such issues in schools has implications for university teacher training programs as well as in-service training programs for current teachers.

College and university training programs for school professionals should assess and address the personal and professional needs of future health educators. They should aim to include information about the detection, prevention and treatment of eating disorders and obesity in such a way that dispels popular myths and negative attitudes. It has been suggested that a combined primary and secondary prevention approach is ineffective in the college setting (Mann et al., 1997). Research has recommend that the knowledge, attitudes and behaviours of all school professionals be addressed using a didactic, psycho-educational approach to training about nutrition and eating disorders rather than an information-giving approach (Drake, 1989; Higgins & Gray, 1998; Springer et al., 1999; Zabinski et al., 2001). This should include training in prevention science and preventive techniques, and preparation for teaching about weight control and weight-related issues. Students at high risk of disordered eating problems may also need to be identified and given specialised psycho-educational interventions to improve their body image and eating behaviours. The importance of school professionals having appropriate body image and weight control knowledge, attitudes and behaviours should also be emphasised in terms of the potential for students to view teachers and school professionals as appropriate role models.

In-service training for school professionals should be directed at their personal and professional needs. It has been suggested that the use of a school resource person would be an efficient method of in-service training and implementation of prevention programs (Piran, 2004; Smolak et al., 2001; Yager, 2003). Smolak and her colleagues argue that there is at least one person within every school who has an interest in body image, eating disorders and child obesity. The existing motivation and knowledge of this person is then put to use, and they should receive appropriate, controlled and planned training, which would allow them to conduct staff training sessions and act as a resource if students or staff have any questions (Smolak et al., 2001).

The prevention programs developed and tested by eating disorder prevention specialists and child obesity prevention experts should make certain to include a teacher training component to their programs. Teacher training may be addressed by providing accurate and up-to-date information, factual content, attitudinal testing activities or continuing education classes. Grant applicants would be well advised to write such budget requirements into their grant proposals and grant reviewers should identify the obvious need to train those who are expected to undertake intervention roles.

Teachers and school personnel have a very valuable contribution to make in the prevention of eating disorders and child obesity but school-based personnel have been largely under utilised as such potential change agents. In fact, failure to investigate the nutrition, dieting and weight control knowledge, values, attitudes and behaviours of teachers and other school professionals involved in the treatment or prevention of obesity and eating disorders in schools may be one factor that could explain the modest success of some of these prevention programs. It is possible that school professionals are poorly trained about nutrition, prevention science and appropriate methods of prevention for eating disorders and obesity. They may also be susceptible to body image and weight-related problems themselves, especially if they are young and female. Furthermore their professional role and experience may not necessarily protect them against having significant levels of anti-fat bias. The combination of these factors may have a significant impact on the success of prevention initiatives, in particular, due to the potential for inappropriate role modelling and transference of these attitudes and behaviours.

In order for future prevention of eating disorders and child obesity to be successful, pre-service and ongoing training for the various school professionals involved is urgently required. This training must increase their knowledge of nutrition, eating disorders, obesity and preventive techniques. Taking a psycho-educational approach as a form of secondary prevention is also likely to improve the personal weight-related attitudes and behaviours of school professionals. Finally, teacher-training programs should stress the importance of school professionals having a healthy body image and address appropriate weight control practices in order to assure the appropriate modelling and transference of these attitudes and behaviours to the many students in their care. These coordinated measures are required in order to fully utilise schools as a setting for prevention initiatives, to improve the success of future prevention initiatives and to promote the health of our young people.

Teacher training to enable prevention of eating disorders and obesity

The following activities for teacher training or retraining tutorials or workshops, provide suitable activities to help trainee teachers become aware of the many issues involved in being able to implement school-based prevention programs for body image improvement and obesity prevention.

The following is a list of weekly lessons from my university course for trainee physical education students at the University of Sydney.

The course outline covers ways of addressing self-esteem development, media literacy development, knowledge of weight issues and ways of avoiding harmful and undesirable outcomes among groups of trainee physical education or home economics teachers.

Naturally, these activities can also be used in retraining or professional development courses for teachers involved in in-service training, professional development or preparation for return to the workforce.

TABLE 9.1 Course content of a teacher training program that addresses body image, self-esteem development and psychosocial health issues

Health, personal awareness and self-concept   Revision of health, its meanings, its many dimensions and the importance of a holistic approach to teaching about health. Mapping types of social support and identifying social support networks, analysis of self-concept in children, adolescents and adults, factors influencing self-concept and self-esteem throughout various life stages. Gender and cultural influences on personal awareness and self-concept.
Interpersonal skills   Types of communication, expressing feelings and needs, importance of effective communication, barriers to effective communication, improving the effectiveness of communication, conflict resolution, types of relationships, how groups satisfy personal needs, role of the peer group, acceptance of responsibilities in relationships, acknowledgment of individual rights in relationships.
Lifespan development   Growth and development: patterns of growth and development, influence of heredity and environment, diet and exercise, disability, illness and disease on growth and development, pubertal development, issues in teaching sensitive topics.
Mental health and social health   Exploring mental and social health, factors influencing psychological and social health, the role of the brain, enhancing psychological health, common psychological problems, effect of life changes on psychological health, managing psychological health, suicide prevention.

A detailed outline of the weekly course content and due dates for assignments is given in Table 9.2.

Case study activities for use in tutorials

Following is the outline for tutorial activities for the program.

All case studies are true stories, but the names and places have been changed and all characters have pseudonyms.

- Divide class into pairs, using the fruit technique. Pick two fruits (for example, apple, banana) and designate students as either an apple or banana. They then have to stand up and walk around to find a partner of the opposite fruit.
- In pairs, students read through the true case studies and discuss:
  - What is your initial reaction to this real life story?
  - What was positive about this teacher's approach?
  - What was potentially harmful?
  - How this would make the students feel?
  - How would you do things differently as the teacher?

TABLE 9.2 Outline of weekly course content of a teacher training program that addresses body image, self-esteem development and psychosocial health issues

Week	Lecture	Tutorial
1	Dimensions of health in children and adolescents Physical, mental, social, spiritual health and related issues. See Chapter 8 for an outline of the multidimensional nature of health.	Introduction to WebCT • 'What is health?' Lucky Dip task as tutorial activity • See health activities from Chapter 8 • Include the what is health quiz, definitions of health lucky dip activity, health opinion cards, and the debate or discussion topic about 'Good health is a matter of luck'
2	Growth and development in children and adolescents • Physiological changes during puberty • Teachers need to teach this in a factual but sensitive manner • See Chapter 6 for a detailed review of this topic	Pubertal change • Lucky Dip activity—description of your most memorable experiences during puberty, anonymous learning activity—include age and gender • See activities in Chapter 6 for classroom activities
3	Growth and development • How is weight for height decided? • Set point theory, genetic influence, body weight composition diagram, growth in puberty • See Chapter 6	How was height and weight taught at your school? • Group discussion of positive and negative teaching and learning experiences • Case studies of the ways teachers have approached weight issues in the classroom are given below • Examine each of these case studies in tutorials or as online discussion activities
4	Weight assessment methods • BMI—what is it? • Outline the many limitations of the BMI among growing children and adolescents • See Chapter 8 for information about determinants of weight and height in growing children and adolescents	Weight Issues • Calculate your own BMI • Discuss limitations of BMI (See Chapter 8, pages 230–1) • Discuss 'weight for health vs weight for fashion' • Reiterate multidimensional 'health' • Brainstorm on the board other ways we could measure 'health' rather than focusing on weight—heart rate, blood pressure, blood glucose, mental health, physical activity etc. • Have students in tutorials participate in the heart rate activities, Chapter 8, pages 265–6 Discussion—should BMI be taught in schools or are there better ways to deal with health and weight issues in schools?
5	Social health—media literacy definitions—see Chapter 5 • Aims of media literacy • Examples of media literacy interventions (Chapter 3)	Media literacy • Explore the social construction of the gender and media stereotypes using magazines and covers • Group discussion (Where does the ideal come from? Is it realistic? Who benefits? What are the costs? How does it impact on 'health'?) • Implement some of the media literacy activities from Chapter 5 such as My 24-hour media diary, Stereotypes in the media and 'Sending up the stereotypes', Retouching exposed and Male magazine makeover • These activities easily lend themselves to online versions of the activities
6	Self-concept and self-esteem development in children and adolescents • Definitions of self-concept and self-esteem (see Chapter 4 for fact files) • Difference between self-confidence and self-esteem • Risk behaviour related to poor self-esteem • Benefits of high self-esteem • Interventions to improve self-esteem and body image (see Chapter 3)	Exploration of students' own self-concept and body image • Mindmap: Write down the score out of 10 that you give yourself for how your body looks. Now write down the three negative influences and the three most important positive influences on your body image. • Each student places their anonymous answer in a hat and selects another to read to the class • Group discussion focuses on: What influences your own body image? What are the major negative and positive influences? • What improves your body image and why? How can you implement these ideas with your students • Web task or essay—How will you teach in order to build self-esteem and a positive body image in your students?

TABLE 9.2 (Continued) Outline of weekly course content of a teacher training program that addresses body image, self-esteem development and psychosocial health issues

Week	Lecture	Tutorial
7–8	Self-concept and self-esteem (see Chapter 4 for information and fact files about self-concept and self-esteem and social support) • Readings about self-esteem and mental health—Mann et al. *(2004).*	Building self-esteem workshop—activities from Chapter 4 • Relaxation activities, What makes up a person?, Classroom bingo, Hand outline activity, Self-advertisements, What do I admire in others?, Positive perspectives cards, Communication and conflict resolution
9	Nutrition (see Chapter 7) Nutritional requirements for children and adolescents. Major food groups then major macro and micro nutrients from different food groups. Outline of how the healthy eating pyramid incorporates all of the food groups in the right proportions.	Teaching nutrition in a positive way • Food group activities, taste tests • Nutrition, quizzes and games (see Chapter 7) • Quick and healthy snacks • Play nutritional pursuit
10	Case study presentations (30%)	Case study presentations (30%)
11	Case study presentations (30%)	Case study presentations (30%)
12	Exam (40%)	Exam (40%)

Case studies

Samantha and Barry, aged 13, Year 7

At the start of the Year 7 school year, all new students were encouraged to participate in the yearly school play. That year the play was 'Sheik, Rattle and Roll' and the drama teachers were looking for many students to play guards, harem girls and of course, the leads.

Many students were auditioning under the watchful eyes of the two drama teachers, Mr Harvey and Ms Boyle. Both teachers were excited about this year's play; being a popular state high school, they were always keen to find new stars coming from the local primary schools.

During the auditions, several shy, new, young Year 7s gradually made their way to the top of the stage where the auditions were proceeding. The next girl to audition was Samantha.

Samantha was a pretty girl with a head of long red hair, but was a little plump. Her audition, however, was excellent. She knew her lines off by heart, delivered them well and could even move. It was evident she had taken some dance lessons. The two teachers conferred briefly before Mr Harvey announced: 'That was actually very good Samantha. But, you are not the right size to be a harem girl; we need someone much smaller. Leave it to us, we should be able to find you another role, more suitable to your, um, shape'.

Samantha, eyes welling with tears ran from the stage before any student could comment further.

Next was Barry. He was a tad effeminate and very skinny. Barry was incredibly quiet. His audition was quite good; he had remembered his lines but needed to talk much more loudly if all the viewers down the back were to hear him. Mr Harvey was interested; however, Ms Boyle was sceptical. She said to Barry, 'Well done, you had a lot of feeling in those lines which was good. You are far too skinny though to be on stage. However, your voice is quite feminine sounding, so if you can sing as girlie as you sound, perhaps we can cast you in the choir'.

Barry left the stage in a frenzy, he was mortified that the teachers had picked on his voice, none of his friends' had broken yet either. Additionally, their concentration upon his weight was also upsetting. 'They don't pick on skinny girls', Barry thought.

Both children went through their secondary education watchful of their weight, one wishing to lose it, another wishing to gain it. Both turned to abusive methods of to try and achieve their goal.

Ms Cawdry, Year 12 coordinator

Ms Cawdry had been teaching for over 15 years. Additionally she was the Year 12 coordinator at a private, coeducational, Anglican high school.

Ms Cawdry came from a line of girls who had all fought their weight during their youth. Being at a healthy and comfortable weight now, she tried to encourage healthy eating of her students, supporting their dieting and exercise routine. She could be found most mornings walking to school or riding her bike.

She disliked students bullying others about their weight and tried to discipline those students caught commenting. However, deep down, she also disliked students who ate without any regard for their bodies.

On 'Jeans for genes' day all students were permitted to wear casual dress for a coin donation. Ms Cawdry herself went to work in jeans.

During the lunchtime break, Ms Cawdry bumped into two of her the Year 12s, Bradley and his friend, Martin. After a few minutes of chat, Ms Cawdry noted what both boys were wearing, commenting on their attire. 'You boys look nice today', she started, much to the pleasure of both teenagers.

However, this wasn't all she wanted to say. She continued 'Gee, you two are not as fat as I had thought. Perhaps you both should purchase a smaller uniform, I am sure you could exchange your current one for a size or two smaller.' The boys both taken aback, exchange puzzled glances, so Ms Cawdry took this as a prompt to explain further 'Well, you both get picked on because of your weight, perhaps if you showed that you were not that fat, the kids would lay off you both'. With that she smiled and wandered off.

The next morning she walked down the corridor finding the parents of both Brad and Martin waiting for her outside her office. Ms Cawdry thought that both boys must have spoken with their parents about her supportive ideas and had come to exchange their uniforms.

However, the parents were there to talk about her hurtful comments. Ms Cawdry couldn't understand how they were upsetting, she believed that she was only protecting the boys from further torments by supporting what she thought was their weight loss.

Penny, aged 12, Year 7

Penny attended a state high school, in the eastern suburbs of Melbourne. The school had a good reputation and a high student population. Penny was a quiet girl; she didn't have many friends. She wasn't very comfortable with her looks, or her size, which wasn't big, but the children teased her anyway, especially since she was shy.

Penny missed a lot of school due to severe asthma. Her favourite subject was English and her worst subject was Physical Education. Penny's PE teacher was Mr Trip. He was in his early 30s and a stern man who demanded healthy, skinny students. He used to roam around on teacher's duty and tell the students off for eating meat pies and sucking on icy poles, commenting on their bad skin or extra weight.

One day, Penny's PE class was ordered to complete a 12-minute run around the school oval. Penny approached Mr Trip and asked if she could either do something else or sit out as she had been having bad asthma due to the summer heat. Mr Trip refused, demanding that Penny participate in the class, he said to her 'I only want skinny students in this class' much to the joy of the nearby students listening to the conversation.

When the run began, Mr Trip stood at the top of the steps and screamed at the students 'Keep going, you need to burn calories', 'What is wrong with you, are you so unfit?' as they past him puffing and panting.

A few minutes in, Penny started to feel her chest tighten. She slowed down to a slow jog, trying to catch her breath. Her wheezing increased and she continually shot her reliever into her mouth, trying to catch her breath. She stopped and stood. The other students, puffed, ran past her, a couple even asked if she was OK. She wasn't. Penny entered into a full asthma attack, she couldn't catch her breath, her chest hurt, she was dizzy and couldn't stop wheezing. Walking slowly to her teacher, Mr Trip yelled at her 'Stop faking it and keep running, you are too big'.

Penny refused. She sat on the steps and only when Mr Trip came down to yell at her, did he hear her wheezing. He simply told her to walk to the nurse, Penny at this point, had stopped wheezing, and entered into the 'silent' attack stage, the most dangerous.

Penny took a week to recover from that severe asthma attack, but she has never recovered from the comments Mr Trip made about her weight.

Case study activity—discussion guide and answers for lecturer or tutor

As a class group, groups share their case study by reading it aloud, and presenting their response to the rest of the group. Other members of the class may add comments/questions, and the tutor facilitates discussion.

Appropriate responses to the case studies may be found below.

Samantha and Barry

- Unnecessarily negative comments caused deep harm.
- The teachers did not have to say those things in order for the audition process to continue.
- By saying that was 'actually' very good showed that his expectations were not high due to physical impression.
- Teachers were conforming to gender stereotypes and showed a sheer lack of knowledge about growth and pubertal development.

Ms Cawdry

- Her previous struggle with weight may lead to a saviour/overhelpful approach that may be harmful to students.
- She was completely unaware that her comments were inappropriate and could be hurtful to the boys.
- Need to be extremely careful with any comments made about students' weight/shape/appearance. Best to stay positive or avoid commenting altogether.
- May be more constructive to target the students who were bullying the boys.

Penny

- Mr Trip displayed a dangerous lack of knowledge about weight loss and asthma, and about the individual capabilities and medical requirements of his students.
- These days this scenario would most likely end in a legal battle for negligence.
- It is important to know students individually, to be aware of, and acknowledge their medical conditions/injuries, and incorporate them appropriately.
- He probably believed that by guilt/shaming/blaming all students into doing the run, he was helping to reduce their body fat and increase their health. However, all he was doing was helping them to associate exercise with struggle, pain and boredom, which would not be conducive to them adopting lifelong physical activity habits.
- His assumptions about fatness equating with lack of fitness is outdated. This could lead to incorrect assumptions about slim students' fitness levels as well.

Discussion activities for tutorials

'Did anyone have a PE teacher whose teaching style or teaching approach was particularly inappropriate or potentially damaging?'

Students give accounts of personal experiences in PE.

Discussion: What makes a good PE teacher?

Discussion: Ask students to give qualities of a good PE teacher in a quick brainstorm.

Discussion, homework activity or written assignment: How will you role model a healthy body, a healthy body image and a healthy attitude to life?

Course assignment and assessment guide

The content of this teacher training course may be placed online or delivered in various ways. The suggested course assessment is outlined below in Table 9.3.

Summary

This chapter has presented issues in the prevention of childhood obesity and body image improvement in schools. It summarises the issues that teachers and trainee teachers need to be aware of before they embark on any school based prevention initiatives.

Teachers and other school staff will inevitably become involved in preventive activities at some level, but it is important to recognise that they will probably need some specific training in order to do so. This chapter has outlined how teachers and school personnel may be best trained and prepared for such a preventive role; whether they currently feel willing and able to undertake such a role and whether some groups of teachers may be personally susceptible to body image and eating problems.

Discussion in this chapter focuses on what may need to be done in order to enable teachers and other school-based educators to perform most effectively in the implementation of school-based eating disorder and child obesity prevention programs. In particular, those involved in the training of teachers may implement any of the evidence-based strategies outlined in Chapters 3–8 as well as the activities suggested in those activities. In this way, teachers are 'work-shopped' in how to deliver these classroom activities as well as covering the content of the activities.

TABLE 9.3 Course assignments and assessment for a teacher training program that addresses body image, self-esteem development and psychosocial health issues

1 Seminar presentation or case study of an adolescent (30%)
2 WebCT online quizzes and online activities (30%)
3 Exam (40%)
Assignment Topic—exploring and understanding issues in psychosocial health   **Choose EITHER an oral seminar presentation OR a case study of a teenager**
• Choose a topic of interest from one of the major topics covered in this course.
• Choose a working group of 4–5 people if you choose an oral seminar presentation.
• Work in pairs if you choose to do a case study of a teenager.
• Make contact with people working in the area of your chosen topic and research the topic via your community contacts, as well as the library research databases.
• Make a class presentation on your selected topic. Remember to make your presentation creative, interesting, interactive, informative and fun.
• Make a one-page summary (double-sided) handout with references for each class member. This material will be examinable.
• Assessment is made during your presentation but you will be required to submit all relevant materials including references, overheads, video, resources etc.

The course outline of my program for trainee health education, home economics and physical education teachers is also presented in this chapter to allow those involved in teacher training or professional development to use some of these activities.

References

Bandura A (1986), *Social Foundations of Thought and Action: A social cognitive theory*, Prentice Hall, Englewood Cliffs, NJ.

Barbarich N (2002), 'Lifetime prevalence of eating disorders among professionals in the field', *Eating Disorders*, *10*, 305–12.

Barr SI (1986), 'Nutrition knowledge and selected nutritional practices of female recreational athletes', *Journal of Nutrition Education*, *18*(4), 167–73.

Bassler E (2001), 'Challenging future nutritionists to promote normal eating', *Healthy Weight Journal*, *15*, 25–46.

Bloomgarden A, Gerstein F & Moss C (2003), 'The last word: A "recovered enough" therapist', *Eating Disorders*, *11*, 163–7.

Brownell KD, Rodin J & Wilmore JH (1992), 'Eating, body weight and performance in athletes: An introduction', in Brownell KD, Rodin J & Wilmore JH (eds), *Eating, Body Weight and Performance in Athletes: Disorders of modern society*, Lea & Febiger, Philadelphia, PA, 3–16.

Bryan J & Walbek N (1970), 'Preaching and practicing generosity: Children's actions and reactions', *Child Development*, *42*, 329–53.

Campbell K, Waters E, O'Meara S, Kelly S & Summerbell C (2004), 'Interventions for preventing obesity in children', *The Cochrane Database of Systematic Reviews*, *1*.

Cardinal BJ (2001), 'Role modelling attitudes and physical activity and fitness promoting behaviours of HPERD professionals and pre professionals', *Research Quarterly for Exercise and Sport*, *72*, 84–90.

Clark D, Blair S & Culan M (1988), 'Are HPE teachers good role models?', *Journal of Physical Education, Recreation and Dance*, *54*, 76–80.

Connolly C & Corbett-Dick P (1990), 'Eating disorders: A framework for school nursing initiatives', *Journal of School Health*, *60*(8), 401–6.

Crawford DA & Worsley A (1988), 'Dieting and slimming practices of South Australian women', *Medical Journal of Australia*, *148*, 325–31.

Crisp AH, Gelder M, Rix S, Meltzer H & Rowlands O (2000), 'Stigmatisation of people with mental illnesses', *British Journal of Psychiatry*, *177*, 4–7.

Crockett SJ & Littrell JM (1985), 'Comparison of eating patterns between dietetic and other college students', *Journal of Nutrition Education*, *17*, 47–50.

Davis T (1999), 'Health educators as positive role models', *Journal of Health Education*, *30*, 60–1.

Donelly JE, Jacobsen DJ, Whatley JE, Hill JO, Swift LL & Cherrington A (1996), 'Nutrition and physical activity program to attentuate obesity and promote physical and metabolic fitness in elementary school children', *Obesity Research*, *4*(3), 229–43.

Drake MA (1989), 'Symptoms of anorexia nervosa in female university dietetic majors', *Journal of the American Dietetic Association*, *89*(1), 97–9.

Drummond M (2002), 'Men, body image and eating disorders', *International Journal of Men's Health*, *1*, 79–93.

Epstein LH, Gordy CC, Raynor HA, Beddome M, Kilanowski CK & Paluch R (2001), 'Increasing fruit and vegetable intake and decreasing fat and sugar intake in families at risk for childhood obesity', *Obesity Research*, *9*(3), 171–8.

Garner DM (1985), 'Iatrogenesis in anorexia nervosa and bulimia nervosa', *International Journal of Eating Disorders*, *4*, 701–26.

Gortmaker SL, Peterson K, Wiecha J, Sobal AM, Dixit S, Fox MK & Laird N (2000), 'A school-based, interdisciplinary curriculum in grades 6 and 7 reduced obesity in girls', *Evidence Based Nursing*, *3*, 13.

Graves KL, Farthing MC, Smith SA & Turchi JM (1991), 'Nutrition training, attitudes, knowledge, recommendations, responsibility, and resource utilization of high school coaches and trainers', *Journal of the American Dietetic Association*, *91*, 321–4.

Gurney VW & Halmi KA (2001), 'Developing an eating disorder curriculum for primary care providers', *Eating Disorders*, *9*, 97–107.

Higgins LC & Gray W (1998), 'Changing the body image concern and eating behaviour of chronic dieters: The effects of a psychoeducational intervention', *Psychology and Health*, *13*, 1045–60.

Hill A (ed) (2002), *Prevalence and Demographics of Dieting*, The Guilford Press, New York.

Jenkins A & Olsen L (1994), 'Health behaviours of health educators: A national survey', *Journal of Health Education*, *25*, 324–32.

Johnston CS & Christopher FS (1991), 'Anorexic-like behaviours in dietetics majors and other student populations', *Journal of Nutrition Education*, *23*, 148–53.

Joseph A, Wood IK & Goldberg SC (1982), 'Determining populations at risk for developing anorexia nervosa based on selection of college major', *Psychiatry Research, 7*, 53–8.

Kenardy J, Brown W & Vogt E (2001), 'Dieting and health in young Australian women', *European Eating Disorders Review, 9*, 242–54.

Kinzl J, Traweger C, Trefalt E, Mangweth B & Biebl W (1999), 'Dietitians: Are they a risk group for eating disorders?', *European Eating Disorders Review, 7*, 62–7.

Kirk D & Tinning R (1994), 'Embodied self-identity, healthy lifestyles and school physical education', *Sociology of Health and Illness, 16*(5), 601–24.

Kushner RF (1995), 'Barriers to providing nutrition counselling by physicians: A survey of primary care practitioners', *Preventive Medicine, 24*, 546–52.

Larson B (1989), 'The new epidemic: Ethical implications for nutrition educators', *Journal of Nutrition Education, 21*, 101–3.

Mann T, Nolen-Hoeksema S & Huang K (1997), 'Are two interventions worse than none? Joint primary and secondary prevention of eating disorders in college females', *Health Psychology, 16*, 215–25.

Mann M, Clemens MH, Herman PS & deVries NK (2004), 'Self-esteem in a broad-spectrum approach for mental health promotion', *Health Education Research, 19*(4), 357–72.

McArthur A & Howard A (2001), 'Dietetics majors' weight-reduction beliefs, behaviors, and information sources', *Journal of American College Health, 49*, 175–84.

McCarthy M (1990), 'The thin ideal, depression and eating disorders in women', *Behavioural Research Therapy, 28*, 205–15.

Melville DS & Cardinal BJ (1997), 'Are overweight physical educators at a disadvantage in the labor market? A random survey of hiring personnel', *The Physical Educator, 54*, 216–21.

Melville DS & Maddalozzo JGF (1988), 'The effects of a physical educator's appearance of body fatness on communicating exercise concepts to high school students', *Journal of Teaching in Physical Education, 7*, 343–52.

Mishkind M, Rodin J, Silberstein L & Striegel-Moore R (1996), 'The embodiment of masculinity: Cultural, psychological and behavioral dimensions', *American Behavioral Scientist, 29*, 545–62.

Mond JM, Hay PJ, Rodgers B, Owen C & Beumont PJV (2004), 'Beliefs of women concerning the severity and prevalence of bulimia nervosa', *Social Psychiatry and Psychiatric Epidemiology, 39*, 299–304.

Mo-Suwan L, Pongprapai S, Junjana C & Puetpaiboon A (1998), 'Effects of a controlled trial of a school-based exercise program on the obesity indexes of preschool children', *American Journal of Clinical Nutrition, 68*(5), 1006–11.

Muller MJ, Mast M, Asbeck I, Langnase K & Grund A (2001), 'Prevention of obesity is it possible?' *Obesity Reviews, 2*, 15–28.

Neumark-Sztainer D (1996), 'School based programs for preventing eating disturbances', *Journal of School Health, 66*, 64–71.

Neumark-Sztainer D, Story M & Coller T (1999), 'Perceptions of secondary school staff towards the implementation of school-based activities to prevent weight-related disorders: A needs assessment', *American Journal of Health Promotion, 13*(3), 153–6.

Neumark-Sztainer D, Story M & Harris TR (1999), 'Beliefs and attitudes about obesity among teachers and school health care providers working with adolescents', *Journal of Nutrition Education, 31*(1), 3–9.

O'Dea J (1999), 'Cross-cultural, body weight and gender differences in the body size perceptions and body ideals of university students', *Australian Journal of Nutrition and Dietetics, 56*, 144–50.

O'Dea J (2000), 'School based interventions to prevent eating problems: First do no harm', *Eating Disorders, 8*, 123–30.

O'Dea J (2002), 'Can body image education programs be harmful to adolescent females?', *Eating Disorders, 10*, 1–13.

ODea J (2005), 'Prevention of child obesity: First, do no harm', *Health Education Research, 20*(2), 259–65.

O'Dea J & Abraham SF (2000), 'Improving the body image, eating attitudes, and behaviours of young male and female adolescents: A new educational approach that focuses on self-esteem', *International Journal of Eating Disorders, 28*, 43–57.

O'Dea J & Abraham SF (2001), 'Knowledge, beliefs, attitudes and behaviours related to weight control, eating disorders, and body image in Australian trainee home economics and physical education teachers', *Journal of Nutrition Education, 33*, 332–40.

O'Dea J & Abraham SF (2002), 'Eating and exercise disorders in young college men', *Journal of American College Health, 50*, 273–8.

O'Dea J & Maloney D (2000), 'Preventing eating and body image problems in children and adolescents using the health promoting schools framework', *Journal of School Health, 70*(1), 18–21.

Palmquist-Fredenberg J, Berglund P & Dieken H (1996), 'Incidence of eating disorders among selected female university students', *Journal of the American Dietetic Association, 96*, 64–6.

Parcel G, Green L & Bettes B (1988), 'School-based programs to prevent or reduce obesity' in Krasnegor N, Grave G & Kretchmer N (eds), *Childhood Obesity: A biobehavioural perspective*, Telford Press, Caldwell, 143–57.

Phillips J & Drummond M (2001), 'An investigation into the body image perception, body satisfaction and exercise expectations of male fitness leaders: Implications for professional practice', *Leisure Studies*, *20*, 95–105.

Piran N (1998), 'A participatory approach to the prevention of eating disorders in a school', in Vandereycken W & Noordenbos G (eds), *The Prevention of Eating Disorders*, Athlone Press, London.

Piran N (2004), 'Teachers: On "being" (rather than doing) prevention', *Eating Disorders*, *12*, 1–9.

Price J, Desmond SM, Price JH & Mossing A (1990), 'School counsellor's knowledge of eating disorders', *Adolescence*, *25*(100), 945–57.

Price JH, Desmond SM, Ruppert ES & Stelzer CM (1987), 'School nurses' perceptions of childhood obesity', *Journal of School Health*, *57*(8), 332–6.

Price JH, Desmond SM & Stelzer CM (1987), 'Elementary school principals' perceptions of childhood obesity', *Journal of School Health*, *57*(9), 367–70.

Puhl R & Brownell KD (2001), 'Bias, discrimination and obesity', *Obesity Research*, *9*(12), 788–805.

Reinstein N, Koszewski W, Chamberlain B & Smith-Johnson C (1992), 'Prevalence of eating disorders among dietetics students: Does nutrition education make a difference?', *Journal of the American Dietetic Association*, *92*, 949–54.

Rodin J, Silberstein LP & Striegel-Moore RH (eds) (1985), *Women and Weight: A normative discontent*, University of Nebraska Press, Lincoln.

Rutz S (1993), 'Nutrition educators should practice what they teach', *Journal of Nutrition Education*, *25*(2), 87–8.

Schwartz M, O'Neal Chambliss H, Brownell K, Blair S & Billington C (2003), 'Weight bias among health professionals specializing in obesity', *Obesity Research*, *11*, 1033–9.

Smolak L, Levine M & Schermer F (1998), 'A controlled intervention of an elementary school primary prevention program for eating problems', *Journal of Psychosomatic Research*, *44*, 339–53.

Smolak L, Harris B, Levine MP & Shisslak CM (2001), 'Teachers: The forgotten influence on the success of prevention programs', *Eating Disorders*, *9*, 261–6.

Soper J, Carpenter RA & Shannon BM (1992), 'Nutrition knowledge of aerobic dance instructors', *Journal of Nutrition Education*, *24*, 59–66.

Sours J (1980), *Starving to Death in a Sea of Objects: The anorexia nervosa syndrome*, J Aronson, New York.

Spencer A (1988), 'Physical educator: Role model or roll the ball out?', *Journal of Physical Education, Recreation and Dance*, *69*, 58–63.

Springer E, Winzelberg A, Perkins R & Taylor CB (1999), 'Effects of a body image curriculum for college students on improved body image', *International Journal of Eating Disorders*, *26*, 13–20.

Stang J, Story M & Kalina B (1997), 'School-based weight management services: Perceptions and practices of school nurses and administrators', *American Journal of Health Promotion*, *11*(3), 183–5.

Stewart A (1998), 'Experience with a school-based eating disorders prevention program', in Vandereycken W & Noordenbos G (eds), *The Prevention of Eating Disorders*, Athlone Press, London.

Stice E (1998), 'Modeling of eating pathology and social reinforcement of the thin-ideal predict onset of bulimic symptoms', *Behaviour Research and Therapy*, *36*, 931–44.

Stice E & Shaw H (2004), 'Eating disorder prevention programs: A meta-analytic review', *Psychological Bulletin*, *130*(2), 206–27.

Story M, Neumark-Sztainer D, Sherwood N, Holt K, Sofka D, Trowbridge F & Barlow SE (2002), 'Management of child and adolescent obesity: Attitudes, barriers, skills, and training needs among health care professionals', *Pediatrics*, *110*(1), 210–14.

Teachman BA & Brownell K (2001), 'Implicit anti-fat bias among health professionals: Is anyone immune?', *International Journal of Obesity Related Metabolic Disorders*, *25*, 1525–31.

Tomeo CA, Field AE, Berkey CS, Colditz GA & Frazier AL (1999), 'Weight concerns, weight control behaviours and smoking initiation', *Pediatrics*, *104*(4), 918–24.

Vertinsky P (1985), 'Risk benefit analysis of health promotion: Opportunities and threats for physical education', *Quest*, *37*, 71–83.

Westcott WL (1979), 'Physical educators and coaches as models of behaviour', *Journal of Physical Education and Recreation*, *50*, 31–2.

Worobey J & Schoenfeld D (1999), 'Eating disordered behaviour in dietetics students and students in other majors', *Journal of the American Dietetic Association*, *99*, 100–4.

Yager Z (2003), *Body Image, Dieting and Disordered Eating Behaviour in School Professionals Dealing with Body Image Issues and Eating Problems*, University of Wollongong, Wollongong.

Zabinski MF, Pung MA, Wilfley DE, Eppstein DL, Winzelberg AJ, Celio A & Taylor CB (2001), 'Reducing risk factors for eating disorders: Targeting at-risk women with a computerised psychoeducational program', *International Journal of Eating Disorders*, *29*, 401–8.

A whole-school approach to body image and obesity

Introduction

This chapter outlines the 'whole-school approach' and how it may be implemented in schools for preventing body image problems and child obesity. Discussion focuses on the efficacy of preventive school-based strategies, and on the safest and most successful interventions. The framework encompasses three major areas of intervention in the school and community: 1) school curriculum, teaching, and learning; 2) school ethos, environment, and organisation; and 3) school-community partnerships and services. Suggested strategies for implementing the framework are outlined. Case studies of how several primary schools and high schools have adapted the new approach for dealing with the issues of eating disorders prevention, body image improvement and child obesity prevention are presented.

Several authors worldwide have called for preventing eating disturbances and body image problems among children and adolescents using school-based programs (Collins, 1988; Moreno & Thelen, 1993; Neumark-Sztainer, 1996; Piran, 1995; Rosenvinge & Gresko, 1997; Shisslak et al., 1987; Smolak & Levine, 1994). Various preventive and educational approaches have been suggested. Several authors recommended use of self-esteem building strategies (Button et al., 1997; Moriarty et al., 1990). Others suggest activities such as peer involvement (Paxton, 1996), parental involvement (Graber & Brooks-Gunn, 1996), a focus on sport activities (Patton et al., 1999), and addressing feminist issues such as cultural stereotypes and empowerment of women (Fallon et al., 1998; Patton et al., 1999; Striegel-Moore & Steiner-Adair, 1998). Identifying adolescents at greatest risk for eating problems, such as ballet students, athletes and overweight students, also has been suggested (Lindeman, 1994; Piran, 1998). Other potential approaches include teaching students to analyse and deconstruct social body image ideals and media messages (Levine & Smolak, 1998), and implementing screening programs for high-risk students (Schoemaker, 1998).

Several large, randomised and controlled trials have examined whether school-based programs could prevent disturbed and unhealthful eating and body dissatisfaction among adolescents and these are outlined in detail in Chapter 3. Results from many of these interventions have demonstrated that school-based health education programs, when properly planned and evaluated, can have a positive and lasting impact on body image, eating behaviours, attitudes and self-image of adolescents.

To develop effective and sustainable strategies to prevent eating and body image problems in schools, professionals must first exclude approaches and practices proven ineffective or harmful. The potential exists for certain educational approaches to do more harm than good (Garner, 1985). School and college-based education programs that provide information about eating disorders, particularly activities led by recovered eating disorder patients, may inadvertently increase student knowledge and symptoms of eating disorders such as dieting, vomiting and laxative abuse (Carter et al., 1997; Mann et al., 1997). School-based programs also may inadvertently create potentially harmful outcomes by providing direct instruction and information about disordered eating behaviours and may introduce students to beliefs, attitudes and behaviours known to precede eating problems. Instruction about eating disorders also may glamorise (Garner, 1985) and normalise (Mann et al., 1997; O'Dea, 2000) disordered eating behaviours, thereby creating the belief that these activities are common and 'normal'. In addition, school-based programs may treat food and nutrition issues negatively by referring to 'good' foods, 'bad' foods, and 'junk' foods (O'Dea, 1999; 2000). The negative focus contributes to an underlying fear of food, dietary fat and weight gain, which precipitate eating problems.

School-based programs to prevent overweight and obesity may also unintentionally create harmful effects if teachers and school staff transfer negative beliefs and attitudes to students including poor body image; prejudices about body weight; and bias towards students, as in prejudice towards overweight students. In addition, teachers may be poor role models for students if they are obsessed about having the 'perfect' body themselves or if they believe that fitness and health can only be achieved at a slim body weight. Those implementing school-based programs should examine potentially harmful outcomes before beginning school activities. The previously mentioned suggestions for effective and safe school-based preventive strategies may prove most effective when coordinated and encompassed within the health promoting schools framework.

A health promoting schools framework

The World Health Organization (WHO) health promoting schools framework (Nutbeam, 1992; WHO, 1998a) outlines a holistic approach to foster health within a school and its local community by engaging health and education officials, teachers, students, parents and community leaders in making common efforts to promote health. A health promoting school has an organised set of policies, procedures, activities and structures designed to protect and promote the health and wellbeing of students, staff and wider school community members.

The health promoting schools concept is based on the premise that education and health are inseparable and that health supports successful learning, and successful learning supports health. The ideology of the health promoting schools framework states that the school and its surrounding community must implement policies, practices, and other measures that respect individual self-esteem, provide multiple opportunities for success and acknowledge good efforts and intentions as well as personal achievements. A health promoting school also strives to improve the health of school personnel, families and community members as well as students, and it works with community leaders to help them understand how the community is influential in affecting health and education.

Table 10.1 contains the WHO guiding principles for developing health promoting schools. Important features include the holistic nature of health, gender equity, involvement and ownership of the whole school community, participatory decision making, sustainability, cultural appropriateness and inclusion of measures to increase health literacy. WHO defines health literacy as the cognitive and social skills that determine the motivation and ability of individuals to gain access to, understand and use information in ways that promote and maintain health (WHO, 1998b). Thus, the health promoting school promotes empowerment of students, teachers, parents, school staff and community members because they learn to obtain and use health information.

School curriculum, teaching and learning

The framework outlines requirements for a planned and sequential health education curriculum across all age groups and the need for it to be inter-sectoral and cross-

TABLE 10.1 Guiding principles for the development of health promoting schools

• Good health supports lifelong learning, living and wellbeing.
• Students grow and learn in a safe, caring, responsive and empowering environment.
• Health promoting schools view health holistically, addressing the physical, social, mental, intellectual and spiritual dimensions of health through comprehensive programs.
• Equal access by male and female students from all population groups to educational opportunities is essential for promoting quality of life.
• Health promoting schools ensure a coordinated, comprehensive approach to health and learning by linking curriculum with the school ethos/environment and the community.
• Health promoting schools are inclusive—the whole community of students, parents, staff and local agencies are engaged in school activities.
• Active participation is based on respecting skills, values and experiences of parents, students and staff.
• Collaborative, participatory decision making and personal action provide the conditions for the empowerment of individuals and the school community.
• Staff and parent wellbeing is an integral part of health promoting school activity.
• Partnerships result in action which is more effective, efficient and sustainable.
• Addressing health literacy is an important component of a health promoting school.
• The contribution of diverse cultures and groups is supported and valued.

Reproduced with permission from the Australian Health Promoting Schools Association, http://www.ahpsa.org.au/files/framework.pdf

curricular. An example of this concept includes focusing on dieting prevention in health education classes (skill development to reduce the influence of peer group pressure), English classes (the impact of persuasive advertising) and science (normal composition of the human body). The cross-curricular approach ensures health messages remain consistent across subject areas. In addition, the framework emphasises teacher training in specific areas and the opportunity for teachers to reflect on their own values, beliefs, prejudices and life experiences to be effective role models. In terms of preventing eating disorders, body image problems and obesity, teachers and other school and community personnel may require training to better understand these issues, as well as training in effective and safe preventive strategies, and access to counselling and referral services.

School ethos, environment and organisation

This section of the framework includes beliefs, attitudes and norms within the school and local community that form the overall 'ethos' of the school environment. The area includes school structures, policies and practices that contribute to a healthful environment. To foster a healthful school environment, health promotion policies of the school must be examined. For example, the school may need to examine its school meal policy (for-profit or not-for-profit basis) and may need to introduce policies about teasing, bullying, dress codes, prejudice and the need for special programs such as school sport programs specifically suited to the needs of girls or overweight students.

School–community partnerships and services

Part of the health promoting schools holistic approach involves developing collaborative relationships with students' families, school and community health workers, youth and educational services, and non government agencies. Resources in school and the community can complement healthy attitudes and activities promoted in school that can be reinforced in the community. In regard to preventing eating and body image problems, examples of this exchange of resources between school and community include providing health services for students, teachers, school nurses and families, such as mental and allied health services. Complementary educational activities such as training programs for preventing eating and body image problems for parents, school nurses, youth workers, coaches, dance teachers, journalists and health workers may be designed to maximise the impact of school-based curricula. A comprehensive collaborative approach between the school and community will enable implementation of policies, procedures, activities and structures required to promote a healthy body image and healthy eating behaviours in children, teachers, parents and community members.

Ecological and environmental considerations

Development of student self-esteem in the prevention of obesity, eating problems and the improvement of body image should not be confined to the individual or to the school classroom. A child's self-esteem and sense of self-worth, while certainly affected by school curricula and teaching style (for example, authoritarian teaching versus student-centred, interactive, inclusive teaching), is also impacted on by peers (for example, teasing), family, teachers, coaches, school environment, community factors (for example, the media, advertising, sports involvement) and culture (for example, feminist issues, cultural stereotypes, social norms and stigma about weight and shape) (see Shisslak & Crago, 2001 for a detailed and thorough review of risk and protective factors in the development of eating disorders).

A holistic environmental approach to the prevention of body image and eating problems as well as child overweight, such as the health promoting schools framework (O'Dea & Maloney, 2000), theorises that whole communities need to be involved in fostering overall health within school and community environments.

Eating disorders researchers have suggested various ecological, empowerment and activism approaches to the prevention of eating problems (Levine & Smolak, 2005; Piran, 1995; 1998; 1999; 2001; Streigel-Moore & Steiner-Adair, 1998).

Piran (1999; 2001) describes 'a participatory action project' in a school environment where the main aim of the project is focused on changing the whole school including addressing school policy, developing 'girls' critical voice' and the overall empowerment of girls in the school. In implementing this participatory approach, Piran first met with a group of girls at the ballet school to try and assess, in their experience, aspects of the school environment that they felt had contributed to their poor body image and their eating problems. The students reported school-based adverse effects such as comments from boys, comments from teachers, a focus on weight and shape, and a school 'ethos' of perfectionism and strict body image norms.

After gaining the 'voice' Piran was then able to work with the whole-school environment to make it a more body friendly environment.

Likewise, the innovative community-based training programs developed by Friedman (2002) in Canada are also aimed at building resilience and self-esteem among young women, using a predominantly feminist approach in order to foster empowerment.

Media literacy and media advocacy interventions are also encouraged in order to encourage self-acceptance and help to reduce the internalisation of the thin ideal and the pervasive body image norms for males and females which are constantly promulgated and reinforced by the media (Field et al., 1999; Levine & Smolak, 1998; Levine et al., 1999). The impact of media literacy programs is believed to be most powerful in an environment where the whole school is supportive and when the final result is one of rejection of the thin ideal which serves to facilitate self-acceptance and results in having participants derive an overall sense of self-worth from the media literacy program. In this way, media literacy programs may encompass an overall self-esteem building approach. This area of research warrants further study to clarify the most effective components of the media literacy approach to prevention.

Hence, whole systems such as families, schools, communities, governments and corporations need to be aware of, involved in and committed to the protection and enhancement of child health and the prevention of these pernicious body image and eating problems which are currently burgeoning among our children and our youth.

Case studies— applying the health promoting schools framework

The following case studies illustrate how some schools have addressed the improvement of body image and the prevention of eating disorders and obesity using a whole-school approach. All of these case studies are true stories.

McKillop Girls High School

McKillop Girls High School experienced a problem of laxative abuse among 20–30 students. School staff contacted a local physician and requested that she address the students about harmful effects from abusing laxatives. Asking medical experts to 'come and do the scare talk' is common in schools where eating disorders are identified as a problem. Fortunately, the physician sought advice from local health educators and, through the team at the community health centre, the school addressed the problem in a comprehensive and effective manner. Using principles of health promoting schools and facilitation by a local health educator, the teachers, students and parents identified three key questions to address: 1) What were they teaching in the curriculum?; 2) Did the school environment promote a slim ideal body image?; 3) What did they know about the issue and where to get help for eating problems?

Curriculum

Previously, the school curriculum focused on presenting case studies of eating disorders. They used a work sheet with a picture of a young female with anorexia nervosa that included a list of symptoms of eating disorders. They used this work sheet in a class discussion to encourage girls not to diet and not to use other eating-disordered behaviours. A new curriculum was developed using ideas from students, teachers, parents, school staff and community leaders to focus on body image issues. To reduce the stigma attached to eating disorders, and to avoid possible glamorisation of eating problems, the curriculum did not focus on eating disorders. Rather, the new curriculum explored societal expectations of females, the media and its influence on the ideal body image, people's internal messages about their body image, coping mechanisms for problems and the responsibility of individuals as advocates of change towards a more realistic body image. Students, teachers, parents, school staff and community leaders brainstormed ways to influence others to accept a healthier attitude towards their bodies and dieting. Similar complementary activities occurred in English and media studies classes.

School ethos

A critical analysis of values and attitudes towards body image by teachers and other school staff occurred at a full staff meeting. Staff discussed the influence of their own attitudes about the slim ideal and they critically analysed their practices in terms of how they encourage students to participate in physical activity. Physical education teachers in particular examined whether they were unnecessarily focusing on the larger girls and whether they might inadvertently be projecting a slim ideal onto students.

It was important to look across the curriculum into areas such as home economics as well as health classes to ensure that consistent messages about nutrition were delivered. Again, teachers, school staff and parents discussed whether they were portraying sensible messages about food. Teachers reconsidered their use of the terms such as 'junk' food and 'bad' foods, and they took a more positive approach to nutrition focusing on positive language rather than 'scare tactics'.

Community

Teachers and other school staff participated in training about eating and body image problems, referral systems and treatment. Links were established with local resources, including health care and clinical services, and this approach helped facilitate access to help for some students. Two students were referred into clinical treatment from the process.

Students, teachers, staff, parents and community members were asked to act as advocates to change the slim ideal. They wrote letters for the school newsletter and actively advocated for changes to the canteen to improve food selection. A more balanced approach to food and eating is currently reflected in the school canteen. The school continues to implement health promoting schools activities.

Successful aspects of this health promoting schools approach

This approach was successful for several reasons. First, rather than ask a medical expert to come in and 'do the scare talk', the whole school community took responsibility for what was happening at their school. They utilised the skills of a local health education specialist and they looked at the curriculum, the school's environment in relation to body ideals and what the local community could offer. The process involved teachers, parents and students, and was facilitated by a local community health centre. The success of the program was largely due to this sort of collaboration.

What they implemented also affected the success of the program. They deliberately included a curriculum that did not focus on eating disorders but addressed the following key causes of body image concerns:

- societal expectations of females
- media and its influence on body ideals
- people's internal messages about their body image
- problem solving and coping
- individuals as advocates of change towards more realistic body image.

A strength of the program was the cross-curricular nature of the changes where they were able to deliver similar complementary activities in other school subjects. These activities were implemented in English, Media Studies, Health and Home Economics classes and included discussions at staff meetings about the whole school's ethos addressing:

- influence of the staff's attitudes about the slim ideal
- physical activity practices and inadvertent focus on body size
- consistent messages about nutrition in Health and Home Economics classes
- positive language about food and avoidance of terms such as 'junk' and 'bad' foods, and changes to the school canteen to offer more choice.

The new links with the community led to:

- teacher training about body image
- identification of local resources
- advocacy action related to changing the slim ideal (e.g. letters to newspapers).

The success of this approach reinforces the view that school-based strategies using this whole-school 'health promoting school' framework provide an efficient and effective way to approach body image issues of concern to schools.

Healthy body image through social education at Siena College

This case study is reproduced with permission from the Children's Health Development Foundation, *Virtually Healthy* newsletter, no. 29, p. 7, 2003.

Siena College is a Catholic girls' high school in Adelaide, South Australia. The school has a Social Education program operating throughout the whole school. It is closely linked with the school's Catholic philosophy and vision of educating the whole child, and aims to promote self-esteem, self-respect and confidence so that students can make the best possible choices in every area of life. The program has a different focus at each year level (8–12) and at Year 9 the focus is on body image. It became obvious through discussions with students and the ideas they were expressing in their writing that important areas of learning were not covered by the formal curriculum, and there was a need to address body image issues.

Body Image Program

The Body Image Program has evolved over a number of years. We have attempted to make it a positive, broad program without the traditional narrow focus on eating disorders.

The objectives are to:

- empower young women to feel good about themselves and to make positive life choices
- develop strategies that help young women identify and address the messages they receive about their bodies
- examine ways women are portrayed in the media and the impact on young people.

In 2003, for the first time we ran the Body Image Program as a camp workshop at the end of Term 1. We included a session on food and physical activity due to the current focus on childhood obesity and declining physical activity. Using the workshop format enabled us to intersperse the Body Image Program with fun physical activity sessions including belly dancing, tae-bo and tai chi. We invited an artist to work with our students to produce some beautiful paintings, in which all our students had input. Night time entertainment consisted of karaoke singing and a visit by Innerbody, an interactive drama group that deals with body image issues. The students had some free sessions during the day in which they were able to do physical activity sessions outside, watch videos or use a computer program that enables them to scan their faces and manipulate certain features on the screen, as magazines do. In Term 2, the Year 9 students undertook phase 1 of the three phases Alcohol Program. Phase one targets students prior to the time a high proportion of students start drinking. This allows them to gain alcohol harm reduction skills and strategies immediately prior to the potential adoption of a new behaviour.

Whole-school approach

While our Social Education Program and Body Image Programs stand alone, we take a whole-school approach and closely link them with the formal curriculum and other programs and policies in the school. School policies that support the Social Education Program are the 'Drug and Alcohol Policy', 'Behaviour Education Policy' and the 'Anti-bullying and Harassment Policy'. Curriculum areas covered include the 'Friends' Program and a smoking unit with an emphasis on refusal skills (Year 8), more of the Alcohol Program, and study related to the school, future, community, relationships and illicit drugs (Year 10). The Year 11 and 12 students look at a range of issues including workplace matters, parenting, driver education, self-defence and coping skills.

Community links

Our program is supported by many community organisations. Recently Year 9 students participated in current surveys with the University of South Australia and Adelaide University, which investigated physical activity and garment sizing. The students had just completed their work on Body Image and their involvement with the university helped them identify some community concerns regarding this topic. Several students and teachers were interviewed recently by the ABC TV Stateline program which highlighted recent work on garment sizing.

The success of the Social Education and Body Image Programs are largely due to the way they are integrated into many aspects of school life and the strong support they receive from school management, teachers, students and the many participating community groups and individuals.

V.I.K.—Very Important Kids anti-teasing program in Minnesota, USA

The program is aimed at reducing teasing and unhealthy weight control behaviours among students in Years 4–6 using a broad spectrum approach that involves students, school staff, teachers and parents and incorporates a broad range of factors. Student participation in this program was high and the evaluation was positive. The implementation of this program (Haines et al., 2006) significantly reduced teasing, particularly weight-related teasing. A description of the program is given below.

Individual factors

After-school program

Ten sessions that incorporated interactive activities to address factors, such as body image, skills to intervene on impact weight-teasing situations, media literacy, healthy eating and physical activity. Each session was preceded by one hour of physical activity and the provision of a nutritious snack.

Theatre program and production

Students worked with a local theatre company over 10, one-hour sessions to develop and perform a theatre production, in which students used their own experiences with teasing to develop scenes that communicated messages about why it is not appropriate to tease and about strategies to address teasing situations when they occur.

Environmental factors

School-based intervention components

School staff training Half-day training for all teachers, administrators and school support staff that used interactive activities to help staff identify their own prejudices regarding weight, and how they can be positive role models to their students by addressing teasing, modelling a healthy body image, and refraining from talking about weight and shape.

No-teasing campaign Students developed and implemented a no-teasing campaign at the school, which involved posters, buttons and intercom announcements promoting the message that teasing is not acceptable.

Book-of-the-month All classes read a fictional book about one youth's experience with teasing, followed by a discussion led by teachers using questions designed by the research team.

Theatre production Performance of the *V.I.K.* theatre production was held for all students and school staff.

Family-based intervention components

Family nights Two family nights were held at the school: the first was an interactive session on body image; and the second was a hip-hop dance demonstration and lesson.

Parent postcards Postcards addressed similar topics to those covered in the curriculum for the after-school program including weight-related teasing, media's impact on body image and being physically active with your family.

Booth at parent teacher night Research staff attended two parent–teacher conference nights at the school to answer questions about *V.I.K.* and distributed promotional material, such as pamphlets and *V.I.K.* magnets.

Theatre production Families were invited to attend an evening performance of the *V.I.K.* student theatre production.

Pennington Primary School

This case study illustrates how music can be incorporated into a whole-school approach to develop health literacy skills in young children.

In the same way that advertising jingles and tunes are remembered—health messages can be easily learned and retained when presented in chants, rhythms, poems and songs.

At Pennington Primary School, songs are used to enhance learning in the area of health as well as to support language acquisition in the school's large English as a Second Language and Newly Arrived community. A wide variety of musical forms are used and children's attention can be held with both simple and more complex songs. Some examples include: 'Breakfast, water, healthy food ... sleep'—an echo song with a very simple repetitive chorus to enable easy learning of these four key ideas, 'Rubbish is yuk'—a rap, 'Yummy scrummy fruity fun'—a Calypso tune and 'When you cross the road' a Zydeco tune. Songs can be simple or more complex. They can be written to particular themes and events and can be original or innovations on a well-known tune. They are particularly effective if devised by the students themselves. And most of all they are a lot of fun and easy to learn.

Canteen makeover at Burton School Campus

The following case study illustrates how a broad coalition of parents, students, teachers and other school staff can successfully work together to promote a more healthy school environment.

During 2005 Burton school community focused on creating a canteen with even more healthy foods. Student Canteen Committee members attended a half-day workshop along with parent volunteers and selected staff. Together the team came up with exciting make-over initiatives to improve the look of the canteen, and had input into healthier and more creative menu options. By creating large colourful collages and providing glossy coloured photographs and posters, the canteen underwent a complete facelift during the October school holidays. In order to capture the students' attention, catchy names were given to the various healthy menu packs along with attractive presentations of the food. The 'CCC' pack included chicken, corn cob and juice. The 'Sun and Surf' packs contained grilled fish and oven baked wedges. These were just two of a range of six new exciting packs. With relevant marketing, term 4 started off exceptionally well. Word of mouth saw the 'Sun and Surf' pack orders go from five on Monday to forty on Friday! While we were delighted with the take up of the new, healthy food packs, we soon realised that demand far outweighed the resources we had at the time! The homemade fare required more 'hands on deck' to prepare, heat and present the packages. What became apparent very quickly was the need for a much larger commercial oven, a bain marie and additional volunteer support.

We were thrilled with the response from students, knowing that the marketing was successful and that the healthy food options 'were a hit'. But due to issues around kitchen equipment and volunteers, we unfortunately had to stop the sale of the packs. Our immediate priority then became the purchase of necessary equipment to cope with the increased demand. In 2006 we are now at a stage where we are ready to reintroduce the packs.

Reproduced with permission from Centre for Health Promotion, CYWHS, *Virtually Healthy* newsletter no. 40, p. 5, 2006, http://www.chdf.org.au/

Interview with the principal of Enfield Primary School

How would you describe the health promoting schools (HPS) approach?

We describe it in our school plan as an ethos; as a set of health promoting principles and values that drive the organisation. To me, what a health promoting school does is to constantly look for opportunities to adapt the school's practices to the health promoting ethos.

What has been your experience of using the HPS approach?

We started about 10 years ago with a grant. We were looking at quite basic issues then such as what we were selling in the canteen and what we were doing in the curriculum—areas you could look at quickly and make changes towards healthier lifestyles for students. But then for the long haul, we had to look at changes we could make over a period of time— changes that would make a lasting difference. We identified practices we had in the school that supported making Enfield a health promoting school. We realised we had a sound basis for development. As a staff we formulated a core plan of what we would implement each term to support our goal. We have continued to review and adapt our plans each year. One aspect that is an annual event is our 'Healthy Lifestyles Day'. Everyone in the community and the school works together to celebrate and demonstrate our commitment to working towards the wellbeing of students and staff.

How have you developed a shared vision for HPS in your community?

We write it into the 'contextual influences' of our Site Plan, so that everyone can see this is a priority of the school. Each year we include core aspects of our program into induction for new staff. We use signage throughout the school to make overt what we believe. I think this is very important in developing a shared vision for the whole community.

Do you think parents have appreciated this approach?

Parents do see it as a positive development. We began with a set of behavioural expectations for students. For example we were saying that 'we will play safely and keep others safe'. To have an appropriate whole-school community message we have changed it to 'we will keep ourselves safe and consider the safety of others'. At Enfield we now have an ethos for the whole-school community—parents, students and staff—that includes and values everyone. This whole-school community approach has meant that parents now see that the school considers not only the students' wellbeing as important, but everyone's wellbeing as important. This in turn encourages whole-school decision making which recognises the diversity of the community. Different cultures and customs are brought together in a safe environment for all.

You have identified planning and communication as key strategies; are there any others?

Our curriculum has moved on. Aspects of health promotion are not taught in isolation. As in Aboriginal perspectives across the curriculum, the health messages are not just included in the Health curriculum. In activities such as daily fitness, healthy eating and Program Achieve, we find the messages are implemented across the curriculum. We all understand that we have to be organised and get along well to be successful and these values form the core of our learning program. We also allocate funds annually from our budget to support the core activities of our plan.

How do you think using the HPS approach benefits students' learning?

One of the biggest benefits for students is the delivery of an integrated curriculum across the whole school. Staff work together to create a safe and caring environment. I know this sounds like jargon, so our school practices must reflect a commitment by all to live healthy lives. An example of this in practice has been our daily fitness program where senior students have planned and led activities for all classes three times a week. Senior students model taking turns, sharing and being considerate of others. Having responsibility for promoting the health of others develops a culture where all students can have input, share and give feedback to each other.

Student voice

We have dramatically increased student voice across the school and the role of the SRC in keeping the school healthy is really strong. Recently the SRC asked for a particular brand of popular ice cream to be sold in the canteen. They did some investigation about healthy eating and decided this brand would not meet the healthy criteria. Recommended ice creams were considered and have now been added to the menu. They wanted better smelling soap in the toilets. We investigated the options and realised that for a small price we could have higher quality soap. They wanted the toilets to smell better, so we have had the walls painted and the floors will soon be tiled. Automatic air fresheners have been installed in all the toilets. It's about empowering students to become more aware of what they are doing for their own health through being able to impact on the school. When we started 'Fruity Friday' this year the parents, staff and students all realised that a safe food preparation area was needed that was more hygienic than using the existing wet area of the unit. Students wanted hot water to wash dishes. One side of the wet area is now a kitchen area with hot water and power supply. Parents now use the area, including one father who takes cooking sessions for students in his son's class. Students have the facilities they require to be successful in moving towards healthier lifestyles. These quite small changes bring huge benefits.

What would you say to others about the HPS approach?

The strongest message is about developing a whole-school approach and ethos. We are looking for generational change and improvement in lifestyles rather than believing there is a quick fix. Just start somewhere. It is amazing how a few small changes can drive and sustain practices over a period of time. We have never stopped finding small things to change.

The whole way through, it's not the leadership of the school saying this is what you need, it is building from parent, student, community, and teacher ownership of what they want to do.

Reproduced with permission from Centre for Health Promotion, CYWHS: *Virtually Healthy* newsletter, no. 38, pp. 2–3, 2005, http://www.chdf.org.au/.

Ascot Park Primary School

The principal of Ascot Park Primary School shares some of his experiences of working with a health promoting schools approach.

When I first started using the HPS approach way back in 1996, we deliberately set out to have programs fitting the model of the three areas—linking together the curriculum, school environment and community—and to involve students, parents and teachers. After several years of that way of looking at things it becomes the way you look at everything all the time. For example, we recently joined the Data in Schools and Data for Learning Collection Program looking at SACSA and students' standards of literacy.

Our philosophy was not to jump in but to consider:

- how can we get kids involved?
- how to make sure the community knows why we are doing this and inform them through a reporting process

- how to look at the process of involving teachers—is there a sense of fairness and equity?

It would be the sort of program six years ago I would have thought—that's not health promoting schools—that's literacy—we'll look at HPS when we do Health and PE. My experience has gone from that very narrow 'this is a health promoting school program' to 'now let's try to look at this whole school in terms of a health promoting school'. I hope everything we do, from behaviour management to introducing our two-hour literacy time, uses HPS approaches and improves students' learning and wellbeing. I have tried to elevate aspects of 'we are all in this together' and it is 'all actually part of health'. It is not about individual programs. It is a headset about:

- involving everybody where you possibly can
- relationship building
- listening to people
- implementing changes that are going to benefit people through their involvement not only because you think it is a good thing
- teaching that learning and wellbeing are linked. If you are not well, you are not learning.

Don't get hung up with the word 'health'. People see 'health' as in Health and PE, so they think it is about PE programs and sex education, and growth and development.

In my experience, some of the key strategies are:

- Take time to look at what the HPS framework is talking about—it is the benefit of knowing the philosophy and applying it 'subconsciously'.
- 'Hasten slowly' so that there is always forward momentum, but be prepared to go backwards sometimes. You get a whole-school momentum by small things over time— slowly it turns people around.
- It is important to have people on board with you. Getting people on board and developing shared vision is half the battle. If you use the idea 'I've got to get this into place' as your reason for being, then you've lost the battle. If the reason for being is actually to get people on board, and what you get out of it is what you originally set out to, then good luck to you for achieving both. If you try to dominate and say 'I'm going to put this program in' without getting people on side, then you might achieve the program and don't achieve the other bit. In the early days I prepared a five-year plan, and at the end of the third year we planned to have everyone on board, which we did. At the end of five years, I could have walked out the door and it would have continued to happen without me.
- Involve people by gathering their views. Last year we surveyed parents and students with results from both groups being quite similar. Many didn't see the school as 'academic' but both groups rated the school really highly on relationships. Students saw their teachers as really caring for them. We have now taken steps to improve the academic perspective of the school, introduced literacy programs, collected data, offered support for students' academic wellbeing at the same time as talking with them about their emotional wellbeing.
- Give students an authentic voice. We used the HPS checklist to see what we do that fits under the HPS banner. We did that with school council, teachers and students. What grew out of it with the Year 6–7s was that notion of what it means to be a successful learner at Ascot Park. We developed student statements: 'at the end of my time at Ascot Park I would like to know ...', and teacher statements: 'therefore, as teachers we will ...'
- We use them on documents, in our school vision and as part of our induction process for new teachers. Years ago it was the notion of 'action competence' in topics that are relevant to students' lives that enthused me about HPS. It was difficult to start, but in time at Ascot Park PS it became part of teachers' ordinary programs. And yes, giving students

a realistic say about their learning took us to diverse areas ... 'Why is the footpath outside my house never fixed?' ... 'Why do you bleed when you are stabbed?'

- The whole concept is to put the context first, then work out the content that students want to learn.
- Teachers are very good at involving students. Sometimes you can start with small groups of students rather than whole classes.
- Encourage people to be involved. It is sometimes difficult to encourage the wider school community to be involved in things. I have encouraged teachers to have a say on a range of things going on at the school (for example, cleaning contracts) and it has worked really well. Parents are now also invited to provide input through a feedback section of the newsletter. This has worked well too, with the number of responses growing. We are also involved in the Commonwealth Government's Strengthening Families project which is providing programs to engage parents.
- Support with funding and resources. You need to back up actions with funding and other resources. Empower people who are going to do the implementing.
- Offer strategies. All teachers are interested in children's wellbeing and if you offer specific strategies, solutions and resources to make things happen, people will give it a go.
- Have whole-school programs so the kids get consistent messages and consistent approaches.
- Talk to people all the time and use the terminology about what you are doing.
- Listen and involve others in decision making. You have to have a collaborative leadership group—and model that to the students.

This case study is reproduced with permission from Centre for Health Promotion, CYWHS, *Virtually Healthy* newsletter, no. 38, pp. 4–5, 2005, http://www.chdf.org.au/.

Deputy Principal, Hackham East PS

I have been really passionate about health promoting schools probably all my teaching life. It becomes part of your psyche—putting people first. For me a health promoting school is a well functioning, safe, happy school for students, parents, teachers and everyone who comes in.

Nothing delights me more than people saying 'this is a lovely school to come in to'. It's not my doing that it's a lovely place. The people here really do care about each other, and the leadership team has really put a focus on people.

We have gone through the process of identifying the staff's values, and have now canvassed the whole school community. 'Care' came up clearly as the top value, followed by 'expressiveness and joy' and 'success'. So this community wants people to care about their children.

HPS provides an umbrella for coordinated strategies and programs to support the learning and wellbeing of students. It values all people and educates and caters for the whole being.

For me, the first thing is to get your students on board and then involve the school community. Some of the things we are doing at the moment are:

- involving a student leadership team in making decisions about things in the school
- using student initiated curriculum in some classes, with shared responsibility for learning
- emphasising discussion of values and children making choices
- some students are investigating healthy eating, with student representation on the canteen committee.

It is really important to find out about the health of a school, and you will find out a lot through the students. You can create your own survey (for example, in the annual report) about how students are feeling. It is really good if you can get them involved in what could be happening, making predictions—what is it going to be like here in a few years time and what do we need to be doing now? You can also ask parents and staff. We won a major environmental grant at my previous school. I think we won it because we had 'authentic student voice'. Students identified the problem with our sprinklers, did the investigations and applied for the grant to underground them. I have also had students involved in purchasing for and running the canteen which was highly successful.

Have a collective understanding of what it is to be a healthy school. Think about the future. Know where you want to go. It's about the big picture and working towards a future you want.

Communication is really important. It's a matter of finding out where people are at in their understanding and ensuring that you communicate with all groups.

Build relationships. Understand and value each other's strengths and identify areas where we can further develop.

Take small steps towards your goals. Make sure that everything you do in the school, every decision you make, every policy you write fits with the philosophy.

Have a core group of people to drive a shared vision. It may include staff or counsellors, people interested in student leadership or student initiated curriculum, or maybe even keen parents meeting for another purpose!

Collect data. That's something I would like to do more of—analyse it and see what is really happening. For example when making changes in the canteen—see what is really going on.

Encourage optimism. Students who are optimistic and can see where their future is going—their whole health is catered for.

Curriculum. Make sure that every area of the curriculum reflects the HPS philosophy, and that all students' learning needs are catered for. Offer stimulating and rewarding activities.

Involve your community. At a previous school, I was involved in arranging for a student who was experiencing difficulties to take up what he was interested in—work experience at a local piggery. This boy had the support of the piggery and many others were involved in making it happen. It evolved into an exciting experience for a student whose learning was turned around.

At Hackham East we have a range of positive wellbeing programs including 'The Shed'. This is a local workshop run by adults who help students to make things, and talk to them too, just like a grandpa would. It's been very successful and the students have something to look forward to at the end of the week.

Jump in and take risks!

Never say, 'Oh, we can't do that.'

This case study is reproduced with permission from Centre for Health Promotion, CYWHS: *Virtually Healthy* newsletter, no. 38, p. 6, 2005, http://www.chdf.org.au/.

HPS activities that may attract funding grants

The following initiatives have attracted some funding and been successfully initiated in schools.

Curriculum

- Developing whole-school health curriculum and related activities, supported by local health services.
- Developing a Health Focus in the curriculum with strong links to other educational institutions.
- Increasing students' positive feelings about themselves and their learning.

School ethos

- Collecting data from the whole-school community to support the development of strategies to address bullying.
- Developing health promoting practices across the school.
- Raising awareness of the health promoting school approach in the school and community.
- Raising awareness in the school of the importance of wellbeing.
- Establishing an online 'student voice' facility for isolated students.
- Surveying the school community on food and nutrition issues.
- Whole-school involvement in planning and lead-up activities for a 'Health and Harmony Day'.

Environment

- Involving students in planning the use of outdoor areas to encourage physical activity.
- Promoting physical activity.
- Improving healthy food choices in the canteen and raising awareness of healthy eating.

'Feel'n Good' at Karcultaby Area School

Karcultaby AS is using the health promoting school framework and taking a holistic approach to health and learning at the school. The school was keen to raise awareness of the HPS approach in the school and community, and has done much to publicise and promote the school as a health promoting school.

Some of the activities undertaken are:

- forming the 'Feel'n Good' committee of staff, students, the principal, a parent, the local police officer and youth development officer to identify, plan and implement activities
- linking with the SRC to gather students' ideas (for example, about interesting ways to make students more active at the school)
- producing a health promoting schools brochure
- launching the brochure at an afternoon of fun health activities at the school. The event emphasised the link between good health and good learning and a holistic approach to health—hence our motto 'Feel'n Good in the Head, Feel'n Good in the Heart and Feel'n Good in the Body'
- producing a HPS resource package including a CD-ROM of the school's HPS journey, the brochure and school information for other schools and community services
- including a survey in the newsletter to gather the community's ideas about 'health' and what being a health promoting school means
- preparing a health promoting school policy
- brightening up a dull corridor with a 'Feel'n Good' display of health brochures and posters
- displaying a wall chart in the staff room of current activities and structures within the HPS framework
- developing a canteen policy and forming a student canteen committee
- becoming a SunSmart school
- staging a 'Rural Road Crash' mock accident on an intersection near the school, in conjunction with many other agencies and schools.

Being a health promoting school is forming the basis of the school's 'student involvement and wellbeing' priorities for 2005–08, and involving students in the decision-making processes has been an essential part of our successes so far.

Students' comments:

- 'I learnt that you can have fun by doing everything healthy.' Year 5
- 'Being healthy is not just about being fit.' Year 6
- 'You have to have a healthy heart, mind and body.' Year 3
- 'Fitness is good for people and it's not hard.' Year 3
- 'It's more than just physical health.' Year 8
- 'Feeling healthy makes ya feel good.' Year 8

This case study is reproduced with permission from Centre for Health Promotion, CYWHS: *Virtually Healthy* newsletter, no. 38, p. 7, 2005, http://www.chdf.org.au/.

Woodville High School, South Australia

'How do we see ourselves as a health promoting school?' The staff at Woodville High School in Adelaide, South Australia, are well aware of the stresses that both the school and the wider community place on our young people, and we have been seeking to create ways of giving our young people the skills to cope and thrive.

Creating a vision

Resilience has been a key word in our discussions over a couple of years, and in a day-long staff conference in 2000, local community experts informed us all about what it means to be resilient. They also gave us the hard facts on what our young people are facing in our community today.

Among the local community experts were a doctor, Vietnamese street worker and local council youth worker. These people were also members of a drug education strategy project team, formed at the beginning of 2000.

Developing action plans

We had foreshadowed the government's decision that all schools will be mandated to develop a drug education strategy, and the project team was already arguing about whether we should be developing a drug education strategy or a student resilience strategy.

The team, which also consisted of a student, parent and three teachers, finally agreed that much of what we would eventually develop would be aimed towards building student resilience, but our focus would remain with drug issues.

The members of the project team had much to learn from each other:

- The student knew exactly what was going on in the student culture.
- The parent voiced the concerns of caregivers.
- The doctor had up-to-date knowledge of drug issues in our local community.
- The youth worker spoke of the risks young people are facing.

Finally, the teachers spoke of curriculum needs and the realities of supporting student welfare in a school setting.

Plans into action

A widespread information gathering process, which took six months to complete, had a dual purpose.

Firstly, it provided data on the knowledge base and opinions of students, parents, staff and community agencies on a variety of drug issues.

Secondly, it began to engage the full spectrum of the school community in this prominent health issue. It raised awareness that the school was taking some initiative and that everyone's opinion would contribute towards the action to be taken.

We tried very hard to avoid the connotation that, because we were moving forward on this issue, then we must have a drug problem in the school. We acknowledged that drugs are an issue for young people in every school, and our priority was to provide our school community with the best quality support that we could muster. It has taken a full year, from setting the scene with the project team to preparing a final report, which contains enough recommendations to keep staff, students, parents and community agencies busy for a considerable time.

Health promotion is already one of the school's priorities and will be strengthened in areas that relate to student resilience and drug education.

Recommendations

- The curriculum review will see the inclusion of drug issues across the curriculum, with the teachers undergoing training to equip them with appropriate responses to whatever students may raise. A broader range of curriculum materials, available nationwide, will be used.
- The student welfare review will see the expansion of personal development programs, and appropriate training for staff with designated student welfare roles.
- Protocols for working with government and community-based agencies will be strengthened.
- The surveys of students, parents and staff will see the development of new activities to engage students in thinking about their relationship to alcohol and other drugs and the training of peer drug educators.
- Parent information sheets (which will include many of the ideas suggested by parents through the survey), and parent information and activity nights will be organised.
- Staff from our local agencies have already volunteered to facilitate these.

Staff will need to be involved in training and development activities ranging from drug information updates; familiarisation with school welfare procedures; a review of teaching and learning strategies on drug-related issues; and learning how to identify and respond to students at risk from a wide variety of harm.

All this will have the effect of changing the way all members of the school community see their approach to drug issues.

The over-arching principle is one of harm-minimisation, a difficult one to accept when we (teachers and parents) wear our 'parenting' hat.

However, it is the reality that we must work with, and we all, including students, need to gain the communication skills and confidence to work together.

The future

Implementing the recommendations becomes the next phase of the project. This will involve a wide variety of groups within the school: committees, staff-parent groups and combined staff/agency teams. It will be by far the most demanding phase since it will involve a greater number of people being pro-active with programs, the evaluation and subsequent use of classroom activities, and the involvement of all staff, all students, many of our parents and many community agency personnel.

A structure modelled on the health promoting school concept will be in place and will be self-sustaining. It will include teacher training and development programs; curriculum materials; school policies, procedures and protocols; parent education programs and well-developed links with service providers in the community. While our teachers will be better skilled at working with our students, and parents will be more confident in communicating with their young people, it is that each young person is making good decisions with regard to their use or otherwise of alcohol and other drugs that is our ultimate aim.

This case study has been reproduced with permission from Centre for Health Promotion, *Virtually Healthy* newsletter, no. 20, 2001, http://www.chdf.org.au/

Summary

Research reinforces the suggestion that educators need preventive strategies for eating and body image problems and prevention of obesity, and that school-based programs may provide an efficient and effective way to approach these problems. The health promoting schools framework offers a suitable approach because it encompasses a range of influences internal and external to the school environment. The holistic focus of the framework targets numerous aspects of eating and body image problems, including school curricula, policies and attitudes, as well as the local environment and community activities, services and resources. Collaboration among school, home and community, which is central to implementing the framework, enables a shared language and a shared way of working and understanding each other (WHO, 1998a).

This new approach provides a structure that offers the flexibility required to suit individual school needs and a diversity of problems. Implementing the health promoting schools framework for preventing eating and body image problems as well as obesity prevention may provide schools and local communities with a safe, effective and long-term solution to these pernicious and burgeoning community problems.

This chapter has provided an outline of the theoretical framework behind the health promoting schools approach and has illustrated how several schools have successfully implemented strategies to promote overall health within their school and community.

References

Australian Health Promoting Schools Association, vision statement for health promoting schools in Australia. Available at: http://ahpsa.org.au/files/framework.pdf

Button L, Loan P, Davies J & Sonuga-Barke E (1997), 'Self-esteem, eating problems and psychological well being in a cohort of school girls aged 15–6: A questionnaire and interview study', *International Journal of Eating Disorders*, *21*, 39–47.

Carter JC, Stewart A, Dunn VJ & Fairburn C (1997), 'Primary prevention of eating disorders: Might it do more harm than good?', *International Journal of Eating Disorders*, *22*, 167–72.

Collins ME (1988), 'Education for healthy body weight: Helping adolescents balance the cultural pressure for thinness', *Journal School Health*, *58*, 227–31.

Fallon P, Katzman MA & Wooley SC (1998), *Feminist Perspectives on Eating Disorders*, Guilford Press, New York.

Field AE, Cheung L, Wolf AM, Herzog DB, Gortmaker SL & Colditz GA (1999), 'Exposure to the mass media and weight concerns among girls', *Pediatrics*, *103*(3), E36.

Friedman SS (2002), *Body Thieves: Help girls reclaim their natural bodies and become physically active*, Salal Books, Vancouver.

Garner DM (1985), 'Iatrogenesis in anorexia nervosa and bulimia nervosa', *International Journal of Eating Disorders*, *4*, 348–63.

Graber J & Brooks-Gunn J (1996), 'Prevention of eating problems and disorders: Including parents', *Eating Disorders: Journal of Treatment and Prevention*, *4*, 343–63.

Haines J, Neumark-Sztainer D, Perry C, Hannan P & Levine M (2006), 'V.I.K. (Very Important Kids): A school-based program designed to reduce teasing and unhealthy weight control behaviours', *Health Education Research*, *21*(6), 884–96.

Levine M & Smolak L (1998), 'The mass media and disordered eating: Implications for primary prevention', in Vandereyken V & Noordenboos G (eds), *The Prevention of Eating Disorders,* New York State University Press, New York, 23–56.

Levine MP & Smolak L (2005), *The Prevention of Eating Problems and Eating Disorders: Theory, research and practice,* Lawrence Erlbaum Associates, Mahwah, NJ.

Levine MP, Piran N & Stoddard C (1999), 'Mission more probable: Media literacy, media activism and media advocacy in the prevention of eating disorders', in Piran N, Levine M & Steiner-Adair C (eds), *Preventing Eating Disorders: A handbook of interventions and special challenges*, Brunner/Mazel, Philadelphia, 3–25.

Lindeman AK (1994), 'Self-esteem: Its application to eating disorders and athletes, *International Journal of Sports Nutrition*, *4*(3), 237–52.

Mann T, Nolen-Hoeksema S, Huang K, Burgard D, Wright A & Hanson K (1997), 'Are two interventions worse than none? Joint primary and secondary prevention of eating disorders in college females', *Health Psychology, 16*, 214–25.

Moreno AB & Thelen MH (1993), 'A preliminary prevention program for eating disorders in a junior high school population', *Journal of Youth and Adolescence, 22*(2), 109–24.

Moriarty D, Shore R & Maxim N (1990), 'Evaluation of an eating disorders curriculum', *Evaluation and Program Planning, 13*, 407–13.

Neumark-Sztainer D (1996), 'School-based programs for preventing eating disturbances', *Journal of School Health, 66*(2), 64–71.

Nutbeam D (1992), 'The health promoting school: Closing the gap between theory and practice', *Health Promotion International, 7*(3), 151–3.

O'Dea J (1999), 'Children and adolescents identify food concerns, forbidden foods and food-related beliefs', *Journal of the American Dietetic Association, 99*(8), 970–3.

O'Dea JA (2000), 'School-based interventions to prevent eating disorders: First do no harm', *Eating Disorders, 8*, 123–30.

O'Dea J & Maloney D (2000), 'Preventing eating and body image problems in children and adolescents using the Health Promoting Schools Framework', *Journal of School Health, 70*(1), 18–21.

Patton GC, Selzer R, Coffey C, Carlin JB & Wolfe R (1999), 'Onset of adolescent eating disorders: A population based cohort study over 3 years', *British Medical Journal, 318*, 765–8.

Paxton SJ (1996), 'Prevention implications of peer influences on body image dissatisfaction and disturbed eating in adolescent girls', *Eating Disorders: Journal of Treatment and Prevention, 4*(4), 334–47.

Piran N (1995), 'Prevention: Can early lessons lead to a delineation of an alternative model? A critical look at prevention with school children', *Eating Disorders: Journal of Treatment and Prevention, 3*(1), 28–36.

Piran N (1998), 'A participatory approach to the prevention of eating disorders in a school' in Vandereycken W & Noordenbos G (eds), *The Prevention of Eating Disorders*, Athlone Press, London, 173–86.

Piran, N (1999), 'Prevention in a high-risk environment: An intervention in a ballet school', in Piran N, Levine ML & Steiner-Adair C (eds), *Preventing Eating Disorders: A handbook of interventions and special challenges*, Brunner/Mazel, New York, 148–59.

Piran N (2001), 'Re-inhabiting the body from the inside out: Girls transform their school environment', in Tolman D & Brydon-Miller M (eds), *From Subject to Subjectivities*, New York Press, New York, 219–38.

Rosenvinge JH & Gresko RB (1997), 'Do we need a prevention model for eating disorders? Recent developments in the Norwegian school-based prevention model', *Eating Disorders: Journal of Treatment and Prevention, 5*(2), 110–18.

Schoemaker C (1998), 'The principles of screening for eating disorders', in Vandereycken W & Noordenbos G (eds), *The Prevention of Eating Disorders*, Athlone Press, London, 187–213.

Shisslak CM & Crago M (2001), 'Risk and protective factors in the development of eating disorders', in Thompson JK & Smolak L (eds), *Body Image, Eating Disorders and Obesity in Youth*, American Psychological Association, Washington, 103–25.

Shisslak CM, Crago M, Neal ME & Swain B (1987), 'Primary prevention of eating disorders', *Journal of Consulting Clinical Psychology, 55*, 660–7.

Smolak L & Levine MP (1994), 'Towards an empirical basis for primary prevention of eating problems with elementary school children', *Eating Disorders: Journal of Treatment and Prevention, 4*, 293–307.

Striegel-Moore RH & Steiner-Adair C (1998), 'Primary prevention of eating disorders: Further considerations from a feminist perspective', in Vandereycken W & Noordenbos G (eds), *The Prevention of Eating Disorders*, Athlone Press, London, 1–2.

World Health Organization (1998a), '*Health Promoting Schools: A healthy start for living, learning and working*', *WHO/HPR/HEP/98.4*. WHO, Geneva.

World Health Organization (1998b), *Health Promotion Glossary*. WHO/HPR/HEP/98.1. WHO, Geneva.

Summary and conclusions

This book is a summary of my 25 years of practice, research and teacher training in the field of body image education, eating disorders prevention and, more recently, child obesity prevention. It is clear that the role of schools, teachers and teacher training for the prevention of these weight issues among young people is now more important than ever, but it has also become very clear that teachers need to approach these issues in an informed, positive and effective manner, as any unplanned approach is likely to do more harm than good to already body-sensitive young people. The intention of this book is to assist teachers and school administrators to implement health promoting activities within their school and community for the encouragement of healthy eating, physical activity and overall health and wellbeing.

The major focus of this book is to promote positive body image development by giving teachers and university lecturers ways of promoting self-esteem, self-acceptance and acceptance of others to improve general health and to improve body image among children, adolescents and university students. The book focuses on self-esteem development and media literacy to promote a positive body image and prevent eating disorders and obesity in young people.

In addition to development of individual self-esteem, the self-esteem approach of this book helps teachers to challenge the current Western belief system that we are valued for our appearance in Western society. How we look and how slim we are, or how muscular for males, correlates with how successful we are considered to be. This is a very narrow ideal for men and women to achieve and the inevitable failure to achieve these extreme body ideals results in failure, shame, guilt, hopelessness, dissatisfaction and worthlessness—all of which constitute low self-esteem. Low self-esteem predicts eating disorders, depression, anxiety, drug and alcohol abuse, risky behaviours, teen pregnancy and suicide.

Hence the title of this book and the message of the educational program is 'Everybody's Different'—consistently giving teachers, students, parents and health educators the message that we are all supposed to have different, varying and unique body shape and size as well as many other different features. All people are born to be different and we must learn to embrace our own diversity and uniqueness and be tolerant of differences in others. This major message forms the basis of my self-esteem building approach and the approach has a proven track record in research studies for body image improvement and eating disorders prevention as well as quite obvious relevance for the promotion of racial and religious tolerance and prevention of other forms of intolerance in any school setting.

The benefits of positive body image in boys and girls

The development of a positive body image in boys and girls is desirable because it helps to promote general mental and social health and involvement in physical activity. Children and teens who have a positive body image are likely to be positive about themselves in general and positive about their lives. A positive body image is associated with having a healthy social life and general self-esteem. Research shows that exercising people of all ages are generally more positive about their bodies than non-exercisers. Physical activity also helps young people 'feel better' because of its stress-reducing, 'relaxing' effect, but young people will not become involved in sports or physical activities if they have a poor body image or if they feel self-conscious about their bodies and their weight.

Positive body image also protects boys and girls against dieting and weight loss attempts. Research has repeatedly shown that 'dieting' is not a harmless activity and that it is likely to lead to further body dissatisfaction, disordered eating and eating disorders. Dieting also leads to binge eating when dieters 'go off' their diet. Hence, dieting has been shown to predict weight gain in teenage girls. A positive self-image protects young people against eating disorders, drug and alcohol abuse, truancy, depression, youth suicide, teenage pregnancy and other risky behaviours. Having a positive sense of self, a sense of self-respect, tolerance and respect for others is a very 'healthy' thing to promote among young people. Unfortunately, some teachers incorrectly believe that self-esteem building is unnecessary or even dangerous among young people because they mistakenly perceive self-esteem to equate with egotism, narcissism and over confidence. This book helps teachers to understand the true meaning of self-esteem development and its value in producing self-assured, self-satisfied, tolerant and productive young people.

Summary of chapter content

The first chapter of this book describes body image trends and it outlines the many factors that are related to body image in children and adolescents, including historical influences, social developments, health implications and the relationship of body image to self-concept and self-esteem. It is important for teachers to be able to identify how body ideals are constructed and perpetuated in Western society and how they can affect self-concept and self-esteem, so that we can convey this information to our students. Our students may then in turn learn to expose these social and cultural stereotypes and reject them.

In Chapter 2, I have presented an outline of the major body image problems and disorders which are present among boys, girls and young adults. Teachers and tertiary educators can use this information to detect developing problems among students and refer students for early intervention. Body image problems present among our students as body dissatisfaction including the desire to be slimmer among boys, girls and young women and the desire for greater muscularity among boys and young men. Body dissatisfaction may lead to physically damaging behaviours such as dieting, disordered eating, excessive weight lifting, obsessive exercise and steroid abuse and may also lead to more pronounced and life-threatening psychological problems such as eating disorders such as anorexia nervosa and bulimia nervosa. Each condition is characterised by low self-esteem and, hence, the focus of this book is the prevention of such problems using a self-esteem enhancing approach.

This chapter provides an overview of the whole spectrum of body image issues among adolescents and young adults and can certainly be a helpful reference guide for teachers' personal use. This information should not be used to teach students about these disorders as direct instruction about disordered eating behaviours is known to provide susceptible young students with ideas about weight losing behaviours. Many eating disorder patients recount how they first thought of using vomiting as a means of weight control when advised of this technique by their teachers. It also provides very valuable information for teachers and tertiary educators to learn how to understand the development of these common problems among our students, but teachers must resist the temptation to deal with educating students about these problems using a 'chalk and talk' approach or didactic instruction about these problems. The whole focus of this book is about implementing self-esteem development, media literacy skills and positive education about pubertal body changes, food and nutrition and positive approaches to child obesity prevention, rather than simply talking about the problems at hand.

Research findings from studies of body image among young people are presented with a focus on recent Australian data. Case studies of young people with body image concerns and eating problems are also presented to illustrate the many individual, family, social, cultural and biological factors associated with the development of these problems. While the use of these case studies with school students is not recommended, their use among trainee teachers is recommended as this sort of problem-based learning helps student teachers learn how important and influential their role is. The case studies in this chapter and those in Chapters 8 and 9 are very useful activities for university lecturers to use in tutorials or for other educators to use for teaching training or in-service training activities.

Chapter 3 describes how body image concerns and eating problems among children and adolescents are becoming increasingly targeted for preventive health education and health promotion programs in schools and universities. The chapter focuses on the current co-occurrence of increasing body image concerns and disordered eating with increasing rates of child obesity and how this trend makes the role of teachers and health educators complicated because of concerns that we must 'do no harm' in our efforts to ameliorate both issues in schools and universities. Teachers and health educators need to be very careful to ensure that the implementation of programs for the prevention of child obesity do not inadvertently create food concerns, body image issues, weight stigma, prejudice or eating disorders. Similarly, eating disorder prevention programs must take care not to condone obesity or to glamorise or normalise dieting or disordered eating. This chapter therefore summarises activities from body image programs and eating disorder prevention programs in schools and outlines self-esteem and media literacy approaches, which have produced positive results in some large, randomised and controlled interventions. Several suggestions for safe and successful school-based activities and strategies are outlined and discussed in this chapter so that teachers and school administrators can make informed, evidence-based choices about which approaches are most helpful in school settings.

Clearly, a major aim of school-based programs to improve body image, eating problems and prevent child obesity is to encourage healthy eating and physical activity among children and adolescents of all shapes and sizes without promoting weight concerns, fad diets, weight loss attempts and the diet-binge cycle.

Chapter 4 describes how to approach the promotion of overall child health and the prevention of body image problems and obesity by implementing a self-esteem approach—the Everybody's Different program.

This chapter describes how developing a broad positive sense of self promotes a positive body image among children, adolescents and young trainee teachers, which in turn reduces their risk of eating problems.

It contains details of research interventions that have tested predominantly self-esteem approaches for the improvement of body image and the prevention of eating problems, which have produced support for the efficacy, safety and suitability of a self-esteem and self-acceptance approach.

Several recent studies utilising strong self-esteem components as part of their controlled prevention interventions have produced improvements in body image, dieting, internalisation of the thin ideal and attitudes associated with the eating disorders and these are outlined in Chapter 4 along with my Everybody's Different program.

The chapter discusses self-esteem as one of the important risk and protective factors in the development of body image concerns and eating disorders and describes the subsequent use of the Everybody's Different self-esteem program for improvement of body image and prevention of eating disorders. Interventions containing strong self-esteem components from around the world are discussed in relation to their impact on the body image and eating behaviours of adolescents. Applications of the self-esteem approach for the prevention of child obesity are also discussed. Program activities and work sheets for use in the school or university classroom are given.

Chapter 5 extends the use of self-esteem development for body image improvement and eating disorders prevention by showing teachers how to implement media literacy lessons to help students identify and then reject these media constructed social norms. The purpose of this chapter is to first show teachers how to educate students about media literacy and then, finally, how to help students become more self-accepting and more accepting of others. In this way, the media literacy chapter incorporates both media literacy approaches and a self-esteem approach.

Media literacy and media advocacy interventions are effective in the promotion of a positive body image. The major aim of media literacy for body image improvement is to encourage self-acceptance and help to reduce the internalisation of the thin ideal and the pervasive body image norms which are constantly promulgated and reinforced by the media.

The media promotes a slim ideal for young females and a mesomorphic muscular ideal for young males. The impact of media literacy programs is most powerful when the final result is rejection of the thin or muscular ideals and the facilitation of self-acceptance. Participants in media literacy education derive an overall sense of self-acceptance and self-worth from the media literacy program. In this way, media literacy programs may encompass an overall self-esteem building approach.

Chapter 6 illustrates how important it is to teach students about their growth, development and pubertal changes in a factual, positive and reassuring manner. Students need to learn the facts about pubertal changes, but they also have many questions and concerns about these particular topics.

Teaching growth and pubertal development in a positive manner is very important because the onset of the pubertal growth spurt often results in body image dissatisfaction, especially for girls. One of the facts of pubertal development for both boys and girls is that their slim, 'low fat' preadolescent body is re-formed to become naturally covered with a layer of fat. In essence, it is true that the adolescent is relatively 'fatter' than when they were prepubertal and this increased percentage of body fatness can present a body image problem for some teenagers, especially girls whose percentage of total body weight as body fat increases from about 10–15 per cent to 25–30 per cent during puberty. The roundness and curvaceousness of the natural female form is something that girls and boys can learn in lessons about pubertal development.

While the majority of boys and girls adjust to their pubertal growth and development with little fuss or trauma, some pubertal adolescents may become highly sensitive about their weight, height, body shape and size, and these young people, both boys and girls, can go on to develop any of the following serious problems including poor body image, fad dieting, disordered eating, eating disorders, low self-esteem, depression and social isolation. These body concerns may develop in both boys and girls and can cause physical, emotional and psychological damage during the early teenage years.

Hence, when teaching about puberty, teachers need to focus on the positive outcomes of growth and development—height increase, strength, development towards adulthood—and reassure students that all the changes they are experienceing are normal and that they will soon become used to their newly developed bodies.

Adolescent development occurs in intervals which are known as Tanner Stages and if teachers can learn to comprehend these five Tanner Stages in boys and those in girls, then teaching students about puberty, growth and development will become much more meaningful and productive for students. Chapter 6 outlines and illustrates the Tanner system of staging pubertal development from prepubertal (Tanner Stage 1) to fully adult (Tanner Stage 5) and some fun lesson plans and website addresses provide valuable activities for students to learn about their personal stage of pubertal development. Teaching about growth and development in this particular way helps students to learn where they are in their adolescent development and where they are likely to go from there. This teaching approach also reinforces the theme of this book that 'everybody's different' and that all students are at a different stage of pubertal development. Interestingly, I have found that many of my male first year students are still developing into their early twenties and this sort of activity can also be very reassuring for these young male trainee teachers.

The activities in Chapter 6 also provide many different fun and interactive activities for both male and female students and this approach to teaching about sensitive body issues is an effective and engaging strategy for getting the message across in a direct, but sensitive approach.

Chapter 7 of this book focuses on teaching about food and nutrition in a positive way and it provides a lot of new research information about the importance of sound nutrition, healthy eating and exercising behaviours for the health of young people. Nutrition is essential for growth and health in childhood and adolescence as many of our adult eating and exercise behaviours and habits are well entrenched in childhood. Good nutrition provides energy, immunity, brain function and physical performance. Children's eating habits and attitudes are now becoming increasingly scrutinised with the exponential rise in child and youth obesity, so it is very important for teachers to teach nutrition in a positive way. In my experience, many teachers focus mainly on what students should not eat, rather than motivating them towards choosing more healthy options.

Teaching nutrition in a positive way cannot occur without some knowledge of foods and food groups which is then followed with some information about nutrients. Finally, teaching about food and nutrition in a positive way is most valuable and meaningful when it incorporates some form of realistic, practical aspect such as identifying different foods, food tasting or simple cookery.

This chapter outlines the many important benefits of childhood nutrition, including the promotion of growth, development, immunity, brain function, dental health, resistance to adult diseases and the development of sound eating habits for life. While weight control and the prevention of overweight and obesity are valid factors in teaching about healthy eating, they are not the only factors and they should not dominate lessons about food and nutrition. In fact, the most effective way to teach about food and nutrition is to engage the students with some sort of personal relevance and personal interest so that they learn to apply the nutrition theory to their everyday lives. The chapter therefore includes some information about the benefits of healthy eating from a large survey of 5000 school children from primary and secondary schools. Students learn to become motivated towards healthy eating because of the many personal advantages it may confer on them as individuals. It also provides teachers and school principals with the original survey used in the research study so that it can also be applied as a learning activity in individual schools.

There is also detailed nutritional information about the content of foods and in particular, the protein, iron, calcium and fibre content of foods. Vegetarian diets are discussed and lessons about vegetarian eating are included. A detailed account of sports nutrition is also given with several classroom activities for students of various ages. Finally, this chapter includes several quizzes, work sheets and lesson ideas to teach students about food groups, nutrients, major nutrients from foods, a food diary, factors effecting food habits, how to read a food label, the content packaged foods, fad diets and a card game called 'Nutritional pursuit'.

Chapter 8 explains how child obesity is defined, how it is measured and the many limitations of using the body mass index (BMI) among young people. In fact, this is a chapter full of information about the BMI, but I discourage teachers from measuring weight in class because it is a very limited and imperfect measure of body composition and it is more than likely not going to be a helpful activity for students. While studies in a number of different countries have shown increases in the worldwide prevalence of overweight and obesity among children over the past three decades, and these increases have given rise to concern about children's health and wellbeing, particularly in regard to the risk of Type 2 diabetes, teachers and school administrators need to think seriously about whether it is our role as educators to measure children's weight status.

In this chapter, I outline the facts about child overweight and obesity, but I recommend that teachers leave the assessment of weight status (essentially what I believe to be a medical diagnosis) to a doctor or trained health professional. I think teachers should be very careful to avoid taking on any 'treatment' role instead of our identified preventive role.

There are many other issues for teachers and school administrators to consider before they embark on any obesity prevention activities and these are outlined in this chapter. An important consideration is the potential to inadvertently create or worsen body image concerns among students, particularly among overweight students or those who perceive themselves as overweight. Several case studies of real students in real life situations are outlined in Chapter 8 to illustrate how, despite our very best intentions, teachers can sometimes do more harm than good when attempting to deal with issues in nutrition education, physical education and child obesity prevention.

Similarly, some true case studies of positive student experiences are also given in Chapter 8 to illustrate how effective teachers can be in the positive body image development of students. As mentioned before, these case studies are not suitable for use in the school classroom, but they are important ways to educate teachers and trainee teachers about the influence they have as educators and role models. I use these case studies to train young teachers about how to effectively approach issues of weight, shape and body image with students.

Finally, the holistic approach to teaching about these health issues is outlined in Chapter 8 and some suggested activities and classroom lessons are presented including activities to teach about health in a multidimensional way rather than focusing on weight, a quick quiz about overall health status, a discussion of health statements, a school health survey and lessons about bullying and harassment, including an activity about cyber bullying. Teasing and bullying are huge issues in the school-based prevention of body image problems, eating disorders and child obesity prevention. As teachers, we want to do all we can to motivate self-esteem and physical activity among all young people, but especially among those students who are overweight or inactive. Controlling weight-related teasing and bullying is essential for the production of a health promoting school environment in which students feel encouraged to participate in sports and physical activities.

Chapter 9 outlines the important role of teachers in positive body image development and prevention of eating disorders and obesity.

Many education and health professionals have a role to play in promoting a positive body image in students and this chapter examines the important contribution that teachers, health educators, school nurses, school counsellors, school psychologists, dieticians and sports coaches have to offer in the prevention of eating disorders and child obesity.

It is important to recognise that while school staff have an extremely important role in health promotion and prevention of body image concerns and obesity, there is also a current need to specifically examine how teachers and school personnel may be best trained and prepared for such a preventive role; whether they currently feel willing and able to undertake such a role and whether some groups of teachers may be personally susceptible to body image and eating problems themselves. The issue of teacher training or retraining to enable them to be most effective in their role as health promoters is an issue that is sure to become very obvious over the next few decades when more and more people start to call for schools to 'do something' about rising obesity rates and disordered eating among children and adolescents. Now is the time to start to consider what schools, teachers and other educators may need as far as training is required.

It is also vital to understand the knowledge, behaviours, attitudes and expectations of teachers and other educators who will be implementing any child obesity or eating disorder prevention programs in order to ensure that they are personally and professionally capable of carrying out such prevention initiatives in schools.

Research shows that individuals involved in food and exercise-related careers have been identified as being at risk for body image and eating problems, and it may be possible that they chose their career path due to their own personal experience with eating disorders or weight issues. In such cases specific training or assistance may be required in order to enable the educators to conduct effective preventive activities.

Discussion in this chapter focuses on what may need to be done in order to enable teachers and other school-based educators to perform most effectively in the implementation of school-based eating disorder and child obesity prevention programs.

I also provide an outline of my course and training program for trainee health education, home economics and physical education teachers so that people involved in teacher training can utilise some of my resources and ideas.

Chapter 10 deals with the important issue of how schools can become better prepared as sites for prevention of body image problems and obesity.

While schools have certainly been recognised as an appropriate setting for the prevention of eating disorders and child obesity due to the continual and concentrated access to a large number of individuals at a developmentally appropriate age, school staff also need to realise that what is taught in the classroom needs to also be reinforced in the whole-school community and at home. The theme of Chapter 10 is, therefore, how to create a school environment that supports healthy eating, physical activity and a healthy body image so that students can develop overall physical, mental, social and general health and wellbeing.

This chapter outlines the whole-school approach and how it may be implemented in schools for preventing body image problems and child obesity. Discussion focuses on the efficacy of preventive school-based strategies, and on the safest and most successful interventions. The framework encompasses three major areas of intervention in the school and community: 1) school curriculum, teaching and learning; 2) school ethos, environment and organisation; and 3) school-community partnerships and services. Suggested strategies for implementing the framework are outlined.

Luckily, I am able to include some excellent real life case studies of how several primary schools and high schools have adapted the new approach for dealing with the issues of eating disorders prevention, body image improvement and child obesity prevention. I am very grateful to the school principals and teachers who wrote their stories and I am also very grateful to the Centre for Health Promotion of South Australia (http://www.chdf.org.au/) for allowing me to include the stories from schools which were originally posted on their website. The case studies from schools illustrate how a long-term, whole-school commitment to an overall health promoting schools philosophy has resulted in a very 'healthy' and productive school community.

Controversial issues in this book

This book points out several controversial issues that teachers, school principals and other members of the school community need to consider before embarking on any body image promotion programs or obesity prevention activities. These controversial issues include whether or not to become involved in the routine screening for overweight and obesity; how to prevent any unintentional harmful outcomes from programs; and how to best prepare teachers and other educators for the important role as health promoters when they are likely to possess the same body image ideals and unrealistic body image expectations as their students and other young people exposed to the narrowly defined ideas of beauty in Western society.

The first issue, whether or not schools should become involved in the routine screening for overweight and obesity, is a very controversial issue at present. The biggest issue about screening for overweight is whether or not this is a role that teachers and school staff should be expected to undertake. I think not. School teachers are trained to implement educational initiatives and health diagnosis in not one of these activities. Screening for overweight or obesity using the very limited BMI definitions has inherent problems such as the uselessness of a one-off measure of BMI in growing children; the lack of any other health indices or a family history of disease (which predicts health outcomes much better than any measure of weight); the lack of properly trained staff to undertake what is basically a medical diagnosis; and the minefield of questions around what to do with the data once it is collected. For an excellent recent review of this particular topic I refer the reader to Ikeda et al. (2006), 'BMI screening in schools: Helpful or harmful?', *Health Education Research, 21*(6), 761–9.

The second issue addressed in this book is equally controversial, yet easier for schools to handle because there is a solid research base on which to base decisions. It is well known and well reported that both eating disorder prevention programs and child obesity prevention programs have the potential to do more harm than good.

To develop effective and sustainable strategies to prevent eating and body image problems in schools, professionals must first exclude approaches and practices proven ineffective or harmful. The potential exists for certain educational approaches to do more harm than good. School and college-based education programs that provide inform-ation about eating disorders, particularly activities led by recovered eating disorder patients, may inadvertently increase student knowledge and symptoms of eating disorders such as dieting, vomiting and laxative abuse. School-based programs also may inadvertently create potentially harmful outcomes by providing direct instruction and information about disordered eating behaviours and may introduce students to beliefs, attitudes and behaviours known to precede eating problems. Instruction about eating disorders also may glamorise and inadvertently normalise disordered eating behaviours, thereby creating the belief that these activities are common, that 'everybody is doing it' and that it is 'normal.' In addition, school-based programs may treat food and nutrition issues negatively by referring to 'good' foods, 'bad' foods, and 'junk' foods. The negative focus contributes to an underlying fear of food, dietary fat and weight gain which precipitate body image concerns and eating problems.